D0986784

Why Science Needs Metaphysics

Why Science Needs Metaphysics

A Plea for Structural Realism

ELIE ZAHAR

OPEN COURT
Chicago and La Salle, Illinois

To Helen Zahar
and to Isabelle and Lucas Erbe

To order books from Open Court, call toll-free 1-800-815-2280, or visit www.opencourtbooks.com.

Open Court Publishing Company is a division of Carus Publishing Company.

Copyright ©2007 by Carus Publishing Company

First printing 2007

All rights reserved. No part of this publication may be reproduced, stored in a retrieval system, or transmitted, in any form or by any means, electronic, mechanical photocopying, recording, or otherwise, without the prior written permission of the publisher, Open Court Publishing Company, 315 Fifth Street, P.O. Box 300, Peru, Illinois 61354.

Printed and bound in the United States of America.

Library of Congress Cataloging-in-Publication Data

Zahar, Elie.
    Why science needs metaphysics / Elie Zahar.
        p. cm.
    Summary: "Arguing against subjectivist epistemology, the author aims to revive a rational metaphysics for the practice and understanding of science" —Provided by publisher.
    Includes bibliographical references and index.
    ISBN-13: 978-0-8126-9603-5 (trade paper : alk. paper)
    ISBN-10: 0-8126-9603-4 (trade paper : alk. paper) 1. Science—Philosophy. 2. Science—Methodology. 3. Metaphysics. I. Title.
    Q175.Z24 2007
    501—dc22

                                                                                    2007001429

Table of Contents

Introduction

It is hoped that the present treatise will be of interest both to scientists and to philosophers of science, if only because it brings together, corrects, and transcends important strands of classical epistemology; also because it puts *rational* metaphysics back at the heart of the scientific enterprise. It is based on a series of lectures delivered by the author in Paris in 1996–1997; which were in turn a synopsis of various courses—on the history and logic of the sciences—given at the London School of Economics and Political Science between 1969 and 1995.

The prospective reader might well ask him or herself: why yet another book on epistemology at a time when the market seems saturated with such treatises? One answer is that the standpoint to be defended in the present work is the result of a synthesis of views which seemed *prima facie* irreconcilable. Note that 'synthesis' does not mean a simple juxtaposition but the modification in depth of theses most of which go back to Duhem, Poincaré, Mach, Brentano, Russell, Schlick, Popper and Lakatos. These modifications are intended not only to reconcile various conflicting viewpoints but to do so in a content-increasing way. For example, it will be shown that the 'justification' of scientific theories is not as divorced from the process of discovery as Popper, the Neopositivists and even Lakatos claimed it to be. The proposed methodology—a variant of Lakatos's Methodology of Scientific Research Programs, or MSRP—will thereby acquire a coherent and highly unified structure. In this way, I hope to have fulfilled a dialectical requirement put forward by Popper in his (1979); namely that a new methodology should contain, as 'moments' within its structure, all those aspects of its predecessors which have been transcendentally confirmed by the development of the sciences; it should moreover conform more closely to actual scientific practice in those areas where criticism has undermined its rivals (Popper 1979, §§ 9, 47). This dialectical method bears an obvious resemblance to the Correspondence Principle used in physics: a new hypothesis should both explain the facts which refuted its rivals and yield the latter as limiting cases in those areas where the old laws proved empirically successful (See below Chapter VI).

Let me describe, in somewhat more detail, the theses defended in this work.

(1) Thanks to the adoption of Popper's demarcation criterion, metaphysics reemerges not only as a meaningful discipline but also as one which is of essential significance both in the sciences and in methodology. More particularly: an important metaphysical doctrine, namely Structural Realism, is found to play a central role in the progress of science. While being consistent with the theses advanced by Poincaré, Russell and Popper, this conclusion flies in the face of doctrines propounded by practically all modern positivists.

(2) Structural Realism finds its formal expression in the thesis that the epistemological import of a scientific theory H lies in its Ramsey sentence H*. As a consequence of a mistake made by Russell in his *Analysis of Matter*, structuralism laid itself open to a seemingly devastating objection leveled at it first by Newman and then, more recently, by Demopoulos and Friedman; the objection being that H* expresses a mere consistency or cardinality constraint. Through altering Russell's position—while remaining within the spirit of Russellian philosophy—it can however be shown that Structural Realism can definitively be vindicated.

(3) Protocol sentences are given a phenomenalist and hence infallibilist interpretation; which turns out to be consistent with Mach's and Schlick's positions but incompatible with Duhem's, Neurath's and Popper's conventionalist theses about the empirical basis. Yet the incorrigibility of basic statements offers a *rationale* for the requirement that empirical tests should be repeated wherever and whenever possible; the aim being that of providing a—tentative—solution of the Duhem-Quine problem.

(4) Against Reichenbach and Popper, it is maintained that the context of discovery not only is susceptible of, but also positively calls for a rational reconstruction. It is demonstrated that the process of scientific creation largely rests on the application of mathematical techniques such as the Correspondence Principle, the adjustment of parameters to known facts and the imposition of symmetry constraints on putative physical laws. Should the context of discovery display a non-rational aspect, then the latter will be no more mysterious than that inhering in any deductive process.

(5) Because hypotheses can be adjusted to known empirical results, the context of discovery plays an important—albeit indirect—role in the assessment of the degree of inductive support of theories by facts. I shall

however also try to explain the sense in which Popper's notion of corroboration retains its essentially logical character.

(6) The book ends with two short case studies demonstrating the important role played by metaphysics in the progress of the sciences: Chapter VIII deals with the problems faced by classical atomism, problems which were not only of an empirical, but also of a metaphysical nature. The last Chapter examines the way in which realism exerted a determining influence on Einstein's scientific work.

I

How Respectable Is Metaphysics?

Aversion to metaphysics is a philosophical malaise which appeared in different guises in the development of modern thought. Through dividing all meaningful propositions into analytic sentences and statements of fact, Hume rejected metaphysics in all its forms. For his part, Kant threw doubt on the validity of all the metaphysical doctrines proposed by his predecessors and by his contemporaries; he did so most explicitly in the Introduction to his *Prolegomena*. In this connection, it should be remembered that despite being non-derivable from experience, the Kantian Categories are applicable only to the phenomena, i.e. to what is in principle observable. As for the metaphysical thing-in-itself, it remained wholly unknowable. It ought next to be pointed out that Mach, who had initially been an orthodox Kantian, gave the first chapter of his *Analysis of Sensations* the revealing title: *Antimetaphysical Considerations*. More recently, the phenomenologists proposed to go back to the 'things themselves' (*zu den Sachen selbst,* where the *Sachen* are not to be confused with the things-in-themselves), thereby renouncing ontological as well as scientific presuppositions. As for the Marxists, they felt nothing but contempt for the metaphysical dogmas propounded by their allegedly benighted opponents. This brings to mind Sartre's justified remark that while blindly subscribing to a materialist version of metaphysics, his Marxist opponents—correctly— accused him of being a metaphysician. However, until the emergence of the Vienna Circle whose avowed aim was to eliminate all metaphysics, the latter remained a badly defined term which vaguely referred to an occult reality lurking behind the phenomena. Everything seemed to change with the arrival on the scene of the Neopositivists. In view of what was said above, it is hardly surprising that the logical empiricists should have counted Kant among their precursors. But like most modern philosophers, the Neopositivists had stopped believing in the validity of the synthetic apriori principles which formed the cornerstone of Kantianism; they held that meaningful propositions were either analytic and hence logically true, or else synthetic aposteriori; so only the former could be regarded as apriori in the sense of being independent of experience. More precisely: according to the Vienna Circle, a synthetic proposition is meaningful only to the extent that it proves fully empirically decidable, i.e. only if it is verifiable *and* refutable by observation (Needless to say, it cannot be both verified and falsified). This dichotomy clearly relegates ontology to the domain of nonsense. (It should be added that the logical empiricists—wrongly—held all mathematical postulates to be analytic. See Schlick 1968c and Schlick 1938, pp. 145–46. Also Zahar, E. 2001, chapter 5.)

Popper, who stood close to the Vienna Circle without ever becoming one of its members, soon realized that no contingent universal law can be experimentally verified. In order to be useful, a scientific theory must enable us to predict; which clearly implies that the time coordinate occurring in the theory must have future import. This explains why most laws are universal with respect to the time variable; so that in order to serve as a guide to action, scientific hypotheses must always remain unverified by experience. Thus the Neopositivists had excluded not only 'metaphysics' but also natural science from the domain of rational discourse. Admittedly, one essential point remained ungainsayable: no matter how tentative, a conjecture can legitimately be termed empirical only if it somehow comes into contact with experience. From what has just been said, it follows that the only form of contact is one of possible conflict with observation; whence Popper's well-known demarcation criterion: a consistent proposition H should be regarded as scientific if it is empirically refutable; should this not be the case, then H will be termed 'metaphysical'. Let us immediately note that Popper's definition was not intended to be a meaning-criterion. On the contrary: an unfalsifiable but syntactically well-formed sentence M does not only convey a meaning; it can also act as the metaphysical principle underpinning a whole research program. It can therefore be said that Popper gave a renewed dignity to metaphysics.

Popper's criterion leaves open two possibilities for a well-formed sentence M to be metaphysical: though irrefutable, M could be empirically verifiable; or M might be totally independent of experience, i.e. M might be both unverifiable and unfalsifiable by experience. In the first case, M will be called metaphysical 'in the narrow sense', or more simply 'narrowly metaphysical'; and in the second, M will be described as synthetic apriori. M might furthermore be considered a priori in the psychological sense of our being unable to cease believing in it; but then rationality would still demand that M be *objectively* irrefutable and hence metaphysical in Popper's sense. This subjective concept of the apriori will anyway be of little interest to us.

Note here that in the above 'apriori' does not have the Kantian connotation of 'necessarily true'. It is equivalent to: fully empirically undecidable; so that even though, unbeknown to us, M is actually false, we could still hold on to it come what may (Note that this conclusion applies to all metaphysical theses and not only to synthetic a priori propositions). For example: despite being acknowledged as synthetic, some mathematical postulates are wholly empirically undecidable and hence apriori in the above sense. Though irrefutable, mathematics could nonetheless be indirectly undermined by experience; for sophisticated mathematical principles form part of almost every scientific system S. As pointed out by Quine, considerations of simplicity or, alternatively, a serious experimental failure of S might lead us to alter not only the physical but also the mathematical postulates of our system (See Quine, W.v.O. 1980c). It can therefore be asked: are there any propositions which, unlike the mathematical axioms, are synthetic a priori in some absolute or intrinsic sense? In what follows, I propose to show that the Principle of Induction is synthetic as well as *absolutely* apriori: despite knowing Induction to be fallible, there is no situation in which we might be prepared to give it up. We therefore fully sympathise with Poincaré when he admits to being as incapable of defending induction as of doing without it.

As for those propositions which are narrowly metaphysical, they include every existential sentence of the form $(\exists x)P(x)$, where P is a conjunction of observational predicates. It is e.g. clear that the statement 'There exists a diamond whose diameter exceeds 10 metres' is both verifiable and empirically irrefutable; where, in the present context, 'diamond' denotes a cluster of observationally ascertainable properties. But here again, though strictly unfalsifiable, $(\exists x)P(x)$ could form part of a scientific system S; so that should S be empirically undermined, then we might have grounds for rejecting $(\exists x)P(x)$; this proposition would thus have been indirectly condemned by experience. For example: assuming the existence of an extra planet might cause our astronomical theory to be falsified by observation and hence lead us to reject this existential assumption. $(\exists x)P(x)$ thus proves to be metaphysical not only in the narrow, but also in a very relative sense. There exists nevertheless a different class of narrowly metaphysical propositions: apart from being verifiable, these are absolutely irrefutable in that no conceivable situation can arise which might lead us to regard them as having been empirically undermined. Such are all statements of the form $(H^* \rightarrow H)$ which express the difference between a scientific theory H and its Ramsey-sentence H^* (See below, Chapter VII).

II

The Problem of Induction

(A) A MODEST SOLUTION OF THE PROBLEM OF INDUCTION (POINCARÉ, POPPER AND LAKATOS)

When thinking about the logical invalidity of Induction, two names come to mind, those of Hume and Popper. As is well known, Hume held that we have an irrepressible but unjustified belief in inductive inferences. Popper's attitude to this problem is both more ambiguous and more sophisticated than Hume's. In 1934, Popper laid down a set of rules for scientific research, rules which had little to do with the notion of truth; so that *The Logic of Scientific Discovery* had no truly epistemological dimension. Popper had of course already espoused realism—at least at the intuitive level. The Correspondence Theory of Truth had unfortunately fallen into disrepute; that is: until the time when Tarski proposed his truth-schema $[\mathrm{Tr}(p^*) \leftrightarrow p]$; where p is an arbitrary sentence of the object-language and p^* is a name of p. Basing himself on Tarski's work, Popper put forward a notion of verisimilitude according to which, of two theories A and B, A possesses a higher degree of verisimilitude than B iff: $[((T_A \supseteq T_B) \wedge (F_A \subset F_B)) \vee ((T_A \supset T_B) \wedge (F_A \subseteq F_B))]$, where: a theory K is defined as any set of sentences closed under the relation of logical consequence; T_K and F_K are, respectively, the truth-content and the falsity-content of K; i.e. T_K is the set of all true members of K, and F_K that of all its false members. Hence: $T_K = \{X: (X \in K) \& (X^* \text{ is true})\}$;

$F_K = \{X: (X \in K) \& (X^* \text{ is false})\}$; $K = T_K \cup F_k$ and $T_K \cap F_K = \emptyset$. (Note: in what follows, we shall not distinguish scripturally between X and X^*; so that we shall e.g. say of X, rather than of X^*, that it is true). This definition clearly constitutes a good formal rendering of our intuitive notion of verisimilitude, i.e. of truth-likeness. This is why Lakatos urged Popper to adopt an inductive principle which would synthetically link verisimilitude to corroboration. Such a principle should enable us to assert—tentatively— that a theory having withstood severe tests stands a good chance of being truth-like; or at any rate: a better chance than an empirically undermined rival (See Lakatos, I. 1978b).

As is by now well known, David Miller and then Pavel Tichy showed that no false theory can have have a degree of verisimilitude higher than that of *any* other. One elegant proof, to which David Miller drew my attention and whose central idea goes back to C. Hempel, goes as follows.

Let J be any interpretation of the language in which A and B are expressed. J, which will be kept fixed throughout the proof, enables us to speak of the truth or falsity of all the members of A and of B. Suppose that A is false, i.e. that $F_A \neq \emptyset$; also that A has a higher degree of verisimilitude than B; i.e. $[((T_A \supseteq T_B) \wedge (F_A \subset F_B)) \vee ((T_A \supset T_B) \wedge (F_A \subseteq F_B))]$; so that we anyway have $[(T_A \supseteq T_B) \wedge (F_A \supseteq F_B)]$. We shall show that A = B.

Since A is false, there exists at least one false consequence f of A. I.e. $f \in F_A$; hence $f \in F_B$ since $F_A \subseteq F_B$; B is therefore also false. Let $X \in A$. Given that $f \in F_A \subseteq A$, we have $A \supseteq \{f, X\} \} (f \wedge X)$; whence $(f \wedge X) \in A$, for A is closed under logical consequence. But since f is false, then so is $(f \wedge X)$; i.e. $(f \wedge X) \in F_A$. But $F_A \subseteq F_B$; so $(f \wedge X) \in F_B$; *a fortiori*: $(f \wedge X) \in B$. Thus: B $\{f \wedge X\} \} X$. Since B is also closed under logical consequence, it follows that $X \in B$. We have thus shown that $A \subseteq B$.

Conversely, let $Y \in B$. Thus: $B \supseteq \{Y\} \} (\neg f \vee Y)$; so $(\neg f \vee Y) \in B$, for B is closed under logical consequence. But since f is false, $(\neg f \vee Y)$ is true. Hence, by definition of T_B: $(\neg f \vee Y) \in T_B$; so $(\neg f \vee Y) \in T_A$ since $T_A \supseteq T_B$. But by definition, $T_A \subseteq A$. Therefore $(\neg f \vee Y) \in A$; so that: $A \supseteq \{f, \neg f \vee Y\} \} Y$; whence $Y \in A$ since A is closed under logical consequence. Thus $B \subseteq A$. Together with $A \subseteq B$, this yields: A = B; whence $T_A = T_B$ and $F_A = F_B$, which contradicts the relation: $[((T_A \supseteq T_B) \wedge (F_A \subset F_B)) \vee ((T_A \supset T_B) \wedge (F_A \subseteq F_B))]$.

Of two false theories, neither can therefore have a degree of verisimilitude greater than that of the other; which defeats the whole purpose of Popper's notion of verisimilitude.

Precisely because Popper's definition closely captures our presystematic concept of verisimilitude, Miller's negative result constitutes a serious setback for epistemological realism as a whole. Yet Popper—rightly—continued to hold that scientists are entitled to go on making use of the intuitive notion of truth-likeness (See Popper 1983, Introduction). But it seems to me that his views had by then rejoined those of Duhem, according to whom the whole of science tends asymptotically towards a natural classification. The latter is taken to reflect the ontological order which it cannot however directly signify. Through atomizing the domain of discourse of a proposition, Tarski's approach, which lies at the foundation of the above definition of verisimilitude, might after all prove inapplicable to physical science (See Duhem, 1954, Part 1, Chapter II).

The problems besetting verisimilitude reemerge, albeit in a somewhat different form, in connection with the technological reliability of scientific hypotheses. Had Popper's definition been appropriate, then the degree of corroboration of a law could legitimately have been regarded as an index of its verisimilitude. This would have enabled us to assert that a highly corroborated theory A is likely to be more reliable than an empirically undermined rival B; for the ratio of the truth-content T_A of A to its falsity content F_A is, in an intuitive sense, higher than that of T_B to F_B; by choosing to apply A, we are therefore more likely to be making use of true propositions than in the case of B. The notion of verisimilitude can nonetheless be short-circuited and the following problem posed: degrees of corroboration pertain to the past record of theories and say nothing about their future performance. In fact, starting from intuitively self-evident assumptions, it has been proved that no matter how many empirical facts support a universal hypothesis, the latter's probability never rises above zero; and yet, in technology, we normally decide to apply the most highly confirmed theories; provided, of course, that the latter's relevant predictions be actually derivable. It can therefore be asked whether this decision is rational; more precisely: whether it is *zweckrational* in the sense of being the means most appropriate to some given—practical—end. Could we not just as rationally, or just as non-rationally, opt for another criterion of choice or even choose our theories at random? Note that in technology a decision is termed rational only if it can be linked, in one way or another, to the question of the reliability of certain laws; as long as the latter remains outside the domain of methodology, every technological decision, no matter how arbitrary, is permissible. This is why Popper was often urged to accept, independently of any notion of verisimilitude, an inductive principle which would treat the degree of corroboration as an index of reliability. This suggestion leads me to put forward the following proposition—henceforth denoted by J(H, K, Δ)—where H , K and Δ are to be treated as free variables:

Let H be a theory which has withstood the severest form of criticism; more particularly, suppose that H is a unified and non-ad hoc scientific system which has been systematically corroborated in some domain Δ Then, with regard to the future, H is (in the long run) less likely to break down in Δ than any rival hypothesis K which has succumbed to severe criticism or which has more particularly been empirically undermined in Δ (See Appendix 5; and for an alternative approach to the problem of induction, see Appendix 4).

In view of the universal quantification over H and K, $(\forall H, K, \Delta)J(H, K, \Delta)$ is unverifiable; and because of the occurrence in it of the locution 'less likely (in the long run)', $(\forall H, K, \Delta)J(H, K, \Delta)$ is also strictly irrefutable. Induction—as expressed by $(\forall H, K, \Delta)J(H, K, \Delta)$ —is therefore unfalsifiable and uncriticisable, hence synthetic apriori in the new sense explained above. One can of course try to argue for the rational acceptability of $(\forall H, K, \Delta)J(H, K, \Delta)$ by appealing to the improbability of coincidences, or to what Alain Boyer calls the non-existence of a malicious demon bent on deceiving us (See Boyer 1997). Let us note that Poincaré had already used the first type of argument in support of the truth–likeness of highly confirmed physical laws. But this seems to me to shift the problem—in an admittedly interesting way—but not really to solve it in the sense of reducing it, say, to a logical principle (Poincaré, 1906. Chapter XI, p. 184). For our refusal to accept the presence of a deceitful demon or of long series of coincidences constitutes a principle essentially equivalent to $(\forall H, K, \Delta)J(H, K, \Delta)$. This does not mean that the attempts to derive Induction from other propositions are worthless; for alternative versions of induction might be intuitively more convincing than, or at least as convincing as $(\forall H, K, \Delta)J(H, K, \Delta)$. Different but convergent intuitions would thus reinforce each other. In order to illustrate this point, let me adduce two examples borrowed from pure mathematics. In logic, three intensionally different definitions of computability were put forward; namely Gödel's and Turing's definitions, as well as a characterization by means of μ-recursiveness. That all these approaches proved equivalent lent intuitive support to each one of them, as well as to Church's thesis that all mechanically calculable functions are recursive (See Hermes, 1965. Chapters 4 and 5). Despite being the easiest criterion to apply, μ-recursiveness at first seemed ad hoc, especially when compared with the other two definitions. But given the equivalence of the three criteria, logicians could from then on restrict themselves to the condition of μ-recursiveness. A second example is provided by set theory. In most branches of mathematics, e.g. in topology as well as in algebra, Zorn's Lemma turns out to be more useful, though intuitively less transparent than either the Axiom of Choice or Zermelo's Well-ordering Theorem. As in the case of general recursiveness, the proven equivalence of these three principles reinforces each one of them taken separately. With regard to Induction, the non-existence of a malicious demon and the improbability of coincidences, where the latter appears to be based on quasi-logical considerations, similarly reinforce our belief in $(\forall H, K, \Delta)J(H, K, \Delta)$.

Let us look more closely at Poincaré's arguments in support of the Principle of Induction. These are given in the more general context of his defense of Structural Scientific Realism (SSR). Poincaré's reasoning always involves the following inference (See below, Chapter VII). To begin with, the principle of unity is regarded as a transcendental condition to be imposed on all scientific hypotheses. So let H be a unified system, i.e. one whose various parts are closely knit; and let D be a domain in which H can be empirically put to the test. (For the sake of simplicity, we have dropped the inverted commas and identified H with 'H'). Should one part of H diverge considerably from the truth, then thanks to the unity of H, the falsity of this one component will have repercussions throughout the system, more particularly in those parts yielding basic statements. H can thus be expected to get the facts wrong in whole subdomains of D. Suppose however that H has actually been confirmed whenever and wherever it was tested. Only finitely many tests could admittedly have been conducted; and it could be argued that even a hopelessly false theory accidentally gets some of the facts right. But we should then be compelled to assume that an evil demon made us test H only at those points where this hypothesis happened to make correct predictions. Otherwise, the chances are that we would have stumbled on one of the many falsifiers of H. In order to illustrate this point, Poincaré considers a fictitious example in which Tycho imagined himself to have observed Mars only when the real path of this planet happened to intersect an ellipse. Poincaré argued that this kind of conspiracy theory is highly unlikely, for it relies on the existence either of an evil demon or of an improbable sequence of coincidences. It is therefore likely that H is at least approximately true. He concludes:

> For this purpose let us see what part is played in our generalizations by the belief in simplicity. We have verified a simple law in a considerable number of particular cases. We refuse to admit that this coincidence, so often repeated, is a result of mere chance and we conclude that the law must be true in the general case.
>
> ... This simplicity, real or apparent, has always a cause. We shall therefore always be able to reason in the same fashion, and if a simple law has been observed in several particular cases, we may legitimately suppose that it will still be true in analogous cases. To refuse to admit this would be to attribute an inadmissible role to chance. (Poincaré 1902, pp. 149–150)

Poincaré realized that through his no-conspiracy argument he was simultaneously addressing the problem of induction, which he nonetheless admitted being unable to solve:

I do not at all wish to investigate here the foundations of the principle of induction; I know very well that I shall not succeed; it is as
difficult to justify this principle as to get on without it. I only wish
to show how scientists apply it and are forced to apply it. (Poincaré
1906a, p. 133)

No matter what one thinks of Poincaré's intuitive anti-conspiracy argument, it remains a central tenet underpinning the whole of scientific practice. For example: Poincaré could not bring himself to believe that only the
first and second-order effects of the earth's motion systematically failed to
materialize; so he concluded that Relativity is a universally valid principle.
Maxwell similarly refused to accept that light should have exactly the same
velocity as all electromagnetic disturbances and yet differ fundamentally
from the latter. Finally, Einstein could not believe that despite being caused
by absolute velocities, electromagnetic processes systematically give rise to
phenomena dependent only on relative motions; and he found it odd that
despite expressing two essentially different properties of matter, gravity and
inertia seemed always to remain in unison at the observable level (See
below, Chapter IX). To repeat: in all these situations, scientists refused to
believe that some Cartesian demon set out to deceive them about what
really happens behind the scenes; which in turn led them to found induction
on the rejection of conspiracy theories.

Let us go back to discussing the theses put forward by Popper and
Lakatos. The latter considered the difference between his viewpoint and
Popper's so small as to be purely verbal. Lakatos held that the rationality of technological praxis flows from the acceptance of some inductive
assumption. But he also realized that induction cannot be vindicated
without resorting to a principle of the same kind, albeit of a higher-order;
which obviously lands the epistemologist in an infinite regress, thus
showing that induction cannot be justified. The rationality of technology
has therefore to be paid for by the non-rational acceptance of induction.
This is why Lakatos rightly believed that he and Popper differed only
over the levels at which non-rationality has to be admitted into the sciences: according to Lakatos, this occurs at the level of an unjustifiable
inductive principle which justifies technological practice; and according
to Popper: at the level of technology itself. Popper's position clearly
implies that every time we decide to apply a scientific theory we take an
'existential risk'. What Lakatos did not know was that in 1930–33,
Popper had already dealt with this problem by proposing the following—
clearly inductivist—solution:

We unquestionably believe in the probability of hypotheses. And what is more significant: our belief that many a hypothesis is more probable than another is motivated by reasons which undeniably possess an objective aspect (*Gründe, denen ein objektiver Zug nicht abgesprochen werden kann*). (Popper 1979, beginning of §15. My translation)

And again:

The subjective belief in the probability of hypotheses can be based on their corroboration, but it goes beyond what corroboration can effectively do. According to this belief, a corroborated hypothesis will again be corroborated. Clearly, without this belief, we could not act and hence could not live either. There is in this belief nothing which should further intrigue us. Its objective motives are clarified by the notion of corroboration to such an extent that this belief should not give rise to the deployment of any further epistemological questions. (Popper 1979, end of §16. My translation)

Thus Popper's position is indistinguishable from Poincaré's. Through conceding the need for a belief in the probability of hypotheses, Popper moreover goes well beyond the acceptance of a proposition like ($\forall$H, K, Δ)J(H, K, Δ). And it is no use objecting that *Die beiden Grundprobleme der Erkenntnistheorie* is the early work of an author who subsequently altered his views about the principle of induction; for *Die beiden Grundprobleme* was first published in 1979, at which point Popper took the opportunity of indicating, in various footnotes, the problems and solutions about which he had changed his mind during the intervening years. One of these—very important—footnotes concerns the nature of allowable criticism. In 1930, Popper regarded only transcendental—as opposed to transcendent—criticism as legitimate. Transcendental or immanent criticism holds only two methods to be allowable: first, the logical method which examines whether a given position M is coherent; secondly, an internal analysis whose aim is to examine how well or how badly M accounts for its basis, whether the latter be empirical or quasi-empirical, more particularly: methodological. In the case of a scientific theory M, the basis consists of the negations of M's potential falsifiers. Where M is a methodology, the basis consists of the descriptions of those procedures which have been used in what is normally taken to be successful scientific practice (See below, Chapter VI). In this sense, methodology is a science of the sciences. Transcendent criticism, which Popper rightly rejected in 1930, consists of pitting M against a position M' whose main characteristic is its incompatibility with M. For example: M could be Newtonian physics and M' the Cartesian metaphysical thesis that no forces act instantaneously at a distance; or M might be Quantum Mechanics and M' the Einsteinian requirement a theory should provide a complete description of physical reality; finally, M' might be the condition that all scientific laws should be deterministic and M any methodology according to which statistical hypotheses are allowable, provided they yield the accepted facts. In a footnote Popper indicated that, by 1979, he had changed his views about the nature of permissible criticism; for he had come to consider the transcendent method as permissible (Popper 1979, p. 53, footnote). This was, to my mind, an unfortunate decision which turned criticism into something ill-defined, all-pervasive and amorphous; for from now on, any 'plausible' metaphysical thesis M' could be regarded as constituting a legitimate criticism of any hypothesis M which, though empirically successful, has the misfortune of being irreconcilable with M'. Be it as it may, such widening of the scope of allowable criticism might have led one to believe that Popper had concurrently altered his views about the need for an unavoidable, albeit unjustified principle of induction: because of the new scope given to criticism, successful resistance to the latter might have been expected to render all inductive concessions expendable. Popper seems however to have realized that this could by no means be the case; for criticism, and resistance to it, are always past-orientated; which is no doubt why the above passage occurs, without any disclaimer, in all modern editions of *Die beiden Grundprobleme*.

(B) DAVID MILLER'S RADICAL SOLUTION

Although David Miller claims to have drawn his conclusions from Popper's theses, his solution—or rather dissolution—of the problem of induction is far more radical than Popper's. In view of the revolutionary, not to say the startling, character of Miller's proposal, the latter deserves to be examined in some detail. Let me say, right from the start, that I hold Miller's position to be coherent but ultimately unacceptable.

Miller distinguishes sharply between science and technology; also between the different roles which induction is alleged to play in these two disciplines. Let us start with the case of science. Miller writes:

> It suffices to recall that if an agent accepts some set Y of propositions then, whether he appreciates it or not, he accepts all the logical

consequences of Y. In particular, if the agent accepts some laws of nature or other spatio-temporally universal generalization—in this paper, calling a generalization a law is understood not to imply its truth—that is, accepts them to be true—then, like it or not, he accepts that in some respects the future will resemble the past. . . . No metaphysical principle of induction is needed. . . . (Miller 2002, p. 85)

This whole argument seems to me to trade on the ambiguity of the word 'accept'. In the absence of an inductive principle, a critical rationalist—call him **C**—accepts neither as true nor even as truth-like any universal proposition H. Before testing the hypothesis H or having it tested by somebody else, **C** merely entertains, envisages or contemplates H. If the outcome of the test is negative, i.e. if H is observationally refuted, then **C** is in my opinion committed to accepting the truth of ¬H, i.e. the falsity of H. Should H be confirmed and even if H is both unified and non-ad hoc, then *unless* **C** *subscribes to some inductive principle*, he will continue to abstain from regarding H as true or even as verisimilar; and so **C** will certainly not commit himself to the view that the future will resemble the past in the way described by H. Thus **C** has absolutely no reason to make technological use of H rather than of any other hypothesis. **C** is in fact entitled to only one assertion, namely that H is—to date—not known to be false. All this is nothing but trivial, albeit fully justified Popperian orthodoxy arising from the asymmetry between confirmation and empirical refutation. So when Miller claims that 'The procedure of acceptance plays an ineliminable role in deductivism, since a hypothesis cannot be rejected until it has been accepted', a Popperian of my ilk cannot but be startled; until, that is, he realizes that the author explicitly equates 'accept' with 'conjecture' (Miller 2002, pp. 98–97). Needless to say, this definition considerably weakens the meaning of 'accept'. In as far as it conveys something like 'provisionally assume to be true', even the word 'conjecture' is a misnomer which ought to be replaced by verbs like 'consider', 'entertain' or 'envisage'. Of course, in order for H to be tested, it must previously have been entertained and understood. Many scientists moreover believe—at least provisionally—that their theories are true or at least that they will escape refutation. But this belief, which is normally based on the realization that the envisaged theory H explains some of the known phenomena and hence *already* has a measure of empirical support, is no part of the testing process; where the latter might anyway issue in the rejection of H. After all, the theoretician might ask an experimental physicist to test H, where the experimentalist could well adopt a totally agnostic attitude with respect to H. In other words:

H can be tested without in any way presupposing that the future will resemble the past *modulo* H.

Let me again try to explain why a principle like $(\forall H, K, \Delta)J(H, K, \Delta)$ cannot be circumvented. Suppose that H and K yield the generalizations $(\forall \underline{x}, t)[A(\underline{x}, t) \rightarrow C(\underline{x}, t)]$ and $(\forall \underline{x}, t)[B(\underline{x}, t) \rightarrow C(\underline{x}, t)]$ respectively; where $(\underline{x}, t)$ is a 4-tuple of spatio-temporal coordinates. We assume that A, B and C are observational predicates; moreover that—unlike $C(\underline{x}, t)$—both $A(\underline{x}, t)$ and $B(\underline{x},t)$ can be actualized at will. Suppose further that in the domain Δ, K has been refuted through the verification of $[B(\underline{x}_0, t_0) \wedge \neg C(\underline{x}_0, t_0) \wedge B(\underline{x}_1, t_1) \wedge \neg C(\underline{x}_1, t_1) \wedge \supset \wedge B(\underline{x}_n, t_n) \wedge \neg C(\underline{x}_n, t_n)]$; while H has been corroborated by $[A(\underline{y}_0, t_0) \wedge C(\underline{y}_0, t_0) \wedge A(\underline{y}_1, t_1) \wedge C(\underline{y}_1, t_1) \wedge \supset \wedge A(\underline{y}_n, t_n) \wedge C(\underline{y}_n, t_n)]$. Consider the future, i.e. some instant t' such that $t' > \text{Max}(t_0, t_1 \supset , t_n)$; and suppose that we are interested in bringing $C(\underline{x}', t')$ about; i.e. our intention is that C should obtain at $(\underline{x}', t')$, where $(\underline{x}', t')$ lies in Δ. Should we then make use of H or of K, i.e. should we actualize $A(\underline{x}', t')$ or $B(\underline{x}', t')$? As conceded by Popper in the above passage taken from his (1979), any normal person would intuitively attribute to H a probability higher than that of K; and such a person would certainly refuse to trust K, which he instinctively expects to be refuted—yet again—at $(\underline{x}', t')$. In other words, he takes the hypothesis R for granted; where $R \equiv_{\text{Def.}} (\forall \underline{x},t)[((\underline{x}, t) \in \Delta) \wedge B(\underline{x}, t)) \rightarrow \neg C(\underline{x}, t)]$. This is precisely why Popper held a theory to be refuted not by a single basic statement but by the latter conjoined with a low-level hypothesis such as R. R is however not verified, but merely supported by the $[B(\underline{x}_j, t_j) \wedge \neg C(\underline{x}_j, t_j)]$'s. Barring a principle of induction, we therefore have no reason for accepting R as true and are thus caught in a circle: we should like to replace induction by a falsificationist criterion, but falsification cannot be achieved without induction. Taken by itself, the falsification of K through $[B(\underline{x}_0, t_0) \wedge \neg C(\underline{x}_0, t_0) \wedge B(\underline{x}_1, t_1) \wedge \neg C(\underline{x}_1, t_1) \wedge \supset \wedge B(\underline{x}_n, t_n) \wedge \neg C(\underline{x}_n, t_n)]$ neither entails nor probabilifies $[B(\underline{x}', t') \rightarrow \neg C(\underline{x}', t')]$. So nothing prevents us from making use of K, i.e. from actualizing $B(\underline{x}', t')$ rather than $A(\underline{x}', t')$, and then waiting for $C(\underline{x}', t')$ to materialize. According to Popper, the choice of H in preference to K is however "'rational' in the most obvious sense known to me: the best-tested theory is the one which, in the light of our *critical discussion,* appears to be the best so far, and I do not know of anything more 'rational' than a well-conducted critical discussion." But he then back-pedals by adding: ". . . in spite of the 'rationality' of choosing the best-tested theory as a basis of action, this choice is *not* 'rational' in the sense that it is based upon *good reasons* for expecting that it will in practice be a successful choice: *there can be no good reasons* in this sense, and this is precisely Hume's result." These two passages, taken from *Objective Knowledge*, are quoted by Miller, albeit in the order opposite to that in which they occur in Popper's text (Popper 1972, p. 22). It follows that the second quotation describes Popper's definitive position on the problem of induction. Still, we have here two theses which give rise to a confusion due to the ambiguity of the adjective 'rational'. Unless his intention be to extend or modify the meaning of 'rationality', Popper was being somewhat disingenuous. Be it as it may, the two quotations taken from Popper's (1972) lend some credence to A. Musgrave's construal of *what might have been* Popper's solution of the Problem of Induction; that is: had Popper explicitly endorsed Musgrave's interpretation. According to the latter:

> . . . But suppose our critical endeavors fail and [the hypothesis] H stands up to our efforts to criticize it. Then this fact is a good reason to believe H, tentatively and for the time being, *though it is not a reason for the hypothesis H itself.* (Musgrave 2004, p. 21. Italics in the original text)

It seems to me that Musgrave's proposal constitutes a purely terminological 'solution' based on the following dubious principle: one can have a good reason for *believing* that a proposition H has some property P (e.g. truth, approximate truth, likelihood of being true, or even falsity), although this is no good reason for H possessing P. Note that I have added 'falsity' to the list; for according to Popper, all basic statements are theory-dependent, so that even an empirical refutation of H does not establish the falsity of H. Nothing in what follows will however depend on 'falsity' figuring in the list.

Musgrave's construal is in effect tantamount to a semantic redefinition of the notion of 'good reason'. If, despite H having withstood very severe tests, there is no good reason why H *itself* should even be approximately true, then I might just as well, or just as rationally, act on any theory K chosen at random. Should I decide to behave in this way, then I should naturally be confined to a mental asylum; and this by virtue of the general acceptance of a principle like $(\forall H, K, \Delta) J(H, K, \Delta)$ which links criticism with actual, approximate, or likelihood of, truth. Imagine telling an engineer that there are good reasons for his *believing* in the reliability of H but not for H being actually reliable. He will certainly be unimpressed by such an assurance; for he will be concerned about the bridge he is about to construct not falling down, not about his *beliefs* concerning the solidity of the bridge. Musgrave's 'solution' would moreover turn the undeniable technological breakthroughs achieved by the sciences—as distinct from any *beliefs* about these breakthroughs—into a series of miracles.

As already mentioned: in technology, acting on the best-tested hypothesis can be termed rational only if it is *zweck*rational, i.e. if bestness can somehow be linked to the likelihood of practical success. Having excluded this possibility, Popper admits to being incapable of going beyond Hume's insight on this subject. But he had already altered the very meaning of 'rationality' which, given the present context, is the only relevant one. He had thus given the impression, or rather the illusion of having shown induction to be expendable, and hence of having solved Hume's problem. And David Miller—as well as Alan Musgrave—urge us to accept such a solution at face value. We should however refuse to be fobbed off by being called 'rational' in a purely honorific sense, i.e. a sense which has absolutely no technological clout. Miller in fact asks us to renounce any quest for good reasons and simply follow certain procedures which are labeled 'rational'; to which our only reply should be that such rituals are devoid of both real interest and practical relevance. Let me illustrate, by means of a concrete example, the *tour de passe-passe* we are invited to swallow. Assume that I prefer 'red' to all other colors and that I set out to buy a mechanically reliable vehicle. Suppose further that a salesman offers me a choice between two cars, one red and the other black, while being unable to provide me with any information about the comparative reliability of the two vehicles. Given that I prefer 'red' to 'black', it is in a sense 'rational' for me to opt for the red car; but this kind of rationality is totally irrelevant to my primary aim, which is to reduce the likelihood of breakdowns. Had I preferred 'black' to 'red', then my choice would—just as rationally—have been different. In the absence of an inductive assumption, the two cars can be made to stand for two scientific hypotheses; while 'red' and 'black' could respectively be interpreted as 'written in verse but (having been) empirically undermined' and 'written in prose and (having been) empirically confirmed'. To repeat: in the absence of an inductive assumption such as $(\forall H, K, \Delta)J(H, K, \Delta)$, there is no question of one choice being practically more *zweck*rational than another.

This having been said, I still hold that in theoretical science, only the notion of truth-qua-correspondence plays the role of an essential regulative idea. We could—if we so wished—dispense with all inductive principles; we could attribute different degrees of corroboration to our laws without passing judgment on their future performance. If the theorist's latest conjecture K happens to be refuted, then the only thing he henceforth needs to keep in mind is that K is false. Since he aims at the truth, he is committed either to modifying K or else to starting his researches afresh. So far, no induction needs be presupposed. All the same: the scientist's next move will normally be based on considerations of truth-likeness; he would be ill-advised to continue working on the same research program after the latter has suffered a long sequence of degenerating shifts, the latest one being the breakdown of K. Such degeneration usually indicates that the core of the program—e.g. Aristotelian Dynamics, the Phlogiston Theory or Newton's Laws—is false; which accounts for the repeated failures of the program. For instance, it would be foolish for a modern physicist to work on a new version of Ptolemaic astronomy rather than on an Einsteinian type of cosmology. Still, in theoretical science, an inductive principle like $(\forall H, K, \Delta) J (H,K,\Delta)$ remains optional: after falsifying K, then as long as he avoids empirical refutation, the scientist is free to do whatever he deems fit. Miller is however reluctant to admit that matters are very different in technology, about whose nature he holds views widely differing from mine.

(C) HOW DIFFERENT IS SCIENCE FROM TECHNOLOGY?

Under the heading 'Applied Science', Miller writes:

> Given the initial condition that the predicate A is satisfied at a spatio-temporal location k, the agent may accordingly use the generalization $[(\forall k)(Ak \rightarrow Ck)]$ to conclude that C is satisfied at k. But for this he needs to know not only the generalization $(\forall k)(Ak \rightarrow Ck)$ but also the initial condition Ak. It should be clear that if it is Ck that is the agent's known goal, then it is a generalization of the form $(\forall y)(Cy \rightarrow Ay)$ that would give him the instructions on how to proceed, rather than one of the form $(\forall y)(Ay \rightarrow Cy)$. Yet it is rare for a temporally prior condition A to be necessary for an event C. Sufficient conditions for C, in contrast, often abound, but are unknown . . . It is more likely that he [the agent] knows all the science in the world, yet does not know a single generalization with the required consequent C. . . .
>
> As almost any academic engineer will remind you if you ask 'what is your field of research?', technology is a different business from pure science. The main business of technology (and practical action of all kinds) is not the formulation and critical assessment of generalizations, but the formulation and critical assessment of useful initial conditions or plans or proposals. . . . The fundamental laws

and generalizations are taken for granted. (p. 90). . . . In any case, the solutions are highly conjectural, and not implied by, nor even suggested by, our scientific knowledge.

These trite logical considerations do not entail that scientific knowledge is of no use to technology. On the contrary: what they indicate is that when theories are practically applied, they are applied not positively but negatively. Theories proscribe, they do not prescribe. (Miller 2002, pp. 89–90)

Far from being trite or logical, these considerations strike me as totally unacceptable. Miller's point that a technologist knows his goal, namely the consequent C, but that the antecedent is as yet unknown to him seems to me to reduce to the following uncontroversial claim: given a hypothesis H and a formula $C(\underline{x}, t)$, it may well be impossible *mechanically* to find an $A(\underline{x}, t)$ such that $A(\underline{x}, t)$ is realizable and $\vdash [H \to (\forall \underline{x}, t)(A(\underline{x}, t) \to C(\underline{x}, t))]$; where the emphasis should be placed on the word 'mechanically'. But this kind of undecideability has never prevented scientists from constructing proofs. Anyway, Miller's remarks apply not only to $\vdash (H \to (\forall \underline{x}, t)(A(\underline{x}, t) \to C(\underline{x}, t)))$ but equally well to $\vdash (H \to (\forall \underline{x}, t)(C(\underline{x}, t) \to A(\underline{x}, t)))$, i.e. to $\vdash (H \to (\forall \underline{x}, t)$ $(\neg A(\underline{x}, t) \to \neg C(\underline{x}, t)))$; where $\neg A(\underline{x}, t)$ is unknown whereas $\neg C(\underline{x}, t)$, like $C(\underline{x}, t)$, is known. Miller's objection moreover hits the very notion of the empirical testability of all hypotheses, whether these be theoretical or applied. As pointed out by Duhem, H is testable only within the context of a larger system S, some of whose components describe the behavior of the instruments meant to be used in testing or in applying the central hypothesis H. Thus one of the creative tasks of a physicist **E** is to enlarge H into a coherent system S and then to tease out of S a consequence of the form: $(\forall \underline{x}, t)[A(\underline{x}, t) \to C(\underline{x}, t)]$; where A is realizable, while both A and C are observational. (Note that $C(\underline{x}, t)$ might be of the form $C^*(\underline{x}, t+a)$, a being the time-interval between cause and effect). Hence the physicist might well find himself in a position worse than that of the technologist; for in his case, both A and C could initially be unknown. Yet only after withstanding severe criticism, e.g. through being shown to be non-ad hoc, and only after being strongly corroborated by statements of the form $[A(\underline{x}_j, t_j) \wedge C(\underline{x}_j, t_j)]$ can H be used in practical applications. As shown above, the latter could in turn be based on the deduction, from S, of statements of the form $(\forall \underline{x}, t)[A'(\underline{x}, t) \to C'(\underline{x}, t)]$ where A' and C' have properties similar to those of A and C respectively. (There is in fact no reason why we should not have $A = A'$ and $C = C'$). As correctly pointed out by Miller, the technologist will generally take S, or rather the generalization

$(\forall \underline{x}, t)[A'(\underline{x}, t) \to C'(\underline{x}, t)]$ for granted; but Miller fails to add that the technologist should be reminded—by all conscientious Popperians—that his confidence is not founded on logic but on the acceptance of something like the metaphysical principle $(\forall H, K, \Delta) J(H, K, \Delta)$; for $(\forall \underline{x}, t)[A'(\underline{x}, t) \to C'(\underline{x}, t)]$ is not verified but merely corroborated by past experience. He should also note that though subscribing to $(\forall H, K, \Delta) J(H, K, \Delta)$ be unjustified, it is so only in the trivial sense that any premise is presupposed rather than justified by an argument. Though unjustifiable and even uncriticizable, Induction is in fact precisely that which allows us to assess science and hence to put it to technological use. In the absence of an inductive principle, there exists at best a psychological difference between, on the one hand, the technologist who applies a hypothesis H and, on the other, the physicist who sets out to test H: the former feels certain that the result C will materialize once the state of affairs A is actualized, while the latter is genuinely ignorant about the outcome of his experiment. As for the fundamentalist Popperian who genuinely abjures induction, he is committed to regarding every application of a theory as a fresh test of the latter; so Miller is in effect unable to distinguish between science and technology. His position actually entails that not only technological applications but also all tests are helped exclusively negatively by the presence of the theory to be tested; which is a patently untenable consequence.

Let us now turn to the question of the heuristic relevance of science to technology and to the claim that:

> . . . it would be a deductivist fantasy (not to mention an insult to many inventors of genius) to suggest that these inventions are suggested, except in the most dreamy and impracticable fashion, by the laws that explain them *post hoc*.
>
> . . . The [Baconian] doctrine perversely confuses science with technology, thus masking the true relationship between the two. As several writers . . . have observed, for most of their histories science and technology proceeded independently of each other; although sometimes science gained from technological advances (in the grinding of lenses, for example), not much was achieved in the other direction. . . . The plain answer (not offered by any of the authors mentioned) is that science has very little to contribute to the advance of technology except for criticism; and that this criticism can always in principle be replaced by empirical rather than theoretical criticism; that is, by practical testing. (Miller 2002, pp. 92–93)

Note that the above theses should not be attributed to Popper according to whom we should, and hence *can* act on our best-tested hypotheses (See Popper 1972, p. 22). This clearly implies that theories have direct technological import. We have seen that technology differs from science as regards emphasis rather than method. Anyway Popper himself held science to be commonsense writ large. So even if technology could be treated as a separate enterprise, it would certainly lie somewhere between commonsense and science. Putting it slightly differently: technologists are somewhere between the amœba and Einstein, and it seems to me that they are somewhat nearer the latter than the former. Should we believe Popper—as I think that we ought to—then all living beings apply essentially the same method, namely that of trial-and error; which in no way implies, as some would have us believe, that the trials are uninformed by past experience. Thus: the statement that repeated friction between two pieces of a special kind of wood produces fire (where some bound is placed on the time needed) is already a scientific generalization, albeit on a rather modest level; and so is the proposition that heat softens iron. No intrinsic difference can be detected between such generalizations on the one hand, and Boyle's or Hooke's law on the other. All these universal propositions are tested and then accepted or rejected according to the same rules. As for science playing an exclusively negative role with respect to technology, this also appears to me to be a false thesis. Even though some academic engineers might claim that 'technology is a different business from pure science' and Rutherford asserts that 'anyone who expects a source of power from the transformation [of the nuclei] of atoms is talking moonshine', such remarks have only psychological import; and Rutherford's prophecy anyway turned out to be false. The only relevant question is: do the fundamental laws of physics play—qua premises—an essential role in the derivation of those quantitative results which govern applications? The answer is emphatically affirmative; for the elimination of the laws from among the premises of the derivations—as presented—would invalidate the latter. And the fact that some basic principles are taken for granted does not mean that they thereby cease to play a central role in the prediction of technological results; nor, by the same token, that they remain forever shielded from refutation; i.e. from being undermined, if only indirectly, by experience. Think, for example, of Newton's laws which have been empirically falsified—while being still used in the determination of the orbits of satellites.

Heuristically speaking, one can naturally wonder whether any fundamental laws actually *suggested* any technological applications. There appears to be no single answer to this question. Many mechanical devices were of course known long before the discovery of Newton's laws. So there arose the question whether the latter imply—rather than merely prove compatible with—these mechanical rules of thumb. In other words: the relationship which was sought for—if not always achieved—was one of entailment rather than of mere logical consistency. For example: the law of the conservation of energy, which is at the heart of most technological applications, was discovered independently of Newtonian theory. Subsequently however, the conservation of mechanical energy had not only to be squared with, but also to be deduced from, the classical equations of motion. This was achieved through showing that under standard conditions, the Hamiltonian function remains constant over time.

Other examples however show that the underlying theory actually suggested its own applications to physical reality. Consider Faraday's law of electromagnetic induction which entails something like the following generalization: when the flux of a magnetic field **B** through a surface bounded by a wire is altered, an electric current arises in the wire. This proposition, which can be written in the form: $(\forall k)[A(k) \rightarrow C(k)]$, is both part of Faraday's theory and a straightforward consequence of Maxwell's equations; and it enabled engineers to transform mechanical into electrical energy: if we modify the flux of **B**, i.e. if we actualize A, then C will ensue, i.e. electricity will be created. We have of course to 'know' that we *can* realize certain boundary conditions; e.g. that the flux of **B** can be altered *mechanically* by moving a magnet relatively to a loop. It would however be absurd to claim that this trivial piece of 'practical knowledge', rather than Faraday's or Maxwell's hypotheses, suggested any technological breakthrough, let alone made it possible. It is moreover clear that the equation $\int \mathbf{E}.dl = -\partial \Phi / \partial t$ governing electromagnetic induction played an essentially positive role, namely that of a central premise, in predicting the creation and the actual magnitude of the electric current. A second example is also provided by electromagnetic theory. Given that the equations discovered by Maxwell failed to be Galileo-invariant, it was hardly an accident that Maxwell was among the first to suggest a concrete way of detecting the supposedly absolute motion of the earth. He was obviously guided by the mathematical structure of his theory; more particularly, by the occurrence in it of the velocity c which, given the Galilean transformation, was held to be constant only in the ether frame. New technical refinements, together with the adjunction of phenomenological laws, were of course needed before an appropriate instrument—the so-called interferometer—could be designed. This further illustrates Duhem's point about the need of appealing to low-level generalizations which govern the behavior of the apparatus used in an experiment. It was thus left to Michelson to test Maxwell's conjecture. Michelson's interferometer was regarded as a great technological achievement designed to tell us whether the earth moves effortlessly through the ether or else drags this medium. Note that like any 'technologist who takes certain laws for granted', Michelson at no moment doubted that wave motion can take place only in a quasi-material medium, i.e. in the 'ether'; and nobody expected the experimental outcome not only to render the ether superfluous but also gradually to lead to the abandonment of Newton's laws, and hence of classical physics as a whole (See below, Chapter IX). Once again, the distinction between test and technological application proves hazy.

Let us now consider Einstein's celebrated equation "$E = mc^2$," which was deduced from the fundamental postulates of Special Relativity. This law was revolutionary in at least two respects. It showed that far from being a mere mode of existence of an invariable substance, energy is in effect continuous with matter. Furthermore, it entailed that irrespective of its origin, mass is interchangeable with energy, c^2 being the conversion factor. Some 19th century scientists had wondered whether chemical reactions involve any gain or any loss of weight. Experiments were carried out but none of them yielded any positive results. It was concluded that Lavoisier's law concerning the conservation of mass had, once again, been confirmed. After 1905, the advantages offered by the newly-found relation "$E = mc^2$" were twofold. First, this equation followed directly from the central postulates of a highly corroborated theory, namely from Einstein's Special Relativity. Secondly, the presence of the negligible factor $(1/c^2)$ in "$m = E/c^2$" accounted for the null outcomes of the experiments just mentioned: the anticipated effects were taken to have fallen below some observational threshold. But by 1907 radioactivity had been discovered; so Einstein conjectured that "$E = mc^2$" could lead to the prediction of detectable effects in the case of radioactive substances; where the latter were assumed to suffer considerable losses of energy. He furthermore knew that in all practical results a central role would be played by the ratio $(M—\sum m)/M$, which still figures in the design of atomic reactors and atom bombs. Against David Miller, it can therefore be maintained that "$E = mc^2$" more than dreamily suggested to working scientists the possibility of certain applications. True, Einstein modestly conceded that he "did not in fact foresee that it [atomic energy] would be released in my lifetime. I believed only that it was theoretically possible" (See Calaprice 1996, pp. 125–26). This does not however mean that "$E = mc^2$" had become a superfluous premise when it came to determining the order of magnitude of the energy released during an atomic explosion. The quotation simply reminds us that other hypotheses—which Einstein himself might not have anticipated—had to be adduced before an atomic bomb could be built; for example, the laws governing atomic fission and chain reactions. Putting it somewhat pedantically: we are, once again, being reminded of the Duhem-Quine problem: in testing as well as in technologically applying a scientific system, numerous hypotheses are involved; which incidentally implies that none of these hypotheses is eliminable from the deduction of the empirical results—at least in the form in which the latter are presented by the scientist.

General Relativity again shows how narrow a difference separates the experimentalist from the theoretical physicist. It can be claimed that Einstein was the first scientist to corroborate the new hypothesis. He carried out no new experiments; but neither did he need to, for he was aware that his hypothesis had to explain the precession of Mercury's perihelion. In other words: in the symbolism used above, he identified the $C(k)$ which had to be explained; but the antecedent $A(k)$ was also known: it consists of certain obvious boundary conditions, e.g. the spherical symmetry of the sun's gravitational field, the sun being assimilated to a mass point or to a homogeneous sphere. As for the core theory H which is under test, it consists of Einstein's field equations. Schwarzschild was admittedly the first physicist to find an exact solution of H; but Einstein's approximate solution had already satisfactorily accounted for Mercury's anomalous motion. Be it as it may: it was not—as alleged by Miller—the choice of appropriate boundary conditions which posed the greatest challenge, but the construction of a mathematical proof leading form the field equations to one of their symmetric solutions, and then on to the explanation of Mercury's known motion.

The same considerations apply to the star-shift prediction. It might *prima facie* look as though thinking of the right boundary conditions—more specifically: of the solar eclipse—were the creative moment in Eddington's reasoning. This however is an illusion. First: it has often been claimed that predicting the bending of the light rays resulted from a new revolutionary conjecture, namely from the Principle of Equivalence as illustrated by Einstein's lift experiment; where the latter can be made accessible to every layman. But Newton himself had put forward a similar principle in the form of the identity $m_i = m_g$ between a body's inertial and its gravitational mass. So classical physics itself implies that a gravitational field would deflect a light ray conceived as a stream of moving particles (photons). In view of the equation $m_i = m_g$, such a deflection would be independent of the mass of the photon—which happens to be zero. So far, there is near equivalence between Einstein and Newton. Secondly however: a real breakthrough occurs when it is *mathematically*—and far from trivially—proved that the curvature of space, when it is 'added' to the Principle of Equivalence, leads to an Einsteinian prediction double that entailed by Newtonian Theory. Whence the possibility of a crucial experiment between Einstein and Newton. The difficult path is again the one leading from Einstein's field equations to Schwarzschild's solution: $ds^2 = (1 - 2m/r)$ $.c^2.dt^2 - [1/(1 - 2m/r)].dr^2 - r^2.(d\theta^2 + \sin^2\theta.d\varphi^2)$; where: r, θ and φ can be assimilated to the ordinary spherical polar coordinates; c is the speed of light, $m = GM/c^2$, G = the gravitational constant; M = mass of the attracting body (e.g. the sun).

Eddington carried out a rigorous *theoretical* analysis of the Schwarzschild formula (See Eddington 1920, Chapter VI). To begin with, he had to show that all the relevant clauses of the Correspondence Principle were satisfied. Trivially, as $r \to \infty$, ds tends to the Minkowskian metric, which is therefore a limiting case of Schwarzschild's solution. As for the coefficient $(1 - 2m/r).c^2$ of dt^2, it ensures that Newton's theory is a limiting case of Einstein's. Thus only the coefficient $[1/(1 - 2m/r)]$ of dr^2 yields an experimental correction of the Newtonian predictions. Furthermore, in the normal case of *slowly* moving particles where dr is very small in comparison with c.dt, the above expression of ds shows that any deviation from Newton would be imperceptible; whence the desirability of considering cases where dr is of the same order of magnitude as c.dt. The prime example of such a fast process is of course that of the propagation of light. Einstein's hypothesis would therefore be crucially tested against Newton's in the case of a light ray (or stream of photons) moving in a gravitational field. The Einsteinian prediction would roughly consist of the Newtonian deflection—as represented by the term $(1 - 2m/r).c^2.dt^2$ in the expression of ds^2—together with the quantity represented by $[1/(1 - 2m/r)].dr^2$, which arises from the curvature of space. This mode of speech, which seems to presuppose the separability of time from space, is of course strictly illegitimate; but it gives an intuitive description of the fact that Newton's observational prediction is half that of Einstein.

It was finally well known that while remaining weak, the gravitational force increases with the mass of the attracting body. One of the largest masses accessible to man is of course that of the sun, the main problem being that the latter normally—i.e. in the absence of an eclipse—masks the other stars; whence the obvious desirability of waiting for an eclipse. By itself, the choice of the eclipse as boundary condition did not therefore constitute the solution to a major problem facing physicists of Eddington's calibre. The central difficulties were all of a theoretical nature. Hence I cannot share Miller's view that in applying a hypothesis, it is the determination of boundary conditions and not any theoretical considerations which poses the greatest difficulties. The latter have much more to do with the solution of theoretical, and more specifically of arduous mathematical problems, which in turn largely dictate the boundary conditions.

Another example showing the positive nature of the relationship between theory and practice is that of the discovery of DNA, which was followed by that of DNA-fingerprinting. Such examples can in fact be multiplied at will. So I shall stop here and draw some general conclusions.

Two points can be made. First, many important logical consequences of a scientific theory H, all of the form $(\forall \underline{x}, t)[A(\underline{x}, t) \rightarrow C(\underline{x}, t)]$, are generally known; so that we have:

$\vdash [H \rightarrow (\forall \underline{x}, t)(A(\underline{x}, t) \rightarrow C(\underline{x}, t))]$. Secondly, it is highly misleading to describe the relationship between science and technology as purely negative—except in the following trivial sense: $[H \rightarrow (\forall \underline{x}, t)(A(\underline{x}, t) \rightarrow C(\underline{x}, t))]$, i.e. $[H \rightarrow G]$ where $G \equiv_{Def.} (\forall \underline{x}, t)(A(\underline{x}, t) \rightarrow C(\underline{x}, t))$, can of course be rewritten as $\neg[H \wedge \neg G]$. $\neg[H \wedge \neg G]$ could then be rendered as: H 'proscribes' $\neg G$. It is however G, i.e. $(\forall \underline{x}, t)[A(\underline{x}, t) \rightarrow C(\underline{x}, t)]$, and not $\neg G \equiv (\exists \underline{x}, t)[A(\underline{x}, t) \wedge \neg C(\underline{x}, t)]$ which constitutes a scientific generalization. Of course: in view of $\vdash [(\forall \underline{x}, t)(A(\underline{x}, t) \rightarrow C(\underline{x}, t)) \rightarrow (A(\underline{x}_0, t_0) \rightarrow C(\underline{x}_0, t_0))]$, we must also have $\vdash [H \rightarrow (A(\underline{x}_0, t_0) \rightarrow C(\underline{x}_0, t_0))]$; i.e. $\vdash \neg[H \wedge (A(\underline{x}_0, t_0) \wedge \neg C(\underline{x}_0, t_0))]$, so that H 'proscribes' the event $[A(\underline{x}_0, t_0) \wedge \neg C(\underline{x}_0, t_0)]$. Should we however choose to actualize $A(\underline{x}_0, t_0)$—as we normally know that we can—then H will 'prescribe' the only state-of-affairs which is of interest to us, namely $C(\underline{x}_0, t_0)$. It is finally mistaken to hold that such logic-chopping clarifies the relationship between science and technology.

(D) Can Induction be Rendered by a Prescriptive Statement?

David Miller seems to have anticipated something like the above criticism of his position; for despite his rejection of all inductive principles, he—rightly—feels the need to supplement his methodology with the following injunction:

All that may be derived from the empirical report that T_1 is refuted and T_2 is not refuted (together with a statement of our preference for truth over falsity) is not that T_2 *should be preferred to* T_1 but that T_1

should not be preferred to T_2. No attempt to justify this latter claim is made, but manifestly no justification is needed. Anyone who denies it exposes himself at once to deadly criticism. (Miller 2002, p. 99)

To the extent that our aim is to choose a hypothesis having a chance of being true, I cannot but agree with Miller: once the theory T_1 has been falsified, it becomes impossible for us to prefer it to any unrefuted proposition, no matter what the latter is. Let me nonetheless demonstrate that this choice can be overturned as soon as we try to select a hypothesis intended for technological use. First, it is difficult in such a case to appreciate what is gained by saying: *T_1 should not be preferred to T_2* rather than: *T_2 should be preferred to T_1*. In most practical situations, we have to opt for one from among a finite number of hypotheses $T_1,..., T_n$; where these give rise to mutually incompatible strategies, and only one of them, T_2 say, has been empirically confirmed. Thus preferring neither T_1 nor T_3 nor ... T_n comes down to preferring T_2. Miller's injunction, as opposed to that which would positively advise us to apply the most highly corroborated law, might moreover mislead us into making the wrong choice between two applicable theories. For let the points $P_1,..., P_r$ and Q represent a sequence of observational results, where Q is well outside the interval Δ determined by $\{P_1,..., P_r\}$. Suppose that the theory T_1 is given in the form of a graph C_1 going through $P_1,..., P_r$ but not through Q. Thus T_1 is empirically refuted by the observational result Q. Assume furthermore that at the points $P_1, P_2,..., P_r$, the hypothesis T_1 has been confirmed in a non-ad hoc way. It can even be supposed that, throughout Δ, C_1 is observationally indistinguishable from the 'true' curve C^* (T_1 could be the Rayleigh–Jeans law: $\delta u_v = 8\pi k\tau v^2.\delta v/c^3$, where δu_v denotes the spectral energy density, τ the absolute temperature, and v the frequency. This law is confirmed for values of v small relatively to τ, and refuted for higher values of v. [See Sears and Salinger 1975, §13-3].) Let us now cook up any wildly oscillating broken line C_2 which passes through $P_1,..., P_r$ and Q. Denote by T_2 the law whose graph is C_2. Unlike T_1, T_2 subsumes all the known facts and is therefore unfalsified. Most engineers would nonetheless take it as self-evident that they ought to rely not on T_2 but on T_1, at least within the interval Δ. It is of course likely that not long after being proposed, T_2 will be experimentally refuted; but the same construction can just as immediately be repeated, leading to the same methodological conclusions. It might be objected that nobody would anyway bother to envisage as ad hoc a theory as T_2; so why mention it at all? To this objection, which has often been made, we can reply first that the construction of C_2 might well be part of the solution of a *purely mathematical problem*; secondly, that if—as is undoubtedly the case—T_2 is not taken seriously as a *physical hypothesis*, then this is so precisely because of our instinctive belief in the principle of induction. What is important is therefore not the *negative* fact that T_2 is unrefuted, but the *positive* result that T_1 has been genuinely corroborated in an interval Δ comprising the point at which the theory is to be applied. This example demonstrates, once and for all, the impossibility of obviating an inductive principle such as $(\forall H, K, \Delta)J(H, K, \Delta)$.

III

Protocol or Basic Statements?

(A) THE PROBLEM-SITUATION

We have seen that by capturing what it is for a theory to be scientific, Popper rehabilitated metaphysics. Let us point out that Popper's criterion clearly weakens the constraint imposed on scientific hypotheses—from decidability to one-sided refutability. Hence any criticism leveled at the notion of falsifiability is tantamount to an attack on empiricism as a whole, whether it be of the neopositivist or of the Popperian kind. This is why I have decided to single out the hypothetico-deductivist scheme, namely H, p $\vdash$ q, or equivalently [H $\Rightarrow$ (p→q)], as the expression of the very essence of rational empiricism; where: H is a scientific system, p a description of boundary conditions and q an observational prediction; it being understood that both p and q are decidable statements. It was therefore natural for any critique of this scheme to be directed at at least one of its three fundamental aspects; namely:

(i) the structure of the hypothesis H, which has given rise to problems like those of Duhem-Quine, of the adjustment of parameters and of the distinction between analytic and synthetic propositions;

(ii) the nature of the inferential relation $\vdash$; whence the question whether a 'deviant' rather than classical logic might not be more appropriate for dealing with empirical theories;

(iii) the status of the statement (p → q), or rather of its negation (p∧¬q); whence the problem of the reliability of the empirical basis.

In this section we shall start by addressing the third problem, namely that posed by the status of the empirical basis. We have just seen that a hypothesis H is to be considered scientific iff it is refutable by a so-called basic statement b; i.e. iff H $\Rightarrow$ ¬b, where: b is of the form b $\equiv$ (p∧¬q), p describes some initial conditions and q expresses a prediction. Should H be refuted, then its falsification would be conclusive only if the truth-value of b can be effectively decided. This is however the point at which a serious criticism was leveled at Popper's conception of the empirical basis.

Let me define a few terms which will often be used in the rest of this section. A singular sentence p is said to express a level-0 proposition if p describes, in the first person, the immediate contents of a speaker's consciousness. Examples of such sentences are: 'I feel pain (now)', 'I seem to be perceiving a red patch', 'It seems to me that the arm of the galvanometer (i.e. what I take to be the arm of the galvanometer) has just moved', 'I seem to be perceiving a group of pink elephants', etc. It will be taken for granted that *the truth-value of such a proposition p is logically independent of all transcendent states-of affairs,* i.e. of all events occurring outside the speaker's consciousness. This is why level-0 statements are also referred to as immanent, autopsychological or phenomenologically reduced sentences. Finally: an entity will be called transcendent if it goes beyond the present contents of the observer's mind; i.e. if it is non-immanent.

Before going into the detail of Popper's position, let me describe it in broad terms. The formulation of the demarcation criterion might lead one to believe that the impossibility of verifying a hypothesis has to do with the physical impossibility of performing infinitely many operations; while the possibility of falsification rests on the possibility—in principle—of carrying out finitely many observations which decide the truth-value of a basic statement. However, both in his (1959) and in his (1979) Popper goes out of his way to assert that observation as commonly understood, i.e. as a process grounded in perception, bears no epistemological relation to basic statements. Sense-experience might motivate or cause us to accept a basic statement, but it provides no *reason* for doing so. Potential falsifiers can be, and normally are, objective statements about the external world. Not only are they theory-laden but, as already noted, they consist of low-level hypotheses containing dispositional terms; their verification is therefore impossible and it certainly has nothing to do with any observer's perceptions. Thus the basic statements which test scientific theories are not, and in fact should not be of the autopsychological kind; they are acceptable if and only if there is intersubjective agreement about their truth-value. Such an acceptance can be revised and is therefore non-dogmatic. But if carefully examined, such 'revisions' simply mean that the previously accepted basic statement, when taken in conjunction with other hypotheses, can be rejected as a result of a fresh agreement about some other falsifier. At no point does this potentially infinite process bring in epistemological considerations, i.e. any considerations which might link the truth-value of the basic statement either to the act of observation or to that of reaching a consensus. This is why Popper's view of the empirical basis will henceforth be referred to as the *conventionalist thesis* (This is in fact the way he described it in his [1979]).

Following independent routes, John Watkins and I reached the conclusion that Popper's conventionalist thesis is mistaken; also that level-0 statements play an important role as explananda of scientific theories. Our positions were largely constrained, if not dictated, by the intrinsic difficulties besetting Popperian methodology. The main problem facing falsificationism is that the conventionalist thesis threatens to destroy the asymmetry between verification and refutation; for the epistemologist will now typically find himself facing a situation in which a conjecture, called 'theory H', confronts another conjecture labeled 'basic statement B'; where such labels notwithstanding, all he is entitled to assert is that H and B are logically incompatible. The relationship between H and B is therefore perfectly symmetric.

Despite acknowledging the epistemological importance of autopsychological statements, John Watkins held them to be the concern of psychology or of psychobiology, but not of physics proper. He stratified all propositions belonging to a scientific system into various levels: 0, 1, 2,.... As already explained, level-0 reports describe the results of introspective processes, while level-1 propositions typically assert the existence of material objects. Higher-level sentences may refer to more abstract entities; they may also involve universal quantifications. Watkins held that only level-1 statements form the empirical basis of physics, which ought therefore to contain no autopsychological statements. The latter can nonetheless be appealed to—as a last resort—in cases of litigation. We shall see that this thesis bears a close resemblance to that of Schlick, which will be examined below.

In what follows, I propose to defend a more radical view, henceforth referred to as *the phenomenological thesis*. It asserts that only level-0 reports should count as the *basic* statements of *all* the empirical sciences. It will be shown that in epistemology only one fundamental dichotomy is called for, namely that demarcating all autopsychological propositions from the rest; where the latter consist of sentences referring to at least one transcendent entity or containing a universal quantifier. Naturally, all propositions are partially ordered by the logical consequence relation; but from the viewpoint of the theory of knowledge, only the dichotomy between the zero and all other levels is of any significance.

Let me begin by giving a historical account of this *Problematik*; an account which seems to me methodologically instructive. In the 1930s a debate raged, especially among members of the Vienna Circle, about the status to be conferred upon protocol sentences, i.e. upon statements of the form $b \equiv_{Def.} (p \wedge \neg q)$. This debate, which opposed Schlick to Neurath, was moreover laced with ideological undertones.

(B) Neurath's Position

Neurath was an (un)orthodox Marxist ideologue who paradoxically ended up defending a radical form of conventionalism. He set out not only to eliminate metaphysics but also to replace it by what he regarded as the only acceptable alternative; namely by a form of *linguistic* physicalism. It will be shown that he was thereby forced to espouse an extremist version of relativism.

Neurath started by rejecting, as unacceptably metaphysical, the correspondence theory of truth. In *Sociology and Physicalism,* he wrote:

> It is always science as a system of statements which is at issue. *Statements are compared with statements,* not with "experiences," "the world," or anything else. All these meaningless *duplications* belong to a more or less refined metaphysics and are, for that reason, to be rejected. Each new statement is compared with the totality of existing statements previously coordinated. To say that a statement is correct, therefore, means that it can be incorporated in this totality. What cannot be incorporated is rejected as incorrect. (Ayer 1959, p. 291)

In other words: Neurath subscribed to a coherence theory, if not of truth as such, then at any rate of scientific correctness; for he intended to dispense with the very notion of 'truth' which he held to be metaphysics-laden. This extremist viewpoint determined his conception not only of the empirical basis but also of the nature of logic and mathematics. He claimed:

> But, in the system of radical physicalism, even the expression "2 times 2 is 4," a *tautology,* is linked to protocol sentences. Tautologies are defined in terms of sentences which state how tautologies function as codicils appended to certain commands under certain circumstances. For instance: "Otto says to Karl 'Go outside when the flag waves *and* when 2 times 2 is four'." The addition of the tautology here does not alter the effect of the command. (Ayer 1959, p. 200)

Ignoring Leibniz's, Bolzano's and Frege's seminal insights, Neurath was thus prepared to empiricize logic in order to steer clear of 'metaphysical' concepts like those of *truth* qua correspondence, as well as of tautologies conceived as statements *true* under all interpretations of their descriptive terms. His conception of logic and mathematics is clearly untenable. For let S be the conjunction of all the postulates of some finitely axiomatized theory, e.g. of Gödel's system as presented in his (1940); and let F be any complex mathematical proposition, e.g. the continuum hypothesis. Consider the two commands: "Carry out X" and "If [S $\Rightarrow$ F], then carry out X." If we are to believe Neurath, then in order to decide whether or not F is a mathematical theorem, all we have to do is observe whether or not these two commands have the same effect on any person to whom they might be addressed; which is patently absurd. Already at this stage, two conclusions can be drawn. First, Neurath was driven to a crass form of behaviorism by an ideological dislike of metaphysics. Secondly, like most positivist purists, he had very little insight into the nature of mathematical truth; so that Gödel's incompleteness results came as a severe shock to logical empiricists of his ilk.

In the name of physicalism, Neurath moreover gave up the notions of an ego and of a conscious observer which he regarded as overly 'idealistic'. With respect to the empirical basis of physics, he maintained that *"There is no way of taking conclusively established pure protocol sentences as the starting point of the sciences."* But this objection seems to me to be aimed at a straw position; for according to Schlick against whom this remark is directed, the *Konstatierungen* do not stand at the beginning of the scientific enterprise; on the contrary, they constitute observational end-points at which our theories, having come into unmediated contact with experience, are either undermined or provisionally confirmed. Popper, who shared Schlick's fallibilism, nevertheless followed Neurath in refusing to accept autopsychological reports as suitable candidates for the status of basic statement. Yet Schlick had the merit of realizing that unless the latter enjoyed an epistemologically distinguished status, then every attempt at refuting or at corroborating scientific hypotheses was bound to end in failure. As a result, Popper's demarcation criterion would become inapplicable.

Let us now examine Neurath's formal definition of a protocol sentence:

Protocol sentences are factual sentences of the same form as the others, except that, in them, a personal noun occurs several times in a specific association with other terms. A complete protocol sentence might, for instance read: "Otto's protocol at 3:17 o'clock: [At 3:16

o'clock Otto said to himself: (at 3:15 o'clock there was a table in the room perceived by Otto)]." This factual sentence is so constructed that, within each set of brackets, further factual sentences may be found. . . . These sentences are, however not protocol sentences. . . . That is, in a full protocol sentence the expression within the inner-most set of brackets is a sentence which again features a personal noun and a term from the domain of perception-terms. . . . (Ayer 1959, pp. 202–203)

Note that Neurath [i] eliminates all indexicals from his protocol sentences, i.e. all words such as 'I', 'now' and 'here', for which he substitutes proper names or spatio-temporal coordinates; and [ii] nonetheless insists on perceptual terms like 'see', 'hear', etc. occurring in his protocol statements. But since the latter no longer contain any indexicals, they have in effect become 'objective' and hence fallible, thereby shedding their special epistemological status. This is why, qua 'objectivist', Popper could consistently drop condition [ii]: he took every singular report b to be an allowable basic statement provided a consensus be reached about the acceptability of b. As for Neurath, it is hardly surprising that he took a coherence view of the truth of *all* scientific propositions:

In unified science, we try to construct a non-contradictory system of protocol sentences and non-protocol sentences (including laws). When a new sentence is presented to us, we compare it with the system at our disposal, and determine whether or not it conflicts with the system. If the sentence does conflict, we may discard it as useless (or false). . . . The fate of being discarded may befall even a protocol sentence. No sentence enjoys the *noli me tangere* which Carnap ordains for protocol sentences. (Ayer 1959, p. 203)

Thus Neurath's visceral hatred of metaphysics and his rejection of 'psychologism' drove him into a vulgar form of relativism; and this as regards not only high-level hypotheses, but also all protocol sentences and mathematical truths.

The best way of showing the absurdity of such a coherence theory is as follows. Let S be any scientific theory; i.e. S is a falsifiable set of sentences closed under logical consequence. Take S to be consistently axiomatizable and contain ordinary arithmetic. It is by now well known that S must be incomplete. So there exists at least one formula d such neither d nor ¬d is entailed by S. Both $S \cup \{d\}$ and $S \cup \{\neg d\}$ are therefore consistent.

Depending on which of these sets we decide to accept—and note that according to Neurath, each one of them is acceptable—we can decree that d or that ¬d is true; i.e. that d is true or that d is false. No objectivist, whether Marxist-materialist or not, can or should find such a conclusion acceptable.

(C) SCHLICK'S SOLUTION

In the debate about the status of protocol sentences, Neurath's main opponent was none other than Moritz Schlick, the founder and head of the Vienna Circle. To the end of his life and despite coming under Wittgenstein's fateful influence, Schlick remained a realist according to whom science aims at discovering propositions true of the physical world:

> If attention is directed upon the relation of science to reality, the system of its statements is seen to be that which it really is, namely a means of finding one's way among the facts; of arriving at the joy of confirmation, the feeling of finality. The problem of the "basis" changes then automatically into that of the unshakeable point of contact between knowledge and reality. (Ayer 1959, p. 226)

Schlick could therefore accept neither Neurath's nor even Popper's conventionalist view of basic statements; a view which he correctly regarded as inevitably leading to relativism or to out-and-out skepticism. The following quotation shows that according to Schlick, the empirical corroboration of every theory entertained by any scientist rests on the latter's mental and perceptual experiences. As already mentioned, these were called 'constatations' (Konstatierungen) and will sometimes be referred to as 'confirmations'.

> Whether and to what extent we hold a statement to be corrigible or annullable depends solely on its origin, and (apart from very special cases) not at all upon whether maintaining it requires the correction of very many other statements and perhaps a reorganization of the whole system of knowledge. . . . In the ordering of statements according to their origin which I undertake for the purpose of judging their certainty, I start by assigning a special place to those that I make myself. And here a secondary position is occupied by those that lie in the past, for we believe that their certainty can be impaired

by 'errors of memory'. . . . On the other hand, the statements which
stand at the top, free from all doubt, are those that express facts of
one's own 'perception', or whatever you like to call it. . . . The
Cartesian cogito ergo sum is the best-known of the destinations to
which this path has led—a terminating point to which indeed
Augustine had already pushed through.

. . . Well, under no circumstances would I abandon my own
observation statements. On the contrary, I find that I can accept only
a system into which they fit unmutilated. (Ayer 1959, pp. 217–19)

. . . We have come to know these absolutely fixed points of contact, the confirmations, in their individuality: they are the only synthetic statements that are not hypotheses. (Ayer 1959, pp. 226–27)

Thus Schlick seems to have fully subscribed to the phenomenological
view of basic statements. But as pointed out by Hempel, Schlick's account
turns out to be incoherent. This incoherence will presently be shown to flow
from the verificationist theory of meaning.

[a] In the above passage, Schlick treats confirmations as *synthetic* but
non-hypothetical propositions. He goes on to draw a parallel between tautologies and observation statements:

While in the case of all other synthetic statements determining the
meaning is separate from, distinguishable from, determining the
truth, in the case of observation statements they coincide, just as in
the case of analytic statements. However different therefore 'confirmations' are from analytic statements, they have in common that the
occasion of understanding them is at the same time that of verifying
them. (Ayer 1959, p. 225)

Let me show that Schlick is deeply mistaken about the nature of both
tautologies and observation statements. 'Tautological' will henceforth be
given the more general meaning of 'logically true'. In the case of a formula
like $\neg(p \wedge \neg p)$, we can of course immediately see that we have here to do
with a trivially analytic statement. However, not only are there logical
truths much more complex than $\neg(p \wedge \neg p)$ but, as later shown by Church,
the property of being logically true turns out to be undecidable: it is impossible to specify an effective method, no matter how complex and hence how
non-immediate, for deciding whether or not a given sentence is analytic. Of
course, Schlick can hardly be blamed for not having anticipated Church's
result, but the following considerations ought to have made him aware of

the untenability of his views. Again, let M be the conjunction of all the postulates of a finitely axiomatized mathematical theory, and let F be any conjecture; M might stand for set theory and F for Fermat's last 'theorem', with which Schlick was no doubt familiar. Proving F thus reduces to establishing the tautological character of (M→F). Hence Schlick's position entails that all mathematical proofs are *immediate verifications* of analytic statements; which is clearly untenable. Note that (M→F) has by now been demonstrated to be logically true, but only means of a very sophisticated proof. The proof of a tautology need consequently not be trivial. Schlick in effect confuses the lack of content of the sentence (M→F) with the alleged *immediacy* of ascertaining its analytic character, i.e. of *verifying* that (M→F) lacks content. But to repeat: we have no direct insight into the logical character of (M→F). More importantly: to claim that the meaning of (M→F) consists in its being immediately recognized as universally valid would lead to the absurd conclusion that the mathematician who proved F, i.e. showed (M→F) to be analytic, did not know what he was doing until he actually did it; for prior to establishing the analyticity of (M→F), he did not know what he was embarking on. These absurd conclusions flow from Wittgenstein's verification principle according to which the meaning of a proposition consists in its method of verification; where, in the case of logical truths, the verification depends exclusively on the meaning of the connectives and is therefore held to be immediate. Anyway, should S be an ordinary synthetic statement, then as admitted by Schlick himself, there is no a priori certainty that S will be verified; so we must somehow be able to understand the proposition S before setting out to verify it. As shown by Frege, meaning must therefore be strictly distinguished from verification—which depends on reference.

[b] Let us now go back to Schlick's 'confirmations' (*Konstatierungen*). It has to be admitted that expressions like "Here now red" can be verified only at the moment at which they are uttered. My claim however is that this kind of verification in no way constitutes the meaning of the corresponding *Konstatierung*. Well in advance of carrying out an experiment and of either verifying or falsifying an utterance like "Here now red," I have a clear idea of what 'here', 'red' and 'now' mean, or rather: of what such words *will mean* at the moment of observation. Of course, prior to performing the experiment, I am not in possession of the Fregean *referents* of these terms, or more precisely: of those referents which I *shall* assign to these terms during observation. And it is only by carrying out the experiment, i.e. by going through a sequence of actual *Erlebnisse*, that I ascribe denotations to such words as 'here', 'now' and 'red'. But far from being necessarily verified,

"Here now red" could be refuted, say by the occurrence of the referent of 'blue' which I experience as being different from that which I would have attributed to 'red'; or so it would have seemed to me at the time of performing the experiment; where such 'seeming' lies at the basis of all the incorrigible descriptions of my instantaneous mental states and where the descriptions are issued by my secondary consciousness (See below, section I). Be it as it may, the meaning of "Here now red" in no way coincides with its verification; which again underlines the perverse character of the verification principle.

Generally speaking, most Neopositivists were what Popper called *criterion-philosophers*. As a result, they faced the insuperable task of constructing a universal truth-criterion; for they would—at least initially—have rejected any non-effective definition of truth as some sort of correspondence between statements and states-of-affairs. And yet they stood in urgent need of something like Tarski's semantic theory which would, among other things, have enabled them to define a sentence S as analytic if it proves true under all interpretations of its descriptive terms. There would then have been no need to mention anybody's ability immediately to ascertain the truth-value of S; for since the semantic definition does not constitute a criterion, it does not run foul of the undecidable character of analyticity.

[c] It seems at first sight that Schlick held 'confirmations' (*Konstatierungen*) to be empirical sentences which can be fully decided by our *Erlebnisse*. But on closer examination, doubts arise as to whether he regarded 'confirmations' as possessing any propositional status at all.

> . . .What I call observation statement cannot be identical with a genuine protocol statement, if only because in a certain sense it cannot be written down at all—. . .
>
> . . . In reality what is actually expressed in protocols stands in a less close connection with the observed, and in general one ought not to assume that any pure observation statements ever slip between the observation and the "protocol". . . . (Ayer 1959, p. 221)

And again:

> . . . A genuine confirmation cannot be written down, for as soon as I inscribe the demonstratives "here", "now", they lose their meaning. . . .

. . . [But] all the statements of science are collectively and individually hypotheses the moment one considers them from the point of view of their truth value, of their validity. (Ayer 1959, p. 226)

In these passages, Schlick takes 'confirmations' to consist in ineffable *Erlebnissen*. They would then constitute mental events which might occur, or else fail to occur, but could not be said to be true or false, certain or dubitable, etc. Schlick in effect regards 'confirmations' as happenings towards which theories tend, but which are 'consumed' (*verzehrt*) as soon as scientists get hold of them. After the occurrence of such events, the scientific enterprise has to restart—as it were from scratch. So it looks as though 'confirmations' are left behind immediately after they have been grasped.

. . . They [confirmations] do not in any way lie at the base of science; but like a flame, cognition, as it were, licks out of them, reaching each but for a moment and then at once consuming it. And newly fed and strengthened, it flames onward to the next. (Ayer 1959, p. 227)

Schlick thus adopted a quasi-existentialist approach to confirmation, which was bound to issue in a fallibilist conception not only of universal propositions but also of the empirical basis of the sciences. His position was therefore hardly distinguishable from Neurath's or from Popper's conventionalism. I shall nonetheless try to show that the ineffability thesis points to a genuine problem which was unfortunately misrepresented by Schlick.

As already explained: when Schlick claims that after carrying out a 'confirmation' we forego the meanings of our indexicals, he is simply mistaken; for what we leave behind are not the *meanings* of words like 'here' and 'now', but only their *referents* with which we admittedly become acquainted only while making an observation. So we can write down and understand the expression "Here now red" well before and well after performing the experiment which determines its truth-value. To repeat: even after it takes place, a verification does not constitute the meaning of the above expression—which might anyway have been, not verified, but refuted. Thus 'confirmations' either are, or else can be captured by genuine propositions. And we must anyway be able subsequently to rely on the truth of these propositions in order legitimately to regard the theories yielding them as more likely to be true or truth-like—and hence more reliable—than their disconfirmed rivals. But we then face a genuine problem to which Schlick alluded, albeit in an inappropriate manner: we have to rely on our fallible memory in order to maintain that a hypothesis H can legitimately be put to technological use because of its having been corroborated by past 'confirmations'. Let us illustrate this point by going back to our previous example. Consider a hypothesis K which predicts that in well-defined circumstances a piece of litmus paper will turn red. Thus K, taken with certain psycho-physical assumptions and with the description of appropriate boundary conditions, entails that in well specified circumstances I shall verify the expression "Here now red." As already explained: well in advance of carrying out the experiment, I know what is meant by 'here', 'now', 'red', 'blue', etc. Performing the experiment might issue in one of the following mutually exclusive *Erlebnissen*:

[i] I observe, or rather: I experience, not a red but a blue patch, thereby falsifying "Here now red" while simultaneously refuting K .

[ii] I perceive a red patch—thus verifying "Here now red"—while being instantaneously aware that K has been confirmed.

Suppose that [ii] actually obtains. Am I entitled to claim that K is reliable when I *subsequently* decide to prefer K to a rival S which, as far as I can *recall*, has been disconfirmed? My conclusions will clearly be predicated on my having correctly remembered the outcomes of past tests. But I know my memory to be fallible. The reliability of my short-term memory can of course be checked, i.e. tested. Suppose that in an overwhelming number of cases, the thesis of the reliability of my short-term memory is inductively supported by expressions of the form "Here now X." I still have—subsequently—to rely on my memory in order to conclude that the latter has been shown to be reliable and hence that K has actually been confirmed. Note that we have here a regress but not a vicious circle: assuming my memory to be reliable, I conclude that it has been reliably checked and that K has been strongly corroborated by past evidence. I could of course try to break out of the regress by denying—à la Descartes—the existence of a malicious demon bent on deceiving us; where only He can make any of us systematically believe that K has often been confirmed in the past even though K has actually been undermined. Unfortunately, such malicious demons occasionally exist in the form of mental illnesses which distort our memory. So the success of our procedures—and even our survival —depend on the existence of a largely healthy social and physical environment; which seems to be the one and only *naturalistic* presupposition of the theory of knowledge. That is: unless we resort, once again, to Poincaré's no-miracle argument. Thus consider a society most of whose members seem to remember that the theories underpinning their technology have been strongly confirmed. Assume that this society not only survived but achieved sustained technological break-throughs; where such successes are phenomenologically—and individu-ally—ascertained by the overwhelming majority of members of the group. Suppose moreover that the latter regularly communicate with one another, or so it seems to each one of them. The thesis that each of these members has been systematically deceived by an evil genius as to the reliability of the group's *collective* memory is clearly blocked by the no-miracle argument; for the simultaneous awareness of such (alleged) technological achieve-ments would constitute a very unlikely miracle—unless the confirmations really took place and were correctly remembered.

Be it as it may, going back to expressions of the form "Here now X": because these phenomenologically reduced statements refer to our present *Erlebnissen*, their truth-values can be immediately ascertained; for we can grasp their meanings while simultaneously experiencing their referents. This enables us to decide whether a truth-correspondence obtains between such reports and the state-of-affairs they putatively describe. Their mean-ings do not however consist in their being verified for they might anyway be refuted; and their verification—if and when it occurs—rests on the tra-ditional correspondence-theory being *applied* to descriptions of some of our mental states (For more details, see below section I).

Let us conclude by reasserting that science cannot content itself with homing in on Schlick's *Konstatierungen*, which are alleged to be instanta-neously 'consumed' and then forgotten; for this would entail that such con-firmations do not belong to the body of scientific knowledge. This is inadmissible since science makes retrospective use of experimental results both in its applications to the natural world and in assessing the verisimili-tude of its hypotheses. Should science have at its disposal, not any indu-bitable 'confirmations', but only their transcriptions into 'hypothetical' and hence fallible 'protocols', then it cannot but look upon its theoretical and technological progress as an ongoing miracle (See below, section H). Despite being on the right track, Schlick's proposed solution cannot there-fore be pronounced a success; which might explain why, after initially shar-ing Schlick's viewpoint, Carnap finally adopted Neurath's and then Popper's conventionalist theses concerning the empirical basis.

(D) CARNAP'S AMBIGUOUS POSITION

As shown by the following passage, Carnap initially inclined towards Schlick's autopsychological conception of the empirical basis:

Of first importance for epistemological analyses are the *protocol* language, in which the primitive protocol sentences (in the material mode of speech: the sentences about the immediately given) of a particular person are formulated, and the *system language*, in which the sentences of the system of science are formulated. A person S *tests* (verifies) a system-sentence by deducing from it sentences of his own protocol language, and comparing these sentences with those of his actual protocol. The possibility of such a deduction of protocol sentences constitutes the content of a sentence. (Ayer 1959, pp. 165–66)

At first sight, it looks as though, according to Carnap, the only reliable protocol statements are those about the immediate contents of the observer's consciousness. These are descriptions of primary conscious acts; where such descriptions are issued by secondary (reflexive) consciousness. As already explained, a phenomenological reduction aimed at eliminating all references to transcendent entities must be carried out prior to formulating any protocol sentence. However, it quickly becomes clear that Carnap's approach is incoherent in many respects.

[i] Carnap claims that the only universal language is the physicalist one:

To every sentence of the system language there corresponds some sentence of the physical language such that the two sentences are inter-translatable. It is the purpose of this article to show that this is the case for the sentences of psychology. Moreover, every sentence of the protocol language of some specific person is inter-translatable with some sentence of physical language, namely with a sentence about the physical state of the person in question. The various protocol languages thus become sub-languages of the physical language. The *physical language is universal and inter-subjective*. This is the thesis of physicalism. (Ayer 1959, p. 166)

This passage clearly implies that the physical language will not contain any expression like "Here now red" ($\equiv$ p), but a sentence ($\equiv$ P) describing the physical condition of a person who sees red. P and p are then claimed to be inter-translatable, from which it should follow that these two propositions are equivalent. P is however not logically, but at best materially, equivalent to P. That is: for some theory H, we might have $\vdash [H \rightarrow (P \leftrightarrow p)]$, where H contains at least part of the protocol vocabulary in which p is expressed. It can now easily be demonstrated that H must be synthetic; for as convincingly established by Descartes, the existence and properties of our mental states do not *logically* presuppose those of our bodies; i.e. Not $[p \Rightarrow P]$; i.e. there exist logically possible worlds in which p is true and P false. It follows that since $H \Rightarrow (P \leftrightarrow p)$, then H must be contingent. H will generally be a scientific hypothesis consisting of a set of physical, psycho-physical and psychological laws. Hence H could in principle be falsified; in which case the equivalence between P and p might no longer obtain (See below, Chapter IV, section B). The Neopositivists could of course counterargue as follows: should it turn out—as it well might—that the method of verifying P coincides with that of verifying p, then P and p will have the same meaning. But as already explained, we are far from being under any logical obligation to accept this verificationist criterion of meaning. Since P and p are not logically equivalent, they anyway fail to have the same consequence class and they moreover possess very different epistemological statuses: p can incorrigibly be ascertained as true or as false, whereas P remains fallible through and through. We naturally remain at liberty to accept the synthetic hypothesis H mentioned above; which would entitle us to interchange P and p within any formula B. Note that the acceptance of H entails acknowledging the phenomenological terms occurring in H as part of the scientific vocabulary. It should incidentally be remarked that this methodological conclusion in no way implies any genuine adherence to a dualist metaphysics. For all we know, the universe might consist of entities all of the same type—energy, say—some of whose complex configurations possess a property which we call 'consciousness'. This attribute proves capable of reflecting on itself, i.e. of purviewing its own acts and of infallibly describing them. Admittedly, there exists at present no theory which explains all of these facts in a satisfactory way. There are nonetheless confirmed laws implying that some physical processes are correlated with specific perceptual experiences; e.g. some electromagnetic frequencies give rise to a person 'seeing red' while also being detectable by nonvisual means; other frequencies, though detectable by these same means, are accompanied by no visual sensations, etc. Moreover, some alterations of the brain states are known to be systematically accompanied by specific modifications of our mental processes; all of which supports, if not any identity between mind and brain, then at any rate a monistic form of ontology.

These questions are however not the theme of the present work. So let us go back to Carnap's view of the empirical basis, a view which can be seen as mediating between Schlick's and Neurath's positions. Carnap actually oscillated between two very different unitary theses.

[ii] According to the first thesis, each observer has his own protocol reports, or rather his own protocol 'utterances'; these are non-statements which, despite being in some sense 'incorrigible', do not belong the domain of science proper. Each protocol p can nonetheless be 'translated' into a physicalist proposition P, the method of translation being alterable at will. Since it depends not only on the 'content' of p but also on the mode of the latter's translation into a physicalist language, P remains fallible; which clearly reposes the problem of the testability and confirmability of physical hypotheses.

[iii] The second thesis admits—into an allegedly physicalist language—statements like $p_0 \equiv$ (There is a red ball on the table); where 'red' can be given its ordinary observational meaning; except that Carnap henceforth abstains from alluding to any 'meanings' or to any semantic aspects of his language: he systematically adopts not the material, but the formal mode of speech. In other words: he takes account only of the syntactical structure of language and makes no reference to any extra-linguistic entities. He requires the vocabulary of science to contain predicates like: 'red', 'sharp', 'hard', . . . while abstaining from any mention of the referents of these words. He then claims that all protocol languages can be made into parts of one comprehensive physicalist vocabulary, *P* say. It should however be pointed out that *P* can hardly be regarded as intersubjective in the sense intended by the Vienna Circle; for my protocol statements, though understood by other people, can be verified only by me; which flies in the face of the verificationist principle according to which the meaning of a proposition consists in the method of its verification by *anybody*. Had he unreservedly opted for this second thesis, then Carnap would therefore have had to give up intersubjectivity. In return, he would have retrieved the incorrigibility of all observation sentences; and somewhat like Schlick, he could rightly have maintained that a theory is to be considered empirically successful if it entails basic statements which are infallibly, albeit only instantaneously verified by some observer. As it was, Carnap caved in to Neurath's criticism according to which protocol statements, being both objective and fallible, are subject to a mere coherence requirement.

As has already been said, the question concerning the form of protocol sentences is to be answered by means, not of an assertion, but of a stipulation. This also holds within the second form of language, hence applies to the question as to what concrete sentences of the physicalist system language are to be taken as protocol sentences. There are essentially *two paths* between which a choice has to be made: A) with a *constraint*: it is stipulated that concrete sentences of this and this definite form should serve as protocol sentences; B) *without constraint*: it is decided that that every concrete sentence may, in certain circumstances, be taken to be a protocol sentence. Neurath chooses path A). . . .

In what follows, path B) will be followed. The possibility of this procedure was elaborated by Karl Popper during talks we had together. (Carnap 1932, p. 223. My translation)

Thus Carnap adopted Popper's radical view that protocol sentences need contain no 'observational' terms at all; where such a perceptual ingredient was a constraint on which Neurath still insisted. Note that from a 'physicalist' viewpoint, Popper's more permissive attitude is well-founded: once the incorrigibility of basic statements is given up, there is no reason left for requiring that observational terms occur in them; for according to both Neurath and Popper, such terms have no epistemic clout; so their occurrence in a sentence in no way increases the latter's chances of being true. As admitted in the above passage, Carnap accepted the theory-ladenness of factual propositions together with the conventionalist thesis that protocol sentences are to be fixed by a stipulation. Hence any statement can be looked upon as basic provided it be—in some unspecified sense—'concrete'.

Let me repeat that in the absence of an argument for the incorrigibility either of Popper's potential falsifiers or of Schlick's protocol sentences, we remain free to *decree* what statements should count as basic. But from an empiricist viewpoint, this is clearly the wrong attitude to adopt with respect to the basis of the sciences; for both the Neopositivists à la Carnap and the falsificationsts à la Popper had a vested interest in singling out decidable propositions through which high-level hypotheses could *genuinely* be confirmed, or at least refuted.

(E) A Synopsis of Popper's Position

Let me start by playing Popper's advocate—through showing that from his own viewpoint, he had solid reasons for rejecting 0-level sentences as suitable candidates for membership of the empirical basis of science. Popper argued as follows.

[A] Level-0 statements are incorrigible only in the sense of being *psychologically* indubitable. But we know that no matter how strong, feelings

of conviction are often misleading: they neither establish nor even probabil-
ify the propositions towards which they are directed.

> I admit again that the decision to accept a basic statement and to be
> satisfied with it is causally connected with our experiences—espe-
> cially with our *perpetual experiences.* But we do not attempt to *jus-
> tify* basic statements by these experiences. Experiences *can motivate
> a decision,* and hence an acceptance or a rejection of a statement, but
> a basic statement cannot be *justified* by them—no more than by
> thumping the table. (Popper 1959, p. 105. For the rejection of the
> view that experiences confer a degree of certainty onto protocol
> statements, see Popper 1959, p. 104, footnote 1.)

[B] Autopsychological reports have the added disadvantage of being
private to the persons uttering them. They cannot be subjected to repeated
checks, so that their veracity is not independently testable. No intersubjective agreement regarding their truth-value or their general acceptability can
therefore be reached.

[C] Psychology is an empirical science which investigates—among
other things—the feelings of certainty accompanying certain utterances;
and it demarcates the cases where such feelings mislead us from those
where they are more or less justified. Thus testing psychological hypotheses by means of level-0 statements—where the latter are supported by feelings of conviction—would land us into a vicious circle; for we might be led
to rely exclusively on those experiences of certainty which, according to the
hypothesis under test, are justified. But the latter might be questionable,
which is precisely why we may have decided to perform the test in the first
place (Popper 1979, p. 123).

[D] It is therefore preferable to choose intersubjectively testable sentences as constituents of our empirical basis. Such sentences refer to pub-
licly observable entities and, more particularly, to physical objects which
can be inspected at different times and by different persons. These
objects—grasped largely by means of theory—are transcendent in the sense
of lying beyond the reach of the observer's consciousness. This is why basic
statements are fallible on at least two counts. On the one hand, they refer to
external objects which may either be non-existent or else possess properties
different from those attributed to them by the observer; for the latter confronts these entities, as it were from the outside. On the other hand, basic
statements are theory-laden or theory-dependent in a sense to be explained
below. For the time being, suffice it to say that objective statements involve

universal and hence conjectural hypotheses; so their truth-value cannot be determined with any degree of certainty.

[E] Thus accepting a basic statement constitutes a decision, and a conventional one at that. But such conventions are not arbitrary; they rest on consensual decisions where regard is paid to the feelings of various experimenters. According to Popper, a consensus about the acceptability of a statement b should be regarded as having been reached when divergences no longer exist between the feelings of certainty experienced by various observers. Popper then regards b as being both verifiable and falsifiable (Popper 1979, pp. 125, 130). The context makes it nevertheless clear that these two terms have little to do with the truth-value of b; they could just as well be replaced by 'acceptable' and 'rejectable' respectively (Popper 1979, p. 127). Thus the non-arbitrariness of the conventions governing the choice of basic statements has to do, not with the latter's presumed truth-value, but with the uniformity of certain procedures. It is also to be noted that these procedures are partly psychologistic: the feelings of conviction of various experimenters play a crucial role in arriving at a consensus. This is another reason why such a consensus, which founds the intersubjective character of a basic statement b, has little to do with the truth-value of b.

(F) The Structure of Popper's Argument

In what follows, clause [A] will often be referred to as *the psychologistic view of level-0 statements* or, more briefly, as *the psychologist thesis*: it constitutes the linchpin of Popper's argument in support of his conventionalist conception of the empirical basis. It will be shown that clauses [B]–[E] are all consequences of the psychologist thesis, where the latter is conjoined with some self-evident principles. I shall postpone my criticism of [A] until the next section and start by examining the ways in which the other clauses follow from [A].

First note that [B] is a trivially true proposition; for almost by definition, an autopsychological assertion q is private to one speaker only, and only at the instant at which he utters 'q'. We have moreover seen that as soon as an observer relies on his memory in order to describe his past experiences, his statements become fallible; for he is now referring to transcendent states-of-affairs and hence trying to grasp events beyond the reach of his present consciousness.

Next, let us remind ourselves that according to [A], autopsychological sentences are supported exclusively by *subjective feelings* of conviction.

Hence clause [A] entails [C]; for psychology does in fact investigate various feelings of conviction; so should it decide to found *its* methodology on basic statements underwritten only by such feelings, then it would face a problem of vicious circularity. From all this it follows that in order for our conjectures to be testable, it is preferable for us to settle on 'basic' statements of a non-immanent sort.

[D] is also a consequence, albeit an indirect one, of the psychologist thesis [A]. For a statement is either immanent or transcendent; where, to repeat, 'transcendent' means: involving at least one reference to some entity external to our mental operations. Thus, should immanent propositions prove unsuitable for the role of basic statements, then we have to resort to sentences some of whose referents are mind-independent, i.e. to transcendent propositions. Since the latter have an unknown truth-value, their acceptance or rejection depends on a methodological decision; whence [E]. We now have to turn to the problems posed by the alleged theory-ladenness of such propositions.

(G) IN WHAT SENSE OR SENSES ARE OBSERVATION STATEMENTS THEORY-DEPENDENT?

Duhem was among the first epistemologists to underline the theory-dependence of scientific propositions which he distinguished from singular commonsense statements:

> An experiment in physics is the precise observation of phenomena accompanied by an *interpretation* of these phenomena; this interpretation substitutes for the concrete data really gathered by observation abstract and symbolic representations which correspond to them by virtue of the theories admitted by the observer. . . It is not correct to say that the words "the current is on" are simply a conventional manner of expressing the fact that the magnetized little bar of the galvanometer has deviated. . . . This group of words does not seem to express therefore in a technical and conventional language a certain concrete fact; as a symbolic formula, it has no meaning for one who is ignorant of physical theories; but for one who knows these theories, it can be translated into concrete facts in an infinity of different ways, *because all these disparate facts admit the same theoretical interpretation.* . . . Between the phenomena really observed in the course of an experiment and the result formulated by the physicist there is interpolated a very complex intellectual elaboration which

substitutes for the recital of concrete facts an abstract and symbolic judgment. (Duhem 1954, Chapter IV, Section1)

I have quoted this long passage for two reasons. First, it provides a synopsis of Duhem's position on the status of factual scientific statements. It secondly hints at two different notions of theory-ladenness; the one is objective-logical, the other psychological. But more of this later. For the time being, let us note that according to Duhem, commonsense propositions like 'There is a white horse in the street' possess truth-values which can be infallibly ascertained. Such reports are however alleged to lie outside the domain of science proper. As for the descriptions of genuinely scientific facts, they are precise, symbolic and theory-laden. At times, Duhem seems on the point of denying any truth-value to such propositions; at others, to hold that their truth-value cannot effectively be determined. Be it as it may, he claims that any increase in scientific precision is paid for by some loss of certainty; so that, between science and commonsense, there exists a hiatus which contemporary French thinkers call 'coupure épistémologique'.

Popper broadly shared Duhem's conception of the empirical basis, but he rightly underlined the continuity between science and commonsense, hence the fallibility of both types of knowledge (*Science is commonsense writ large*). Thus 'There exists a white horse in the street' and even 'I see a white horse in the street' can both be false; for I may be hallucinating. Even if my perception were 'veridical', the concept of horseness would still be theory-dependent; for it rests on a hypothetical assumption about the existence of certain animal species.

Let me now turn to the concept of theory-ladenness which has recently been overworked, and therefore stands in need of clarification. As indicated in the quotation above, theory-ladenness is sometimes equated with the proposition that the meanings of observational terms are theory-dependent. This thesis seems to me totally unconvincing. Let us first note that if a scientific system is to entail testable consequences, it must contain at least some observational predicates. Secondly: according to usual Tarskian semantics, the truth-value of the system is founded on the meanings, or rather on the referents of its primitive concepts; *not* the other way round. It is thus difficult to see how the meaning of an observational term can presuppose the truth of a theoretical premise or, for that matter, of any premise whatever. Saying that the meanings of certain terms are theory-dependent sounds like putting the cart before the horse; unless, by meaning, one meant something like a verbal or dictionary definition, whereby a single word is treated as shorthand for a much longer description formulated in terms of an underlying primitive vocabulary. But in such a case, no

theory need anyway be presupposed, which brings me to the central point
of this section; the point namely that in the thesis of theory-ladenness two
distinct claims are often conflated: (a) a logical principle according to
which all so-called observational terms are definite descriptions containing
occurrences of universal theoretical statements, and (b) the cognitive-psy-
chological thesis that what we observe does not directly depend on any theory, but indirectly on our *believing* or *entertaining* certain hypotheses.

Let us start with the logical thesis. It is claimed that the sentence 'The
current is on' looks like a singular proposition because 'the current' is
instinctively treated as a proper name; but it actually represents a definite
description which, when properly unpacked, is found to involve a sophisticated electrical theory. E.g. 'the current' might denote: the movement of
electrons in this well-defined spatio-temporal region where the electrons are
subject to electrodynamic forces. Similarly, in Popper's favorite example
'Here is a glass of water', 'water' stands for something like: a substance
resulting from the combination of one oxygen and two hydrogen atoms,
where the combination is effected by certain cohesive forces. Thus the verification of such basic statements would presuppose that of a universal proposition and is therefore impossible. A parallel can in fact be drawn between
these basic scientific statements and 'The present king of France is bald'
which stands for: there exists exactly one present king of France and, for all
x, if x is any present king of France (say, in 1912), then x is bald. The longer
sentence contains quantification over individual variables and is therefore
non-singular (non-atomic). Needless to say, the universal assumptions
involved in genuinely scientific factual propositions are more complex than
those in 'The present king of France is bald'; which makes the ascription of
any truth-value to such propositions all the more intractable. Thus basic
statements possess only a *superficially singular syntax* but a *deep universal-
theoretic* structure. In this sense, they are theory-dependent and hence fallible. Popper himself admits that his basic statements constitute hypotheses,
albeit of a low-level kind. Because of their scientific character, they are however susceptible of being further tested: they can be adjoined to other theories and will thus give rise to new predictions over whose truth-value the
scientific community may find it easy to reach agreement. But the adjective
'low-level' has little cash-value: in the examples above, the assumptions
involved in basic statements are among the most fundamental laws we possess. This is why I cannot but differ from John Watkins when he maintains
that hypotheses can be tested by level-1 propositions. The basic statements
mentioned above, which are taken to be level-1 sentences, are highly theoretical and must therefore belong to a level far higher than the first one. So

all we have before us is a logical conflict between conjectures all of whose levels are on a par; and only our attitude decides which hypothesis is under test and which does the testing. This is why the only legitimate *epistemological* divide seems to me to be the one separating level-0 reports from the rest, i.e. from all transcendent propositions.

Let me now turn to the psychological thesis (b). It says that observation largely depends on the theories entertained, or held to be true by the observer. The latter typically jumps from a visual experience of whose intricate details he remains unaware, to a description of the assumed cause of his perceptions. Such a cause is therefore inferred against a background of theoretical assumptions instinctively made by the experimenter. The latter will thus observe different things depending on his theoretical prejudices. Schopenhauer rightly maintained that even animals make an instinctive use of an inborn principle of causality in order to adjust to their surroundings. He should have added that whereas the intuited causes are, in the case of animals, always the same in the same immediate circumstances, humans seem to be more flexible and hence more adaptable than other species. Note that even if sense-data are regarded as the only proper objects of perception, the latter are far from being passively given: each possesses a focus towards which our preconceived ideas direct our attention. Thus both focus and attention depend on our beliefs and, more generally, on the overall state of our knowledge; so that a sense-datum is largely structured by the mental acts which intend it. This is why Duhem spoke of a scientist *interpreting* his experiences in the light of a theory (See last quotation). 'Interpretation' however seems to me to be a misnomer. As already mentioned, we do not *interpret* our perceptions but immediately *infer their presumed causes,* where the latter largely depend on our background knowledge. Let us give a few examples. Michelson claimed to have ascertained ether drag. He took it for granted that light was a wave phenomenon presupposing a carrier called 'ether'. This medium could therefore either be dragged, i.e. pulled along by the motion of the earth; or else, there was slippage between earth and ether. Hence Michelson could not help concluding that his null result revealed ether drag. Nowadays, we have good reasons for assuming that no ether exists; so Michelson could not have observed any medium being dragged by the earth's motion. His 'experimental' claim is consequently false, thus establishing Duhem's and Popper's theses about the fallibility of 'basic' statements (see below, Chapter IX).

Galileo's discovery of the Jupiter moons provides another illustration of the theory-dependence of experimental results. In his famous play, Bertolt Brecht claimed that when invited to look through the telescope and thus observe these moons, Galileo's opponents refused point blank to carry out this simple experiment; they had allegedly decided a priori that objects such as the Jupiter moons could not exist (See Brecht 1963, Act 4). This story may well be apocryphal; but even if they had looked through the telescope, Galileo's critics might not have changed their minds; they would probably have failed to focus on the four luminous spots, or else have 'interpreted' them in a way very different from Galileo's. In other words, they would have told *a different causal story*: given their Aristotelian background, they might have claimed that the spots emanated from the telescope itself. Note that Galileo had his own—Copernican—prejudices: believing the world to be polycentric, he 'jumped' to the conclusion that he was observing the satellites of Jupiter.

Thus beliefs in different theoretical systems give rise to incompatible *transcendent* basic statements. Could we nevertheless not maintain that despite there being major differences between the 'interpretations' of the facts, there exists a fixed perceptual core which does not depend on the experimenter's prejudices? After all, Michelson must have seen the *same* interference fringes which a modern relativist, were he to repeat the experiment, would observe. And would not Galileo's enemies have seen the *same* four spots which he claimed to have observed?

In answer to these well-known objections, let us first note that we have already changed from speaking about physical entities to describing perceptual experiences. In other words: we have shifted towards a more phenomenological position. Even then, sameness of perceptual content cannot always legitimately be claimed. We have already remarked that focus and attention are largely determined by preconceived ideas. On a chest X-ray a trained doctor will notice details which escape the attention of the layman. The latter will—at best—recognise the normal contours of the patient's ribs amid areas of varying shades of grey; whereas the physician's attention will be drawn to a dubious patch indicating the presence of a tumor or of some infectious disease. Even after limiting our discourse to a phenomenological language, we have to admit that the doctor and the layman see *different phenomenal objects*: the doctor, but not the layman, homes in on the 'diseased' patch which forms a central point of his sense-datum. Since focus and attention form essential parts of every intentional entity, the two sense-data, the layman's and the physician's, are different. As for the real objects which are said to be either directly observed or inferred—namely the diseased as opposed to the allegedly normal lung—these are clearly different in the two cases.

To sum up: in all the cases cited above, we mistakenly speak of the *theory*-dependence of observation reports rather than of the dependence of experimental results on the experimenter's *beliefs* and, more generally, on his *state of mind.* Though seemingly pedantic and somewhat trivial, this point underlines the crucial role played by psychological assumptions in the derivation of basic statements. This brings physics into line with the social sciences where it was long realized that the prediction of some phenomena depends on the subject being aware of certain theories, and more particularly of the hypothesis under test.

Important methodological consequences flow from this so-called 'theory-dependence' of observational results; consequences which are grist to my phenomenological mill. We have seen that Michelson's claim to have observed ether drag is false. Yet the basic statement: 'There exists ether drag (at some point of the earth's surface)' was taken to have refuted classical electrodynamics, which is nowadays also thought to be false. We have here a clash between two propositions both of which are not only fallible but actually false. Hence there was no good reason for concluding that classical electrodynamics and, more particularly, its transformation rules had been refuted by Michelson; we were lucky in rejecting a false hypothesis but had no really sound reason for doing so. Note that our decision becomes much more rational if we switch attention to what ought to have been Michelson's more guarded *autopsychological* claim: 'I believe that I have detected ether-drag' which we still take to be true—of Michelson's state of mind. But in order to deduce such statements, or their negations, from classical electromagnetism, we have to adjoin to the latter auxiliary hypotheses which include assumptions about the experimenter's beliefs. In this way we obtain, as premises for our derivation of phenomenological basic statements, a greatly expanded scientific system consisting not only of some *core physical theory* but also of psychological and psycho-physical hypotheses. We must furthermore resort to descriptions both of boundary conditions *and* of the experimenter's mental state. As a result, there is a considerable increase in the magnitude and complexity of the Duhem-Quine problem; but in return, we should now be in a position to know, or rather Michelson should then have known that his premises, taken as a whole, had been falsified by the ether *seeming* to him to have been dragged.

(H) CONSEQUENCES OF [B]–[E] FOR POPPER'S POSITION

In the last few paragraphs I seem to have jumped the gun. So let me now go back to Popper whose position becomes coherent once clause [A], i.e. the psychologistic conception of level-0 reports, is accepted. For we have seen that [A] entails [B], [C], [D] and [E]. (Note that [E] merely expresses the *stipulation* that basic statements should be accepted as a result of a consensus. Strictly speaking, [E] does not therefore have to follow from *any other proposition.* The other clauses nonetheless provide a rationale for adopting [E]).

We shall now show that [B]–[D] have serious consequences for Popper's overall position which, contrary to his own intentions, is thereby turned into out-and-out skepticism. Throughout this section and barring indications to the contrary, the psychologist thesis will be presupposed. Basic statements—also called potential falsifiers—are taken to be objective and hence theory-laden propositions; *theory-laden* both in the logical and in the psychological senses described above. Potential falsifiers are therefore doubly fallible and can therefore be accepted only through a consensus among scientists. In Popper's own words, basic statements constitute dogmas, albeit temporary and hence harmless ones. They are harmless because they remain revisable: being in the nature of low-level hypotheses, they can be adjoined to other assumptions and hence tested. But by what? By further potential falsifiers which are, in their turn, to be accepted through the fiat of some consensus. As already mentioned, at no point does this potentially infinite process involve genuinely epistemological considerations; i.e. *considerations pertaining to the truth or falsity of factual propositions* (See section A above).

According to Popper, traditional conventionalism and his own brand of empiricism differ over the kind of statement which the two positions are prepared to accept as a matter of convention (Popper 1979, pp. 129–130). Conventionalism holds on to high-level theories while Popper gives methodological priority to the potential falsifiers of such theories. This definition might provide an interesting criterion for demarcating between conventionalism on the one hand and Popperian empiricism on the other, but hardly any reason for preferring the latter to the former. In fact, Popper's view of the empirical basis threatens to destroy the presumed asymmetry between verification and falsification. For we now face a typical situation in which one hypothesis, labeled 'theory H', confronts another hypothesis, labeled 'basic statement B'. All we are however entitled to assert is that B is logically incompatible with H; so the relationship between H and B is perfectly symmetrical. As already mentioned, Popper describes B as a *low-level* hypothesis, but this appellation is of little help; for since neither of the two propositions H or B logically implies the other, the levels of H and B are strictly non-comparable. More seriously: as explained above, nothing tells us that the theories impregnating B are less risky than H; yet we arbitrarily regard H rather than B as being under test. All we can say is that, over the last 400 years or so, science has pursued a largely empiricist policy; i.e. physicists have reached agreement over statements which have *superficially* the same form as B rather than over statements *resembling* H. But as Popper himself admitted in his (1979), no scientific explanation can be provided for the success of this empiricist strategy (p. 132). Worse still: we cannot explain why the pursuit of such a policy since the beginning of the scientific revolution issued in undeniable *technological breakthroughs.* Such breakthroughs are taken to depend, if only in part, on the truth or approximate truth of some consequences of our theories. Yet the notion of truth has so far played no role in Popper's methodology: though rejecting H in favor of B, we have so far offered no good reason for supposing that we have thereby eliminated error, let alone approximated truth. Thus sustained technological progress is again turned into a perpetual miracle. As so far depicted, Popper's position thus leads to skepticism about every item of knowledge save logic and mathematics. And the only criticism we can level at any theory H is of the transcendent type, which Popper had firmly rejected in his (1979): against H we simply pit another assumption B which happens to be logically incompatible with H. (Popper 1979, p. 53).

It is well known that Popper's fallibilist attitude with regard to the empirical basis provided Paul Feyerabend with his major argument in favor of epistemological anarchism. As set out in Feyerabend's (1975): since Galilean theory was supported exclusively by *Galilean factual statements* while Aristotelianism rested on *Aristotelian observational results,* Galileo could—and did—win a mere propaganda war against the Aristotelians. No observation report adduced by one of the schools could be accepted by the other. It follows that *anything goes,* provided it be defended by means of a powerful and persuasive rhetoric. So the best that even the greatest scientific minds can achieve are propaganda victories.

We have explained why, according to Popper, a level-0 approach to the empirical basis would lead straight into psychologism. But Popper also acknowledged the sociological character of his own conventionalist view. Let us recall that his concept of objectivity is founded on the twin conditions of repeatability and consensus; this means that science is entitled to ignore observation reports which cannot be intersubjectively ascertained (Popper 1979, p. 122). But would it not then follow that descriptions of dreams can no longer provide tests for psychological hypotheses? A dream is an intrinsically private phenomenon whose repetition, even in the case of one and the same person, poses practically insuperable problems. Certain aspects of a dream might admittedly recur, but one can hardly speak of repetitions in the sense in which a physical experiment can be rerun in a controlled way. As for the question of intersubjectivity, it is difficult to see how it could even arise in the case of purely subjective phenomena. For example, in a laboratory, any number of technicians can look through the same microscope at the *same* blood sample and arrive at the same conclusions; but it would clearly be absurd to ask these technicians to 'observe' or experience the same dream. Yet Popper would surely not want *a priori* to deny scientific status to psychology.

There is another objection to the conventionalist thesis which is also mentioned by Popper in his (1979), namely the 'Robinson Crusoe Objection'. Note that as a result of Popper's demarcation criterion, no person on his own, e.g. if stranded on a desert island, can do any science:

> One can imagine a person, a Robinson Crusoe, who though completely isolated, would master a language and develop some physical theory (possibly in order to gain better mastery over nature). One can imagine—though this is far from being plausible from the viewpoint of the psychology of knowledge—that his physics coincides, so to speak literally, with our modern physics; furthermore that such a physics was experimentally tested by Crusoe who has built himself a laboratory. Such a process, no matter how improbable, is at any rate thinkable. Consequently, so concludes the Crusoe objection, the sociological aspect is of no fundamental significance for science. . . .
>
> With respect to this argument, one must concede that continued testing by one individual is already similar to intersubjective testing (the sociological aspect is thus, at any rate in many cases, of no decisive significance for science). Furthermore, the concept of intersubjectivity, of the multitudes of subjects, is in certain respects not sharply defined. Yet the Crusoe objection does not hold water: that which Crusoe constructs under the name of physics is not a science; this is so not because we arbitrarily define science in such a way that only intersubjectively testable theories can be termed scientific, but because the Crusoe objection starts from the false premise that science is characterized by its results rather than by its methods. . . .
> (Popper 1979, p. 142. My translation)

To my mind, this whole argument betrays a certain embarrassment. Let us first remark that Robinson Crusoe need not invent sophisticated hypotheses comparable to those of modern physics; he may construct simple laws about regularities thought to obtain in his environment, then use these laws in order to survive. He would thereby be implicitly testing his hypotheses and hopefully surviving the successive tests. Thus Crusoe's discoveries and successes need not be miraculous. Should he regrettably succumb as a result of his first test, then his hypotheses would certainly qualify as scientific; for they would have been refuted, thus sadly preventing him from repeating the experiment. This conclusion holds good even in cases where the test can *in principle* be performed only once. So even the possibility of having an experiment *repeated* by the same person constitutes no *essential* requirement for a hypothesis to qualify as scientific. Notice secondly that in the passage above Popper backpedals by granting that intersubjectivity can sometimes be equated with the repeatability of the same test by the same person. He then annuls his concession by claiming that the Crusoe objection is anyway invalid because, in it, science is mistakenly defined by its results and not by its methods: according to Popper, Crusoe does not practice science because he does not apply any genuinely scientific method. But this is precisely where the problem lies: if we build repeatability and intersubjectivity into the very definition of a basic statement, then Robinson Crusoe can, *by definition,* no longer do science.

Let us recall that should we accept the psychologist thesis, then we would have no option but to accept objections [B]–[E], hence all the counterintuitive consequences mentioned above. But these consequences *are* intuitively unacceptable. As its name indicates, physical science ought to be founded on man's relation to a physical world which acts on man through his senses and his brain, thus finally affecting his consciousness. Only at this level is man's contact with nature direct; which is why most scientists instinctively subscribe to the phenomenological, as opposed to the consensual view of observation. To the extent that Crusoe tries out his hypotheses, then corrects and uses them in mastering his physical environment, he should be considered as practising empirical science. He does not of course possess as efficient a method for eradicating error as we do. If he is color-blind, he may well perish in circumstances in which we should have a greater chance of surviving; but he could conceivably develop a theory enabling him indirectly to distinguish between all frequencies. He is in greater need of luck than we are, but we collectively need a lot of luck too. Thus specific social conditions may provide additional means of detecting error, i.e. of unraveling the Duhem-Quine problem; but they are not of the essence. Methodologies should anyway remain neutral vis-a-vis such contingencies.

Now consider one last difficulty which flows from the psychologist thesis i.e. from clause [A] above. According to [C], psychology would face a problem of vicious circularity if it decided to base its methodology on an observer's feelings of conviction with regard to basic statements. This argument is undoubtedly valid; it should however be realized that sociology fares just as badly under Popper's conventionalist thesis. Sociology investigates how collective agreements come about and, more particularly, whether they are due to purely psycho-social factors or are at least partially based on objective considerations; e.g. on the acceptance of a scientific theory which might have led to a collective agreement about a fact like the earth's motion. Thus sociology might examine whether, and under what conditions, the conclusions reached through consensual agreement are rational. But according to Popper's conventionalist view of basic statements, a sociological hypothesis ought in turn to be tested by reports underwritten by a consensus. Of course, a sociological theory might tell us that the consensus is objectively well-founded; but this theory may well be the one undergoing the test, so that its status is highly uncertain; or else it might claim that only superstitious beliefs led to the consensus in question. Hence the allegedly factual report cannot be used in order to confirm the hypothesis under test. Popper was aware of this paradox when he wrote:

> Knowledge is thus possible because there are "unproblematic" basic statements (an analogue to the intuitively certain propositions about sense-data), i.e. basic statements which need not be tested any further and which should not be questioned after intersubjective agreement has been reached. That such propositions can exist, that we have had luck with such decisions and with such experimental propositions, that we are not thereby led into contradictions is to be noted as a fundamental methodological fact; a fact about which we can naturally never know that it will obtain at all times and in all cases. (Why there are such propositions, why objections are not raised against every decision or why the decisions do not lead to contradictions, this *question*, like all questions about the grounds of the possibility of knowledge is scientifically impermissible and leads to metaphysics, to metaphysical realism and not to a realism of method). (Popper 1979, p. 123. My translation)

Despite the coherence of Popper's position, I find his conclusions puzzling. There ought to be no good reason for excluding the possibility for science of explaining the occurrence and consistency of intersubjective agreements in terms, say, of the observers' common biological make up and their shared social environment. Should we succeed in refuting the psychologist thesis, then the phenomenological view will be seen to give us a free hand in scientifically explaining the occurrence of consensual agreements and of feelings of certainty regarding basic statements.

That Popper later recognized the problematic character of his conventionalist thesis is shown by his response to Ayer's criticism. In the following passage, Ayer argues that subjective experience provides not only a motive or cause, but also a reason for accepting objective experimental results:

> None of this prevents it from being true that my having this 'observational experience' supplies me not only with a motive but also with a ground for accepting the interpretation which I put on it. . . .
>
> It is to be noted that in arguing that basic statements can find a justification in experience, I have not found it necessary to cast them in the form of statements which refer exclusively to present sense-data. This is not because I have any objection to such statements in principle; I am not even convinced that it is wrong to treat them as incorrigible, in the sense that they do not leave room for anything other than merely verbal mistakes. It is rather that I do not think that they are strictly needed for the role which has here been assigned to them. (Popper 1974, p. 689)

My main objection to this argument is that in it, Ayer tries to circumvent any recourse to level-0 sentences by holding that experience directly confirms objective factual statements. But a proposition is justified either by the known existence of the state-of-affairs which it purports to describe or by way of other—verified—propositions. Popperian basic statements are not deduced from propositions known to be true; they are moreover about public events, hence cannot have private experiential referents. The latter correspond to level-0 reports, i.e. to Ayer's sense-datum statements. We must therefore take Ayer to be claiming that perceptions verify sense-datum propositions which in turn justify some 'interpretations' of our experience, i.e. some Popperian basic statements. By 'justification' Ayer clearly means something like inductive confirmation, which falls short of proof. Given his global anti-inductivist stance, Popper could therefore have rejected Ayer's thesis while remaining consistent with his own position. But short of accepting full-blown skepticism, Popper ought also to have admitted sense-datum statements as explananda within a hypothetico-deductive scheme. In other words: given his anti-inductivism, Popper should have held descriptions of sense-data to be basic statements, or rather: negations of observation reports deducible from an expanded scientific system. Instead of making this move which would have been consistent with his own position, he chose to cave in to Ayer's argument.

> Nevertheless, most organisms act upon interpretations of the information which they receive from their environment; and the fact that they survive for some considerable time shows that this apparatus usually works well. But it is far from perfect. . . .
>
> . . . Our experiences are not only motives for accepting or rejecting an observational statement, but they may even be described as inconclusive reasons. They are reasons because of the generally reliable character of our observations; they are inconclusive because our fallibility. (Popper 1974, pp. 1112–14)

Thus Popper's agreement with Ayer about observation supplying us with—inconclusive—reasons for accepting basic statements turns on the following argument. External states-of-affairs causally give rise to experiences which motivate us into holding certain basic statements to be true. The latter are however not about the experiences themselves but about their external causes. So far, this chain is a purely causal one: we directly respond to the *external* world because of our need quickly to adjust to it in order to survive. At this point, a Darwinian twist is given to the argument: in many if not in most cases, natural selection sees to it that our basic statements correspond to, or at least approximately model their transcendent causes which thereby become their true referents; for otherwise, we could not have survived long enough to start our present philosophical discussion. Like Ayer, Popper obviates all recourse to level-0 reports; but he does so at high cost to his own anti-inductivist position. This is not to say that Popper's claims are false, only that they presuppose Darwinism; they are circular and thus constitute no *argument* for the reliability of basic statements. If we believe Darwinism to be largely correct, this is only because some of its aspects have been strongly corroborated. The observation reports supporting Darwinian theory ought however not to be predicated on Darwinism itself; so the latter should not be presupposed in any epistemological argument. Note that in his (1979) Popper himself realized the necessity of avoiding such vicious circularity; he agreed with Leonard Nelson that a *theory* of knowledge, conceived as a system of true-or-false statements, is impossible; for it leads either to circularity or to an infinite regress (p. 110). This is precisely why Popper intended his methodology to be a set of proposals rather than of genuine propositions; for no *transcendent* thesis can be invoked prior to fixing some methodology, since any argument in support of such a thesis involves theories whose confirmation presupposes a methodology.

Both Ayer's and Popper's positions are therefore vitiated by their refusal to take account of the special status of autopsychological reports. These will be shown to rest not on any *science* in the ordinary sense but on phenomenological analysis. And phenomenology, which was intended by its founders to yield the principles of both logic and mathematics, may well prove to be an irreducible bastion of *the synthetic a priori* (where the latter does not imply *necessary truth*).

(I) REFUTATION OF THE PSYCHOLOGIST THESIS

It has to be admitted that Popper had sound *historical* reasons for holding a psychologistic view of autopsychological reports. This last phrase anyway has a pleonastic ring to it. As explained in the chapter of Popper's (1979) devoted to Kant and to Fries, the latter realized that on pain of falling into vicious circularity or some form of infinite regress, we have to give up any idea of justifying *all* synthetic propositions. In order to avoid dogmatism, Fries accepted experiential statements as something which, as a matter of brute psychology, we cannot help believing in. Thus Fries openly subscribed to the psychologist thesis.

Towards the end of the 19th century, Franz Brentano tried to account for the certainty of level-0 reports in non-psychologistic terms. He thereby developed a so-called 'Evidenzlehre' or theory of self-evidence. The latter is an attempt to draw a distinction between the blind compulsion which misleads us into believing, even in cases of hallucination, in the existence of allegedly external objects and of their qualities; and genuine self-evidence which is the objective hallmark of such indubitable propositions as the logical and mathematical principles, the axioms of probability and our autopsychological statements (which Brentano called statements of secondary or inner perception. See his (1930), section 4). The latter are however known to be contingent; so they cannot be established without appealing to some synthetic principle. Once again, the twin problems of infinite regress and of vicious circularity rear their ugly heads. Brentano envisaged two solutions to these problems. The first consisted in giving a laundry list of propositions which were declared, by fiat, to be self-evident (Brentano 1930, section 4). This is tantamount to postulating what is needed and, as well-known, represents the advantages of theft over honest toil. The second 'solution' treats self-evidence as a property which can be infallibly grasped by direct insight: though self-evidence be an objective attribute of certain propositions, we have to rely on a psychologistic criterion in order to identify it (Brentano 1930, Introduction). Hence Popper should be excused for regarding such 'Evidenzlehren' as thinly disguised forms of psychologism. But it seems to me that Brentano's thesis can be rescued by methods somewhat similar to those used by his follower Anton Marty. As already mentioned, in attempting to demonstrate the truth of level-0 propositions, one has to stop somewhere, where this 'somewhere' is necessarily synthetic and hence questionable. So why not follow Brentano by halting the process of justification at the level of the autopsychological reports themselves which could, without further ado, be dubbed self-evident?

Where one decides to break off the analysis is nevertheless not a matter of indifference. In the present case, in order to establish the certainty of level-0 statements, it might prove possible to single out a principle which links up with other components of the philosophical system one proposes to defend. In other words: despite being ultimately invoked without any justification, this principle might be needed in other areas of a global position, which thereby becomes more unified. In what follows, I shall argue that the certainty of level-0 sentences rests on an intuitive version of the Correspondence Theory of Truth; and it is significant that Brentano resorted to his 'Evidenzlehre' precisely at a time when he expressed doubts about the Correspondence Theory. Remembering that Truth—qua some form of correspondence—became a central theme in Popper's later philosophy, my move will show the phenomenological view of the empirical basis to be a natural complement to falsificationism. Putting it briefly: I propose to demonstrate that level-0 reports can be recognized as true, not through being derived from self-evident propositions, but by our having a direct access both to their referents and to the meanings of all the concepts occurring in them. Only in such epistemologically privileged situations can it be ascertained that a correspondence relation obtains—or fails to obtain—between a sentence and the state-of-affairs it supposedly signifies (Note also that only at the observational level can the notion of such a strict correspondence definitely be *known* to hold).

First, we have to analyze the kind of referent which an autopsychological proposition can reasonably be said to possess. Ayer wrote:

> The next step, continuing with our example, is to convert the sentence "it now seems to me that I see a cigarette case" into "I am now seeing a seeming-cigarette-case." And this seeming-cigarette-case,

which lives only in my present experience, is an example of a sense-datum . . . .

. . . the expression must be used in such a way that the experience of the physical object which appears to be referred to remains an open question: there is no implication either that it does exist or that it does not . . . What appears most dubious of all is the final step by which we are to pass from "it seems to me that I perceive x" to "I perceive a seeming-x", with the implication that there is a seeming-x which I perceive . . . For to talk of someone's sensing a sense-datum is intended to be another way of saying that he is sensitively affected; the manner in which he is affected reappears as a property of the sense-datum. (Ayer 1956, pp 106, 111, 115, 118)

In these passages Ayer mentions, as if in passing, one of the central problems with which Brentano grappled throughout his life. Brentano underlined the intentional structure of consciousness, which is always a consciousness *of something*. Every mental act intends, i.e. it is directed towards some object or other. Such objects need not exist independently of the mental operations which generate them; which explains why they are called 'intentional' or 'immanent'. This does not mean that no transcendent entity exists over and above the intentional one; only that the latter is always present, whether or not the former is. Given the phenomenological continuity between hallucination and veridical perception, all perceptual objects must belong to the same category and are therefore non-physical. In view of the above quotation, Brentano's perceptual intentional objects can be identified with Ayer's sense-data. But can immanent entities be said to exist in any legitimate sense? Note that the answer must be in the affirmative if 'I see a seeming-x' is to count as a true level-0 report.

Initially, Brentano half-heartedly ascribed to intentional entities a kind of existence which he misleadingly called 'inexistence in consciousness'. Thus sense-data were not supposed to exist in the ordinary realist sense but to remain private to one mind. Still, they were *objects* which could act as bearers of such phenomenal properties as color, smell and shape; being interposed between the mental acts on the one hand and the external world on the other, they could in principle reflect the properties of transcendent entities; but they existed only 'in the mind'. Should this thesis prove tenable, then we could identify level-0 statements with propositions of the form 'I perceive a seeming-x', where x is some definite description. The intended referent of 'seeming-x' will therefore be a sense-datum. Since the latter is an immanent entity, then provided it really exists, we should be able directly to apprehend it and check whether it has the phenomenal properties expressed by x. Level-0 statements would thus have ascertainable truth-values.

With time, Brentano grew dissatisfied with his shadowy intentional realm; and this for a variety of reasons. To begin with, he became more of an empiricist and hence doubted the existence of such ethereal entities as sense-data. And he later came to fear the logical paradoxes which the postulation of 'ideal' objects might engender. He baulked at the prospect of being compelled to accept the existence of logically impossible entities like round squares. In this, he was undoubtedly mistaken. There is of course nothing to prevent us from conjoining squareness with roundness and from thus obtaining the empty class; but we can neither perceive nor even have to imagine round squares. Hence the principle of non-contradiction is not threatened by the introduction of objects of thought.

All the same, Brentano seems to have had an unerring instinct regarding the logical inadmissibility of intentional entities; for these are both richer and less determinate than ordinary objects. They are richer in that they present themselves theory-laden; thus, the same physical object can give rise to infinitely many different sense-data: what was said above concerning the theory-ladenness of Popperian basic statements can be transferred to all descriptions of primary intentional entities. We have already noted that sense-data have a focus which is fixed by the observer's attention; so that the same chest X-ray can be integrated in several different ways.

Two-dimensional objects, e.g. a painting or an image on the television screen, are automatically observed as possessing depth. Only through an effort of reflection can I bring myself to 'see' them as two-dimensional pictures. The photo of an object taken from an unusual angle will, on the contrary, appear first as a two-dimensional arrangement of colors and shapes; the object might subsequently be identified, and the new sense-datum will not only supplant but also suppress the old one. In the case of a dot on a radar screen, both the expert and the layman will be aware of a two-dimensional picture, to which only the expert will instinctively add some information about the distance of a flying object; and only through an act of will can he suppress this theoretical admixture and 'retrieve' a purely visual image. Since every transcendent object may thus give rise to any number of sense-data, admitting the existence of the latter will lead to ontological inflation. But there are even worse dangers; for intentional entities are less determinate than their physical counterparts: they possess only those properties which are explicitly projected on to them by our mental acts. A sense-datum is after all a phenomenal entity, i.e. some *object-as-perceived*. A speckled hen is apprehended as having a finite number of speckles but neither as having 100 speckles nor as not having 100 speckles. Should we transform this innocuous sentence into a statement about sense-data, then we would clearly violate the law of the excluded middle: the phenomenal hen will have a finite number of speckles, but it is not the case that this number will be either equal to or else different from 100. In this respect, the hen is on a par with Hamlet who cannot be said to be either 1.75 metres tall or not 1.75 metres tall; for Hamlet was not *intended* to have any specific height. Thus an intentional entity will lack every property which is not explicitly attributed to it by some act of consciousness. Husserl expressed this principle by asserting the existence of a strict correlation between, on the one hand, the noesis and, on the other, the noema together with the corresponding intentional object. I take this to mean that all talk of intentional entities, and more particularly of sense-data, is shorthand for a more complex description of the underlying mental operations. This problem could alternatively be solved by decreeing that even sense-data should obey the law of the excluded middle; but they will then escape our control and cease to be immanent entities. For we may be unable to count the number of speckles on the 'phenomenal' hen; and any mechanical device for counting them will, if applied, alter the corresponding sense-datum. Finally, should the hen have been hallucinated, then to assume that it still possesses a well-defined number of speckles is nothing short of fantastic. Thus, for any intentional object y and any property P which might subsume y: P(y) holds iff y is intended by the corresponding noesis to possess P; but then the law of the excluded middle will be violated in certain cases.

Brentano was therefore right to look for another solution out of this logical *impasse*, a solution which he first put forward at the turn of the century and then held on to until his death in 1916. Before discussing Brentano's thesis in any detail, let us examine a concrete example. Consider the proposition 'I see a red house' and assume that there is no physical house out there at all; that is: suppose that I am hallucinating. If 'red house' is given its ordinary realist meaning, then my proposition will clearly be false. It could conceivably be turned into a true sentence if 'red house' were to denote a sense-datum. But as already explained, we have good reasons for denying the existence of all intentional entities; so the truth-value of my proposition becomes problematic. Fortunately for the philosophy of science, the sentence 'I seem to be perceiving a red house' has a truth-value which is independent of the existence or non-existence of the referent of 'red house'; which is all that is needed in order to secure a phenomenological basis for the sciences.

Let us now turn to Brentano's definitive solution according to which all acts of consciousness are described by sentences having a form similar to 'I seem to be perceiving a red house'. Consciousness is furthermore claimed always to possess two indissolubly connected components (it is *zwei-strahlig*; i.e. it consists of two rays). There is first a primary conscious act directed at a primary object, e.g. the red house. But in no sense can a primary intentional object like the red house be said to exist qua sense-datum. There simply is no *immanent* red house. Only the ego with its various directional activities exists. As for any statement about the phenomenal red house, it is shorthand for a description of certain modes of the underlying conscious activity. Secondly, the primary act is always accompanied by an inner or *secondary* consciousness which takes the primary conscious activity for its object; this latter—immanent—entity exists in the ordinary sense and, through it, secondary consciousness obliquely intends the non-existent primary object, e.g. the red house qua sense-datum. That is: whenever I primarily seem to be perceiving a house which is red, I am at the same time secondarily aware of so seeing it. Finally, this inner awareness is aware of itself as well as of primary consciousness. (See Grossmann 1984, Chapter 2). Thus every (perceptual) conscious act is such that:

(1) There exists a primary conscious activity directed at a non-existent primary intentional object (This does not of course imply that no corresponding transcendent object exists).

(2) There is a secondary conscious activity which directly targets the (existent) primary act and, through the latter, obliquely refers to the (non-existent) primary object.

(3) Secondary consciousness is finally aware of itself. Hence tertiary, and with it all higher levels of consciousness fall back onto the secondary level.

There is clearly something wrong with Brentano's final solution but it can, to my mind, be altered into an acceptable thesis. Note first that level-0 reports should be put in the form 'I seem to be perceiving x' rather than 'I am perceiving a seeming-x'. We are thus dealing with descriptions—issued by secondary consciousness—of primary mental acts; in this way, we avoid being entangled in discussions about the ontology of sense-data, i.e. of seeming-x's. Secondly, we find Brentano defending the view that *every* mental act must be accompanied by secondary consciousness and should therefore be self-aware. I find this thesis unconvincing. Not only does it exclude all subconscious activity; it also entails that animals must either be capable of reflection or be altogether devoid of any form of consciousness; which is patently false. There is anyway direct evidence—supplied by memory—for the fact that in everyday life we are not always reflexively conscious of perceiving something. In other words, we do not always observe ourselves perceiving, but merely perceive, i.e. intend exclusively *primary* objects. It is of course also true that through reflection, the primary acts can be made into the existent objects of higher mental activities; that is: of inner or of secondary consciousness. This gives rise to level-0 reports like 'I seem to be seeing a red house' or 'I believe that there is a red house in front of me', whose intentional objects, viz. my seeing the red house or my belief in its physical existence, are both immanent and known to exist while under the scrutiny of secondary consciousness. Having admitted that a conscious act can take place at a definite level without necessarily involving any higher one, we no longer need Brentano's assumption (3) which was no doubt introduced in order to block an infinite regress: if every conscious level presupposed a higher one, then we should have to postulate an actually infinite number of strata in every mental act; which is clearly absurd. Brentano arrested this regress at the secondary stage by identifying the secondary level with the tertiary one. For our part, we can accept that every level could *but need not* be made into the existent object of a higher-order activity. Everyday experience occurs exclusively at the primary level and issues in statements like 'Here is a glass of water', which will be fallible if 'glass' and 'water' are given their usual transcendent meanings. All levels above the primary one have immanent and hence existent intentional objects. More precisely: once the higher act is performed, then its object must exist and the corresponding proposition become incorrigible. Of this kind are the level-0 reports which describe the findings of secondary consciousness. Thus the testing of scientific theories takes place at the level of inner consciousness—through statements of the form 'I seem to be observing a glass of water (i.e. a glass of a liquid which I take to be composed of H_2 and of O)' or 'I seem to be seeing a red house'. Note that the modes of primary consciousness remain dependent on the theories entertained by the observer; but the role of *secondary consciousness* should be exclusively descriptive of these modes. As for philosophical reflection which examines the relationship between our primary and our inner mental activities, it takes place—at the very least— on the tertiary level.

Before accounting for the infallibility of level-0 reports, let me dispel the myth—propagated by Neurath—that propositions can be justified only by means of other propositions; a view shared by Alan Musgrave:

Suppose, as is traditional, that the thing believed is a *proposition*. What might a reason for a proposition be? Logic tells us. A conclusive reason for a proposition P is another proposition R that entails that P is true. . . .

. . . Only a proposition can be a reason for a proposition. (Musgrave 2004, pp. 19–20)

But Logic 'tells us' no such thing: there is no logical principle according to which 'only a proposition can be a reason for a proposition'. By contrast, semantics tells us that a statement is true if and only if the state-of-affairs putatively described by the statement exists. Let me clarify this point further. Once a statement q has been deduced from another, p say, then we of course know that the truth of p must entail that of q; for all (valid) deductions are designed to transmit truth. Neurath's myth asserts something like the converse of this trivial deductive principle; namely that all we can effectively know is the transmission of truth, not the truth of any single proposition. Of course, given the structure of the correspondence theory of truth, such a correspondence can never be infallibly established between a realist hypothesis and the transcendent state-of-affairs it supposedly denotes. For remember that the external world is not something we can directly apprehend; it is known, if at all, not by acquaintance but through the medium of conjectures which are not effectively verifiable (See Russell 1984, Part I). This conclusion does not however apply to the relationship between level-0 statements and the immanent states-of-affairs they describe. And Musgrave himself seems to rely on the decidability of certain level-0 reports in order to confirm some level-1, and hence also some theoretical claims:

Perceptual experience causes us to acquire perceptual beliefs. Having a table-experience or seeming to see a table causes us to come to believe that there is a table in font of us.

. . . A good reason for believing that there is a table in front of you is that you seem to see one. Perceptual beliefs are not necessarily true beliefs. . . .

. . . What is the relation between the proposition 'I have a table-experience' (E) and the proposition 'There is a table in front of me' (T)? Obviously, E does not entail T. . . . But T, combined with other assumptions, does entail or predict or explain E. So E represents the results of a successful test of H. (Musgrave 2004, p. 20)

So the relation between E and T is not only causal, but also logical (predicated, of course, on background assumptions); and Musgrave seems—rightly—to attribute a special status to the autopsychological report E. There are in fact two features of autopsychological propositions which make them epistemologically privileged:

(a) They signify states-of-affairs which German-speaking philosophers appropriately call '*Erlebnisse*'. As their name indicates, *Erlebnisse* can be *lived through*; so that we have an unmediated access to them and can thus check a level-0 statement against its referent. For example, I can directly compare the sentence 'I seem (or seemed) to be seeing a red house' either with a present or with a remembered experience; but I cannot directly apprehend the state-of-affairs described by 'There exists an electromagnetic field in this room'. I am in principle unable to leap out of myself and partake of the state of the field. This privileged access to the referents of autopsychological statements does not however guarantee infallibility; for as already explained, the referent may be a remembered and hence a misremembered one. Whence the necessity of a second condition.

(b) Through inner or secondary consciousness, we become aware of our mental acts *as we perform them*. I can observe, or rather I can sense myself observing some primary object. This eliminates, or at any rate greatly reduces the possibility of my being mistaken in some such claim as 'I now seem to be perceiving a red patch'; provided of course that the claim be made simultaneously with the experience it describes. This is because, without having to rely on my fallible memory, I can directly compare a report about my present state of consciousness with its intended referent. Simultaneity also insures that all my descriptive terms are given the meanings intended at the time of my uttering the report. A truth-correspondence can thus be immediately ascertained (See above, Chapter III, section C).

As remarked by Ayer, verbal mistakes are always possible. We often shout 'Right' when we ostensibly mean 'Left'. In saying 'I seem to be seeing a purple patch', by 'purple' I might now intend what I previously meant by 'red'. These are rather trivial instances of error since what counts is the intended referent of a word, not the word itself. More serious mistakes can however occur. Suppose that I now see a red patch; and that, yesterday, I saw a colored patch which I correctly described as purple but which I now wrongly remember as having had a color identical with my present color-sensation; that I furthermore rightly remember having used the word 'purple' yesterday. As a result, I now claim to be perceiving (or rather seem to be perceiving) a purple patch. Am I not mistaken in a non-verbal way? The answer is in the negative: an illusion of error arises only because no proper phenomenological reduction has been performed. In 'I now seem to be perceiving a purple patch', 'purple' should not be surreptitiously given a transcendent meaning which is not intended by the speaker. His sentence, when properly unpacked, reads: 'I (now) seem to be perceiving a color which (now) seems to be identical with the color which I (now) recall having seen yesterday'. This report, which is properly level-0 in both senses (a) and (b), is certainly true; it being understood that 'recall' is not to be interpreted as a success word.

The two points (a) and (b) have often been conflated—but not by Brentano. Initially, he even thought us incapable of observing ourselves observing; so that we must always resort to fallible memory in order to reach any phenomenological conclusions which have a chance of being correct (Brentano 1924, Chapter 3). Though he later revised his view, he had already made the *logical* distinction between the two points (a) and (b) clear (Brentano 1968, Chapter 1). (a) tells us that in order to be able to decide the truth-value of a proposition not by inferring it from other statements but by confronting it with its presumed referent, we must restrict ourselves to autopsychological reports, whether these describe our past or our present experiences. The reason is that we can directly apprehend only our own mental states. As for point (b), it warns us that should we want to eliminate or greatly diminish the risk of error, then we should further limit ourselves to descriptions of our *present* mental states; for we know our memory to be fallible.

Let us now apply these last conclusions to falsificationist methodology: in order to test scientific laws, it is no use appealing to any of their consequences which describe mind-independent events; for our access to these is exclusively theoretical. We cannot break out of the vicious circle of theories, and of yet more theories, by remaining within the transcendent domain. We have a double access only to those propositions which, on the one hand, flow from some scientific system and, on the other, can be directly checked against the state-of-affairs they are meant to signify. Such statements can only be the level-0 reports discussed above. Should we feel unhappy or unsure about their incorrigibility, then point (a) anyway clearly demonstrates that they are the only possible candidates for the status of basic statement. I have furthermore tried to show that their certainty is founded not on any feelings of conviction on the part of some observer, but on the possibility of directly checking whether they truly correspond to their referents. The psychologistic view of autopsychological statements is therefore false.

(J) An Alternative Approach to the Phenomenological Thesis

With respect to the empirical basis, we shall now adopt an alternative approach based on Tarski's semantic theory of truth. It will be shown that a close examination of Tarski's truth-schema and of its relevance to scientific realism leads, by a route different from the one followed above, to the same phenomenological conclusions (which is not to say that Tarski himself would have subscribed to the latter).

Let us consider the Tarskian scheme: $Tr(\underline{p}) \Leftrightarrow p$ where, for any sentence p, $\underline{p}$ is a name of p. Thus in order to decide the truth-value of p, we must be able to *apply* this scheme to a concrete situation; i.e. we must be in a position to apprehend both a proposition and the state-of-affairs it purports to describe. Since language is of our own creation, we have a direct access to the linguistic entity $\underline{p}$. The main problem lies with the state-of-affairs described by p. As already explained, Descartes showed that we are incapable of directly grasping any transcendent entities. Hence even if the external world existed, we could at best come to know it by description, i.e. via hypotheses whose truth would in turn be subject to the Tarskian scheme (Brentano 1968, Chapter 12, pp. 12–21). The problem of truth would thus be merely shifted, not solved. In the case of a mind-independent reality, we therefore have unmediated access only to language; we have no direct insight into an external state-of-affairs which we might then be able to match with the right-hand side of the truth-scheme above. We must consequently turn to another domain known to us, not by description but by acquaintance (See Russell 1962, Chapter 5, pp. 46–59). This can only be the domain of our mental states. In our inner phenomenological sphere, there occurs a duplication through which the subject turns himself into his own object; he becomes capable of apprehending both his language and his internal states, and thus able to give a 'live' description of his own thought-processes.

To my mind, every carefully conducted experiment involves not only consciousness but also self-consciousness; that is: it brings into play both secondary and primary mental acts. On the one hand, the observer considers a phenomenological prediction of the hypothesis under test; on the other, he will *reflect* on what he observes and, for example, ask himself whether he really perceives a red patch in front of him; i.e. he raises himself to the secondary level. He will moreover carry out a phenomenological reduction by refraining from all assumptions about any transcendent reality. His consciousness will be reflexive. He will not only observe but also watch himself observing. There is in effect a striking parallel between the three levels: Metalanguage – Object Language – States of Affairs and the Sartrian triplet: Reflecting Consciousness – Language – Reflected Consciousness (See Sartre 1981, Chapter 1, pp. 26–37).

The phenomenological reduction adhered to in the course of an experiment ensures the objectivity and neutrality which are essential preconditions to any test being conclusive. Unlike Michelson, a scrupulous experimenter will not assert that he detected ether-drag; he will abstain from emitting any realistic conjecture about the ether and restrict himself to stating that he failed to observe certain fringes move; where "fringes" and "move" are given their *phenomenal* meanings; he can of course affirm that he *took* the ether to have been carried along by the earth's motion; for all these statements are descriptive of his immanent states of consciousness (See Zahar 1989a, Introduction, pp. 5–6).

Let us consider the following example: $p \equiv$ (the current is on), $p' \equiv$ (I see what I take to be the arm of a galvanometer move). Suppose that A is some psycho-physical theory implying the (material) equivalence of p and p'; i.e. $A \vdash (p \leftrightarrow p')$. p and p' obviously possess very different meanings: p refers to a physical state-of-affairs while p' describes a series of observations. Hence p cannot be *logically* equivalent to p'; and a sequence of observations can correspond—in the sense of the correspondence theory of truth—to p' or to $\neg p'$, but never to p or to $\neg p$. Of course, one could by fiat stipulate that $\underline{p}$ is nothing but shorthand for $\underline{p}'$. This was the solution which Poincaré put forward in order to establish the infallibility of crude factual statements (Poincaré 1906, Chapter 10). But the logical connection between p and any physical theory H would thereby be severed, thus defeating the aim of observationally testing H by means of p'. Hence $\underline{p}$ is not another way of expressing $\underline{p}'$; p is *contingently* linked to p' by means of a hypothesis A which often remains implicit. Thus in order for us to know, no matter how tentatively, that a theory has been falsified, we must resort to the phenomenological level which occupies a privileged position both from the psychological and from the epistemological viewpoint; for only at this level can a semantic relation between sentences and states-of-affairs be *ascertained*. Without fear of *formal* contradiction, it could admittedly be maintained that we remain fallible even at this subjective level. But if our decision both to aim at the truth and to accept basic statements in preference to any universal hypotheses contradicting them is to be rational, then we must—for one reason or another—be *less likely to err about our inner experience than about the state of the external world* (See Russell 1962, Chapters 6 and 7). Phenomenology offers such a reason, which also happens to be a good one. Hence a minimal involvement in phenomenology is dictated by scientific realism. And it is because they instinctively adhere to realism and to the correspondence theory of truth that scientists adopt, if only tacitly, the phenomenological view of the empirical basis of all the sciences.

(K) UNMANAGEABLE LARGISM?

One important question remains, namely whether autopsychological predictions can in principle be derived from some—appropriately extended—scientific system. John Watkins has denied this possibility by arguing that a level-0 empirical basis would lead to unmanageable largism (Watkins 1984, Chapter 7). To my mind, Watkins's criticism is the most cogent objection brought against the phenomenological thesis. I nonetheless propose to counter it.

The derivation of autopsychological reports admittedly increases the complexity of the Duhem-Quine problem (See below, Chapter V): for in deducing level-0 statements from scientific premises, we have to postulate not only a central theory taken together with auxiliary hypotheses and descriptions of relevant boundary conditions; but also some conjectures about the effect which certain beliefs have on the experimenter's state of mind and hence on the conclusions he will draw, or rather jump to, from his observations. As part of the boundary conditions, we moreover have to add assumptions about the observer's mental and physical states: if our test involves the identification of certain colors, we may have to suppose that the experimenter is not color-blind. But why bother with all these complications which led Duhem, Popper, Schlick and even Watkins to insist on keeping autopsychological propositions out of the proper domain of physical science? The answer, already given above, is simple: in case of conflict with experience, we want to have some rational ground for holding our premises to be actually false rather than merely inconsistent with a statement which we have chosen provisionally to accept—by means of a consensus. Whence the necessity of the phenomenological thesis. The latter must nevertheless be shown to lead to a feasible strategy.

We have already mentioned a major criticism of the view that 0-level reports should constitute the empirical basis of science; namely that none of Newton's, Maxwell's, Einstein's or Schrödinger's theories refers to anybody's psychological state of mind; so that when taken *by itself*, a scientific hypothesis H entails no autopsychological statement. Thus H appears to be testable by means only of propositions of the form $(e_1 \wedge \pm e_2)$, where: $H \Rightarrow (e_1 \rightarrow e_2)$ and both e_1 and e_2 are said by Watkins to be level-1 statements. Since e_1 and e_2 describe transcendent states of affairs, they are conjectural. Let me nonetheless show that Watkins was mistaken in claiming that H cannot be beefed up so as to become testable by a combination of level-0 reports.

Watkins's critique runs as follows. Let e'_1 and e'_2 be the level-0 correlates of e_1 and e_2 respectively. Our attempt, deemed by him to be unattainable, is to strengthen H into H* in such a way that:

(1) $\vdash [H^* \rightarrow (e'_1 \rightarrow e_1)]$ and $\vdash [H^* \rightarrow (e_2 \rightarrow e'_2)]$

Since H* is moreover chosen to be logically stronger than H, then:

(2) $H^* \Rightarrow H \Rightarrow (e_1 \rightarrow e_2)$; whence:
(3) $\vdash [H^* \rightarrow (e'_1 \rightarrow e'_2)]$.

Thus H* should be refutable by the phenomenologically decidable proposition $(e'_1 \wedge \neg e'_2)$. The reasons why Watkins holds the condition $H^* \Rightarrow (e'_1 \rightarrow e_1)$ to be unfulfillable are best explained by means of an example. Let e'_1 be the level-0 report describing my visual impression of a palm-tree; and let e_1 be the proposition that there exists an actual palm-tree in some spatio-temporal region. The problem is so to strengthen H that e_1 can be validly inferred from e'_1. As a first step, I might be tempted to adjoin to H the thesis K_1 that whenever any subject thinks he perceives a palm-tree, then there exists a corresponding physical object 'out there'. But since Descartes, the proposition K_1 has been known to be false; so it might be replaced by another assumption K_2 consisting of two conjuncts: the first says that whenever a person of sound body and mind experiences an e'_1-like *Erlebnis* (e.g. thinks he sees a palm-tree), then an e_1-like situation obtains (there exists a real palm-tree out there); the second conjunct asserts that whenever a person feels well, cannot remember having taken drugs or drunk to excess during the past six months and moreover feels his ideas to be clear and distinct, then he is actually sound in mind and body (Note that these two assumptions were, more or less, the ones adduced by Descartes in his deduction of the existence of the external world from God's veracity). Now add K_2 to H and define $H_2 \equiv (H \wedge K_2)$. This process can clearly be pushed further, issuing in a sequence of hypotheses: $K_1, K_2, K_3, ..., K_n$.

Hypotheses like $K_1, K_2, K_3, ..., K_n$ are admittedly problematic; for, clearly, none of them is on a par with Newtonian or with Quantum

Mechanics. But *every* scientific theory is problematic in the strict sense of being—not only possibly but even probably—false (General Relativity fails in the subatomic domain; and nonrelativistic Quantum Mechanics is not Lorentz-covariant). More specifically: K_2 is false because healthy people experience mirages; but K_2 can be weakened by strengthening the antecedent of its first conjunct through adding the proviso: "and there is no desert around. . .", or rather: ". . . and the person in question perceives no large yellowish expanse around him. . . ." All this illustrates the following trivial point: since there could have been only finitely many falsifying instances, then through monster- and exception-barring, a hitherto unrefuted hypothesis K_n can always be determined in such a way that:

(4) $\vdash [K_n \rightarrow (e'_1 \rightarrow e_1)]$.

A mirror image operation similarly yields a theory K'_m such that:

(5) $\vdash [K'_m \rightarrow (e_2 \rightarrow e'_2)]$, where K'_m is also unrefuted.

Thus putting:

(6) $H^* \equiv_{Def.} (H \wedge K_n \wedge K'_m)$, obtain
(7) $\vdash [H^* \rightarrow (e'_1 \rightarrow e'_2)]$ from (1)–(6).

(For the notions of monster- and exception-barring, see Lakatos 1976, pp. 86, 41).

We have already pointed out that the assumptions K_n and K'_m are highly fallible; so that in case of empirical refutation, i.e. should $(e'_1 \wedge \neg e'_2)$ be verified, then the falsity of $H^* \equiv (H \wedge K_n \wedge K'_m)$ could be imputed to that of K_n or of K'_m. In other words: the auxiliary assumptions rather than the core theory H are blamed for the failure of the system. This is in fact what very often—and quite properly—happens; and it incidentally explains why dramatic confirmations—rather than falsifications—play an essential role in the progress of science: should $(e'_1 \rightarrow e'_2)$ be verified, then H^*, i.e. $(H \wedge K_n \wedge K'_m)$, is taken to have been globally confirmed; this partly because the chances that the 'falsities' of the disparate hypotheses H, K_n, K'_m should have exactly compensated one another are felt to be negligible (though nonzero). Confirmation is furthermore a temporary affair which can be overturned by any subsequent test. So we risk little by holding a system to have been corroborated by an experimental result. Watkins's unfeasibility thesis is thus refuted.

There is another—less direct—way of showing the untenability of Watkins's criticism. It consists in establishing that the onus of proof rests with the opponents of the phenomenological view; that is: provided a hypo-thetico-deductivist approach be adopted. Using the transcendental method of criticism, I shall demonstrate that the actual practice of science presup-poses, if only implicitly, the phenomenological thesis. Two simple exam-ples will make the point. We all agree that a color-blind experimenter's report can be discounted in test-situations where the perception of color matters. Yet a particular person's inability to distinguish between various colors is logically irrelevant to the objective blueness of a piece of litmus paper, though of course not to the recognition of such blueness. Whether we are aware of it or not, the basic statements which we rely on in chemistry are therefore of the form 'This, which I take to be a piece of litmus paper, looks blue' rather than 'This piece of litmus paper is blue (i.e. reflects light of a certain frequency)'; for this last—objective—proposition can be deduced from hypotheses making no reference to any conscious observer. Such a derivation will therefore not be blocked by altering assumptions about the absence of color-blindness; for no such assumption figures among the premises. Only the corresponding autopsychological report requires, for its derivation, the premise that the observer is not color-blind; which is pre-cisely why ascertaining color-blindness could save our core theory from refutation. Thus only the phenomenological thesis renders the practice of science rational. Similar conclusions apply to the chest X-ray example. The objective existence of some pathological patch on the X-ray image in no way depends on the observer's state of knowledge. Yet we normally feel justified in ignoring an experimental account given by a layman rather than by a trained doctor. There must therefore be some inferential link between the observer's state of knowledge and his report. Hence the latter cannot possibly be an objective statement about some transcendent state-of-affairs; it must rather assume the form 'I notice such and such a patch which, for the following reasons, I take to be evidence for the presence in the lung of active Koch bacilli . . .'. This statement cannot be deduced without recourse to some hypothesis about the observer's professional background; which is why a layman's report constitutes no test of any system comprising both a theory about some illness and certain assumptions about the experimenter's competence. For the layman fails to satisfy these extra assumptions (For more details see Zahar 1989b).

As already explained, repeatability and intersubjective agreement should not be built into the definition of a basic statement. From a phe-nomenological viewpoint, it can nonetheless be seen why, in presumed cases of refutation, the actual repetition of a falsifying experiment, by different people or under differing conditions, makes perfect sense. The main purpose of repeating a test is to render highly improbable a series of coincidences which might have falsified assumptions about experimenter's mental and physical state, or about the non-existence of factors not mentioned by the core theory. Repetition enables us to hive off a number of peripheral premises and thus blame a refutation on some core theory. In this way, the Duhem-Quine problem can be made more manageable; so that the refutation of isolated hypotheses becomes possible, albeit in a fallible-conjectural way. Popper was thus right to underline the conditions of repeatability and intersubjective agreement; not because these conditions are defining characteristics of basic statements, but because they constitute a means of dealing more effectively with the Duhem-Quine problem (See below, Chapter V).

Let me end by advancing a simple logical argument in support of the feasibility of the phenomenological approach to basic statements. As long as level-0 propositions are regarded as explananda and as long as we subscribe to hypothetico-deductivism, then the only way of explaining these explananda is through deducing them from some set of premises, and so, by the completeness theorem, from a finite number of such premises. Each of these assumptions either is derivable from, or else can be adjoined to our core hypothesis, the latter being taken together with certain boundary conditions. In this way, we are bound to obtain a finite system which yields the level-0 statements (viz. their negations) as deductive consequences. Whether or not one chooses to call such a system 'scientific' is a purely terminological issue. The system will certainly be testable against autopsychological reports, which therefore constitute the empirical basis of *all* the sciences.

IV

Falsifiability and Parameter-Adjustment

T.S. Kuhn leveled a global criticism at Popper's demarcation criterion, a criticism which seemed *prima facie* cogent. He held that science consists of successive paradigms each one of which gives rise to a potentially infinite sequence of theories; the paradigm sets its own methodological standards by deciding what questions can legitimately be asked and what answers are to be deemed acceptable; it furthermore reserves the right to shelve recalcitrant instances as anomalies to be dealt with at a later date (Kuhn 1970, p. 6; also pp. 35–41). This is why no empirical result can overturn the paradigm—at any rate during the latter's initial stages. At its inception, the paradigm is in fact ambiguous; and experiments are often carried out in order not to test any of its hypotheses, but to determine the values of certain parameters (Kuhn 1970, pp. 25–27). Moreover, the facts themselves are theory-laden so that renouncing a paradigm might mean giving up the very results which undermined it in the first place. Thus paradigms have built into them those stratagems whose perverse role was exposed by Hans Albert through his notion of an "immunizing strategy" (Albert 1975, section 5, pp. 29–31; also section 15, pp. 91–97). This is in part why Popper added to his falsifiability *criterion* an important methodological *decision*: that of always bowing to the negative verdict of experience and hence of renouncing ad hoc maneuvers (Popper 1959, section 20). I now propose to show that in certain situations, even this kind of voluntarism is of no real help; for despite his metaphorical style, Kuhn based some of his views on sound objective reasons.

(A) The Adjustment of Parameters

While defending the phenomenological view of the empirical basis, we effectively dealt, in the previous chapter, with the question concerning the theory-dependence of factual statements (See Chapter III, section G). So let us once again address the question of the falsifiability of hypotheses by turning to the hypothetico-deductive scheme H, b $\vdash$ p. Kuhn correctly pointed out that far from being implied by H, the facts described by (b∧p) often serve to determine constants occurring in H. This important aspect of *rational* scientific practice seems to have escaped both Popper's and Reichenbach's attentions. Like most members of the Vienna Circle, these two philosophers strictly demarcated between the context of discovery and the context of justification: methodology should concern itself exclusively with the latter while relegating the former to the domain of empirical psychology (See Popper 1959, section 7; also Schilpp 1949, p. 292). The philosophy of science investigates the status of theories laid on the table, for example the relationship between factual statements and fully articulated laws. Given his anti-inductivist stance in both logic and psychology, Popper was anyway averse to granting observation any *positive* role in the construction of new hypotheses: facts can only refute or else corroborate scientific systems; and the process of discovery should certainly play no part in the methodological appraisal of theories (Popper 1972, section 16, pp. 67–70). I find this position untenable; for consider a hypothesis $H(a_1,...,a_n)$ containing the parameters $a_1,...,a_n$, which are unknown prior to experimentation; and let $e_1,..., e_m$ be a sequence of empirical results. Thus each e_j is of the form $e_j \equiv (b_j \wedge p_j)$, where b_j describes some boundary conditions and p_j expresses a prediction. Since $a_1,...,a_n$ have not yet been fixed, we might initially be ignorant as to whether or not $H(a_1,...,a_n)$ subsumes $e_1, e_2,...$ and e_m in the sense of entailing $(b_1 \to p_1)$, $(b_2 \to p_2)$, ... and $(b_m \to p_m)$.

Let us put $\underline{a} = (a_1,..., a_n)$, $F \equiv ((b_1 \to p_1) \wedge (b_2 \to p_2) \wedge ... \wedge (b_m \to p_m))$ and $E \equiv (e_1 \wedge ... \wedge e_m) \equiv (b_1 \wedge p_1 \wedge ... \wedge b_m \wedge p_m) \equiv (\underline{b} \wedge \underline{p})$; where $\underline{b} \equiv (b_1 \wedge b_2 \wedge ... \wedge b_m)$ and $\underline{p} \equiv (p_1 \wedge p_2 \wedge ... \wedge p_m)$. (Note that $\vdash (E \to F)$ is a tautology; i.e. F is a logical consequence of E).

We now face the task of so determining $\underline{a}$ that:

(1) $H(\underline{a})$ is internally consistent and: (2) $\vdash [H(\underline{a}) \to F]$.

Since scientists generally take E for granted while provisionally accepting $H(\underline{a})$, they will postulate the conjunction $H(\underline{a}) \wedge E$ from which they will then draw conclusions as to the possible values of $\underline{a}$. They typically succeed in determining a set K_1 such that: $[EQ] \vdash [(H(\underline{a}) \wedge E) \to (\underline{a} \in K_1)]$, i.e. $\vdash [(\underline{a} \notin K_1) \to (H(\underline{a}) \to \neg E)]$. That is: $\vdash [(\underline{a} \notin K_1) \to H(\underline{a}) \to \underline{b} \to \neg \underline{p}))]$, or $\vdash [(\underline{a} \notin K_1) \to (H(\underline{a}) \to \underline{b}) \to \neg \underline{p})]$.

Thus unless $\underline{a} \notin K_1$, (i.e. if $\vdash (\underline{a} \notin K_1)$), $H(\underline{a})$ will be refuted by the facts E. But scientists are interested in E being not merely consistent with, but also explained by H($\underline{a}$). More precisely: they will construct another set K_2 such that: $\vdash [(\underline{a} \in K_2) \to (H(\underline{a}) \to (b_j \to p_j))]$ for each j. Hence: $\vdash [(\underline{a} \in K_2) \to (H(\underline{a}) \to ((b_1 \to p_1) \wedge (b_2 \to p_2) \wedge \supset \wedge (b_m \to p_m)))]$, i.e. $\vdash [H(\underline{a}) \to F]$. *A fortiori:* $\vdash [(\underline{a} \in K_2) \to (H(\underline{a}) \to (\underline{b} \to \underline{p}))]$; i.e. $\vdash [(\underline{a} \in K_2 \to ((H(\underline{a}) \wedge \underline{b}) \neg \underline{p}))]$.

The next step usually consists in selecting some $\underline{a}_0$ which satisfies $\vdash \underline{a}_0 \in K_1 \cap K_2$. Since $\vdash \underline{a}_0 \in K_2$, then, by the above: $\vdash [H(\underline{a}_0) \to (b_j \to p_j)]$ for each j; i.e. H($\underline{a}_0$) "explains" the facts described by E. As for $\underline{a}_0 \in K_1$, it represents a consistency condition. More precisely: if $\vdash \underline{a}_0 \in K_2$ but $\vdash \underline{a}_0 \in K_1$, then by the above: $\vdash [(H(\underline{a}_0) \wedge \underline{b}) \to \underline{p}]$ and $\vdash [(H(\underline{a}_0) \wedge \underline{b}) \to \neg \underline{p}]$; which means that $[H(\underline{a}_0) \wedge \underline{b}]$ is logically, or rather mathematically inconsistent. In other words: $\vdash \neg [H(\underline{a}_0) \wedge \underline{b}]$ or $\vdash [\underline{b} \to \neg H(\underline{a}_0)]$, so that H($\underline{a}_0$) is already refuted by the boundary conditions $\underline{b} \equiv [b_1 \wedge b_2 \wedge \supset \wedge b_m]$. Thus, choosing $\vdash \underline{a}_0 \in K_1 \cap K_2$ comes down to constructing a (hopefully) consistent theory H($\underline{a}_0$) which is doctored to "yield" the facts $[(b_1 \to p_1) \wedge (b_2 \to p_2) \wedge \ldots \wedge (b_m \to p_m)] \equiv F$.

According to Popper, E nonetheless fails to corroborate H($\underline{a}_0$); for since E was known prior to H($\underline{a}_0$), E formed part of the background knowledge B which was available at the time H($\underline{a}_0$) was put forward. So since $B \Rightarrow E \Rightarrow F$, we have p(E, B) = 1 = p(E, B). A fortiori: p(E, H($\underline{a}_0$)$\wedge$B) = 1 = p(F, H($\underline{a}_0$)$\wedge$B). Therefore: C(H($\underline{a}_0$), E, B) = [p(E, H($\underline{a}_0$)$\wedge$B) – p(E, B)] / [p(E, H($\underline{a}_0$)$\wedge$B) + p(E, B) – p(H($\underline{a}_0$)$\wedge$E, B)] = 0 = [p(F,H($\underline{a}_0$)$\wedge$B) – p(F, B)] / [p(F, H($\underline{a}_0$)$\wedge$B) + p(F, B) – p(H($\underline{a}_0$)$\wedge$F, B)] = C(H($\underline{a}_0$),F, B); where C(H($\underline{a}_0$),E, B) is one expression of the Popperian degree of the corroboration of H($\underline{a}_0$) by E, given background knowledge B (See Popper 1959, Appendix *9, p. 352, footnote 4).

This definition of the degree of corroboration is however clearly unacceptable; for let e.g. E be a description of Michelson's result, of the Balmer series or of the precession of Mercury's perihelion (See Zahar 1989a, pp. 13–17; also pp. 87–92). E would thus have been known prior to Special Relativity, to Bohr's quantum theory or to General Relativity respectively. Hence in each of the three cases, E would have belonged to the background knowledge B; Popper's degree of corroboration must consequently vanish. Yet we have the strong intuition that each of the three E's confirms the corresponding H; the main reason behind this intuition being that H is not of the form H($\underline{a}_0$) where $\underline{a}_0$ was engineered to make H($\underline{a}_0$) yield E (more precisely: to entail F). In other words: what matters is not the whole of B but only that part which was *actually used* in constructing H($\underline{a}_0$); where the construction follows something like the logical pattern described above. Thus the context of the discovery of the hypothesis H has a role to play in the "justification" of H. Let us however note: it does not suffice for a scientist to be *psychologically aware* of E in order for his conjecture to become ad hoc with respect to E; the scientist must furthermore have made some *objective use* of E in determining H. After all, Einstein surely knew about Michelson's results and about Mercury's perihelion before proposing his relativistic theories; but this in no way turns the latter into ad hoc accounts of the known facts.

Finally: even if $H(\underline{a}_0)$ were adjusted, in the manner described above, to yield F, $H(\underline{a}_0)$ could still receive some—reduced—measure of support from E; for it might prove impossible to find any $\underline{a}_0$ such that $H(\underline{a}_0)$ both entails F and is mathematically consistent. This clearly happens whenever $K_1 \cap K_2 = \emptyset$ for some K_1 and all K_2.

There exist two limiting cases in which $K_1 \cap K_2 = \emptyset$ might hold; namely those in which either $K_1 = \emptyset$ or $K_2 = \emptyset$. Concerning $K_1 = \emptyset$: consider the fictitious example in which E refers to a single instance of the addition law of velocities and H(a) to Special Relativity Theory where, for the time being, the speed of light a is treated as a finite adjustable parameter. Then no matter how we vary a, we shall always have $\vdash [H(a) \rightarrow \neg E]$. I.e. $\vdash [H(a) \wedge E] \rightarrow (a \in \emptyset)$. We can therefore take $K_1 = \emptyset$. Note that $\vdash [(\exists \underline{x})H(\underline{x}) \rightarrow \neg E]$ can be inferred from $\vdash [H(\underline{a}) \rightarrow \neg E]$; i.e. $(\exists \underline{x})H(\underline{x})$ already constitutes a scientific theory since it possesses the potential falsifier E.

As for $K_2 = \emptyset$, it represents the case where $H(\underline{a})$ may be compatible with, but is irrelevant to E; so no choice of $\underline{a}$ enables $H(\underline{a})$ to decide F consistently. E.g. take $H(\underline{a})$ to be an economic theory in which we vary some parameter a; and let E be as in the last example. Since economic hypotheses do not bear on any physical laws, there will be no value of a such that $H(\underline{a}) \Rightarrow F$. Thus $K_2 = \emptyset$.

The above procedure for selecting $\underline{a} \in K_1 \cap K_2$ can therefore break down. It follows that $H(\underline{a})$ must derive some measure of support from the existence of at least one element of $K_1 \cap K_2$. Remembering that $\underline{a} = (a_1,...,a_n)$ and $E \equiv (e_1 \wedge \supset \wedge e_m)$, we conclude that the next—unused—experimental result e_{m+1} might serve to test $H(\underline{a})$ severely; where $e_{m+1} \equiv (b_{m+1} \wedge p_{m+1})$. For by hypothesis, $H(\underline{a})$ will have been determined independently of e_{m+1}; thus, if $\vdash [H(\underline{a}) \rightarrow (b_{m+1} \rightarrow p_{m+1})]$, then $H(\underline{a})$ will have explained $e_{m+1} \equiv (b_{m+1} \wedge p_{m+1})$ in a non-ad hoc way. Generally speaking, strong evidential support goes hand in hand with overdetermination: if m experimental results suffice to fix the n parameters $a_1,..., a_n$ in $H(a_1,...,a_n)$, then any number of facts in excess of m can either refute or else strongly confirm $H(a_1,...,a_n)$; for any m data would, in this hypothetical case, uniquely determine $a_1,...,a_n$; while the remaining facts might turn out to be either incompatible with, or else subsumed by $H(a_1,...,a_n)$. In the latter case, $H(a_1,..., a_n)$

will have been corroborated (For more details about empirical novelty and the adaptation of theories to facts, see below Chapter VI).

(B) REFUTATION AND CORROBORATION OF SCIENTIFIC HYPOTHESES

To repeat: according to the phenomenological view of the empirical basis, all basic Statements should be reducible to level-0 sentences; where "reducible" does not mean: logically equivalent. More precisely: let p be a sentence describing some physical process, for example the fact that the current is on; and let p' be the proposition, expressed in a phenomenological language, that a certain spot is seen to move. p' will be regarded as describing a sequence of perceptions correlated with p. p' can be said to result from a reduction which eliminates from p all references to a mind-independent reality. According to the phenomenological view, all experimental results ought to be expressed by sentences having the same form as p' and can therefore effectively verify or falsify such sentences; i.e. the experimental basis of science is strictly experiential. Thus the phenomenological thesis presupposes the existence of psycho-physical laws A such that: $A \Rightarrow (p \leftrightarrow p')$. A will contain clauses about both the reliability of the instruments used in some experiment and the observer's mental and physical state (e.g. the precondition that he is not color-blind). It is important to note that A should be regarded as undergoing the same test as the core hypothesis H to which A is appended. A is therefore contingent, so that p is not logically, but materially equivalent to p'.

In order to test a complex system S one of whose components is A, one extracts from S—conjoined with some boundary conditions p—a prediction q. Thus: $S \Rightarrow A$ and $S \Rightarrow (p \rightarrow q)$. (The core theory in S will generally entail $p \rightarrow q$ without the help of A). To p and q correspond autopsychological sentences p' and q' such that: $A \Rightarrow (p \leftrightarrow p')$ and $A \Rightarrow (q \leftrightarrow q')$. It follows that: $S \Rightarrow (p' \rightarrow q')$. (Note that in order to obtain this last implication, we need only assume $A \Rightarrow (p' \rightarrow p)$ and $A \Rightarrow (q \rightarrow q')$). S is therefore refutable by means of propositions like $(p' \wedge \neg q')$ whose truth-value can be effectively decided. Note that Popper and Neurath, as well as the later Carnap, were prepared to accept the physicalist statement $(p \wedge \neg q)$ as a potential falsifier; whereas, according to the phenomenological thesis, only sentences of the form $(p' \wedge \neg q')$ are admissible as observation reports. But unlike its 'physicalist' rival, this thesis implies that there is practically no possibility of error at the autopsychological level (We could of course content ourselves with explaining why we are *less likely* to be mistaken at the observational than at the theoretical level). Should it be vindicated, then the phenomenological position would reinforce falsificationism at the cost of complicating the Duhem-Quine problem. On the one hand, falsifications would no longer be a matter of convention, for we can now *ascertain* the truth of propositions of the form $(p' \wedge \neg q')$ and hence the falsity of some global system under test. This would block the anarchist conclusions which P. Feyerabend justifiably drew from Popper's position (Feyerabend 1975, Chapter 5, pp. 55–68). On the other hand, we would now have to allow into every scientific theory some psycho-physical laws linking physical processes to mental phenomena; which greatly increases the complexity of the Duhem-Quine problem. The question arises as to which of the two positions gets the balance right.

Having shown the tenability of the phenomenological thesis, let us now demonstrate that it governs scientific praxis; moreover that it contains the valid aspects while avoiding most of the defects of its conventionalist rival. For example: the phenomenological view will be seen to entail that repeatability and intersubjective testability are desirable features arising from the nature of the Duhem-Quine problem; that such desiderata should nevertheless not be built into the *definition* of a potential falsifier (See above, Chapter III, section K).

Let me start by mentioning an example to which the method of transcendental criticism can be applied. In 1926 D.C. Miller claimed to have performed a variant of the Michelson-Morley experiment, thereby establishing a result inconsistent with Special Relativity (henceforth referred to as STR). The experiment was repeated but no results similar to Miller's were ever obtained. According to the conventionalist view, Miller's alleged basic statements have no objective value and need therefore not be taken seriously by science. But far from ignoring Miller's claim, M. Born paid a visit to Miller and inspected his experimental set up; he concluded that the instruments used by Miller were unreliable (See Einstein and Born 1969, pp. 107–128). The phenomenological thesis, as opposed to its conventionalist rival, provides a rationale for Born's attitude. Let e be the result announced by Miller and let e' be its autopsychological counterpart. We have: $(R \wedge A) \Rightarrow (e \leftrightarrow e')$ and $R \Rightarrow \neg e$; hence: $(R \wedge A) \Rightarrow \neg e'$; where R denotes STR, and A some complex hypothesis asserting, among other things, that the instruments used by Miller were reliable. Born's decision to visit Miller can be rationally explained if e' is taken to be true and if Born intended to save R by refuting A. It should by now have become obvious that the Duhem-Quine problem plays a central role in the analysis of complex experimental situations; also that repetitions and intersubjective agreements are intended to exclude the likelihood of random factors nullifying some of the auxiliary assumptions. Let me characterise this test-structure by fixing exclusively on the formal aspect of the above schemes, i.e. by abstracting from the particular meanings of R, A, e and e′.

If ¬e′ is experimentally verified, then (R∧A) is corroborated; so we can provisionally accept (R∧A), hence also ¬e since (R∧A) ⇒ (¬e ↔ ¬e′). In these circumstances, scientists do not normally bother to formulate ¬e′ explicitly; they short-circuit the autopsychological proposition ¬e′ and affirm only its realist counterpart ¬e, thus concluding that (R∧A) has been confirmed. The omission of any mention of ¬e′ gives rise to the impression that despite describing a physical rather than a phenomenal state-of-affairs, ¬e qualifies as a basic statement. But should a refutation occur, i.e. should e′ be verified, then the situation might change dramatically. A double move normally takes place. On the one hand, there is a retreat towards the phenomenological kernel e′ which, being warranted by the experiment, is immune to doubt; but one no longer accepts the "objective" proposition e since the material equivalence between e′ and e is now seen to follow from a falsified hypothesis, namely from (R∧A). On the other hand, one tries to formulate explicitly all the premises used in the derivation of ¬e′ from (R∧A); i.e. one seeks to identify the distinct components of both R and A. This operation, though always possible in principle, often turns out to be difficult in practice; it serves to identify all the hypotheses which might be incriminated by the truth of e′; i.e. it determines the extent of the Duhem-Quine problem. Given the logical force of a refutation, it is highly desirable to repeat the experiment in order to know whether random events might not have falsified the auxiliary hypothesis A, thus accounting for the result e′. Let us analyze in some detail what happens in this situation: for any given e′, A will be expressible in the form: $A \equiv A' \wedge A_1$, where A_1 is a proposition about the reliability of the instruments used in some *specific* experiment and about a *given* observer's mental and physical health, whereas A′ is of a more general nature; A_1 may also contain the *ceteris paribus* condition that, during the experiment, only those factors which are explicitly mentioned by R came into play. Thus: $(R \wedge A) \equiv (R' \wedge A_1)$, where $R' \equiv (R \wedge A')$. Having the experiment repeated at different times, in different places and by different observers comes down to modifying A_1 into A_2, then into A_3, … and finally into A_n; where $A_1, \ldots, A_n$ describe n independent states-of-affairs. At this point we must examine two possibilities:

(a) If each of the n experiments yields a refutation, then, in order to rescue R′, we have to assume the falsity of A_1 and of A_2 … and of A_n; i.e. we must postulate the occurrence of n independent events whose probabilities would have to be multiplied. Hence there is a good reason for supposing that R′ has been refuted; which narrows the scope of the Duhem-Quine problem from $(R′ \wedge A_1) \equiv (R \wedge A′ \wedge A_1)$ down to $R′ \equiv (R \wedge A′)$.

(b) If $(R′ \wedge A_1)$ is falsified (by e′) but all of $(R′ \wedge A_2),..., (R′ \wedge A_n)$ are confirmed, then we could, following Einstein's example, conclude that e′ must have refuted not R′ but the auxiliary assumption A_1. Given the crucial nature of the experiment, Born however wisely decided to go one step further than Einstein: he effectively refuted the premise A_1, more particularly the clause in A_1 stating that the instruments used by Miller were reliable. Be it as it may, both Einstein and Born agreed that Miller truthfully reported what he saw; i.e. they took the autopsychological statement e′ for granted. Thus no repetition of the same experiment was needed in order to confer objective status on e′; instead of which Born effectively dealt with the Duhem-Quine problem.

It has nevertheless to be admitted that the identification of a faulty peripheral assumption like A_1 does not by itself constitute great progress. From a logical viewpoint, Born saved STR without thereby explaining Miller's results; for even if A_1 is refuted, i.e. even if $\neg A_1$ is established, $(R′ \wedge A_1) \Rightarrow \neg e′$ entails neither $(R′ \wedge \neg A_1) \Rightarrow e′$ nor even $(R′ \wedge \neg A_1) \Rightarrow (b′ \rightarrow \neg p′)$; where $e′ \Rightarrow (b′ \wedge \neg p′)$. Thus e′ remains unexplained. All we know is that R′ *need* not be false. Anyway: to try *directly* to account for e′ might be counterproductive and even lead the scientist astray; he may be taken out of the domain of physics and into that of psychology; or he may set himself the impossible task of identifying intrinsically random factors. The situation could however change in an unexpected and dramatically revealing way. Suppose that e′ refutes $(R \wedge A)$ but that we have been unable either to refute A directly or to reproduce e′ (i.e. to falsify $(R′ \wedge A_2)$, or $(R′ \wedge A_3),...,$ or $(R′ \wedge A_n)$). Suppose further that by a route independent of e′, we subsequently construct a theory $(R^* \wedge A^*)$ which explains e′ (that is: yields $(b′ \rightarrow \neg p′)$), explains why b′ could not later be reproduced, and is otherwise observationally equivalent to $(R \wedge A)$. A^* might, for example, take account of meteorological conditions which skew some experimental results; and we might retrospectively realize that very rare and abnormal weather conditions obtained at the time when the experiment yielding e′ was carried out. Though describing a unique event, e′ would then be acknowledged both as having refuted $(R \wedge A)$ and as now supporting $(R^* \wedge A^*)$. In other words: e′ will be regarded as a crucial experiment which confirms $(R^* \wedge A^*)$ *against* $(R \wedge A)$. To repeat: though not reproducible, e′ would have undermined $(R \wedge A)$. Note that corroboration, being logically much weaker than refutation, remains provisional. Whereas falsification is irreversible, the confirmation of (R*∧ A*) by e′ does not protect (R*∧ A*) against being refuted by the next test. This is why we *risk very little* by conceding that the unique event e′ corroborates (R*∧ A*). It is of course preferable to repeat even a confirming experiment in order to reduce the likelihood of its outcome being due to random factors; but repetition plays less important a role in the case of corroboration than in that of empirical refutation (For more details, see below, Chapter V, section D).

To summarize. If an experimental result e′ refutes some conjunction (R∧ A) and even if e′ is not reproducible, such a refutation should be taken seriously; we could, without further ado, impute e′ to ¬A (Einstein's position), but it is preferable effectively to falsify A (Born's decision). If e′ both refutes (R∧ A) and is reproduced several times with the same falsifying effect, we can reasonably conjecture that the central theory, which may well be some proposition R′ stronger than R, is false. The repetition of a refuting experiment e′ is therefore to be strongly recommended, but without ever becoming mandatory; its main role is to enables us to locate errors more precisely, i.e. to limit the scope of the Duhem-Quine problem. If, on the contrary, e′ is explained by (R∧A) (i.e. if (b′ → ¬p′) follows from (R ∧ A)) and even if e′ should in principle be unrepeatable, (R∧ A) is still to be regarded as having been corroborated by e′. Needless to say, it is preferable to confirm (R∧ A) by means of repeated tests. The essential point is that this whole logic of appraisal presupposes both the objective status and the truth of the single autopsychological statement e′.

V

Falsifiability, Duhem-Quine and the Status of Geometry

(A) HISTORICAL BACKGROUND

Having been struck by the steady growth of mathematical knowledge, Duhem wondered whether the same cumulative pattern had been displayed by the development of physical science. In this respect, his conclusions were largely negative: as long as explanatory science relies on metaphysics and as long as the latter is and must remain unstable, progress in physics cannot be viewed as cumulative. But provided physical theories be limited to their purely representative parts, then thanks to the Correspondence Principle, the mathematical structure of scientific systems can be seen to evolve continuously: the old equations, though strictly incompatible with the new ones, constitute limiting cases of the latter (See below, Chapter VI, section I, and Chapter VII, section D; also Duhem 1954, Part 1, Chapter 3).

Let us examine more closely Duhem's negative conclusions regarding the envisaged parallel between mathematics and physics. Duhem took mathematics to consist of *synthetic* theories whose certainty flows from two facts. First of all, the mathematical postulates, for example the axioms of arithmetic and of Euclidean geometry, turn out to be so transparent as to afford a direct and infallible insight into their intended domains. Secondly, the rules of inference used by mathematicians are all deductive, hence infallibly transmit truth from premises to conclusions. It follows that mathematical theorems are established once and for all. Old mathematical truths are never revised, they are simply added to (Duhem 1954, Chapter 1, §3).

This way of viewing mathematics was questioned towards the end of the nineteenth and then during most of the twentieth century. Practically all the logical empiricists took mathematical propositions to be logically true and hence vacuous; there could therefore be no genuine progress in mathematical *knowledge* as such, but at best an increasing *psychological* awareness of the tautologous character of certain statements. This view now lies in ruins; for the most fundamental mathematical system, namely set theory, makes essential use of axioms like those of choice, of infinity and of the power set which are known to be synthetic. (We shall see that this logical fact strongly supports Quine's approach to the Duhem-Quine dilemma. See below, section F). As a result, Duhem's assessment of the status of mathematics nowadays appears to be less wrong-headed than it did fifty years ago: the certainty of mathematics appears to be due, on the one hand, to the deductive nature of its inference rules and, on the other, to the alleged perspicuity of axioms which articulate the meanings of basic concepts like those of 'class' (k) and of 'belonging to a class' (∈). Mathematics is therefore synthetic, so that the difference in certainty between its propositions and those of physics is one of degree rather than kind; but where does this difference really lie? A Duhemian answer has implicitly been given above: physical hypotheses are not only synthetic but also complex and far from self-evidently true; so they provide us with no direct insight into their intended domain. Furthermore, their rules of inference cannot all be deductive; for unlike mathematics, empirical theories must, in one way or another, be based on observation. The question is: in exactly *what way*? Classical answers involve a reference both to induction and to experimentation.

According to Duhem: despite their empirical character, the methods of induction and of crucial testing were intended to parallel the mathematical methods of direct proof and of 'reductio ad absurdum' respectively (Duhem 1954, Part 2, Chapter 6, §§3, 6).

(B) INDUCTION AND DIRECT PROOF

In the first chapter we examined the kind of inductive support a theory can legitimately derive from the empirical tests to which it is subjected. We now have to address a more controversial question, namely that of the presumed heuristic role of induction in the construction of scientific laws. In a direct mathematical proof, we begin by laying down a set of axioms from which we then derive, step by step, a sequence of theorems. As for the inductive process, it supposedly starts from indubitable factual statements from which a general hypothesis is inferred. Duhem showed this method to be invalid on at least two counts. First, unlike their commonsense counterpart, the empirical results on which induction rests are 'symbolic', theory-laden and therefore fallible. For example, in the absence of an electrical theory, a statement like 'the current is on' would be meaningless and hence devoid of truth-value. Thus we have to face the 'vertical' transcendence of factual scientific propositions, which are to be distinguished from commonsense statements like 'there is a white horse in the street'; for the latter can, according to Duhem, be both realistically interpreted and infallibly known to be true-or-false. The fallibility thesis concerning all *objective* empirical statements has a lot to commend it, even though Duhem's views about the incorrigibility of commonsense propositions is highly dubious. (See above, Chapter III, section G. Also: Duhem 1954, Part 2, Chapter 6). There is secondly the well-known Humean or horizontal transcendence of any universal law with respect to any of its instances.

As explained in Chapter III, Descartes made a clear distinction between *autopsychological* sentences like 'It seems to me that I hear a noise' and any *transcendent* proposition which refers to some objective 'external' reality (Descartes 1986, Meditation 2). For example, corresponding to the autopsychological report just mentioned, we have the objective statement that there is—in physical reality—a sound-wave. Descartes realized that only autopsychological propositions are indubitable. Going back to Duhem, let p and p′ be defined as follows: p ≡ (the current is on), p′ ≡ (I see—what I take to be—the pointer of the galvanometer move). Thus p′, but not p, is incorrigible. Let us however note that in inducing laws from basic statements, we need to start from singular propositions having the form, not of p′, but of p. For example: I need to know that iron, and copper, and aluminium etc. conduct electricity, not that *it seems to me* that they do so. Duhem was therefore right about physical induction being neither certain nor theory-independent; or rather about its being fallible precisely because it is theory-dependent; for even the basic statements on which it relies in order to infer laws involve theoretical assumptions and are therefore dubitable. It has moreover been mentioned that experimental laws like 'All metals conduct electricity' are fallible for a second and more prosaic reason: since they proceed from a finite to a potentially infinite domain, generalizations run the risk of being refuted by the next recalcitrant observation. So induction seems to lead from theory-dependent to other fallible statements.

Note that a very different conclusion—namely a hypothetico-deductivist one—can be drawn from this state-of-affairs. We can give up the unacceptable idea of directly inducing laws from facts and look upon an autopsychological proposition like p′ as the only allowable type of basic statement. There is nothing to prevent us from deducing such level-0 reports from high-level theories *taken in conjunction both with boundary conditions and with psycho-physical assumptions*. We shall in fact see that this approach increases the complexity of the Duhem-Quine problem; but indubitable descriptions of sense-experience would, in return, constitute what Quine himself initially regarded as the fixed periphery of our system of knowledge (See Chapter III above; also Quine 1980c).

Having provisionally dealt with induction as a heuristic tool, let us now turn to what Duhem calls the indirect method of proof.

(C) INDIRECT METHOD AND CRUCIAL EXPERIMENTS

Duhem maintained that:

> Those who assimilate experimental contradiction to reduction to absurdity imagine that in physics we may use a line of argument similar to the one Euclid employed so frequently in geometry. Do you wish to obtain from a group of phenomena a theoretically certain and indisputable explanation? Enumerate all the hypotheses that can be made to account for this group of phenomena; then, by experimental contradiction, eliminate all except one; the latter will no longer be a hypothesis, but will become a certainty. . . .; but the physicist is never sure he has exhausted all the imaginable assumptions. (Duhem 1954, Part 2, Chapter 6)

I shall use Popper's demarcation criterion to support Duhem's intuitive argument. Let us recall that a proposition is to be considered scientific if it is universal, non-verifiable and empirically refutable. In the quotation above, Duhem maintains—without advancing any convincing argument—that no disjunction $H_1 \vee H_2 \vee \ldots \vee H_n$ of scientific theories can be known to be true; he simply invokes the psychological fact that the physicist can never be certain of having exhausted the set of all possible hypotheses. Through using Popper's criterion, it can however easily be proved that any disjunction like $H_1 \vee H_2 \vee \ldots \vee H_n$ is scientific and hence unverifiable—in the objective sense.

Without loss of generality, let us restrict ourselves to the case where n = 2. Being scientific and hence universal statements, H_1 and H_2 can be written in the form:

(1) $H_1 \equiv (\forall x) B_1(x)$ and $H_2 \equiv (\forall y) B_2(y)$.

Since the two variables x and y can always be chosen to be distinct, we have:

$\vdash [(H_1 \vee H_2) \leftrightarrow (\forall x)(\forall y)(B_1(x) \vee B_2(y))]$; i.e. $H_1 \vee H_2$ is universal.

If we suppose that H_1 is consistent, then so is the weaker proposition $H_1 \vee H_2$. In order to prove that $H_1 \vee H_2$ is empirically refutable, let a_1 and a_2 be potential falsifiers of H_1 and H_2 respectively. That is:

(3) $\vdash (a_1 \rightarrow \neg H_1)$, $\vdash (a_2 \rightarrow \neg H_2)$. Therefore: $\vdash [(a_1 \wedge a_2) \rightarrow \neg(H_1 \vee H_2)]$.

It can generally be assumed that a_1 and a_2 describe compatible states-of-affairs: given the universality of both H_1 and H_2 with respect to the time parameter t, a_1 and a_2 can be taken to refer to events occurring at different moments; so that $a_1 \wedge a_2$ is a consistent and empirically decidable statement. By (3), $(H_1 \vee H_2)$ is therefore experimentally falsifiable. $(H_1 \vee H_2)$ is finally unverifiable; for any empirical result verifying $(H_1 \vee H_2)$ would have to verify either H_1 or H_2 or both; which, given the scientific character of both H_1 and H_2, is impossible. Thus the scientist is never in a position to know that a disjunction of empirical theories must be true; and this independently of his powers of imagination.

(D) INDIRECT METHOD AND THE DUHEM-QUINE PROBLEM

Let us now turn to the problem posed by the refutability of scientific theories. As explained above, the truth of any disjunction $H_1 \vee ... \vee H_n$ of physical hypotheses must always remain uncertain; but could we not—at least in principle—know with certainty that an isolated theory H_i has definitively been falsified by experience? According to Duhem:

> The prediction of the phenomenon, whose non-production is to cut off debate, does not derive from the proposition challenged if taken by itself, but from the proposition at issue joined to that whole group of theories; if the predicted phenomenon is not produced, not only is the proposition questioned at fault, but so is the whole theoretical scaffolding used by the physicist. The only thing the experiment teaches us is that among the propositions used to predict the phenomenon and to establish whether it would be produced, there is at least one error; but where this error lies is just what it does not tell us. (Duhem 1954, Part 2, Chapter 6, §3)

For example: in order to test his theory about the phases of Venus and hence refute Ptolemy's hypothesis, Galileo had to presuppose optical laws which had not been properly corroborated. This is precisely why Duhem

drew our attention to the undeniable fact that a falsifying experiment undermines, not an isolated theory but a whole system including the theory in
question. Quine reinforced this ungainsayable Duhemian thesis by claiming—for reasons which will be examined below—that:

> My counter-suggestion, issuing essentially from Carnap's doctrine
> of the physical world in the *Aufbau,* is that our statements about the
> external world face the tribunal of sense-experience not individually
> but only as a corporate body. . . . But what I am now urging is that
> even in taking the statement as unit, we have drawn our grid too
> finely. *The unit of empirical significance is the whole of science.*
> (Quine 1980c, §5. My italics)

Note that even in the absence of Quine's globalist thesis, serious problems confront the falsificationist viewpoint. Lakatos showed that certain
boundary conditions, e.g. the assumption that only the gravitational field is
present in a given region, have the character not of singular statements, but
of universal and hence unverifiable hypotheses. This objection however
constitutes no damaging criticism of Popper's falsificationist criterion; for
we can consider all unverifiable boundary conditions as part of the system
undergoing the test. This would admittedly complicate the Duhem-Quine
problem, but without essentially changing its nature.

Lakatos also defended the view that a theoretical system S normally
involves a *ceteris paribus* clause, i.e. the caveat: other things being equal
(Lakatos 1970). This situation can more precisely be rendered as follows.
We have seen that the hypothetico-deductive model of explanation can be
described by means of the scheme: $\vdash (S \rightarrow E)$, where: $E \Rightarrow (b \rightarrow p)$, S is
a theory, b the description of boundary conditions and p a prediction.
According to Lakatos, S consists of some core hypothesis H *taken together*
with an indefinite set Δ of propositions of the form: on some specific occasion, only gravitational forces acted on the test body, there were no random
variations in the weather conditions, etc. Thus, we have: $H, \Delta \vdash E$. Were E
to be falsified, then we should allegedly be unable to decide whether to
blame H or any member of the possibly infinite set Δ. This objection to falsificationism need not however be taken too seriously. As long as we carry
out our deductions in a first-order language, then by the compactness theorem, E will logically follow from some finite subset of $\{H\} \cup \Delta$. Hence
$H \wedge A \vdash E$ will hold, where A is a conjunction of finitely many elements of
Δ. To the extent that $\neg E$ can be observationally verified, $(H \wedge A)$ can be said
to have been refuted. This might admittedly leave us with an aggravated

Duhem-Quine problem; for we cannot a priori decide whether H or any conjunct occurring in A is false. All the same, the single finite proposition S $\equiv$ (H$\wedge$ A) will have been experimentally refuted.

The Duhem-Quine problem can furthermore be partially solved as follows. Let H$\wedge$ A be an empirically falsified conjunction. If successive variants A_1, A_2,..., A_n of A lead to the refutations of H$\wedge$ A_1, H$\wedge$ A_2, ... and H$\wedge$ A_n, then according to both Duhem and Popper, it can *reasonably* be conjectured that the fault lies with H. Popper did not however admit that such *reasonableness* rests—as it clearly does—on the following intuitive probabilistic argument: if, despite all the negative outcomes just mentioned, we decide to adhere to H, then each of A, A_1,..., A_n must be considered false; which yields the unique assignment (t, f,..., f) of truth-values to (H, A, A_1,..., A_n). But should we be prepared to give up H, then each of A, A_1,..., A_n could, for all we know, be either t or f; which yields 2^{n+1} assignments compatible with all the experimental results. Thus: provided the statements H, A, A_1,..., A_n be mutually independent, the chances are that H is false. Note that A, A_1,..., A_n may share a core assumption G such that G is false and H$\wedge$ G testable; which might account for the successive refutations of H$\wedge$ A,..., H$\wedge$ A_n. This is why a caveat of mutual independence has to be entered (For more details, see Zahar 1989a, Chapter 6). Be it as it may, the above—admittedly crude—piece of probabilistic reasoning provides a rationale for our feeling that, barring miracles, H must be the culprit.

Despite this tentative solution aimed at reducing the scope of the Duhem-Quine problem, many questions concerning the conjunction H$\wedge$ A remain unanswered. In Duhem's time the validity of Logic—which was usually identified with the Aristotelian syllogism—was not called into question; and its schemes never explicitly figured among the premises yielding empirical predictions. Logic has since been both enriched and formalized; so that A might well be a logical principle or, more generally, an analytic proposition. In such a case, we should normally feel entitled to regard A as being immune to refutation. The Duhem-Quine problem would then automatically reduce to the question of the falsifiability of H (where the latter might, in its turn, prove to be a conjunction). Quine however rejects the analytic-synthetic distinction and maintains that:

But, for all its a priori reasonableness, a boundary between analytic and synthetic statements simply has not been drawn. That there is such a distinction to be drawn at all is an unempirical dogma of empiricists, a metaphysical article of faith. . . .

Conversely, by the same token, no statement is immune to revision. Revision even of the logical law of the excluded middle has been proposed as a means of simplifying quantum mechanics; and what difference is there in principle between such a shift and the shift whereby Kepler superseded Ptolemy, or Einstein Newton, or Darwin Aristotle? (Quine 1980c, §§4, 6)

If we are to believe Quine, A cannot be hived off even if A is held by most people to be analytic. Thus H∧A would still have to face the verdict of experience *en bloc*. Quine further claims that even mathematics and logic can be revised in the face of recalcitrant empirical evidence. It would then follow that the Duhem-Quine problem cannot be localized. This is why we ought to examine the possibility of demarcating between, on the one hand, all the analytic statements including the principles of logic and mathematics; and on the other, the domain of synthetic propositions including all scientific theories. An important special case is that in which A is a geometrical and hence synthetic hypothesis. This is why we later have to ask whether physical geometry is falsifiable or whether—as claimed by Poincaré—it can always evade the verdict of experience.

(E) KRIPKE'S CHALLENGE

In fact, empiricist methodology faces threats coming from two opposite directions. First: as already mentioned, Quine holds no component of our scientific knowledge to be immune to revision. Observational anomalies can therefore throw doubt on any of our principles, whether these be empirical, mathematical or even logical. This Quinean view which, if correct, would render the Duhem-Quine problem unmanageable, will be examined in the next section.

There is secondly the threat posed by Kripke's thesis that there exist statements which are both necessary and *a posteriori*, i.e. whose necessary truth can be empirically established. 'Hesperus is Phosphorous', 'Cicero is Tully' and 'Heat is a motion of particles' are supposed to be examples of such propositions. Thus, when faced with testable conjunction of premises $H_1 \wedge \ldots \wedge H_n$, we can no longer infer from the *a posteriori* character of some H_i that H_i can in principle be rejected in the light of evidence undermining $H_1 \wedge \ldots \wedge H_n$; for despite being *a posteriori*, H_i might, unbeknown to us, prove metaphysically necessary (See Kripke 1972). This Kripkean thesis has considerable methodological import in that, contrary to Quine's appraisal, it mysteriously and unpredictably restricts the scope of the Duhem-Quine problem. It moreover flies in the face of normal scientific practice. Showing that Kripke's conclusions are at best irrelevant to science, and more particularly to the Duhem-Quine problem, is therefore an important task.

Let us start by granting that the truth of some analytic and hence necessary statements may come *to be known* a posteriori. Before using a pocket calculator, I might have been unaware that $2^9 = 512$; which does not however imply that this equation is synthetic. Kripke's thesis of course goes well beyond this truism. Let us consider an identity between singular terms, for example 'Hesperus = Phosphorous'. In this particular case, Kripke concedes that 'Hesperus' and 'Phosphorous' could be regarded as definite descriptions. We would then be dealing with an identity of the form: $[\iota x H(x) = \iota y P(y)]$, where: $H(x) \equiv$ (x is the Evening Star) and $P(y) \equiv$ (y is the Morning Star). Hence $H(x)$ and $P(y)$ have different Fregean senses. After carrying out a Russellian analysis, the above identity proves equivalent to the sentence $[(\exists x)(\forall z)(H(z) \leftrightarrow (z = x)) \wedge (\forall y)(P(y) \leftrightarrow H(y))]$, which is clearly contingent.

We are nonetheless also told that 'Hesperus' and 'Phosphorous' can be looked upon as proper names; so that 'Hesperus = Phosphorous' assumes the form $[a = b]$, where 'a' and 'b' must now be taken to be distinct individual constants. Kripke maintains that under such a construal, '$[a = b]$' must, if true, be necessarily so. But this *prima facie* startling claim turns out to be a trivial consequence of the stipulation that every proper name 'a' must be treated as a rigid designator; i.e. that if 'a' has a referent, then the latter will be the same in all metaphysically possible worlds. More precisely: let 'a' and 'b' be two distinct primitive symbols, e.g. let 'a' = 'Cicero' and 'b' = 'Tully'. J. S. Mill reasonably maintained that a name might possess a referent but certainly not any (Fregean) sense. The above analysis in terms of the definite descriptions $[\iota x H(x)]$ and $[\iota y P(y)]$ cannot therefore be applied to the identity '$[a = b]$'. The latter will thus hold provided one and only one condition is satisfied; namely that 'a' and 'b' denote the same object. Assume this to be so in our world. Kripke's astonishing conclusion is that '$[a = b]$' would then be necessary in the sense of holding in all possible worlds. Such a bold claim however proves banal since it follows from an arbitrary decision; for according to Kripke:

Possible worlds are *stipulated*, not *discovered* by powerful telescopes. There is no reason why we cannot *stipulate* that in talking

about what would have happened to Nixon in a certain counterfac-
tual situation, we are talking about what would have happened to
him. (Kripke 1972, p. 44; the author's italics)

Thus Kripke demands, by *fiat*, that 'a' and 'b' be treated as rigid desig-
nators; i.e. the class **W** of possible worlds is decreed to be such that our
world belongs to **W**, while each of 'a' and 'b' denotes the same entity in all
members of **W**; from which it trivially follows that if '[a = b]' holds in our
world, then it will be true throughout **W**. Furthermore, this definition of
metaphysical possibility seems doctored to yield this rather bewildering
result.

Scientists have shown little interest in metaphysical, as opposed to logical or mathematical necessity. As admitted by Kripke himself, the identity
'[a = b]' is neither tautological nor analytic. There obviously exist possible
interpretations whose domains contain more than one element and where
'a' and 'b' denote different individuals, thus making '[a = b]' into a false
sentence. And though nothing stops a scientist from postulating [a = b]
where 'a' and 'b' are simple names, there is hardly any reason for him to do
so; for he might just as well systematically substitute 'a' for 'b', thus greatly
simplifying the presentation of his system.

There remains a question concerning the sense in which '[a = b]', as
opposed to the identity '[a = a]', might have some informative content, no
matter how minimal. From what has been said, it would seem to follow that
'a = b' asserts no more than 'a = a', i.e. the statement that a is identical with
itself. This conclusion is highly counter-intuitive for we have the unerring
conviction that 'a = a', as distinct from 'a = b', is totally devoid of content.
The reason however is that when reading a text, we do not remain within
the bounds of the object-language but are also meta-linguistically aware of
the latter's vocabulary and syntax. Thus the sequence of *symbols* in 'a = b'
indicates that the same entity is contingently denoted by the two distinct
names 'a' and 'b'; whereas 'a = a' does nothing but remind us of a convention adopted once and for all; namely that independently of context, the
same primitive sign always refers to the same object. This is one reason
why Frege initially held 'a = b' to be not only about the individuals denoted
by 'a' and 'b', but also about the symbols 'a' and 'b' themselves. No matter
how mistaken this approach might have been, it still reveals an important
psychological fact: our reading of a formula is directed not only at its referents, but also at the sequence of signs constituting the formula. As a
proposition of the object-language, the identity 'a = b' does not tell us that
'a' ≠ 'b' since it talks neither about 'a' nor about 'b'; but 'a = b *exhibits*

the scriptural difference between 'a' and 'b', thus *showing* us that 'a = b' might prove false under certain interpretations and must therefore be synthetic. Once again, a Kripkean analysis turns out to be superfluous. The air of necessity surrounding 'a = b' flows from Kripke's misleading intuition that every equality 'a = b' is either necessary or false.

Let us now turn to more serious examples which allegedly demonstrate the *a posteriori* necessity of some theoretical identities (or identifications):

> . . . One might very well discover essence empirically. (Kripke 1972, p. 110)
>
> ¨. . . Philosophers have, as I've said, been very interested in statements expressing theoretical identifications; among them, that light is a stream of photons, that water is H_2O, that lightning is an electrical discharge, that gold is the element with the atomic number 79. (Kripke 1972, p. 116)
>
> . . . Given that gold *is* this element, any other element, even though it looks like gold and is found in the very places where we in fact find gold, would not be gold. . . .
>
> So if this conclusion is right, it tends to show that such statements representing scientific discoveries about what this stuff *is* are not contingent truths but necessary truths in the strictest possible sense. (Kripke 1972, p. 125)

Let me explain why, despite its seemingly scholastic and innocuous character, Kripke's thesis about the necessity of *a posteriori* propositions threatens the empirical testability of scientific theories. This can most clearly be seen by drawing a parallel between Kripke's position and Kant's views concerning the status of such synthetic *a priori* principles as the law of the conservation of substance; that is: of the conservation of matter (See Kant 1957, section 3, Theorem 2). Kant admittedly regarded his principles as *a priori* propositions while Kripke rightly holds his identities to be *a posteriori* and hence synthetic. Still, both 'Matter is conserved' and 'Light is a stream of photons' are respectively held by Kant and by Kripke to be not contingently, but necessarily true. Thus, under no circumstances in any possible world can such propositions be legitimately regarded as having been empirically refuted. Let us once again note that this conclusion runs counter to the working scientist's intuition. In the post-Einsteinian era, it is well known that the conservation of matter—that is: to the extent that the latter can be regarded as distinguishable from energy—can be rejected without rendering science impossible; which clearly undermines Kantian

philosophy. As for Kripke's views, they have the following paradoxical consequence: given that light *is* a particulate stream of photons, then by proposing that light is a wave process, Huygens, Fresnel and Maxwell
were—albeit unbeknown to themselves—going against a 'necessary truth[s]
in the highest possible sense'; i.e. they were violating something akin to a
logical principle; which also entails that Kripke forecloses the very possibility of accounting for optical processes in continuous field-theoretic terms.

Kripke might of course have meant that *only if true* would a theoretical
identity be necessary. So it looks as though his theses can always be
affirmed with total impunity; and this for two reasons. First: since the identities in question are universal and synthetic, they cannot be strictly verified; so none of them can definitively be asserted as true. Secondly, even if
they could somehow be ascertained as true, then they would *by definition*
hold good in all possible worlds; for the latter are defined in such a way that
if the identity 'Water is H_2O' obtains in one of them, then thanks to rigid
designation, it will automatically be true in all of them. But Kripke is not
out of the woods yet; for his account of essences is too geared to subject-
predicate logic, too *monadic*, to be entirely satisfactory. He neglects rela-
tional properties. For example: it clearly follows from Kripke's theses that
the elementary particles constituting H and O—i.e. the electrons, protons,
etc.—must both belong to every possible world and bear to one another the
same relations which hold in ours. In other words: to the extent that the
electron possesses an essence, the latter must include the relations it bears
to that of the proton, of other elementary particles and of all ambient fields;
for what would the *essence* of an electron be in the absence of positively
charged particles which attract it? Every possible world ought consequently
to be vastly enriched; and so it ends up being governed by the same laws as
ours, while differing from the actual world only by virtue of its boundary
conditions; where the latter will in turn be constrained by the fundamental
laws. Thus Kripke's seemingly bold theory reduces to the classical picture
adhered to by most working scientists; that is: essentially *one* world governed by a fixed system of basic laws but in which different sets of boundary conditions can of course be *envisaged*, the latter being chosen so as to
be compatible with the laws. The entailed generalizations which are sensi-
tive to changes of boundary conditions can be termed 'contingent' while the
remaining laws are dubbed 'necessary'. As for Kripke's identity statements,
they are to be treated as nominal definitions, i.e. as mere abbreviatory
devices. For example: suppose that most of the stuff which had previously
been labeled 'water' on the basis of some phenomenal properties was subsequently found to be composed of two atoms of hydrogen (H_2) and of one

atom of oxygen (O). On the basis of such a composition, of atomic theory, of physiology and of certain boundary conditions, the previously ascertained phenomenal qualities of water should be predictable, at least in principle. This might lead scientists to adopt a new nominal definition according to which 'water' would henceforth stand for: substance consisting of H_2 and of O; i.e. 'water' is now to be treated as an abbreviatory device. This definition admittedly turns 'Water is H_2O' into a necessary statement, albeit a merely analytic one; while the connections between H_2O and the phenomenal properties of water, though predictable, remain synthetic. All this goes to show that the only notion of necessity needed in the sciences is the strictly logical one.

(F) QUINE'S HOLISM AND THE ANALYTIC-SYNTHETIC DISTINCTION

Rather than start by defining the terms 'analytic' and 'synthetic', let us consider an example given by Quine himself. We shall then analyze certain features of this concrete case in order to arrive at a general characterisation of analyticity. Intuitively, the example must of course be unambiguously either analytic or synthetic. Consider the proposition 'No bachelor is married' which is held to be quintessentially analytic; i.e. true by definition, or true exclusively by virtue of the meanings of its terms. For if one were to look up the meaning of 'bachelor' in a dictionary, then one might well find: bachelor $\equiv$ male and unmarried. Through the replacement of 'bachelor' by its verbal or dictionary definiens, the above statement is transformed into: 'There exist no unmarried males which are married' which is logically true, therefore true independently of all empirical states-of-affairs.

Quine rightly claims that *if* there were to be any necessary propositions at all, then these would have to be analytic and hence escape all empirical control. We shall now examine his thesis that no such propositions exist. Let us go back to his concrete example about bachelors being unmarried, while provisionally accepting the following stipulation: a true proposition is analytic if its truth depends exclusively on the meanings of its (non-logical) constituent terms. Thus, by means of the *verbal definition* of 'bachelor':

[α] 'No bachelor is married' is reducible to:
[β] 'No male unmarried person is married', i.e. to $\neg(\exists x)[P(x) \wedge \neg M(x) \wedge M(x)]$, where: $P(x) \equiv$ (x is a male person); $M(x) \equiv$ (x is married).

This last formula is logically true, i.e. true independently of the meanings of its descriptive components P and M. Since logical principles are not only particular cases but also the most important instances of analytic truths, we appear to have reached a paradoxical conclusion; namely that $\neg(\exists x)[P(x) \wedge \neg M(x) \wedge M(x)]$ holds both independently of, and by virtue of the meanings of its terms. This 'paradox' flows from the ambiguity of the notions of 'meaning' and of 'definition'. The dictionary, or verbal meaning of a symbol is the sequence of primitive signs of which the symbol provides an abbreviation. Note that only non-primitive symbols, i.e. those not belonging to the basic vocabulary of a language, possess verbal definitions. In going from [α] to [β], we replaced 'bachelor' by its dictionary meaning, i.e. by 'male and unmarried', thus obtaining the logically true sentence [β].

An expression possesses another 'meaning' or Fregean *Bedeutung*, namely a referent. This is the—normally extra-linguistic—entity denoted by the expression. It will henceforth be called its ostensive meaning since it is often, though not always, fixed by ostension. For example: tables, colors and even elementary particles can often be pointed to with the finger. Though performing an objective function, a logical connective cannot however be singled out by ostension; it can, at best, be partially determined by a number of postulates which circumscribe its use. A Platonist might maintain that even a logical constant refers to an entity inhabiting some World of Forms; which is far from being an absurd claim. None of my theses however rests on the assumption that abstract terms possess actual referents; which is why I chose the agnostic expression 'ostensive meaning' to subsume the referents of all names of physical entities as well as the objective meanings of logical constants and mathematical terms. In what follows, all that matters is our ability clearly to distinguish between the ostensive meanings of words on the one hand, and the dictionary or verbal definitions of nonprimitive expressions on the other.

Quine seems initially to have carried out his critique at the verbal level. We have seen that [α] turns out to be analytic if 'bachelor' stands for 'male and unmarried person'. Quine however asks: how could we possibly know, with any degree of certainty, that we have here the real definition of 'bachelor'? We might of course consult a dictionary, but all dictionaries suffer from one basic defect: since a natural language contains only finitely many words, dictionaries are necessarily circular; for let **V** be any vocabulary and **D** a dictionary of **V**. Thus each entry in **D** is of the form $X =_{\text{Def.}} Y_1 \ldots Y_p$ where X ranges over *all* the members of **V** and each Y_i also belongs to **V**. In such a case, we shall say, for each i, that X is *directly* expressible in terms of Y_i. Thus for every $X \in \mathbf{V}$, there exists at least one $Y \in \mathbf{V}$ such that X is directly expressible in terms of Y. An element A of **V** will be said to be expressible in terms of another such element B iff there exists a sequence $Z_1,\ldots, Z_n$ of members of **V** such that: each Z_j is directly expressible in terms of Z_{j+1}, $Z_1 \equiv A$ and $Z_n \equiv B$; in which case, we shall write: $A \sim B$. Trivially: expressibility is entailed by direct expressibility. Moreover: if $A \sim B$ and $B \sim H$, then $A \sim H$. For let $A \sim B$ and $B \sim H$. That is: for some members $Z_1,\ldots, Z_n, S_1,\ldots, S_m$ of **V**, we have: $Z_1 \equiv A$, $Z_n \equiv B$, $S_1 \equiv B$, $S_m \equiv H$, while every Z_j and every S_q are directly expressible in terms of Z_{j+1} and of S_{q+1} respectively. Thus $A \equiv Z_1,\ldots,Z_n \equiv B \equiv S_1,\ldots, S_m \equiv H$ is a sequence whose every member is directly expressible in terms of the next one; whence, by definition: $A \sim H$. It can now be established, by straightforward induction, that for any positive integer p: $[(A_1 \sim A_2 \sim\ldots\sim A_p) \Rightarrow (A_1 \sim A_p)]$. Finally, **D** will be said be non-circular iff for all elements A and B of **V**, we have:

$[(A \sim B) \Rightarrow (A \neq B)]$, where $\neq$ stands for scriptural difference.

Let us now show that if **D** is non-circular, then **V** must be infinite. Suppose that **D** is non-circular, and let A be an arbitrary member of **V**. By the above, there exists at least one $A_1 \in$ **V** such that A is directly expressible in terms of A_1. Repeating this process, we conclude that there exists some A_2 such that A_1 is directly expressible in terms of A_2; and so on indefinitely. Putting $A_0 \equiv A$, we obtain the infinite sequence: $A_0 \sim A_1 \sim A_2 \sim A_3 \sim \ldots$. Let us show that for any $j \neq q$, $A_j \neq A_q$. Let $j \neq q$. Without loss of generality, suppose $j < q$. Thus: $A_j \sim A_{j+1} \sim A_{j+2} \sim \ldots \sim A_q$; whence, by the above: $A_j \sim A_q$; from the assumption of non-circularity, infer $A_j \neq A_q$. Thus all the elements of the infinite sequence $A_0, A_1, A_2, A_3,\ldots$ are distinct, so that the vocabulary **V** must be infinite. We have thus shown that a non-circular dictionary of a finite language must specify a set of primitive, i.e. of verbally undefined terms. No ordinary dictionary can therefore be relied upon either to give us the correct verbal meaning of a word like 'bachelor' or else to tell us that 'bachelor' is primitive. We could of course go round asking people whether by 'bachelor' they really mean 'unmarried male'; but the answers might well vary from one person to the next; so that the status of 'All bachelors are unmarried' remains uncertain.

Though interesting as questions of applied linguistics, these Quinean considerations do not however bear on any logical or epistemological problems. In its—admittedly idealized—form, theoretical science starts by laying down a primitive vocabulary all of whose terms need not even be ostensively defined. Some molecular expressions may subsequently prove useful and will therefore be fixed by means of verbal definitions, i.e. of abbreviations. Thus all propositions can in principle be reformulated in terms of the basic vocabulary; they will consequently prove, whether effectively or not, to be either analytic or inconsistent or synthetic. Hypotheses are then formulated and basic statements derived. Since the latter are intended to be empirically decidable, their terms must be observational and hence defined directly by ostension. Note that throughout these operations, one logic, together with the fixed *ostensive meanings of its connectives*, is presupposed (Remember that these meanings are embodied in certain principles as well as in the rules of inference). Thus [β] is a logical truth *provided* the universal quantifier, the conjunction and the negation keep their classical (ostensive) meanings. It should be remembered that $(\neg\neg p \rightarrow p)$ and $(\forall x)[\neg\neg M(x) \leftrightarrow M(x)]$ cease to be analytic in intuitionistic logic. In other words: once properly expressed in the primitive vocabulary, an analytic statement will be true independently of the ostensive meanings *not of its logical,* but of its descriptive terms.

So far, nothing has been said in defense of globalism, i.e. of the thesis that experience challenges the *whole* fabric of our knowledge. At this point however, the Quinean critique takes on a radical form. Quine maintains that *any* hypothesis, whether logical, mathematical, contingent or supposedly analytic, can be thrown into doubt by an experimental refutation. For example: as a result of empirical findings, we might decide to reject a *prima facie* analytic premise like 'No bachelor is married'. As explained above, this is tantamount to giving up the verbal definition according to which 'bachelor' is shorthand for 'male unmarried person'; which in turn comes down to enriching our basic vocabulary through adjoining to it the word 'bachelor' as a primitive predicate. This 'solution' would enable us to deny [α] without fear of contradiction. Such an ad hoc move would however be irrelevant to the problem of holism, for it effectively consists in weakening our original theory while leaving its underlying logic intact: treating 'bachelor' as a primitive symbol comes down to giving up the assumption that $(\forall x)[(x$ is a bachelor$)\leftrightarrow((x$ is male$)\wedge(x$ is not married$))]$. Let us note that science hardly ever makes use of such premises except as abbreviatory devices. Moreover: though weakening a hypothesis might ward off an empirical refutation, it would leave Quine's globalist thesis unsupported. In short: altering the verbal definition of words will not lead, beyond Duhem, to the Duhem-*Quine* problem. But what about modifying the *ostensive* meanings of certain terms?

Note that changing the referents of descriptive *non-observational* terms does not stave off empirical falsification. By definition, the relation $S \vdash p$ is syntactical and hence in no way depends on the ostensive meaning of the descriptive symbols occurring in *S* or in p. By changing the referents of certain terms, we may nevertheless change the meaning of p in such a way that p is no longer undermined by experience. But if p is empirical, then it contains exclusively observational predicates; so that only by altering the latter could we conceivably save *S* from refutation. We have however seen that observational notions ought to possess meanings fixed in advance of theory (See Chapter III above). Should this condition be met, then we shall again face the refutability of *S* alone, i.e. of the conjunction of a limited number of assumptions; so that the issue of holism will have been left untouched. This seems to be one reason for Quine's apparent readiness to give up—if need be—a logical truth like $[\neg\neg p \to p]$ or $[(p \wedge (q \vee r)) \leftrightarrow ((p \wedge q) \vee (p \wedge r))]$. But such a move would come down to altering, not the verbal, but the ostensive meaning of certain connectives. We would therefore have modified our logic and—were we to adopt a Platonist stance—the referents of our logical constants. Thus any parallel between the rejection of a banal proposition such as [α] and that of a logical principle vanishes. We might similarly be led to alter mathematical axioms like those of choice or of infinity; which would again be tantamount not to carrying out some verbal redefinition, but to asserting or denying substantive existence claims. *Since logic and—to a lesser extent—mathematics are common to all scientific hypotheses, questioning either of these disciplines might put our whole system of knowledge in jeopardy.* This is in effect the only acceptable version of Quine's holistic thesis; which has however been vindicated at the high cost of modifying either logic, or mathematics, or both. Not only would most working scientists be loath to resort to such drastic measures but, given his attachment to classical first-order logic, Quine himself ought also to have found such a cost prohibitive.

(G) Empirical Content and the Duhem-Quine Problem

In this section it will be shown that many epistemological confusions can be traced back to a misunderstanding, or rather to a faulty diagnosis of the Duhem-Quine problem.

In Chapter III the view was vindicated that scientific systems can be effectively refuted by level-0 reports. Against this 'naïve' falsificationist attitude, Lakatos had argued that a theory H cannot be regarded as having been undermined by a factual proposition $(p \wedge \neg q)$ until and unless a rival hypothesis H* has been proposed, where H* both yields $(p \to \neg q)$ and is incompatible with H. Thus:

While naïve falsificationism stresses 'the urgency of replacing a *falsified* hypothesis by a better one', sophisticated falsificationism stresses the urgency of replacing *any* hypothesis by a better one. Falsification cannot 'compel the theorist to search for a better theory' simply because falsification cannot precede the better theory. (Lakatos 1978a, p. 37)

Paul Feyerabend also mounted an attack on falsificationism. His starting point was however different from Lakatos's. He correctly maintained that in order to be useful, methodologies must have prescriptive import; i.e. they should be normative in the sense of guiding the scientist in his search for, or in his choice of hypotheses. Of course, an alternative definition of a methodology can be adopted according to which the latter's only task is to provide an organon for the *post hoc* appraisal of available theories. Since this sort of academic exercise gives no guidance as to any effective action, it is contemptuously—and understandably—dismissed by Feyerabend. But should prescriptive import be granted, then his claim is that every *known* methodology contains directives which, if systematically followed, would have inhibited the progress of science *at some points* of its historical development. To take but one example: Feyerabend strongly opposes Newtonian empiricism; where the latter is taken to imply that hypotheses can legitimately be criticized by way, not of any theoretical, but only of empirical considerations. Interpreted in this way, Newtonianism entails that in order to be acceptable, every law should be induced from the facts and then held to be true, or approximately true, until such phenomena are discovered as either make the law more precise or else constitute exceptions to it. Feyerabend rightly maintains that this inductivist methodology is reactionary in that, as long as a reigning paradigm encounters no empirical difficulties, inductivism will invariably discourage the formulation of new hypotheses.

In order to combat the conservatism inherent in empiricist philosophy, Feyerabend advanced the view that the empirical content of a theory generally depends on the nature of its rivals. Should this thesis prove tenable, then it would hit not only inductivism but also the very notion of falsifiability; for the latter relies on the existence, for each theory H, of a well-circumscribed set Σ of potential falsifiers such that, should any member of Σ be verified, then H must be regarded as false. Popper called Σ 'the empirical content' of H. But if we are to believe Feyerabend, Σ will in principle depend on all the rivals of H, whether these be actual or potential; so that the appellation 'falsifier of H' ceases to have any univocal meaning. Thus it no longer makes sense even provisionally to accept a theory H on the grounds that unlike its rivals, H is unrefuted; for H might be falsified by some fact which, though well-known, belongs to Σ only by virtue of some rival hypothesis H* which might yet have to be proposed.

In his (1975) Feyerabend put forward two examples which seem *prima facie* to prove his thesis: those of Brownian motion and of the precession of Mercury's perihelion. With some historical justification, he maintained that only after it had been explained in 1905 by the Einstein-Smoluchowski theory, was Brownian motion held to have refuted classical thermodynamics. And yet Brownian motion had been observed long before 1905, i.e. at a time when many physicists looked upon thermodynamics as the very paradigm of a successful hypothesis. Feyerabend concluded that Brownian motion formed part of the falsifying empirical content of classical physics only *after* the emergence of the Einstein-Smoluchowski theory. Similarly: the anomalous precession Mercury's perihelion had been noticed and described long before Einstein put forward the General Theory of Relativity (GTR); but only after GTR appeared on the scene did the motion of Mercury constitute a refutation of Newtonian physics.

Feyerabend has indeed put his finger on a major difficulty resulting from the Duhem-Quine problem; a difficulty which he however misidentifies as pertaining to the empirical content of scientific theories. Let us examine the general test-structure which, according to Feyerabend himself, applies to the case of Brownian motion. Let a system T imply a statement P about some microprocess, which is correctly described by another proposition P'. P' is taken to be both incompatible with, and yet observationally indistinguishable from P. Finally, M' is an observation statement which, though easily verifiable and in fact already verified, remains ignored until a new theory T' is proposed; where T' is such that:

(1) $\nvdash [T' \to (P' \to M')]$ and $\nvdash [T' \to P']$; whence $\nvdash [T' \to M']$.

According to Feyerabend, the methodological status of T is dramatically altered by the appearance of T': M' now confirms T' *and hence* refutes T. Thus the presence of T' has increased the empirical content of T by adding M' to the set of falsifiers of T. For example: M' can now be interpreted as a sentence describing the motion of a Brownian particle, and P' as a proposition about molecular processes. T' is taken to be the Einstein-Smoluchowski theory, and T Classical Thermodynamics.

Despite its superficial plausibility, this example can be shown to be irretrievably flawed. To begin with, Feyerabend commits a simple logical error; for there can be only two possibilities:

(2) Either M′ fails logically to conflict with T , i.e. Not [⊬ (T → ¬M′)]; in which case M′ refutes T *neither before nor after* T′ was discovered;

(3) Or else: for some observation statement M, M is both incompatible with M′ and entailed by T; in which case M′ refutes T *both before and after* T′ was put forward.

Of course, as a matter of psychological fact, people might have realized the importance of M′ only after the 'refuting' theory T′ was proposed; but this fact is relevant neither to logic nor to methodology.

The above considerations suffice to refute Lakatos's and Feyerabend's general theses. But though largely correct, our logical analysis has so far overlooked an important Duhemian point which also escaped Feyerabend's attention; namely that by themselves, i.e. without the adjunction of auxiliary assumptions, such high-level theories as T and T′ entail no observation statements; so that M′ cannot possibly follow from T′ alone. And the fact that Feyerabend mentions Mercury's perihelion and the Brownian motion in the same breath suggests that he might well have had the following situation in mind.

Let T be an old theory, T′ a new rival of T, A some conjunction of (appropriate) auxiliary assumptions, b a sentence describing some boundary conditions. Finally let p and p′ be two predictions. Suppose that:

(4) ⊢ [b → ¬(p∧p′)]; ⊢ [(T∧ A) → (b → p)] and ⊢ [(T′∧ A) → (b∧p′)].

In other words: given the same initial conditions described by b, p and p′ express incompatible predictions; while (b∧¬p′) and (b∧¬p) are potential falsifiers of (T′∧A) and of (T∧A) respectively. Note that in view of the incompatibility of p and p′, (b∧p′) is also a potential falsifier of (T∧A). That is:

(5) ⊢ [(T∧ A) → ¬(b∧p′)] .

Now assume that (b∧p′) is verified, so that (T′∧A) is confirmed and (T∧A) refuted. With regard to (T∧ A), we therefore confront a typical Duhem-Quine situation: we know that (T∧ A) is false but not which of the two conjuncts to blame. There may in fact exist another set of auxiliary hypotheses, A_0 say, such that:

(6) ⊢ [(T∧ A_0) → (b → p′)].

It now looks as though $(T \wedge A_0)$ is confirmed by $(b \wedge p')$ just as strongly as is $(T' \wedge A)$. This is however to forget that A_0 might be a complex assumption whose sole function is to save T from refutation. Compared with A, A_0 may be not only unnatural but also unsupported by independent evidence. Still, it cannot legitimately be maintained that T alone has been experimentally falsified; for the evidence $(b \wedge p')$ conflicts with the *whole* of $(T \wedge A)$. Now suppose that some revolutionary hypothesis T' is put forward which, in conjunction with the 'natural' auxiliary assumption A, explains $(b \wedge p')$; i.e. T' is such that:

(7) $\vdash [(T' \wedge A) \to (b \to p')]$.

Only then would Feyerabend—as well as Lakatos—acknowledge that T has been refuted: because *both* of the presence of T' *and* of the truth of $(b \wedge p')$, we are allegedly entitled to circumvent A and hence, in view of (4), to regard T as false. The crucial step therefore consists in deciding, in the light of (7), that A is true. In other words: given the availability of the new theory T' which, together with A, is corroborated by $(b \wedge p')$, it can now be concluded that A holds good. Neither Lakatos nor Feyerabend seems however to realize that we are here facing a classical Duhem-Quine problem. As an example, consider the concrete case of Mercury's perihelion, where: $T \equiv$ Newtonian Gravitational Theory; $T' \equiv$ General Relativity (GTR) and $A \equiv$ (The Sun is a point mass). Let A_0 be some complicated assumption about the uneven distribution of mass density within the sun, b a statement about the mass, initial position and velocity of Mercury; finally, let p' be a description of the precession of Mercury's perihelion. Then the relations (3)–(6) will be satisfied—naturally within the limits of observational error (For more details, see Zahar 1989a, Chapter 8).

It is probably a historical fact that the precession of Mercury's perihelion was regarded as having refuted Newton only after GTR was proposed. But without violating any logical rules, we can account for this state-of-affairs far more satisfactorily than does either Feyerabend or Lakatos. Although $(b \wedge p')$ is verified, (6) and (4) do not imply that A is true and hence T false; for $(b \wedge p')$ belongs to the empirical content, not of T alone, but of the conjunction $(T \wedge A)$. In other words: $(b \wedge p')$ is not some new falsifier of T created by the emergence of T'. And yet we can explain why, other things being equal, $(T \wedge A_0)$ derives little support from the verification of $(b \wedge p')$: $(T \wedge A_0)$ is ad hoc with respect to $(b \wedge p')$ since A_0 was 'cooked up' in order to accommodate Mercury's perihelion, i.e. to fit $(b \wedge p')$ (See Chapter II above). But suppose—counterfactually—that A_0 had subsequently received some measure of independent factual support; i.e. assume that independently of Mercury's perihelion, we came to have a good reason for holding the sun's density not to be evenly distributed throughout its volume; then from the methodological standpoint defended in Chapter IV—as opposed to that adopted by Feyerabend—the situation would have changed dramatically; for $(T \wedge A_0)$ would have become a serious rival of $(T' \wedge A)$; and I dare conjecture that MSRP (as defined below, in Chapter VI), and not some new-fangled version of sophisticated falsificationism, would then capture the scientists' intuitive value-judgments. Thus Feyerabend's thesis, though psychologically illuminating, depends on a faulty analysis of a historical accident.

(H) Is there a Bayesian solution of the Duhem-Quine Problem?

Let me start by confessing that I find Bayesianism somewhat uncongenial; but I am uncertain as to whether my disagreement with the Bayesians might not, all told, be terminological.

The Bayesians rightly insist on the fact that probabilistic arguments are at the heart of scientific reasoning—a view strongly defended by Leibniz who realized that Logic alone could not solve all epistemological problems. The starting point of Bayesianism is Bayes's theorem, i.e. a straightforward consequence of Kolmogorov's axioms which, in its strong form, asserts that:

$$P(h \mid e) =_{\text{def.}} P(h \wedge e) / P(e) = P(e \mid h).P(h)/P(e) = P(e \mid h).P(h) / [\Sigma_j P(e \wedge h_j)]$$
$$= P(e \mid h).P(h) / [\Sigma_j P(e \mid h_j).P(h_j)]; \text{ where } P(V_j h_j) = 1 \text{ and } P(h_j \wedge h_u)$$
$$= 0 \text{ for } j \neq u.$$

I have written down this cascade of trivial equations in order to underline the fact that Bayes's theorem is an uncontroversial, not to say a trivial proposition accepted by all the protagonists.

Let me go back to the point about terminology. As already mentioned, almost all the philosophers I have read—and this includes Popper—accept Kolmogorov's axioms and hence the relations written down above. For example: the formula proposed by Popper as an expression of the degree of empirical corroboration of a hypothesis is riddled with probability functions of various arguments. So the difference between the Bayesians and their opponents cannot possibly consist in the former's unique acceptance of Bayes's Theorem. From reading various texts, it can be concluded that this difference lies in the subjective interpretation given by the Bayesians to the notion of probability; and this even though Bayesianism is, at least according to Colin Howson, compatible with objectivism. Note that if this were really the case, then Bayesianism would lose all claim to originality; for the difference between it and genuine objectivism would at best be one of degree, not of kind.

Let me give an example which illustrates this point. In their (2003) Bovens and Hartmann claim that $P(R_1, R_2) = 0.10$ and $P(R_1, \neg R_2) = 0.01 = P(\neg R_1, R_2)$; where R_1 and R_2 are the following propositions: $R_1 \equiv$ (the culprit spoke with a French accent), and $R_2 \equiv$ (the culprit drove off in a Renault car). Although these figures seem plausible, no attempt is made to justify them. The context nevertheless indicates not only that these probabilities reflect objective states-of-affairs, but also that they could have been obtained by means of a poll. Clearly, the total number of French men and women, of Renault owners and even of all the people inhabiting a given region could easily be determined. So we have here to do with objective frequencies lying at the basis of allegedly subjective assessments of probabilities. However, the authors also make use of such relations as $P(Rep.R_j | R_j) = p_j$ and $P(Rep.R_j | \neg R_j) = q_j$; where $Rep.R_j$ is the proposition that there exists a report according to which R_j is true (See Bovens and Hartmann 2003, pp. 12–14). But then it is difficult to see not only how p_j and q_j could be estimated but also how they could reasonably be postulated in all circumstances. Consider the case where the truth-value of R_j is unknowable. R_j might e.g. denote some high-level quantum theory, the reporters being Einstein and Heisenberg. Even though both reporters knew the extent to which R_j was empirically adequate, $P(Rep.R_j | R_j)$ would, in all probability, receive widely divergent values; for, unlike Heisenberg, Einstein is not likely to accept reporting R_j as true. Hence a minimal psychologistic element must be allowed for by all consistent Bayesians; which is probably why Howson and Urbach wrote:

> The other notion of probability is epistemic. This type probability is, to use Laplace's famous words, relative in part to our ignorance, in part [to] our knowledge, it expresses numerically degrees of uncertainty in the light of data. (Howson and Urbach 1993, p. 22)

It seems to me that we have here a confusion between two theses: [1] the use of probabilities *arises* from our uncertainty as to the actual truth-value of some propositions; in other words: had we been in a position to know the truth-value of certain statements, then we should never have resorted to the probability calculus; [2] probabilities *express* or *refer to* the degree of our certainty regarding these propositions. This type of reasoning is on a par with the following: Logic owes its origins to our need to learn something about the connections between various state-of-affairs; *ergo*: Logic expresses our desire to acquire such knowledge; which is an obvious *non-sequitur*. There is another *non-sequitur*—of a more sophisticated kind; namely: logical rules are often used in order to infer some truths from other truths; hence Logic is a description of the psychological rules of thought followed by the (healthy) human mind. This of course is the well-known psychologistic fallacy.

Be it as it may, the thesis that probability 'expresses numerically degrees of uncertainty in the light of the data' is admittedly consistent. It is therefore time to examine how the Bayesians use this approach in order to solve the Duhem-Quine problem. Howson and Urbach consider an example cited by Lakatos; namely that of Prout's theory, which will henceforth be denoted by H. H asserts that the atomic weight of every element is an integral multiple of that of hydrogen. As for the auxiliary hypothesis A implicated in the testing of H, it consists of laws about some measuring techniques, about the reliability of certain instruments, about the purity of the chemicals employed, etc. Let e be the verified report that the measured weight of chlorine is 35.83. Thus $e \Rightarrow \neg(H \wedge A)$, which means that $(H \wedge A)$ is empirically refuted. Yet the scientists of the day took e to have undermined A rather than H; a fact which Howson and Urbach set out to explain. They write:

> It seems that chemists of the early nineteenth century, such as Prout and Thomson, were fairly certain about the truth of *t* [= H], but less so of *a* [= A], though more sure that *a* is true than that it is false. . . . For these reasons, we conjecture that P(*a*) was of the order of 0.6 and that P(*t*) was around 0.9, and these are the figures we shall work with. (Howson and Urbach 1993, p. 138)

Following Jon Dorling, the two authors go on to assume that H is independent of A; and then they lay down, without any justification, the following relations: $P(e \mid \neg H \wedge A) = 0.01 = P(e \mid \neg H \wedge \neg A)$ and $P(e \mid H \wedge \neg A) = 0.02$. From all these assumptions they finally deduce $P(A \mid e) = 0.073 \ll 0.878 = P(H \mid e)$.

These operations are however nothing but a series of blatantly ad hoc adjustments of parameters carried out in order to obtain a foreknown result;

namely that in the Prout case, the Duhem-Quine problem was unexpectedly resolved in favor of the high-level theory H rather than in that of the auxiliary hypothesis A.

It cannot of course be denied that many historical events can be 'modeled' through assignments of probability values to various sentences. Such modeling however hardly constitutes an explanation. It even seems to me as though Howson, Urbach and Dorling confuse the explanans with the explanandum. That many chemists attributed to P(H) [= 0.9] a value higher than that of P(A) [= 0.6] is not an explanans but the very fact which, if the Duhem problem is to be solved, ought to be explained. And the same goes for all the other ad hoc assumptions made by the authors. It appears to me that there are two satisfactory methods for explaining why most of the scientists of the day might have been prepared to accept H in preference to A. The first consists in showing that when conjoined with auxiliary assumptions different from A, H had previously been systematically confirmed; which takes us back to the conclusions reached in (D) above. The second method consists in demonstrating that H had introduced unity into a scientific system by establishing unexpected connections between many of its hitherto disparate elements. The scientists would consequently have refused to regard such unity as being due to mere chance or to the existence of a malicious demon bent on deceiving them. All this underlines the relevance of metaphysical considerations to the solution of the Duhem-Quine problem.

Let me end this section by showing that Bayesianism is fundamentally incapable of solving an epistemological problem arising from the ad hoc feature of certain hypotheses; more precisely: of those conjectures arrived at by means of ad hoc maneuvers. None of the statements H, A, e, etc. entering as arguments into the probability functions considered by the Bayesians bears any trace of the methods by which it might have been constructed. In other words, a cooked up law is treated on a par with an ad hoc one. As an illustration, consider an urn Δ containing an infinite number of pairwise incompatible hypotheses, each one of which involves a large number of parameters (i.e. the conjunction of any two hypotheses is inconsistent; and this independently of the values assigned to the parameters). Hence at most one member of Δ can be true. Now let E be any limited set of verified factual statements. Assume that every hypothesis belonging to Δ is known to yield E. Then no matter how sophisticated it might become, Bayesianism will have no machinery for discriminating between the various elements of Δ; and yet if any member of Δ were to be chosen at random, its chances of being true would clearly be vanishingly small. The Bayesians may of course decide to allot higher probabilities to the non ad hoc hypotheses belonging to Δ, but they will be incapable of defending such a decision on Bayesian grounds; all of which is nothing but the generalized version of the above argument which was fielded against the Bayesian treatment of the Proutian case.

(I) REALISM, GEOMETRY AND THE DUHEM-QUINE PROBLEM

Let us now examine the most important example of a synthetic mathematical system, which also happens to be highly relevant to the Duhem-Quine problem; namely that of physical geometry. Going back to (D) above, consider a conjunction G∧P where G is a geometrical, and P a physical hypothesis. We shall discuss Poincaré's thesis—which *prima facie* runs counter to Quine's—that G has nothing to fear from the results of experience.

It ought first to be noted that Poincaré's conception of the conventionality of geometry differs both from Carnap's and from Reichenbach's (See Reichenbach 1958, sections 4 and 8). Poincaré subscribed to an epistemological notion of truth according to which only partially decidable statements possess truth-values. In other words: such statements must be ascertainable at least as true or at least as false (See Zahar 1989a, Chapter 5). All conventions and, more particularly, all geometrical theories are therefore devoid of truth-value. For since space is in principle unobservable, such theories can be neither verified nor empirically refuted; so they are neither true nor false, but more or less convenient. A convention's degree of convenience nonetheless functions as an index of verisimilitude and hence has ontological import: the more convenient a system, the more faithfully it reflects the true nature of things. This principle constitutes the crucial difference between logical empiricism on the one hand, and Duhem's as well as Poincaré's philosophies on the other; for according to the latter, the unity and simplicity of scientific hypotheses bears a relation not only to the human mind but also to some transcendent reality (Duhem 1954, Part 1, Chapter 2, §§4, 5). In Chapter VII below, I shall defend Poincaré's structural realism against Quine's position, which I take to be strictly conventionalistic; but for the time being, let us restrict our attention to Poincaré's philosophy of geometry.

Poincaré's view of the connection between geometry and physics can be rationally reconstructed as follows (See Poincaré 1902, Chapters 4 and 5; also Zahar 2001, Chapter 3). A geometrical system determines a network of relations among well defined objects like points, geodesics, surfaces, distances and angles. Scientific theories then fix the relationships between these ideal entities on the one hand, and certain physical processes on the other. Physicists furthermore subscribe to a principle which can be called the *Generalized Principle of Inertia*, or GPI for short: other things being equal, some natural processes like the motions of free particles and the propagation of light take place along geodesics, i.e. along the privileged paths of the underlying geometry; only deviations from these privileged configurations call for a causal explanation, the latter being normally formulated in terms of external forces.

Consider two material objects, or two physical processes, which will henceforth be denoted by B_1 and B_2. For j = 1,2, let B^0_j be the region of space which, according to GPI, B_j should ideally occupy; i.e. B_j would coincide with B^0_j were it not for certain distorting forces which may be universal, differential, or a mixture of both; where: differential $\equiv$ (dependent on the physical composition of B_j) and: universal $\equiv$ nondifferential. Thus we have the following scheme:

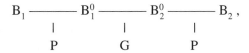

$$B_1 \text{———} B^0_1 \text{———} B^0_2 \text{———} B_2 \text{ ,}$$
$$\quad | \qquad\qquad | \qquad\qquad |$$
$$\quad P \qquad\qquad G \qquad\qquad P$$

in which P denotes a physical theory and G the underlying geometry. Thus G∧P yields a relationship between B_1 and B_2, i.e. between two concrete physical entities. Unlike G alone, the conjunction G∧P is in principle falsifiable and consequently possesses, according to Poincaré, a definite truth-value. Thus we appear to be dealing with a typical Duhem-Quine problem; for we have been led—or misled—into expressing the system under test in the form G∧P and thus into holding that if G∧P were to be refuted, then we could in principle incriminate G or P or both. It therefore looks as though G and the physical hypothesis P were on a par. This is however far from being the case; for whereas G describes the properties of space-time and can therefore be rendered independent of P, the latter *presupposes* G both as a language and as a background theory. It follows that the structure of a scientific system is adequately rendered not by G∧P but by G∧P_G, where the suffix indicates the dependence of physics on some prior geometry. Note that the priority in question is of the logical and not of the genetic or heuristic kind. At one time, it nonetheless looked as though Einstein had undermined the theoretical primacy of geometry, whose dependence on energy seemed written into his celebrated field equations: $R^{ab} - (1/2)g^{ab}R = -kT^{ab}$. The left-hand side of this relation describes the geometrical, and the right-hand side the physical content of space-time. In this way, kinematics and physics appeared to be indissolubly mixed. Let us however recall that these equations were first proposed in the form: $R_{ab} = -k(T_{ab} - (1/2)g_{ab}T)$, where the second member involves both the metric g_{ab} and the energy tensor T_{ab}. Anyway, the basic condition imposed on T^{ab} is the vanishing of its divergence $T^{ab}_{:b}$; where the covariant derivative $T^{ab}_{:j}$ is well known to be dependent on the affine connections and hence on the underlying geometry. It follows that the latter must be *presupposed*. Provided the equations $R^{ab} - (1/2)g^{ab}R = -kT^{ab}$ be construed as providing only a *method for calculating the metric*, Einstein's approach does not jeopardize the primacy of geometry: after using Special Relativity in order to determine T^{ab}, one goes on to solve $R^{ab} - (1/2)g^{ab}R = -kT^{ab}$ for the g^{ab}'s in terms of the tensor (T^{ij}). Any solution will ensure that: $T^{ab}_{:b} = (-1/k).[R^{ab} - (1/2)g^{ab}R]_{:b} = 0$ since the second member vanishes identically. It is worth noting that Einstein himself spoke of the left-hand side of $R^{ab} - (1/2)g^{ab}R = -kT^{ab}$ as being made of marble and of the right-hand side as consisting of low-grade wood (Einstein 1967, p. 81). He moreover conceded that GTR can be given a Euclidean formulation, at any rate in large regions of the spatio-temporal manifold. Thus it looks as though, contrary to Quine's claim, geometry can be lifted above the methodological fray. This is why theoretical physicists like Eddington and Schrödinger went as far as claiming that only geometrical entities exist: asserting the presence of energy at some point $P(\underline{x})$ of space is another way of saying that $R^{ab} - (1/2)g^{ab}R \neq 0$. In other words: geometry alone determines what parts of space-time have a physical content and what parts are empty of all but gravitational energy (See Eddington 1923, p. 120; also Schrödinger 1950, p. 99). This admittedly extremist attitude nonetheless underlines the *logical* precedence of geometry over all other components of a scientific system: proceeding logically, we first settle on some definition of congruence through choosing the values of the $g_{ij}(\underline{x})$'s; these fix our geometry and enable us to express all laws within the framework in which the chosen concept of congruence is held to be applicable. Our decisions in no way debar us from subsequently so redefining the metric (g_{ij}) that our system becomes globally either simpler or more unified. This is in effect what Poincaré proposed that we should do in certain situations: the people living on a 'hyperbolic' disk can achieve Euclidicity through resorting to Poincaré's temperature gradient (See Poincaré 1902, Chapter 4). Thus Poincaré would have granted Quine's point about altering the mathematics of a system so as to give the latter its simplest form; but unlike Quine's conventionalism, Poincaré's position remained structural-realistic (See below, Chapter VII). Let us however repeat that we are here talking about the logical, not about the heuristic or epistemological order of things.

Going back to the conjunction $G \wedge P_G$, we now see why a change in G might induce a change throughout a scientific system, thus allowing it to obviate an empirical refutation. For example: were P_G to state that light travels along geodesics, then it would trivially follow that P_G depends on the underlying geometry G. Should we be faced with an empirical refutation, then we might decide to alter G into G'; for $G' \wedge P_{G'}$ will generally fail to be observationally equivalent to $G \wedge P_G$ and might thus evade the refutation in question. We could alternatively change P_G into P'_G in such a way that: Not $[(G \wedge P_G) \sim (G \wedge P'_G)]$, where "$\sim$" stands for (strict) observational indiscernibility. It might, for example, be assumed that light is deviated from a geodesic of G by some field $\underline{F}$ whose addition alters P_G into P'_G. These considerations show that geometry functions both as a language and as a background theory permeating the whole of physics.

Whenever $(G \wedge P_G) \sim (G' \wedge P'_{G'})$ holds good, Poincaré—rather inappropriately—spoke of the intertranslatability of the two geometries G and G'. But it should by now have become clear that this misnomer actually refers to the observational identity of the two global systems $(G \wedge P_G)$ and $(G' \wedge P'_{G'})$. (See Zahar 2001, Chapter 3). Let us now examine Poincaré's contention—which weakens both Duhem's and Quine's theses—that given any G, P_G and G', there always exists some $P'_{G'}$ such that $(G \wedge P_G) \sim (G' \wedge P'_{G'})$. As remarked above, we can arbitrarily decree any geometry we please not because space as such is amorphous but because it is, and will always be inaccessible to our senses. Hence neither space itself nor any relations between portions of it nor any presumed connection between space and a physical entity will ever be observed. Only the direct connections between concrete objects like B_1 and B_2 could conceivably be ascertained. Let us recall that the relations between the ideal entities B_1^0 and B_2^0 are fixed by the underlying geometry G. As for the connection between B_j and B_j^0 (j = 1,2), it is described by the physical theory denoted by P_G. G' will generally define a new ideal figure $B_j^{0'}$ corresponding to B_j^0. For example, B_j^0 and $B_j^{0'}$ may be geodesics of G and G' respectively (j = 1,2). Very schematically, it can be said that $P'_{G'}$ is obtained by adding to P_G the universal field $\underline{F}$ which effects the transition from B_j^0 to $B_j^{0'}$ (j = 1,2). Thus:

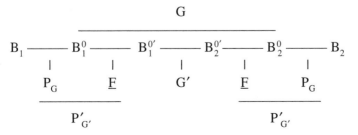

In the above scheme, the net relation between B_1 and B_2 remains unchanged; from which $(G \wedge P_G) \sim (G' \wedge P'_{G'})$ follows.

According to Grünbaum, the introduction of the universal field $\underline{F}$ is tantamount to remetrizing space, thereby altering G into G′. Grünbaum concludes that all talk of universal forces is metaphorical and that $\underline{F}$ can always be made to vanish by resorting to the 'customary means' of determining the $g_{ij}(\underline{x})$'s. On Poincaré's disk for example, we could use material rods in order to measure distances and should thus empirically be led to construct a hyperbolic geometry; all this without having to mention any universal fields at all. This approach however faces two major difficulties, one of vicious circularity, the other of overdetermination.

Let us give a concrete example, which has already been mentioned; namely Poincaré's two-dimensional hyperbolic world (Poincaré 1902, Chapter 4). Denote by w the circle $x^2 + y^2 = R^2$, where R is some positive number; and let Ω be the interior of w. Suppose there exists a temperature gradient which instantaneously affects the dimensions of all bodies in exactly the same way. More precisely: assume that as we move towards the circumference w, all measuring rods are shortened by the factor $h(R^2 - r^2)$, h being a positive constant. Hence the measured distance ds between two neighboring points will be equal to: $ds_e / [h(R^2 - r^2)]$, where ds_e is the ordinary Euclidean interval between the points in question. Thus: $ds_e = \sqrt{(dx^2 + dy^2)}$.

Should the inhabitants of the disk Ω use material rods in order to probe their spatial environment, then they will naturally be led to adopt a hyperbolic metric as the foundation of their global geometry. A creative mathematical physicist might however prefer to use Euclidean geometry on the basis of its being the simplest theory of space: such a physicist could, for example, introduce the temperature gradient described by Poincaré. This gradient typifies what Reichenbach was later to call a 'universal field', i.e. a force which, as already mentioned, cannot be shielded against and which affects *all* bodies in exactly the same way. We should however note that Poincaré's disk example is over-idealized. Even though the temperature gradient be so contrived as to constitute a universal field, all measuring rods have to be corrected for the effects of differential forces, e.g. of electromagnetic variations. This is why Grünbaum rightly remarks that allowances have always to be made for certain inhomogeneous factors (See Grünbaum 1973, Chapter 4, pp. 144–46). The latter are however assessed by means of laws which in turn presuppose some kinematical framework G; and there is no guarantee that G will coincide with the geometry G′ obtained by measurements made with the duly 'corrected' rods (See Zahar 2001, Chapter 3).

For the sake of argument, let us nonetheless assume that allowances have successfully been made for all the inhomogeneous factors. So let us transport our measuring rod to some distant point $P(\underline{x})$; one end of the rod is fixed at P while its other extremity is made to occupy a variable position denoted by some continuous index α. Let $ds_\alpha(\underline{x})$ be the length ascribed to the rod as it stretches from $P(\underline{x})$ to $Q_\alpha(\underline{x} + d_\alpha\underline{x})$, where: $\underline{x} = (x^1,...,x^N)$, $d_\alpha\underline{x} = (d_\alpha x^1,..., d_\alpha x^N)$. Thus: $(ds_\alpha(\underline{x}))^2 = g_{ij}(\underline{x}) \cdot d_\alpha x^i \cdot d_\alpha x^j$, where we agree not to apply Einstein's summation convention to any Greek indices. Since α is a continuous label, there are $2\aleph_0$ independent equations, where $\aleph_0 = $ aleph-zero; but at any given point P, there are only $N(N + 1) / 2$ unknowns $g_{ij}(\underline{x})$ to be accounted for. We consequently have no guarantee that the above equations will turn out to be compatible. The requirement that our space be Riemannian *and* that its metric be realized by certain customary means is far from being innocuous: for we are imposing physical restrictions on the behavior of all measuring rods and are thus dealing, not with a mere stipulation, but with a genuine scientific hypothesis.

At this point, note that the diehard realist proceeds in the direction opposite to that taken by the conventionalist. Let us show that the realist will consequently face fewer epistemological problems. He generally *starts* by putting forward a conjecture about the intrinsic metric of physical space, i.e. about the tensor field $g_{ij}(\underline{x})$; thus he automatically fixes $G = [g_{ij}(\underline{x})]$, where $[g_{ij}(\underline{x})]$ denotes the geometry determined by the metric $g_{ij}(\underline{x})$. He might then ask himself whether some well-known measuring instruments, e.g. a set of identical rods, realize G. Suppose they do not. Would there then be a fact of the matter to be explained? A conventionalist like Reichenbach or Quine must answer in the negative; for according to him, the g_{ij}'s arise from a stipulation which *creates* the metric structure of space. After choosing the g_{ij}'s, the conventionalist simply takes cognizance of a fact which has to do not so much with the physical world, as with his freely chosen convention; namely that the geometry realized by certain customary means, in case it is at all realizable in this way, does—or does not—coincide with the one he has arbitrarily stipulated. If it does, then well and good. If it does not, then there is still nothing to be explained; for according to conventionalism, we are still at liberty to change our minds and remetrize space in conformity with some given set of measuring devices. From a Quinean viewpoint, all that matters is the simplicity of the ensuing system.

The realist answers the above question very differently from the conventionalist. Suppose the rod ascribes different distances to two infinitesimal stretches $\underline{PQ} = (d\underline{x})$ and $\underline{PK} = (\partial\underline{x})$, where: $\underline{x} = (x^1,...,x^N)$, $\underline{x} + d\underline{x} = (x^1 + dx^1,...,x^N + dx^N)$, and $\underline{x} + \partial\underline{x} = (x^1+\partial x^1,...,x^N + \partial x^N)$ are the coordinates of P, Q, and K respectively; suppose further that $g_{ij}(\underline{x}).dx^i.dx^j =$ $g_{ij}(\underline{x}).\partial x^i.\partial x^j$. The realist will conclude that the rod is subject to distorting forces dependent on the directions $\underline{PQ}$ and $\underline{PK}$. Similarly: let two intervals $\underline{PQ}$ and $\underline{UV}$ distant from each other be given different lengths by the rod while $g_{ij}(\underline{x}).dx^i.dx^j = g_{ij}(\underline{z}).dz^i.dz^j$ (or the other way round); where $(\underline{z})$ and $(\underline{z} + d\underline{z})$ are the coordinates of U and V respectively. The realist might conjecture that, during its transport from P to U, the rod was deformed by a field whose magnitude and direction can in principle be discovered. He might alternatively conclude that his initial conjecture about the structure of space was erroneous; he would then try to alter the values of the $g_{ij}(\underline{x})$'s or even postulate a purely affine Nonriemannian structure.

At first sight, it might look as though the clash between conventionalism and realism were of a purely verbal nature: what for the Quinean conventionalist is a change of stipulation turns out, for the realist, to be the refutation of a hypothesis followed by the proposal of an alternative geometry. There remains however an important difference between these two methodologies; a difference which seems to me to be all to the advantage of realism. It has been maintained that conventionalism explains a 'fact' which realism fails to account for, namely the observational indiscernibility of any two physical geometries: according to conventionalism, space is metrically amorphous; so no wonder that no experiment can tell two arbitrarily chosen geometries apart (See Grünbaum 1973, Chapter 1, pp. 29–30). The main problem lies with the status of this presumed 'fact'. My claim is that this fact has a logical rather than a strictly empirical character. For any proposition Y, let us denote by $C[Y]$ the consequence class of Y , i.e. $C[Y]$ is the set of all logical consequences of Y. Put $Z = G \wedge PG$ and $Z' = G' \wedge P'G'$. It can reasonably be assumed that at any given time, there is general agreement as to what constitutes an observation statement O, irrespective of whether O is true or false. Let E be the class of all such O's. Poincaré can be regarded as having established that $C[Z] \cap E = C[Z'] \cap E$. Clearly, this equation, which supposedly expresses the amorphousness of space, describes *no empirical fact*. For though membership of E be in part determined by our perceptual apparatus, no experimental findings—which would of course have to be described by certain elements of E —can either falsify or confirm $C[Z] \cap E = C[Z'] \cap E$; for this equation holds independently of the truth-values of any members of E. Hence the thesis of the amorphousness of space must be either logical or else metaphysical (in Popper's sense); which is incidentally not intended to be a criticism of this thesis. But the equation $C[Z] \cap E = C[Z'] \cap E$ takes on considerable philosophical significance in the light of a positivist principle; namely that where there exists no detectable difference, there ought to be no objective difference either: so since G cannot be empirically distinguished from G', space must lack a metric and the difference between G and G' should be regarded as linguistic.

Needless to say, diehard realism is equally metaphysical. It maintains that there exists an intrinsic spatial metric which, if properly captured, gives rise to a unified, organically compact and hence 'convenient' system; where we ought to remind ourselves that the convenience in question is not of the pragmatic, but of the structural kind.

I shall now attempt to tip the balance in favor of structural realism. As already mentioned: it is generally agreed that without any loss of empirical content, Einstein's GTR can be reformulated in Euclidean terms, at least within vast spatio-temporal domains (See Einstein 1934b, pp. 122–23). Hence classical and Einsteinian kinematics cannot be *experimentally* told apart. Yet scientists feel that the use of a Euclidean metric in GTR is artificial; that this kind of *artificiality* destroys the close coupling between gravitation and the space-time metric. Scientists thus hold that more than a merely linguistic difference separates these two distinct 'formulations' of GTR, hence that kinematics reflects an objective aspect of the real world. This defense of geometrical realism rests on metaphysical assumptions and is therefore far from decisive. It has nonetheless to be added that all rival positions are, by the very nature of the problem, equally metaphysical. Be it as it may, since the realist accepts a merely epistemological thesis concerning the arbitrariness of the metric, he is left free to make a further claim: if G renders the global scientific system $Z \equiv (G {\wedge} PG)$ maximally convenient and if Z predicts or systematically subsumes a whole host of facts, then such a high degree of convenience should not be attributed to mere chance. In other words: Z can be taken to approximate a 'Natural Classification' in Duhem's sense; so that a geometry G which is fully integrated into Z must also reflect true relations between real entities. Such a conclusion—which is consistent with most scientists' intuitive appraisal—cannot be drawn by a conventionalist like Quine, for whom G is a simple *mode of description* of perceptual facts lying at the periphery of our field of knowledge. Poincaré wrote:

It will be said that science is a classification and that a classification cannot be true but convenient. But it is true that it is convenient; it is true that it is so not only for me but for all men; it is true that it will remain convenient for our descendants; it is true finally that this cannot be by chance. (Poincaré 1906, p. 140)

We now see how close Poincaré's position comes to that of the diehard (structural) realist. Thus, summing up: according to realism, space possesses a pre-given metric or, at any rate, an intrinsic geometry which the scientist sets out to capture. Such a background geometry, call it G, cannot be directly tested for. The realist however feels entitled to hold that G will be a good approximation to the true geometry if G provides a coherent kinematical framework for a unified system Z; where Z systematically subsumes some crude facts and successfully anticipates others. In view of his epistemological truth-concept, Poincaré would of course deny that G, or for that matter any isolated convention can legitimately possess a truth-value. His methodological verdict nevertheless parallels that of the realist: Poincaré accepts that Z, together with its components and the way in which these cohere with each other, mirrors real relations obtaining in a transcendent world. And this appraisal can be transferred to the geometry G subtending Z. As explained above, such a verdict remains unavailable to the conventionalist as long as the latter maintains that space is amorphous and that geometry is decreed by the physicist; from which it immediately follows that there exists no structure which geometry could reflect rather than impose.

(J) CONCLUSION

This chapter dealt first with Duhem's ungainsayable, though modest claim that an experimental refutation undermines not one theory but a whole cluster of hypotheses no member of which is singled out as the culprit. Secondly, Kripke's thesis that there exist necessary *a posteriori* truths was discussed; it was shown that in all cases relevant to the empirical sciences, there was an excluded middle between metaphysical (i.e. untestable, yet fallible) hypotheses and scientific (i.e. refutable and hence also fallible) propositions. Thirdly, Quine's holistic thesis that 'the unit of empirical significance is the whole of science' was examined. It was found that throwing doubt on supposedly analytic statements like 'No bachelor is married' comes down to abandoning merely verbal definitions which do not seriously bear on any aspect of knowledge. It is only when one moves towards the centre of the 'field' of science, i.e. towards mathematics and logic, that holism begins to acquire some clout. It is certainly the case that the mathematical and, even more so, the logical axioms are common to almost all physical theories. Altering either logic or mathematics will therefore have repercussions in *practically all* branches of knowledge. This applies more particularly to the geometrical axioms, whose central role in physics warrants a whole section being devoted to them. In this area, Quine's conventionalist conclusions are—to some extent—borne out by the development of mathematical physics; but here again, realism rather than conventionalism provides the best *rationale* for choosing the geometry most appropriate to a given scientific system. And to repeat: holism comes into its own *only* when, as a result of empirical difficulties and in order to increase the simplicity of a system, logic is tampered with; for by its very nature, logic permeates the *whole* fabric of our knowledge. What is however puzzling is that Quine consistently maintained that only one logic, namely classical first-order and hence complete logic, is legitimate. But then one fails to see in what sense the Duhem-Quine problem goes beyond Duhem.

VI

The Methodology of Scientific Research Programs (MSRP)

We have now all the elements needed for the construction of a comprehensive methodological system, henceforth referred to as MSRP (the Methodology of Scientific Research Programs).

(A) Methodological Basic Statements

Instead of giving a 'synthetic', i.e. a dogmatic account of MSRP, let us examine the problem-situation from which MSRP arose; which immediately poses the question: in what sense, if any, can methodologies be problematic? Are there ways in which they can legitimately be criticized and eventually improved?

At first sight, a methodology appears to be a purely normative organon for the appraisal of scientific systems; so that beyond the purely logical question of consistency, such appraisals cannot in turn be assessed or criticized. In other words: apart from being subject to a coherence condition, a methodology must be a priori and is therefore bound to be arbitrary. This argument can however be reversed: because the logical constraints are absurdly weak, methodologies should be expected to yield, or at least to be compatible with the singular value-judgments held by the scientific elite in respect of certain achievements. These evaluative judgments are taken to be 'given' in much the same way as basic statements are accepted in the natural sciences. To take but one example: any methodology which would deem Newtonian Theory inferior to its Cartesian rivals should be rejected. More precisely, one ought to start by fixing two disjoint sets of propositions, A and B: A contains singular positive value-judgments concerning those discoveries which are intuitively regarded as having contributed to the advancement of science; and B consists of negative appraisals of systems and methods held to be pseudo-scientific. A and B need not be exhaustive; i.e. there might be a grey intermediate region C where scientific intuition stalls or breaks down completely. For the sake of argument, suppose that we have no clear idea as to whether some particle theories represented progress or regress in the recent development of physics. This gives rise to uncertain value-judgments all of which belong to domain C. But no matter how C is circumscribed, every methodology must satisfy a minimal requirement: that of including A while excluding B by means of a coherent definition of progress (By excluding B, I naturally mean: yielding the negative value-judgments belonging to B).

This approach appears bound to face two seemingly insuperable difficulties. First: does methodology, which was initially taken to be a normative discipline, reduce to a science of science—in Popper's words: *zu einer Wissenschaftswissenschaft*? The answer is: yes, but not quite; for methodologies are to be based not on empirical but on normative facts. On the one hand, the scientific elite whose attitude determines the two sets A and B is selected by means, not of empirical, but of evaluative criteria. On the other hand, a methodology is expected to yield not factual but normative propositions; for example: the proposition that Einstein's theories are better corroborated than Freud's; that a confirmed hypothesis is preferable to a refuted one; that modern quantum physics represents progress over classical mechanics, etc.

We secondly face what appears to be a problem of vicious circularity. Through using the notion of a scientific elite in order to define the sets A and B, do we not presuppose a host of presystematic normative judgments which we merely retrieve at the formal level? The answer to this question must no doubt be positive: in distinguishing between A and B, there is an implicit reliance on some general criterion, which we might well be unable to formulate or of which we are only half-aware. It is however one of the essential tasks of philosophy to articulate such criteria, to force them—as it were—into the open. This procedure moreover involves no vicious circularity. I shall defend this claim by borrowing two examples from the domain of pure mathematics. Before the ε–δ definition of a limit was put forward, most scientists had a vague conception of continuity; they held the conic sections [set A], but not any step function [set B] to be continuous; they had however no clear intuition regarding the set [C] consisting of all broken lines. Although the ε–δ approach demarcated A from B, it placed C—somewhat unexpectedly —within A. Thus the fit between intuition and formal definition is hardly ever perfect: some people still feel that broken lines ought to be discontinuous; but then rigorous mathematics offers them the possibility of pronouncing such 'abnormal' graphs nondifferentiable, albeit continuous. A similar example is provided by set theory according to which, modulo a definition of a bijection, two intervals of unequal lengths are equinumerous while possessing different Lebesgue measures. Finally, in methodology, one explication of inductive support implies that, given a fact $e \equiv (b \wedge p)$ and a hypothesis H: if $(H \wedge b) \Rightarrow p$, then e *genuinely corroborates* H provided e is novel with respect to H. There can of course be no question of e supporting H if Not $[(H \wedge b) \Rightarrow p]$. However, if $(H \wedge b) \Rightarrow p$ but $(H \wedge b)$ has been adjusted to yield p, then H *subsumes* $(b \rightarrow p)$ and is consistent with, though not strongly supported by e.

Going back to a general consideration of the classes A and B, there is clearly no guarantee that a *unified* and *rigorous* methodology will successfully demarcate A from B; which is why there can be no question of any vicious circularity. Given that A and B are finite, it is of course always possible to fabricate—e.g. by simple enumeration—a criterion disjoining A from B; but we have no assurance that a result obtained in this ad hoc manner will satisfy the condition of simplicity and unity generally imposed on formal definitions. Thus in the case of methodology—as in that of mathematics—we face a problem of informal rigor. Our definitions are required to achieve a reflexive equilibrium between two desiderata; namely those of achieving unity and of maximally accounting for our intuitions, i.e. of demarcating A from B; which will automatically partition C by deciding those fuzzy cases where our intuition fails.

(B) Methodology and History

We have seen that value-judgments concerning some specific episodes in the history of science act as arbiters between competing methodologies. It can conversely be asked whether history has anything to learn from a given methodology. To begin with, historical *reconstructions* are indispensable because historians do not know all the facts. There is one particular type of fact to which they can in principle have no direct access; namely the intuitive system of appraisal which a scientist applies in constructing his theories and in choosing between available research programs. In certain cases, scientists have written about both their methodology and their heuristics. But the scientist's reports cannot always be taken at face value; for he may either knowingly disguise the truth, or else be sincere but have a false consciousness of his own activity. Einstein wrote:

If you want to find anything from the theoretical physicists about the methods they use, I advise you to stick closely to one principle:

don't listen to their words, fix your attention on their deeds. (Einstein
1994b, p. 296)

This passage clearly describes the problem of false consciousness faced
primarily by those scientists who, long after the creative event, try to reconstruct their own path to discovery. The most obvious cases of deception—
as distinct from self-deception—are those in which the scientists knowingly
mislead their readers. It is well known that Newton claimed never to have
framed any hypotheses; but his assumptions about the absolute character of
space and time—which he presented as mere axioms of thought—could not
possibly have been deduced from the phenomena; and he openly admitted
that only clock-time and relative spatial positions could effectively be
ascertained. He also proved that his mechanical laws, i.e. the only theories
he seriously entertained in physics, assume the same form in all Galilean
coordinate systems and cannot therefore be used to fix one unique frame.
Thus Newton must have known that the Absolute Space Hypothesis was
nothing short of a metaphysical assumption (See Newton 1686, Book 1).

As another example of blatant bad faith, we can cite Ampère, who
claimed to have derived his laws from experiments which, by his own
admission, he had not yet carried out. More interesting cases of false consciousness are however those presented by scientists who, despite sincerely
believing that certain philosophical views helped them in their researches,
might have misidentified their own path to discovery. With his usual piti-
less clarity, Pierre Duhem posed the problem in the following terms: it is
not enough for a physicist sincerely to claim that he was a realist in order
for us to conclude that realism cognitively helped him to achieve scientific
breakthroughs; by means of logical and historical analyses, it ought to be
shown that realism provided a heuristic which actually helped the physicist
in question to make specific choices or to embark on putative solutions.
Duhem incidentally maintained that realism as such almost never played
any significant role in scientific discovery; he held that only observation
and mathematical analogy guided scientists towards new successful
hypotheses (See below, Chapter VIII, section D). I shall subsequently try to
refute this claim in as far as it pertains to metaphysical realism. But let us
now go back to the ungainsayable thesis that there might be a large gap
between the intuitive methodology which actually guided the scientist's
activity and the explicit philosophy which he may later have reconstructed
from his fallible memory. The distance between these two methodologies is
likely to be all the greater if the scientist feels compelled, long after the
moment of discovery, to defend his position in the face of various criti-

cisms. For example: Newton's claim to have induced his theory from indubitable facts may have been made in self-defense against the Cartesians' rejection of action-at-a-distance; and let us not forget that Newton himself shared such Cartesian misgivings about the reality of gravitational action. All the same: there remains an objective connection between Newton's explicit philosophy on the one hand, and his implicit methodology on the other; for the former is a crude and exaggerated version, i.e. a caricature of the latter. Since caricatures are relatively easy to grasp, both the historians and the philosophers can hope to learn something from the scientists' reconstructions of their own methods. For example: it is certainly true that despite being uninferrable from the phenomena, Newton's laws are more closely linked to observation and hence more refutable than their rivals. And when the latter are rigorously expressed, say in the form of a Cartesian vortex theory, they are immediately refuted by experience; that is, unless they be saved by ad hoc stratagems. By the same token, we understand why Newton refused to take his own ether hypothesis seriously; not really because it was not derivable from experience, but because it was ad hoc in the sense of not yielding any novel predictions.

Thus reconstructions are not a luxury but a matter of sheer necessity. Of course, an essential condition to be imposed on a reconstruction is that it be consistent with the accepted 'facts', no matter how these are defined. But this again poses the logical problem of how any question of consistency between the facts on the one hand, and some given methodology on the other, can arise. To repeat: methodologies consist either of prescriptive statements or of evaluative judgments constituted into systems of appraisal; they can consequently be neither refuted nor corroborated, let alone verified, by historical 'facts'. But to each methodology can be made to correspond the *value-free* thesis that great scientific breakthroughs took place in accordance with the tenets of the methodology in question. For example: to the inductivist prescription that one ought first to observe and then to 'induce' laws from experimental results, there corresponds the historical thesis that great scientific revolutions were actually achieved by thinkers who made new observations and then derived theories from them.

A historian who attributes an intuitive methodology to a scientist has naturally to do so in a manner compatible with what is generally known about the scientist's discoveries and publications. Consistency with the facts might look like a stringent condition, but it is alas very weak. For example: consider a historian who puts forward a methodology M to which a scientist S is assumed to have adhered *intuitively*. Thus S will in most cases be unable or unwilling to characterize M in general terms. Suppose it is found that in some situations S actually violated M. The historian can always adduce 'external' factors—of the psychological, sociological or even physiological kind—which 'explain' why S's actions did not conform to M. Thus mere consistency with the facts is a weak constraint, which is why the notion of a *rational reconstruction* becomes all-important. A consistent reconstruction is said to be rational if it reduces to a minimum the recourse to external factors for which no independent evidence can be offered; where 'external' means: not subsumed, either negatively or positively, by the methodology in question. Since the choice of problems is at least partly dictated by exogenous and hence by non-methodological factors, reconstructions cannot be entirely rational, but some are more rational than others. Thus a methodology provides a rationality principle whose role is to give a partial account of the scientists' behavior; and it is held to be undermined by the facts if it permits only a non-rational reconstruction of the history of science. Note that history can nonetheless remain value-free provided one essential condition be met: should the historian also be a philosopher of science, then he ought to avoid any intrusion of his own methodological evaluations into his *historiographical* text; or he should otherwise unambiguously indicate those passages in which *he* appraises some past event. Thus imputing a system of values to a scientist—who is an object of study—is and must remain value-free.

Let us now mention one or two methodologies which square badly with the development of the sciences. The version of inductivism according to which laws ought to be strictly deduced from the phenomena fails for purely logical reasons; for no universal proposition can be validly inferred from singular observation reports. Suppose however that the inductivist prescription be weakened to the following, more modest requirement: hypotheses ought to be inferred—whether validly or not—from experimental results. Two episodes in the history of science undermine this mitigated form of inductivism: Newton's espousal of the Absolute Time Hypothesis (ATH) and Einstein's discovery of the Special Theory of Relativity (STR). We have already explained why the ATH could not have been inferred from the facts; for as admitted by Newton himself, the phenomena involve only measured or relative time. But the ATH lies at the foundation of a confirmable, falsifiable and eventually falsified law; namely that of the addition of velocities. Thus banning the ATH on the grounds that it is not induced from the facts would reduce the empirical content of classical mechanics. In other words: the ATH should belong to the set A defined above; and yet the ATH is not characterized by inductivism as truly scientific.

Unlike strict inductivism, falsificationism is logically defensible but it also fails—for more subtle reasons. It asserts that the transition from one theory H_1 to another, H_2, represents progress if H_2 is unrefuted and has moreover greater corroborated content than H_1. According to this criterion, Newton's hypotheses unfortunately turn out to be as unacceptable as, say, astrology or alchemy. Alchemical speculation had of course long been recognized as untenable. But for their part, the Newtonians never succeeded in explaining the motions of the Moon or of Mercury's perihelion in a satisfactory manner; i.e. all conjunctions of Newton's laws and of acceptable descriptions of boundary conditions had fallen foul of experience. It could of course be maintained that when taken in isolation, the Newtonian hypothesis is in fact irrefutable and was therefore unfalsified; which would however mean that Newton's laws are metaphysical and hence cannot— from a falsificationist viewpoint—represent *scientific* progress. At the intuitive level, we are nonetheless deeply convinced that the transition from Copernicus to Newton, not to speak of that from Nostradamus to Newton, was a giant step forward and must therefore fall within the set A. Thus falsificationism breaks down because it fails to characterize the very core of A as progressive.

Let us now consider the case of STR (Special Theory of Relativity). Both from the inductivist and from the falsificationist viewpoint, Michelson's experiment should have played a crucial role in demonstrating that STR was a great improvement over classical mechanics. If we are to believe Reichenbach, Michelson's result inductively established Einstein's second postulate about the invariance of the velocity of light c (Reichenbach 1958, p. 201). Bachelard, who was a falsificationist of sorts, held that Michelson carried out one of the most impressive refuting experiments of all time. Bachelard went on to claim that 'For him [Einstein], the experimental failure of a technique thus scientifically pursued suggested the need for new theoretical information' (Bachelard 1949, pp. 567–68). Einstein himself admitted having read Lorentz's (1895) in which Michelson's experiment is not only discussed but also explained in a non-ad hoc classical way. Einstein moreover consistently denied that Michelson's results played any inspirational role in the genesis of STR. A historian according to whom Einstein was either an inductivist or a falsificationist could say that the latter was simply lying or that he had forgotten the real origins of STR. Holton however convincingly showed that throughout his life Einstein, though an admirer of Michelson, had always stopped short of saying that the discovery of STR had anything to do with Michelson's celebrated experiment (Holton 1969). Thus both the inductivist

and the falsificationist are left with the hypothesis that Einstein systematically lied throughout his life about the heuristic role of Michelson's result.
All that can be said in favor of this explanation is that it is *logically* possible; but the behavior attributed to Einstein is out of character with somebody
known for his intellectual honesty and who, in other circumstances, freely
admitted his debt to other scientists. So the inductivist and falsificationist
accounts are consistent with the facts but there exists no independent evidence for the psychological assumption that despite being otherwise an honest man, Einstein had always lied about the important heuristic role of
Michelson's experiment. There is of course another solution open both to the
inductivist and to the falsificationist historians; they could accept that
Einstein was telling the truth while assuming that some external factor
caused Einstein to act irrationally, i.e. to violate the cannons of inductivism,
viz. of falsificationism. But while such historians would have to specify
these external factors and find some independent evidence for their existence, the historian who presupposes MSRP needs resort to no external considerations at all; he simply takes note of the following fact: Einstein realized
that classical physics postulates theoretical asymmetries which never surface
at the observational level. To adopt Alain Boyer's formulation, it seemed as
though some malicious demon was bent on systematically deceiving us
about the deep structure of reality; so that Relativity proved to be the best
way of ridding both Mechanics and Electrodynamics of this demon, i.e. of
this conspiracy theory (See Boyer 1997). Since the rejection of conspiracy
theories is part and parcel of MSRP, Einstein's evaluative judgments can be
explained internally, i.e. without adducing non-rational factors.

(C) Is Methodology Immutable?

There is one further difficulty besetting our approach to determining a
methodology. In reconstructing the development of the sciences, might not
the historian find himself compelled to impute different methodologies to
different scientists, or even to the same scientist at different points of his
career? Einstein himself conceded that from the philosopher's perspective, the physicist must appear like a lawless opportunist when deciding on
the most fruitful path to discovery (Einstein 1994a, p. 296). And
Feyerabend strongly defended the thesis that there have been not only
numerous scientific, but also many methodological revolutions. He maintained that should methodologies be considered prescriptive and hence
non-vacuous, then they must go beyond mere logic; i.e. they will have synthetic presuppositions. The latter might well change over time, thus induc-

ing an alteration of the correlated methodology (Feyerabend 1972b). Two examples will illustrate this point. Assume we live in an Aristotelian world consisting of finitely many kinds, or even of a finite number of entities; then the decried ad hoc method of fitting parameters to known facts will be perfectly acceptable, for it can in principle lead us to the discovery of all true laws. Alternatively: suppose we adopt Popper's view that science should aim at the truth while avoiding ad hoc maneuvers. In order for these two aims to be compatible, the universe must have been constructed according to some unified plan; so that a proposition like 'All planets except for Mars move along ellipses; but the path of Mars is a square' can be dismissed out of hand as standing little chance of being true. Thus if we are to believe Feyerabend, all methodologies must be dependent on cosmological assumptions (See Feyerabend 1975). This thesis has admittedly a superficial air of plausibility about it. But when its author goes on to claim that before deciding on a methodology, we ought critically to examine the underlying cosmology, he falls into the most vicious of circles; for beyond trivial logical considerations, there is no hope of appraising a cosmology prior to determining the methodology intended to deliver the very instruments of appraisal. In this connection, note that MSRP will be shown to be metaphysics-free: for it puts metaphysical, and hence all cosmological speculation in the hard core of a research program; so that when the latter is assessed—by logical and empirical means—all the components of the hard core are thereby indirectly appraised. No metaphysical theory can therefore rise above the logico-empirical fray. This is one reason why the construction of MSRP was directly based on the singular value-judgments of those people who, by common accord, are held to be great scientists. Without a consensus at this level, there can be no meaningful debate between methodologists. Abstracting provisionally from all normative considerations, MSRP could alternatively be seen as providing a unified characterization of a set of singular appraisals. From a naturalistic viewpoint, MSRP can therefore be construed as a general law subsuming a number of special cases; the latter being regarded as instances of the application of some overriding norm.

Feyerabend deems this method inapplicable—on the grounds that the value-judgments of different scientists concerning the same achievement are often incompatible. For example, the reasons given by Duhem are incompatible with those adduced by Born for the preference given to the Newtonian hypothesis over its rivals: Born claims Newton's theory to have been induced from the 'facts', as described by Kepler's laws; whereas Duhem, who denies the very possibility of such an inductive inference, holds that the Newtonian system, being a more natural classification of the phenomena than its rivals, is preferable to the latter (See Feyerabend 1980; also Born 1964; and Zahar 1989, Chapter 1). Feyerabend's objection however results from a total misunderstanding of the method used in arriving at MSRP. In conformity with Einstein's advice expressed in the quotation above, what is relevant to constructing a methodology is not the *reason given by a scientist* for choosing certain theories but only the bare *fact* that he did choose them. The rationalizations put forward by various scientists anyway involve *general* criteria; so they cannot be the *singular* value-judgments used to test a normative system. By claiming that Newtonian theory is superior to its competitors *because it is induced from the facts*, Born is in effect propounding an inductivist methodology, which incidentally conflicts with Newton's own scientific practice. To repeat: what is relevant to MSRP is the *simple fact* that Newton and Born, Lagrange and Laplace, Duhem and Poincaré, etc. considered Newton's hypothesis superior to its rivals. And to repeat: the task of methodology is to bring to the surface—by means of a general characterization—the deep-seated reasons for this quasi-uniform preference. This is a non-trivial enterprise if only because the explicit reasons given by different thinkers for the *same preference* differ so widely. In other words: if a methodology succeeds in providing a unified *explication* of progress which subsumes all considered cases, then it is reasonable to suppose that apart from its normative role, such a methodology yields a psychological *explanation* of the scientists' agreement over *singular* value-judgments; whence the relevance of methodology to history, which nonetheless remains of secondary importance.

Methodology relates to the empirical sciences in somewhat the same way as logic relates to mathematics. Mathematicians proved theorems and accepted or rejected alleged proofs long before logic was rigorously formulated; and yet the Aristotelian syllogistic, i.e. the only logic then available, could not accommodate the mathematics of the time. We nevertheless know that the old valid proofs—and there are many of them—can in fact be formalized within modern first-order logic. Hence there are good reasons for supposing that even in those early days, mathematicians had a good intuitive grasp of the structure of first-order proofs. One can therefore *apply* a universal criterion without being able to characterize it in *general* terms; which does not of course exclude the possibility for the construction of a general definition of enhancing the scientists' capacity for deriving new theorems. Thus, when interpreted in a naturalistic way, MSRP entails that the presystematic methodology used by scientists in order to judge particular achievements did not change all that much over the centuries, say from

Greek Antiquity to the present day. Of course, the definition of a methodology does not presuppose absolute stability, but only the assumption that
deviations from the norms laid down have been in the nature of local fluctuations very different in magnitude from large-scale scientific revolutions.
After all, even Aristotelian *Logic* was not only extended but also altered,
albeit slightly; for example: the formula $[(\forall x)(P(x) \rightarrow Q(x)) \rightarrow (\exists x)$
$(P(x) \wedge Q(x))]$, as distinct from $[(\forall x)(P(x) \rightarrow Q(x)) \rightarrow (\exists x)(P(x) \rightarrow Q(x))]$,
is no longer held to be universally valid; and logicians still argue as to
whether the laws of distributivity, of double negation and of the excluded
middle ought generally to be accepted. But some minimal or basic logic
has been presupposed; with the result there exists a family resemblance
between Aristotelian and modern classical logic.

The postulate that there have been no methodological upheavals on a
par with scientific revolutions might of course prove too strong; yet the stability thesis remains an interesting working hypothesis which ought to be
further investigated. It is a matter both for historical research and for philosophical reflection to decide whether scientists have, by and large, implicitly subscribed to MSRP or to some other unified methodological system
yet to be formulated. Many philosophers anyway have the strong presump-
tion that, like presystematic logic, intuitive methodology has largely been
stable; so they feel entitled to wonder whether any rationale for such stability exists. One way of accounting for a constant feature of human behavior is to find a biological correlate or a biological function of the constant
in question. The relative stability of our biological make-up, as contrasted
with the numerous social and cultural changes which the human race has
gone through, might then explain the constancy of the considered feature.
Given the role of natural selection in biology, it is not far-fetched to assume
that the theory of evolution might yield answers to some epistemological
questions. Evolutionary solutions of the problem of knowledge have been
given by Mach, Meyerson, Popper and Piaget. For example: in his (1907)
Émile Meyerson maintained that most animal species depend for their survival on their capacity for anticipating certain events. Such high survival
value might therefore explain why the prediction of hitherto unknown facts
was always held to be a mark of excellence in any explanatory hypothesis.
Already in Ancient Greece, the ability to predict facts was highly admired;
and though strongly denying the stability thesis, Feyerabend himself conceded that the allegedly new methodology of the modern scientific revolution had its ancestors in Antiquity. Thus intuitive methodology may well
have been stable over time. This is however a topic which goes well beyond
the scope of the present work.

(D) Heuristics and the Definition of MSRP

One failing of falsificationism is its inability to account for continuity in scientific research. A refuting experiment may tell the physicist that his conjecture is false, but it gives him no clue as to what to do next. This is why, in his logic of discovery Popper remains silent about heuristics or rather about any methodological appraisal of heuristics. It has already been shown that the device of parameter-adjustment yields a method for the construction of new laws, albeit of ad hoc ones. More generally: it has often been felt that there are, and have always been different schools of thought among scientists; for example: the school of Cartesian Mechanists, Newtonian Dynamicists, Electrodynamicists, Relativists, Quantum Theorists, etc. It is well known that these groups approach problems and theory-construction in distinctly different ways. The same considerations naturally apply to the arts where there are, for example, the classical, the impressionist, the cubist and the expressionist schools of painting. In certain situations, it can even be ascertained whether a given artist is a 'genuine' impressionist or merely a precursor, i.e. whether or not his paintings contain elements alien to impressionism; so that speaking about artistic eclecticism is often felt to be justified. Methodology can similarly be expected to account for the continuity in the development of the sciences. But for most of the past century, it was very much part of epistemological orthodoxy that there was no room left for rational heuristics. Popper, Reichenbach and other members of the Vienna Circle agreed about the alleged existence of a sharp distinction between the 'context of discovery' and the 'context of justification'. Only the latter was supposed to lie within the domain of methodology whose proper task is to evaluate hypotheses laid on the table, i.e. theories already constructed. As for the context of discovery, it belongs to the psychology of invention. Neither calling for nor even being susceptible of any rational reconstruction, the process of discovery allegedly rests on what Einstein called 'empathy with nature'. In his (1979) Popper gave an account of the emergence of new hypotheses which he linked to his overall Darwinian world-view: if new theories prove to be explanatory of certain facts, this is due not to any goal-oriented efforts on the scientists' part but to the superabundance of available theories. New conjectures emerge like spontaneous mutations most of which are experimentally falsified, hence subsequently rejected; but given the constant overproduction of hypotheses, some of these will survive. In Popper's words:

. . . There exists no *law-like dependence* between receptions, [i.e.] between new objective conditions, and the emergence of reactions (or rather, there is only *one* form of dependence, namely the *selective* one, which renders the non-adaptive reactions worthless and forces the organism to come up with something new or else go under—a form of dependence). (Popper 1979, p. 27. My translation)

Thus progress is alleged to follow negatively from the elimination, by a process resembling natural selection, of defective alternatives. As for the positive adaptation of laws to facts, it is the effect of chance; there is no intended fit between theory and reality. Only overproduction increases the probability for certain conjectures to escape refutation while simultaneously explaining the past successes of their predecessors. Hence there is really no logic of discovery, only a psychology of invention juxtaposed to a methodology whose only task is to appraise fully fledged theories.

Despite the old orthodoxy, some philosophers have suggested that there is room for some form of heuristics in physical science. It is well known that Kuhn tried to account for continuity in research by means of the twin concepts of paradigm and of normal science. Paradigms provide frameworks—consisting largely of shared assumptions and of puzzle-solving techniques—within which normal science evolves. Kuhn does not however indicate whether his approach is intended to be purely descriptive or to contain normative elements; and he does not tell us exactly how the same 'logic of appraisal' and the same methods of discovery are applied within a given paradigm. All we are asked to accept is the negative fact that there can be no notion of scientific progress cutting across paradigms.

It is my claim that MSRP takes over the positive aspects of Popper's falsificationism together with some of Kuhn's valuable insights, then unifies these elements in a content-increasing way. MSRP is a synthesis which transcends both the Popperian thesis and the Kuhnian antithesis; a synthesis which accounts for the continuity in the development of the sciences in terms of comprehensive research programs. Every research program, or RP for short, is characterized by a hard core and a positive heuristic giving rise to a sequence of hypotheses: H_1, H_2,..... The hard core K of the RP is a conjunction of propositions shared by all the H_n's; that is: $H_n \Rightarrow K$ for all n. The positive heuristic consists of directives, possibly deriving from a metaphysical principle which guides research by indicating the method by which new theories are to be constructed and the manner in which the program should deal with empirical refutations. Thus the development of an RP is governed simultaneously by its hard core and by its positive heuristic; each member of the RP is subject to two conditions: it should logically imply the hard core K while conforming to the positive heuristic (henceforth referred to simply as the heuristic); all of which accounts for the continuous evolution of the sciences. Lakatos's view, which will be contested below, is that K is protected against refutation by the *methodological decision* of never holding it to be falsified even in cases of empirical refutation; Lakatos called this immunization policy 'the negative heuristic of the RP', a terminology which will, as far as possible, be avoided (Lakatos 1978a, p. 50).

Although the hard core and the heuristic do not uniquely determine the sequence of theories H_1, H_2,..., they constitute a genuine logic of discovery; for they provide hints as to what to do in a period of crisis. Lakatos regarded this kind of heuristics as belonging to a limbo half-way between logic and psychology (See Lakatos, 1970). He did not however make this suggestion of a semi-rational heuristics precise. In this chapter, I shall try to remedy this defect by presenting a deductivist thesis which, though strictly inconsistent with Lakatos's position, is in the spirit of his philosophy, while remaining compatible with an non-inductivist view of scientific discovery.

Already at this stage, I should sound a word of warning by sharply distinguishing between two problems. The first concerns the possibility of rationally reconstructing the process of discovery; the second pertains to the question whether such a reconstruction has any role to play in the appraisal of theories after the latter have been generated. We shall see in what sense Popper and Reichenbach were right in answering the second question in the negative. As for the first, I intend to show that the process of discovery is much more rational than it appears at first sight; that it is neither inductive nor purely intuitive; that it does not belong to any kind of limbo but largely rests on deductive arguments from principles which underlie not only science and metaphysics, but also everyday decisions. Different choices of consistent sets of such principles constitute the heuristics of various RP's. Thus I hope to underline the continuity between scientific and commonsense knowledge while showing that the heuristics of RP's operate, not in any mysterious way but deductively —or rather meta-deductively.

(E) THE HARD CORE AS METAPHYSICAL HEURISTIC

As mentioned above, Lakatos claimed that only through a methodological decision does the hard core of a program become unassailable, i.e. observationally irrefutable (Lakatos 1978, p. 50). He was thereby being consistent both with Popper's theses and with his own; for we have seen that according to the former, the basic statements through which a theory is tested are arrived at by a conventional decision; from which it clearly follows that any putative falsifier of the hard core can legitimately be rejected. But having vindicated the phenomenological view of the empirical basis, we are now in a position to assert that independently of any stipulation, every proposition either *is* or *is not* observational; hence every proposition either *is* or *is not* metaphysical. Thus, in order for the hard core to be held on to come what may, it must be unfalsifiable, i.e. metaphysical in some absolute sense. Moreover, the requirement that the hard core be *per se* irrefutable establishes a close connection between MSRP and Popper's notion of a metaphysical research program.

It is a distinctive feature of Popper's philosophy that it replaced the analysis of concepts by an examination of the status of propositions. According to classical empiricist epistemology, e.g. the theory of knowledge professed by Hume and then by Mach, an entity was said to be metaphysical if it could be neither observed nor operationally determined; whence Mach's and Bridgman's operationalist stances regarding all scientific hypotheses. A proposition could then be termed metaphysical in a derivative or secondary sense; more precisely: in the sense of involving 'occult' entities (See Bridgman 1936). By contrast, Popper directly addresses the status of propositions which are declared metaphysical if they possess no empirically decidable consequences. Thus, by virtue of the quantifiers occurring in it, a statement containing only observational predicates might well turn out to be metaphysical. For example, let $P(x, y, t)$ stand for the proposition that the two substances x and y are such that y dissolves x at time t. Then $(\forall x)(\exists y, t)P(x, y, t)$, which asserts that all substances are soluble, is clearly metaphysical.

At first sight, the difference between these two approaches to the problem of metaphysics might seem academic. It nonetheless plays a crucial role in demarcating science from non-science. For example: Mach regarded both Newton's ATH (Absolute Time Hypothesis) and his ASH (Absolute Space Hypothesis) as totally inadmissible on the grounds that these two assumptions involve 'monstrous' metaphysical concepts. But Mach never managed to ban such abstract notions from Classical Mechanics while simultaneously preserving the latter's empirical content. One reason for his failure was his inability to grasp the vast *empirical* difference between the ATH and the ASH. It can in fact easily be shown that the ATH is essential to the derivation of the addition law of velocities; i.e. of a law which is not only testable but whose actual refutation, by Michelson, lent support to STR. Thus let us start by writing down the well-known Galilean transformation equation $x' = x-ut$, where x' is the abscissa in the moving frame. Differentiating with respect to "*the* time", obtain $(dx'/dt) = (dx/dt) - u$, which is taken to be equivalent to $v? = v - u$, i.e. to the addition law of velocities: $v = v' + u$. The relations $(dx'/dt) = v' =_{Def.} (dx'/dt')$, which presuppose $dt = dt'$, are therefore implicitly assumed. Now note that the last equation is nothing but the formal rendering of the ATH, i.e. of the absoluteness of all time-intervals. Hence the addition law depends, in an essential way, on the assumed *absoluteness* of all temporal distances between events (In this context, I have insisted on the notion of *distance* which was later applied by the Relativists to the interval between any two spatio-temporal points).

The Newtonian concept of space has a very different function from that of absolute time. As already mentioned: since the classical Laws of Mechanics are Galileo-invariant, they do not single out any 'absolute' member from the set of all inertial systems. Thus the extra assumption that among the latter there exists a privileged frame is metaphysical in that it adds nothing to the empirical content of classical science; so that it makes *empirical* sense to say of two events that they are simultaneous but not that they occur at the same point of space. Newtonian Time is, so to speak, much more absolute than its spatial counterpart. Thus we have two notions which are unjustifiably treated on a par by traditional empiricist epistemology, but are clearly demarcated by Popper's criterion: whereas the ASH is untestable, the ATH contributes to the degree of falsifiability of classical physics and is therefore scientific. It should be added that Newton himself appears to have been aware of this asymmetry: in Corollary V of the *Principia*, he proves that his laws assume the same form whether the underlying spatial frame be regarded as at rest or in a state of uniform rectilinear motion in Absolute Space (See Newton 1686, Book 1). As for the absoluteness of time, Newton had taken the ATH so much for granted that he did not bother to mention it explicitly. This is not to deny that he also had sound *philosophical*, as distinct from *scientific* reasons for adjoining the ASH to his system: in order for the law of inertia to be intelligible, the impetus or quantity of motion $m\underline{v}$ of a particle had to be made into an attribute of the mobile; the velocity had consequently to be treated as a property of the moving body. But by virtue of the addition law, velocities change from one frame to another. Absolute Space, i.e. a unique frame in which the body would assume its genuine state of motion, had therefore to be posited. Note finally that unlike velocities, accelerations are Galileo-invariant; so even though the postulation of an absolute frame be scientifically expendable, that of a privileged set of inertial systems is not; for only by appealing to the Earth's acceleration against *any* inertial system had Newton succeeded in explaining the flattening of the Earth at the poles. Seen from this perspective, STR is just as 'absolute' as Classical Mechanics; for Einstein also presupposes the existence of a class of inertial frames, whose transformation group is however not that of Galileo but of Lorentz.

The Vienna Circle regarded the above arguments in support of metaphysics as lacking sense; whereas Popper would certainly have held them to be not only meaningful but also highly significant; for according to falsificationism, the difference between physics and metaphysics is no longer the unbridgeable gap between sense and nonsense but the simple difference—in degree rather than kind—between the testable and the irrefutable. As mentioned in Chapter I, Popperian philosophy can thus be said to have largely rehabilitated metaphysics. One essential question however remains: is metaphysics at all answerable to experience?

After taking cognizance of Tarski's truth-definition, Popper realized that syntactically well-formed sentences could be regarded true-or-false without necessarily having to be effectively verifiable or even refutable; more particularly: a metaphysical thesis ought by right to possess a definite, though possibly undecidable truth-value. So Popper felt entitled to affirm the existence, within the history of science, of *metaphysical research programs*, more particularly of those based on one version or other of realism. For example: though initially advanced as a solution to the philosophical problem of being and non-being, Greek Atomism, was gradually turned into a testable hypothesis (See below, Chapter VIII). But what do the words 'turned into' mean in this context? Do modern atomic theories entail, or are they vaguely similar to, the conjectures entertained by the Presocratics? Furthermore: does an experiment which corroborates a theory belonging to a program also support the metaphysics underpinning the program?

Popper did not properly ask, let alone satisfactorily tackle these questions which have largely been answered by MSRP. The thesis that the hard core K of an RP is a metaphysical principle entailed by every member of the program has been vindicated; so the sustained empirical success of an RP can legitimately be claimed to lend some support—if only an indirect one—to its hard core. Conversely, the repeated failure of a program must negatively reflect on its metaphysics. MSRP thus renders the latter accountable to experience. It is not enough for a metaphysical conjecture C to be both coherent and compatible with all accepted scientific systems in order for it to become credible; C must furthermore belong to the core of an empirically successful RP. While keeping an open mind, we therefore ought to be as severe with respect to metaphysics as with respect to science proper. For example: classical science can be held to have supported meta-physical determinism. Similarly: had all their predictions been verified, then unified field theories would have confirmed—though not verified—the Cartesian geometrical conception of physical nature. As against these developments: in as far as it remains the most successful explanation of subatomic phenomena and as long as the most coherent interpretations of its laws are statistical, Quantum Mechanics will continue to support indeterminism at the micro-level; thus it undermines the classical notion of causality, even though, thanks to the Correspondence Principle, determinism still—roughly—obtains at the macro-level. In this way, the development of the sciences is legitimately accompanied by an evolving view of ontology.

Let us remind ourselves that the heuristic of an RP is the motive force of scientific progress. Thus in order for the heuristic to be methodologically appraised, it must somehow be connected to the core, i.e. to the metaphysic underpinning the program. It is my claim that certain components of the hard core have prescriptive counterparts which can in turn be translated into meta-statements about scientific hypotheses; for an ontological thesis clearly imposes constraints on the form assumed by every theory which purports to be a true description of reality. Such constraints form the heuristic of an RP. Hence *metaphysics can be taken to possess prescriptive import*. Should we moreover want the heuristic to operate *deductively* by providing premises for the logical determination of theories, then it is imperative that such prescriptions be translated into propositions, or rather into meta-principles. Thus, we have the following scheme:

**Metaphysics (Hard Core) → Prescriptions →
Meta-Principles (Positive Heuristic)**

The heuristic will therefore reflect certain aspects of the hard core; so the distinction between *negative* and *positive* heuristic is not as sharp as Lakatos seemed to think. Let me give two examples. Part of the ether program's hard core was the thesis that physical reality consists of one medium possessing electro-mechanical properties; whence the prescription that theories should derive all phenomena from the states of the ether. The corresponding meta-principle is that all laws of nature contain only the concepts of position, time, mass and charge. As for STR, it is based on the meta-physical proposition that no privileged inertial frames exist; which leads to the prescription that all hypotheses should assume the same form in all inertial frames. The corresponding meta-statement is that all genuine laws of nature are Lorentz-covariant.

(F) NOVELTY OF FACTS

Before embarking on any general discussion, let us consider a few concrete examples of what are intuitively taken to be novel facts predicted by a hypothesis. Lakatos mentions the return of Halley's comet as a new fact anticipated by the Newtonian program; and it has of course to be agreed that the discovery of any new (type of) fact must be novel. But we have already seen that the converse need not hold; for if we equate novelty with newness, i.e. with *temporal novelty*, then we are driven into a paradoxical situation. Going back to some examples cited in Chapter IV: we should have to give Einstein no credit for explaining the anomalous precession of Mercury's perihelion since this fact was 'old hat'; it had been recorded and fitted into a curve long before GTR was put forward. Similarly, we should say that Michelson's results did not corroborate STR, that Tycho Brahe's data did not confirm Kepler's laws, that neither the latter nor Galileo's experiments on projectiles supported Newton's gravitational theory, etc.; all of which are highly counter-intuitive value-judgments. Lakatos was aware of this difficulty; so he tried to circumvent it through shifting his original view by holding that *in the light of a new theory,* known facts may turn into novel ones. Like Feyerabend, Lakatos was thereby drawing a natural conclusion from Popper's views about the so-called theory-ladenness of observation statements; from which it follows that a change in theory may result in a change of fact. We have already refuted this thesis in Chapter III; but we can now add another fatal objection to it. Every scientific system is a set of propositions connecting different terms and concepts; so the properties of any physical object must include the relations it bears to all other entities within a given theory. On this interpretation, every new hypothesis will, as a rule, ascribe new meanings to old terms; so that practically every old fact will automatically be turned into a novel one. Thus the addition of every new epicycle to Ptolemy's system might transform the most prosaic and well-known observation report into a novel one; which again goes against the methodological judgment of most scientists. Similarly: by expanding a function in terms of spherical harmonics and then adjusting the coefficients of the expansion, the precession of Mercury's perihelion can be accounted for within Newtonian physics (See Adler-Bazin Schiffer 1965, Chapter VI, 6.6). Are we then to count Mercury's motion as a novel fact predicted by Newton? This again is an intuitively inadmissible conclusion.

In Chapter IV it was proved that conjectures can be adapted to known facts by means of parameter-adjustment. Hence the latter constitutes an important heuristic principle, albeit one which systematically leads to the construction of ad hoc hypotheses. More generally: in view of what was said above about the connection between hard core and heuristic, metaphysical principles might well determine a physical theory to within certain constants; the latter might then be fixed by means of observations which, being implicated in the construction of a hypothesis, cannot legitimately be regarded as strongly confirming the latter. The way in which a theory is constructed is therefore relevant to the appraisal of its empirical merits; for if we are given only some theoretical end-product H which subsumes the fact e, we shall generally be unable to decide whether e lends strong support to H or whether H was cleverly engineered to yield e. This suggests the following characterization of a 'novel fact':

[*] *A fact will be considered novel with respect to a hypothesis yielding it if it was not objectively used in the construction of the hypothesis.*

Any temporally new experimental result e will of course be novel with respect to any theory H yielding e, since H could not have been proposed in the light of e. Temporal novelty is thus a sufficient but not a necessary condition of novelty. A genuinely *new* fact may have greater psychological *impact* than some known result; but this, on its own, has no relevance to the objective empirical support which it might lend to a hypothesis.

In order to make the above concept of novelty more precise, a few definitions will be needed. A singular hypothetical statement of the form $(b{\rightarrow}p)$, where b describes some boundary conditions and p expresses a prediction, will be called an empirical implication; and the proposition $(b{\wedge}p)$ will be referred to as the corresponding basic statement. We shall take b and p to be empirically decidable without narrowly specifying the nature of these propositions; and hence without, for the time being, deciding whether or not they are to be level-0 reports.

It follows from [*] that empirical non-ad-hocness is a three-place relation $\Gamma(\beta, H, e)$ between a heuristic ß, a hypothesis H and a fact described by a basic statement e; where e is of the form $e \equiv (b{\wedge}p)$. $\Gamma(\beta, H, e)$ obtains if and only if: $H \Rightarrow (b \rightarrow p)$, where H is constructed in accordance with ß, *and* ß does not (objectively) involve the use of e, i.e. of $(b{\wedge}p)$ or of $(b{\rightarrow}p)$, in the construction of H. If e is moreover verified, then e will support not H alone, but H and ß jointly; the couple (ß, H) will then be said to explain e in a non-ad hoc way.

Here we must guard against a danger of trivialization to which Peter Lipton rightly draws our attention in his (2004). He writes:

... the main weakness of the hypothetico-deductive model is that it is over-permissive, counting almost any datum as evidence for almost any hypothesis. The deductive-nomological model similarly makes it far too easy to explain. . . This comes out most clearly if we consider the explanation of a general phenomenon, which is itself described by a law. Suppose, for example, that we wish to explain why the planets move in ellipses. According to the deductive-nomological model, we can explain the 'ellipse' law by deducing it from the conjunction of itself and any law you please, say a law in economics. (Lipton 2004, p. 27)

Lipton has put his finger on a major difficulty—known as the tacking paradox—which confronts hypothetico-deductivism. In terms of our notation, this can be rendered as follows. Let H be any explanation, or more generally any account of the fact described by the statement e $\equiv$ (b$\wedge$p). That is: H $\Rightarrow$ (b $\to$ p). Then, for an arbitrary proposition M, we also have (M$\wedge$H) $\Rightarrow$ (b $\to$ p). It would however be absurd to claim that e supports the whole of (M$\wedge$H), for M might have nothing to do either with H or with (b $\to$ p). In the simple tacking case, it can admittedly be seen that only H is involved in the derivation of (b $\to$ p); the paradox could therefore be blocked by the removal of M. But the tacking paradox is only the small tip of a large iceberg. For example: let M be any unverifiable metaphysical principle. By definition, M is also irrefutable. The hypothesis (M$\wedge$H) can be regarded as axiomatized by {M, M $\to$ H}; with the result that M is now implicated, in an essential way, in the deduction of (b $\to$ p) from {M, M $\to$ H}; for on its own, M does not entail (b $\to$ p) since M would otherwise be falsifiable, namely by (b$\wedge\neg$p); it is moreover impossible that we should have (M $\to$ H) $\Rightarrow$ (b $\to$ p); for otherwise: (b$\wedge\neg$p) $\Rightarrow$ $\neg$(M $\to$ H) $\Leftrightarrow$ (M$\wedge\neg$H) $\Rightarrow$ M; thus, contrary to our assumption, M would be verifiable by one empirically decidable basic statement, namely by (b$\wedge\neg$p). Both M and (M$\to$H) are consequently needed in order first to deduce H and then, by way of H, to account for e.

At this point let me recall that all these stratagems are blocked by the notion of *natural axiomatization* which I introduced in my (1991). (See also Zahar 2001, Appendix II). Putting it simply: an axiom system Ω for a theory H is said to be natural if Ω is logically independent and if no member of Ω has a proper component which is a theorem of H (Ω is said to be logically independent if no member X of Ω is entailed by $\Omega \setminus \{X\}$). Let us show that no hypothesis H is excluded by this syntactical requirement. Thus suppose that A[B] $\in$ Ω, where B is a component of A[B] such that $\Omega \not\vdash$ B; i.e. such that H $\Rightarrow$ B. Then, without in any way altering H, B can be added to

Ω while A[T] is substituted for A[B], T being an arbitrary tautology. This process can be repeated until a natural axiomatization of H is obtained. Now note that no conjunction is an allowable axiom; for the latter logically implies each of its conjuncts and is therefore 'unnatural'. Thus {M∧H} is not a permissible axiomatization of M∧H. By the method just described, {M∧H} has to be replaced first by {M∧T, H}, then by {T∧T, M, H}, and finally by {M, H} since the tautology T∧T is not logically independent of {M, H}. Thus, instead of (M∧H) $\Rightarrow$ (b → p), we shall write {M, H} $\vdash$ (b → p). Similarly: {M, M → H} offends against naturalness since both M and H are theorems of {M, M → H} and components of M → H. Hence {M, M → H} has to be replaced first by {M, M → T, H}, then by {M, T → T, M, H}, and finally by {M, H} in order for {M, T → T, M, H} to be reduced to a logically independent set. Note that (b → p) follows from a proper sub-class of the axiom set {M, H}, namely from {H} alone; so that M is now clearly seen to be superfluous. By eliminating the superfluous axioms, we obtain {H} $\vdash$ (b → p). These considerations lead us to propose the following convention. Whenever we say of a theory H that it explains or, more generally, that it yields the fact e $\equiv$ (b∧p), we shall henceforth mean the following: H is a universal proposition possessing a *natural* set of axioms Ω such that: $\Omega \vdash$ (b → p) and Not [$\Omega_0 \vdash$ (b → p)] for all proper subsets Ω_0 of Ω; i.e. for all $\Omega_0 \subset \Omega$. This last condition is meant to block the introduction of superfluous premises. (Note that this definition is independent of whether or not H is ad hoc with respect to e).

Going back to the comparison between rival research programs: it is conceivable for two programs Π_1 and Π_2 possessing different heuristics, ß$_1$ and ß$_2$ say, to give rise to the same theory H; and for a fact e to provide strong support for (ß$_2$, H) but not for (ß$_1$, H). In other words: it is possible that Γ(ß$_2$, H, e) but not Γ(ß$_1$, H, e) should hold good. It is therefore more appropriate to speak of an inductive support lent by e to a whole program Π than to an isolated hypothesis H belonging to Π. A first example illustrating this point is that in which Π_1 and Π_2 are the Ptolemaic and the Copernican program respectively, where the former is given its Tychonic formulation; H is a general description of Venus's motion about the earth, and e any basic statement about either the bounded elongation or one of the phases of Venus; in which case H and e are common to Π_1 and Π_2. Yet, according to [*], e clearly and justifiably supports Π_2 but not Π_1. A more problematic example is that in which Π_2 and ß$_2$ are the Relativistic Research Program and Einstein's heuristic respectively; H will denote the Fitzgerald, as distinct from the Lorentz-Fitzgerald, Contraction Hypothesis, and e the result of Michelson's experiment. Γ(ß$_2$, H, e), but not Γ(ß, H, e), would then be satisfied, where ß is the ad hoc method of construction actually used by Fitzgerald. By contrast, both $\Gamma(ß_2, M, e)$ and $\Gamma(ß_1, M, e)$ hold good, where M is the Maxwell-Lorentz theory and $ß_1$ the classical heuristic used by Lorentz in order to explain e (See Zahar 1989, Chapter 2). Thus one and the same hypothesis could find itself at the confluent of two different RP's and might, as a consequence, receive different degrees of support from the same fact. As forcefully pointed out by Leplin, such relativization to programs confronts us with what appears to be a major difficulty: in technology, we have to choose, not between programs, but between competing theories. The solution to this problem is however fairly straightforward; all we have to do is maximize over all the available methods of construction of a given hypothesis H; or even over all the methods judged to be applicable at the time when H was advanced. Thus e will be said to be novel with regard to H *simpliciter* if and only if $\Gamma(ß, H, e)$ holds for at least one ß. In other words: from among all the marks that can justifiably be given to H, the highest one will naturally be chosen.

Criterion [*] implies that the traditional methods of historical research are vital for evaluating experimental support. The historian has to read the private correspondence of the scientist whose ideas he is studying; his purpose will however not be to delve into the psyche of the scientist but to disentangle the heuristic reasoning used by the latter in order to arrive at some new conjecture. Putting it a little differently: the historian has to identify the RP within which the scientist was working. This reconstruction is necessary because only finished theories, as opposed to the heuristic methods leading to them, appear in published form.

It may of course look as though [*] yields a psychologistic, even a person-relative definition of evidential support. But in section (A) of Chapter IV, it has already been shown that the method of adjusting parameters to observational results is an objective one. It might however prove necessary to adjust more abstract mathematical entities, e.g. matrices and operators, to known facts. This is why it seemed preferable to adopt the more general, though admittedly less precise definition [*] of the novelty of predictions. To repeat: this definition should be given an objective construal. Thus Popper and Reichenbach were in a sense right in distinguishing between two contexts, one of discovery and the other of justification; for in the methodological appraisal of scientific hypotheses, it is not the genesis of a theory as such but certain logical relations which play a central role. In certain cases, it can mathematically be proved that the presence of sufficiently many open parameters guarantees that a finite set of facts, which were actually used, could unfailingly be accommodated within a scheme of a given form; for the number of the unknowns was at least equal to that of the independent equations. Since a mathematical theorem tells us nothing about physical reality, the facts which help towards constructing a theory cannot also strongly support it.

(G) A Definition of Scientific Progress

The concept of scientific progress can now be explicated by means of Criterion [*]. Let H_1 and B_2 be hypotheses belonging to the two programs Π_1 and Π_2, whose heuristics are again denoted by β_1 and β_2 respectively. Note that Π_1 need not be distinct from Π_2; so that we shall be able to define progress within one and the same RP (In what follows, it is naturally assumed that each of H_1 and B_2 is consistent).

(i) (Π_2, B_2) is said to represent theoretical progress over (Π_1, H_1) iff the following three condition are met:

[1] Every verified basic statement incompatible with B_2 is also incompatible with H_1. That is: B_2 is no more refuted than H_1.

[2] For each *verified* basic statement $(b \wedge p)$: if $H_1 \Rightarrow (b \to p)$, then also $B_2 \Rightarrow (b \to p)$. That is: B_2 yields all the known facts already yielded by H_1.

[3] For each *verified* $(b \wedge p)$, $\Gamma(\beta_1, H_1, b \wedge p)$ entails $\Gamma(\beta_2, B_2, b \wedge p)$. That is: every ascertained fact novel with respect to (β_1, H_1) is also novel with respect to (β_2, B_2).

[4] There exists at least one basic statement $(b_0 \wedge p_0)$ such that $\Gamma(\beta_2, B_2, b_0 \wedge p_0)$, but not $\Gamma(\beta_1, H_1, b_0 \wedge p_0)$, holds. That is: there exists at least one (actual or putative) fact which is novel with respect to (β_2, B_2) but not to (β_1, H_1).

(ii) (Π_2, B_2) is said to represent empirical progress over (Π_1, H_1) iff, over and above [1]–[3], the following condition is satisfied:

[4'] There exists at least one basic statement $(b_0 \wedge p_0)$ such that $(b_0 \wedge p_0)$ is *actually verified* and: $\Gamma(\beta_2, B_2, b_0 \wedge p_0)$ but not $\Gamma(\beta_1, H_1, b_0 \wedge p_0)$ holds. That is: there exists at least one *ascertained* fact which is novel with respect to (β_2, B_2) but not to (β_1, H_1).

Note first that theoretical progress is not necessarily an antisymmetric relation, thus leaving open the possibility of theoretical Kuhn loss; secondly that empirical progress trivially presupposes theoretical progress.

(iii) Finally (Π_2, B_2) is said to represent heuristic progress over (Π_1, H_1) iff *either* B_2 falls under $ß_2$ while H_1 does not fall under $ß_1$; which in effect means that whereas B_2 genuinely belongs to the program Π_2, H_1 does not really lie within Π_1; *or alternatively*, B_2 is in closer conformity with $ß_2$ than H_1 is with $ß_1$. For example, take: $\Pi_1 \equiv \Pi_2 \equiv \Pi \equiv$ Program of Unified Field Theories; $ß_1 \equiv ß_2 \equiv ß \equiv$ Unity Principle; $H_1 \equiv$ GTR (Einstein's General Theory of Relativity); $B_2 \equiv$ Weyl's Unified Field Theory. Although Einstein coupled gravitation with the structure of space-time, Weyl achieved a higher degree of unification by extracting both the gravitational and the electromagnetic fields from one and the same geometry. This in no way entails that B_2 was bound to be empirically successful. Thus experimental tests are not indispensable for the development—as distinct from the empirical success—of RP's; for since theories can satisfy some metaprinciples to a greater or lesser degree, it is possible to improve such theories purely heuristically, i.e. without reference to observational results. *Note however that actual scientific progress is achieved only if conditions (ii) are satisfied. Hence primacy is still given to empirical considerations.*

Let us repeat that a heuristic can be conceived as a *meta*principle governing the form of the putative laws of nature: so that a change of language *can* be construed as a change of program. For example: though two hypotheses be intertranslatable, one of them, say Einstein's STR, assumes a Lorentz-covariant form while the other, namely Lorentz's theory, does not. Thus the first hypothesis, but not the second, belongs to the Relativity Program. The importance thereby attributed to the choice of a language might enable us to counter some of David Miller's objections to the notion of verisimilitude; where the latter are founded on the principle—which is here rejected—that provided they remain intertranslatable, languages can be altered at will. In rejecting this principle, we follow Poincaré's view according to which Hamiltonian Dynamics differs fundamentally from Newtonian theory, and this despite the empirical identity of the two systems. Thus, Popper's theses notwithstanding, concepts continue to play an essential role in determining the structure of scientific hypotheses; for, within the RP to which they belong, these concepts are meant to denote natural kinds. (See below Chapter VII, section G). We shall not however presently pursue this line of thought any further.

(H) A Rational Account of Heuristics

By means of a few examples borrowed from the history of science, I propose to show that the logic of scientific discovery is not inductive; that, being largely deductive, it does not resemble artistic creation either (See section K below). Against Lakatos, I shall defend the view that heuristics possesses no special status half-way between logic and psychology; for, unlike Reichenbach and Popper, I think that deduction constitutes the most important moment in the process of invention. It has been claimed that deduction itself contains non-rational elements in that hardly any step within a proof is uniquely determined by the previous steps. My answer to this objection is two-fold. First, the objection is consistent with my aim of breaching the dichotomy between the allegedly irrational invention of hypotheses on the one hand, and the deduction of empirically decidable consequences on the other. If my claim holds, then the "irrational" character of the context of discovery will be no different from that of the context of justification; for in both cases, the methods used turn out to be largely deductive. Secondly, it seems clear to me that mathematicians do not produce proofs by a process resembling a sequence of spontaneous mutations; on the contrary: they start by reasoning about what kind of approach is likely to lead them to some desired result. They carry out something like proof-analysis, e.g. a piece of metareasoning based on an analogy with some available proof known to have succeeded in a neighboring domain. Mathematicians generally have an idea about the overall structure of a proof before they fill in the tedious details; so that deductions are far less "irrational" or *sui generis* than they might appear at first sight.

The basis on which the construction of new theories rests consists of precisely the metaprinciples alluded to in (E) above. These almost invariably include the Correspondence Principle and certain symmetry requirements which play a central role in modern physics; all of which will be more fully described in sections (J) and (K) below. Many other metastatements flow from philosophical principles used in everyday life. They may form part of commonsense knowledge; they may well be innate and thus possess a genetic basis. Their emergence might be explicable, along Darwinian lines, in the way in which Popper tries directly but unsuccessfully to account for the invention of new hypotheses; namely through reception-independent mutations most of which are subsequently eliminated by natural selection. In other words: the emergence of consciousness and of its propensities might eventually be explained in Darwinian terms; but once formed, consciousness makes purposive action possible. Such purposive action manifests itself most brilliantly in the sciences, whose development from then on displays not a Darwinian, but a quasi-Lamarckian pattern.

What matters for my thesis is that the heuristic principles mentioned above should have been present before, or concurrently with the birth of science proper; that they have since been largely stable or at any rate as stable as the genetic material of which we are made. Their insertion in the evolutionary process, which leads to the constitution of scientific programs, makes systematic research possible. They are moreover largely non-technical, even vague. Were they all to be simultaneously made precise and conjoined, then they might entail contradictions, for they probably arose from confrontations with vastly different problem-situations. The heuristic of any RP is determined by the *coherent choice* it operates among these principles and by the more or less sharp formulation it gives to each of them. In this effort towards increased precision, mathematical idealizations often plays a major role. As examples, let us cite the mathematical requirements of continuity, of differentiability, of analyticity and of the independence of form vis-à-vis the choice of a reference-frame (covariance). An RP evolves through the application of its heuristic to existing hypotheses some of which might initially have belonged to commonsense knowledge. In this way, new theories are obtained; after these have been pitted against the facts, they might find themselves empirically refuted and then corrected by reiteration of the same methods. As explained in (G) above, empirical refutations are sometimes unnecessary: since hypotheses can fulfill certain conditions to a greater or lesser degree, they can be improved by purely heuristic means.

It is now time to formulate, as clearly as possible, some of the meta-propositions on which the logic of discovery rests. According to Émile Meyerson, the whole of science is informed by the *Identity Principle* which impels the scientist to deny the apparent diversity of the phenomena, or rather to derive the latter from one fixed system of laws. It was already pointed out by Mach that this so-called legal version of the Principle is needed by all species in their struggle for survival. According to the causal version, nature consists of substances whose total quantity remains constant. In this connection, it is worth noting that according to Kant, the conservation of matter is a synthetic a priori law which the transcendental ego imposes on physical reality. For his part, Meyerson regards the human mind as having an irresistible tendency to hypostasize all natural processes, thus turning them into things whose total quantity is then assumed to remain constant. This innate propensity induces in the child a firm belief in the persistence of material objects (See Meyerson 1907 and 1921; also Piaget 1970). Thus the Identity Principle, both in its *legal* and in its *causal* form, precedes science proper. Of course, it also permeates science itself. In the 18th and 19th centuries it led to the discovery of the conservation laws of momentum and energy. The *Unity Principle* (or rather: *Meta-principle*), which played a

central role both in Poincaré's and in Einstein's methodology, clearly derives
from the legal version of the Identity Principle: all phenomena should fall
under one all-embracing law, say under a unique geometry; which entails
that nature does not split into disjoint domains subject to different laws.
Should such a schism appear in science, then one should try to deduce all
extant hypotheses, possibly in a modified form, from a unique premise. A
first and simplest step towards such a unified solution consists in letting one
of the domain annex the others, i.e. in extending the laws governing one
domain to all the others.

The *Principle of the Proportionality of the Effect to its Cause* should
also be mentioned: in everyday life we instinctively hold the magnitude of
the effect to be an increasing function of the intensity of its cause; whence
the assumption of the local proportionality of effect to cause. There is also
the *Principle of Sufficient Reason,* which was clearly enunciated by Leibniz
but had already been implicitly used by the Presocratics. Some arguments
based on *an intuitive notion of probability* must be added to this list; e.g. the
assumption that long sequences of coincidences, being highly unlikely,
hardly ever occur in nature (See Chapter I above). The *rejection of conspiracy theories* belongs to the same order of ideas; e.g. the refusal to accept
theories which postulate deep asymmetries together with compensatory factors which prevent such asymmetries from ever surfacing at the level of
phenomena: an exact and systematic compensation is held to be implausible, because highly improbable. It is also this intuitive notion of probability which leads us to look upon a theory as strongly supported by the distant
and unexpected facts which it predicts: it seems unlikely that this should be
the effect of pure chance, i.e. that this should have nothing to do with the
truth-likeness of the theory (See Chapter VII below).

It has already been pointed out that the principles enumerated above,
though invoked in everyday life, are made more precise by the mathematical techniques used in the sciences. This should not however mask their continuity with commonsense knowledge; furthermore, the desire for precision
which is embodied in mathematics might in its turn be innate and hence precede the birth of science. Let us point out that the deductions starting from
these principles and issuing in the determination of new theories are not
always watertight; they might contain hidden lemmas or assumptions which
are not explicitly formulated. Such gaps are often bridged by simplicity considerations; but they anyway prove less important than some philosophers
like Reichenbach and Popper imagine; and they certainly do not warrant the
view that scientific discovery *consists in such logical gaps*, i.e. in such *intuitive jumps* rather than in deductive reasoning. Moreover, physicists often

recognize that the invoked simplicity requirements are expedients which science should, and often does subsequently shed.

We shall now examine, in some detail, three of the most widely used heuristic devices for the construction of new theories. One of them, namely the *method of parameter-adjustment,* has already been described in Chapter IV; and it was seen to lead—by definition—to the determination of laws ad hoc *vis-à-vis* the facts to which the parameters are adapted. Let us now turn to two essentially non-ad hoc principles, one conservative and the other revolutionary, which have dominated the development of modern physics; namely the *Correspondence* and the *Symmetry Principles.*

(I) THE CORRESPONDENCE PRINCIPLE AS A CONSERVATIVE HEURISTIC METHOD.

Science is classically portrayed as evolving through a succession of improved approximations to the truth. This cumulative view of progress was challenged by the following observation: at the ontological level, the development of science displays an alarming degree of referential discontinuity: as we move from one hypothesis to the next, the same-sounding words are often found to denote, or rather to conflate fundamentally different entities. For example: the term 'electromagnetic wave' referred first to the mechanical states of an underlying ether; then to two oscillating fields deprived of any material support; and finally, to massless particles called 'photons'. The cumulative view can however be rescued by an appeal to two aspects of the development of science, which furthermore turn out to be closely linked. First of all, it is generally agreed that at least at the practical level, our mastery over physical nature has steadily grown. This progress was secondly taken to have been achieved by the systematic application of a continuity requirement; the latter—called the Correspondence Principle—demands that old confirmed laws be either logical consequences or else limiting cases of new hypotheses. This essentially mathematical form of continuity explains why a new theory inherits the degree of corroboration of its predecessors. Let us however note that identity is the most perfect form of continuity; but in the midst of a scientific revolution, identity is the last condition we would wish to impose. In well-specified areas, the new hypothesis is expressly meant to differ markedly from the old one: a new law will normally be required to avoid, or rather to overcome the difficulties encountered by its predecessors.

This tension between continuity and saltation can be resolved by means of the notion of one system being *imbedded in*, rather than forming *a substructure of* another one (See Redhead 1995, Chapter 4). The following examples will clarify this important distinction. Even though the complex plane **C** extends and hence imbeds the real line **R**, the former does not mirror *all* the properties of the latter, *nor vice-versa;* for the linear ordering of **R** cannot be extended to **C** in any natural way; while **C**, but not **R**, is algebraically closed. Another example is provided by hyperbolic geometry; the latter possesses a model in the complex plane **C** in which it is therefore imbedded. It would however be absurd to claim that hyperbolic geometry, which is *non-Euclidean*, constitutes a substructure of the Euclidean plane.

Let me now demonstrate that the possibility of reconciling the gradualist with the revolutionary aspects of scientific progress rests on a topological result; namely on the Heine-Borel theorem which tells us that all closed and bounded subsets of $\mathbf{R}^n$ are compact, n being an arbitrary positive integer. (In the rest of this Chapter we shall write $\Rightarrow$ and $\Leftrightarrow$ for $\rightarrow$ and $\leftrightarrow$ respectively. Thus: $\Rightarrow$ will stand for the notion of material implication, and $\rightarrow$ for that of mathematically tending [to some limit]).

Consider the hypothesis:

(1) $(\forall v, a, b)[Q(v, a, b) \Rightarrow (h(v, a, b) = 0)]$, which is taken to have been superseded by:

(2) $(\forall v, a, b)[Q(v, a, b) \Rightarrow (H(\lambda_0, v, a, b) = 0)]$, where λ_0 is a 'small' constant.

Replacing λ_0 by the variable parameter λ, we shall assume that $H(\lambda, v, a, b)$ and $h(v, a, b)$ are continuous functions of $<\lambda, v, a, b>$ and of $<v, a, b>$ respectively.

Suppose that $[h(v, a, b) = 0]$ has been strongly corroborated in some region Δ, i.e. that this law has withstood a number of severe tests in Δ This number being necessarily finite, we can assume, without any loss of generality, that Δ is of the form:

(3) $\Delta = V \times A \times B$, where V, A and B are bounded closed sets of real numbers.

A could, for example, be taken to be the closed interval $[a', a'']$ where a' and a'' are respectively the minimum and the maximum measured values of a. Similar considerations apply to both V and B. When restricted to Δ, the laws (1) and (2) assume the forms:

(4) $(\forall v, a, b)[(Q(v, a, b) \wedge (<v, a, b> \in \Delta)) \Rightarrow (h(v, a, b) = 0)]$ and:

(5) $(\forall v, a, b)[(Q(v, a, b) \wedge (<v, a, b> \in \Delta)) \Rightarrow (H(\lambda_0, v, a, b) = 0)]$ respectively.

In view of the approximate character of all measurements, we can take (4) to be observationally indiscernible from:

(6) $(\forall v, a, b)[(Q(v, a, b) \wedge (<v, a, b> \in \Delta)) \Rightarrow (|h(v, ab)| \leq \mu_0)]$, where μ_0 is some fixed positive real.

(6) is generally taken to hold not only for the values of v, a and b which have actually been measured but also for all intermediate values; i.e. throughout the domain Δ. Thus, (6) is regarded as true.

In one of its forms, the Correspondence Principle requires that:

(7) for any $<v, a, b> \in \Delta$, $H(\lambda, v, a, b) \rightarrow h(v, a, b)$, as $\lambda \rightarrow 0$.

Given the continuity of H, we must also have: $H(\lambda, v, a, b) \rightarrow H(0, v, a, b)$, as $\lambda \rightarrow 0$.

By the uniqueness of the limit, (7) entails that:

(8) $h(v, a, b) = H(0, v, a, b)$ for all v, a and b such that $<v, a, b> \in \Delta$

We can now describe the way in which the new theory H accounts for the empirical success of h in Δ. Let us provisionally accept (5), from which (6) will presently be deduced. Since λ_0 is small, there exists a real number $k > 0$ such that:

(9) $\lambda_0 \in [-k, +k]$.

Let the parameter λ be confined to the closed interval $[-k, k]$. By the continuity of H and the compactness of $[-k, k] \times V \times A \times B = [-k, k] \times \Delta$, the following theorem about uniform continuity holds good. For any $\mu > 0$, there exists an $\eta(\mu)$ dependent only on μ such that: $|H(\lambda_1, v_1, a_1, b_1) - H(\lambda_2, v_2, a_2, b_2)| \leq \mu$, for all $<\lambda_j, v_j, a_j, b_j> \in [-k, k] \times \Delta$ $(j = 1, 2)$ satisfying: $\sqrt{[(\lambda_1 - \lambda_2)^2 + (v_1 - v_2)^2 + (a_1 - a_2)^2 + (b_1 - b_2)^2]} \leq \eta(\mu)$. In particular:

(10) $|H(\lambda, v, a, b) - H(0, v, a, b)| \leq \mu$, i.e. $|H(\lambda, v, a, b) - h(v, a, b)| \leq \mu$, for all $<\lambda, v, a, b> \in [-k, k] \times \Delta$ such that $|\lambda| \leq \eta(\mu)$.

Taking $\mu = \mu_0$ and $\lambda = \lambda_0$, obtain:

(11) For all $<v, a, b> \in \Delta$: $| H(\lambda_0, v, a, b) - h(v, a, b) | \leq \mu_0$, provided $| \lambda_0 | \leq \eta(\mu_0)$.

Suppose that the numerical value λ_0 actually satisfies $| \lambda_0 | \leq \eta(\mu_0)$. Inequality (11) will then be true for all $<v, a, b> \in \Delta$. Now assume $[(Q (v, a, b) \wedge (<v, a, b> \in \Delta)]$. By (5): $H(\lambda_0, v, a, b) = 0$. By (11), it follows that: $| h(v, a, b) | \leq \mu_0$; whence (6), which is observationally equivalent to (4). I.e. the truth of the new theory accounts for the confirmation of the old one in Δ.

There is another form of the Correspondence Principle which actually possesses greater heuristic power than (7). It requires that for any $<a, b>$, we have: $| H(\lambda, v, a, b) - h(v, a, b) | \rightarrow 0$ as $\lambda v \rightarrow 0$. Fixing v and letting $\lambda \rightarrow 0$, we obtain: $| H(\lambda, v, a, b) - h(v, a, b) | \rightarrow 0$, i.e. $H(\lambda, v, a, b) \rightarrow h(v, a, b)$, as $\lambda \rightarrow 0$. Thus we retrieve condition (7); whence, by continuity: $H(0, v, a, b) = h(v, a, b)$. But we can alternatively fix λ at $\lambda = \lambda_0$ and let v $\rightarrow 0$. This yields: $| H(\lambda_0, v, a, b) - h(v, a, b) | \rightarrow 0$ as v $\rightarrow 0$. By continuity, we must also have: $| H(\lambda_0, v, a, b) - h(v, a, b) | \rightarrow | H(\lambda_0, 0, a, b) - h(0, a, b) |$ as v $\rightarrow 0$. Hence:

(12) $| H(\lambda_0, 0, a, b) - h(0, a, b) | = 0$. That is: $H(\lambda_0, 0, a, b) = h(0, a, b)$ for all $<a, b>$.

From (2) we infer:

(13) $(\forall a,b)[Q(0, a, b) \Rightarrow (H(\lambda_0, 0, a, b) = h(0, a, b) = 0)]$.

In other words: for v = 0, the new law coincides with the old one. As an example, consider the case of STR where: $\lambda_0 = (1/c)$, c = velocity of light, and v = speed of the moving body. It is assumed that as $(v/c) \rightarrow 0$, the relativistic equation of motion 'tends' to the Newtonian one; where both v and $(1/c)$ are now treated as variable parameters. It follows from the above that the classical law $\underline{f} - m\underline{a} = 0$ must strictly hold for v = 0. This desideratum, together with the constraint of Lorentz-covariance, enabled Planck to establish the law $\underline{f} = d[m\underline{v}/\sqrt{(1 - v^2/c^2)}]/dt$. (See Zahar 1989, Chapter 7).

Let us repeat that the above considerations depend on the Heine-Borel theorem, which applies to all closed and bounded subsets D of $\mathbf{R}^n$. This result therefore leaves open the possibility for the two hypotheses,

the old one and the new, to diverge widely outside D; for uniform continuity generally obtains only within *compact* subsets of $\mathbf{R}^n$.

(J) THE REVOLUTIONARY ROLE OF SYMMETRY PRINCIPLES

We have seen that both continuity *and* divergence are of the essence of scientific revolutions; but only continuity—in the two forms of correspondence and of parameter-adjustment—has so far been shown to possess any
heuristic clout. Referring back to the previous section, suppose that (1) has
been refuted outside Δ. If no further information is provided, then all we can
do is modify (1) in some ad-hoc way by restricting it, say, to the domain Δ.
In other words: instead of (1), we might be tempted to adopt (4) as our basic
theory. This method consists in adding extra qualifications to the
antecedents of existing laws. But since (4) is logically weaker than (1), falsification would have been evaded only through a *reduction* of the logical
content of (1).

Physicists however resort to ad-hoc stratagems, which are much more
sophisticated than that of a mere diminution of logical content. Starting
from an old hypothesis such as (1), they construct an equation of the form
$[H(\lambda, v, a, b) = 0]$, where λ is taken to be a parameter so small that in the
domain Δ, the new theory proves empirically indiscernible from (1). Then
they make λ coincide with a value λ_0 chosen in such a way that $[H(\lambda_0, v, a,
b) = 0]$ subsumes some results known to have refuted (1); the hope being
that $|\lambda_0|$ will prove smaller than the $\eta(\mu_0)$ defined above. For example,
Ptolemaic Astronomy was built on the ad-hoc principle of introducing
epicycles doctored to yield both the facts which falsified and those which
confirmed earlier theories of the program. There existed no overall strategy
whereby the extra epicycles could be determined independently of known
observational results (See Lakatos and Zahar 1978). In such cases, the general feeling among scientists is that the new hypotheses possess no greater
truth-likeness than the old ones; which shows that despite being common to
all programs, the Correspondence Principle alone falls short of providing a
comprehensive heuristic for scientific research.

Additional constraints are therefore needed. The latter often take the
form of symmetry meta-principles under which physical laws must be subsumed; all of which confirms Lakatos's views about the essential regulative
role played by mathematics in the development of research programs (See
Lakatos 1978, p. 51). Symmetries however pose paradoxical problems. No
insuperable difficulties arise in the case of two incompatible theories, for

these normally have different symmetry groups. M. Redhead however pointed out that whenever an old law is strictly entailed by the new one, we face a serious problem posed by the so-called Curie-Post Principle. According to the latter, a universal proposition generally transfers its symmetries to its logical consequences and to its special cases (Redhead 1975). This heredity principle seems *prima facie* self-evident: if two situations are not told apart by a strong theory, then they cannot *a fortiori* be distinguished by a weaker one. This however has the unfortunate consequence that as long as it progresses cumulatively, physics can display no new symmetries. Hence no symmetry conditions can help any scientist towards generating new hypotheses; for as long as existing laws get strengthened, new symmetry properties *cannot possibly arise*; and it seems as though neither Correspondence nor any symmetry requirement will enable physics to move away from existing theories. The only heuristic method left for the construction of a new hypothesis appears to be that of modifying—in some ad hoc fashion—an old law so as to force it to fit recalcitrant facts. Whence the need to demonstrate that the Curie-Post principle can be blocked; for only in this way can the *mathematical constraints* of both Symmetry and Correspondence prove to be regulative ideas which help towards constructing new hypotheses strictly stronger than the old ones.

Let $\mathbf{K}(\underline{x}, a, b,...)$ be a law where: $\underline{x}$ is a sequence of spatio-temporal coordinates and a ,b , etc. are specific physical quantities. A symmetry of $\mathbf{K}$ is defined a sequence of functions $<\varphi(\underline{x}), \alpha(\underline{x}, a, b,...), \beta(\underline{x}, a, b,...),...>$ such that, if we put: $\underline{x}' = \varphi(\underline{x})$, $a' = \alpha(\underline{x}, a, b,...)$, $b' = \beta(\underline{x}, a, b,...)$, etc, we have:

(14) $\vdash (\forall \underline{x})(\forall a, b,...)[\mathbf{K}(\underline{x}, a, b,...) \Leftrightarrow \mathbf{K}(\underline{x}', a', b',...)]$.

For the sake of simplicity, we shall henceforth write $(\underline{x}, a, b)$ for $(\underline{x}, a, b,...)$. Thus (14) is shorthand for:

(15) $(\forall \underline{x}, a, b)[\mathbf{K}(\underline{x}, a, b) \Leftrightarrow \mathbf{K}(\varphi(\underline{x}), \alpha(\underline{x}, a, b), \beta(\underline{x}, a, b))]$.

Any symmetry can be *passively* construed as a change from one frame Γ to another—which will be denoted by Γ' — such that: $\underline{x}$ and $\underline{x}'$ are the coordinates of the *same* point, P say; while a and a' denote the values assumed, at P, by the *same* physical quantity when referred to Γ and to Γ' respectively. We could alternatively remain within the same frame Γ and *actively* interpret $\underline{x} \to \underline{x}'$ as a map of Γ into itself which sends a and b into a' and b' respectively.

Note that both construals block Kretschmann's objection to the covariance condition; namely that an arbitrary physical law can be rewritten in a generally covariant form; for α and β are now defined as quantities dependent *only* on ($\underline{x}$, a, b). This caveat forbids the introduction of new entities which might trivially make every law form-invariant under *all* well-behaved bijections. Thus specifying the arguments $\underline{x}$, a and b of the functions α and β lends heuristic efficacy to the symmetry principles (See Zahar 1989, Chapter 8).

We are now in a position to prove that a logical consequence $\mathbf{E}(\underline{x}, a, b)$ of $\mathbf{K}(\underline{x}, a, b)$ *need not* possess the symmetry $<\varphi, \alpha, \beta>$ of $\mathbf{K}$. Thus assume that:

(16) $\vdash$ ($\forall\underline{x}$, a, b)[K($\underline{x}$, a, b) $\Rightarrow$ E($\underline{x}$, a, b)]. Hence, by logic alone:

(17) $\vdash$ [$\mathbf{K}$ ($\underline{x}'$, a$'$, b$'$) $\Rightarrow$ E($\underline{x}'$, a$'$, b$'$)]. So, by (14):

(18) $\vdash$ ($\forall\underline{x}$, a, b)[$\mathbf{K}$ ($\underline{x}$, a, b) $\Rightarrow$ E($\underline{x}'$, a$'$, b$'$)].

(16) and (18) do not however logically entail the relation $\vdash$ [E($\underline{x}$, a, b)$\wedge$ E($\underline{x}'$, a$'$, b)] which expresses the symmetry of $\mathbf{E}$ under $<\varphi, \alpha, \beta>$. As a trivial counter-example, consider the case where $\mathbf{K}$ is self-contradictory and hence implies *all hypotheses*. E.g. let $\mathbf{K}$ ($\underline{x}$, a, b) $\equiv$ [($\underline{x}$ = $\underline{x}$)$\wedge$(a = a)$\wedge$ (b $\neq$ b)]. Since $\mathbf{K}$ ($\underline{x}'$, a$'$, b$'$) $\equiv$ [($\underline{x}'$ = $\underline{x}'$)$\wedge$(a$'$ = a$'$)$\wedge$(b$'$ $\neq$ b$'$)], $\mathbf{K}$ ($\underline{x}'$, a$'$, b$'$) is also inconsistent. Thus (14), i.e. (15), holds good for all φ , α and β; which means that $\mathbf{K}$ admits all functions $<\varphi, \alpha, \beta>$ as symmetries. It is however far from true that an arbitrary $<\varphi, \alpha, \beta>$ defines a symmetry for every physical theory, i.e. for every consequence of $\mathbf{K}$.

Assuming the truth of (14), it is just as important for us to prove that the 'special cases' of the hypothesis $\mathbf{K}$ ($\underline{x}$, a, b) similarly fail to be necessarily symmetric under $<\varphi, \alpha, \beta>$. To this end, it proves convenient to regard every symmetry as a map of the set Ω of all the solutions of $\mathbf{K}$ into itself. By definition, Ω is the class of all tuples $<A(\underline{x}), B(\underline{x})>$ of functions of $\underline{x}$ such that:

(19) $\vdash$ ($\forall\underline{x}$)$\mathbf{K}$($\underline{x}$, A($\underline{x}$), B($\underline{x}$)). By (15):

(20) $\vdash$ ($\forall\underline{x}$)$\mathbf{K}$($\varphi(\underline{x})$, $\alpha(\underline{x}$, A($\underline{x}$), B($\underline{x}$)), $\beta(\underline{x}$, A($\underline{x}$), B($\underline{x}$))).

Substituting $\varphi^{-1}(\underline{x})$ for $\underline{x}$ and then generalizing, we obtain:

(21) $\vdash$ ($\forall\underline{x}$)$\mathbf{K}$($\underline{x}$, A$'(\underline{x})$, B$'(\underline{x})$), where: A$'(\underline{x})$ = $_{\text{Def}}$ $\alpha(\varphi^{-1}(\underline{x})$, A($\varphi^{-1}(\underline{x})$), B($\varphi^{-1}(\underline{x})$)), B$'(\underline{x})$ = $_{\text{Def}}$ $\beta(\varphi^{-1}(\underline{x})$, A($\varphi^{-1}(\underline{x})$), B($\varphi^{-1}(\underline{x})$)).

Taken together, (19) and (21) tell us that if $<A(\underline{x}), B(\underline{x})>$ is a solution of the law **K**, then due to the symmetry $<\varphi, \alpha, \beta>$ of **K**, $<A'(\underline{x}), B'(\underline{x})>$ will constitute another solution of the same law. We can in fact interpret this symmetry as the map of Ω into itself defined by: $<A(\underline{x}), B(\underline{x})> \rightarrow <A'(\underline{x}), B'(\underline{x})>$, where:

(22) $<A'(\underline{x}), B'(\underline{x})> =_{\text{Def.}} <\alpha(\varphi^{-1}(\underline{x}), A\varphi^{-1}(\underline{x}), B\varphi^{-1}(\underline{x})), \beta(\varphi^{-1}(\underline{x}), A\varphi^{-1}(\underline{x}), B\varphi^{-1}(\underline{x}))>$.

It is easily seen that this map does not necessarily send a 'special case', i.e. a solution of **K** of a given type, into another one of the same type, i.e. into a special case. For example: let Ω_0 be the subset of Ω consisting of all tuples of the form $<f(\underline{x}), g(\underline{x})>$, where $g(\underline{x}) = 0 = $ zero function. Thus:

(23) $\vdash (\forall \underline{x}) \mathbf{K}(\underline{x}, f(\underline{x}), 0)$.

The symmetry $<\varphi, \alpha, \beta>$ sends $<f(\underline{x}), g(\underline{x})>$ into $<f'(\underline{x}), g'(\underline{x})>$, where: $g'(\underline{x}) = \beta(\varphi^{-1}(\underline{x}), f(\varphi^{-1}(\underline{x})), g(\varphi^{-1}(\underline{x}))) = \beta(\varphi^{-1}(\underline{x}), f(\varphi^{-1}(\underline{x})), 0)$, since g is the zero function. There is however no reason to suppose that g' vanishes identically; so that we might well have $<f'(\underline{x}), g'(\underline{x})> \notin \Omega_0$, i.e. $g'(\underline{x}) \neq 0 =$ zero function. Here is an example: apply Maxwell's equations to a static system of charged particles; taking $f(\underline{x})$ and $g(\underline{x})$ to be the electric and the magnetic fields respectively, conclude that $g(\underline{x}) = 0$. Let $\varphi(\underline{x})$ be any non-trivial Lorentz transformation. Maxwell's theory is known to be Lorentz-covariant and, i.e. form-invariant under the symmetry φ. As already explained, φ can be *passively* viewed as a change from a stationary frame to a mobile one in which the particles are no longer at rest. The moving frame will therefore contain both an electric and a non-vanishing magnetic field; i.e. $g'(\underline{x}) \neq 0$.

The heredity principle is consequently false. This entitles us to search for hitherto unknown symmetries to be imposed on new hypotheses; where the latter *might*, for all we know, extend or at any rate be consistent with our past conjectures. But how are we to find such symmetries? Going back to (15), it is obvious that if all the relations **K**, φ, α and β were unknown, then it would be impossible for us to begin our search. We could however start *either* by considering a *given* theory **K** and try to determine the class of its symmetries $<\varphi, \alpha, \beta>$, which will then be applied to other hypotheses; *or* from some *available* $<\varphi, \alpha, \beta>$, which could be heuristically exploited in the construction of theories covariant under $<\varphi, \alpha, \beta>$. Note that these two approaches need not be mutually exclusive, not even within the same program. For example: **K** might form part of a more general theory; it could be the set of Maxwell's equations taken within the more general context of classical physics, which includes mechanics. After examining the symmetries of **K**, we might find that they do not extend to the whole system in which **K** is imbedded. Thus Classical Mechanics is not Lorentz-covariant, i.e. it does not possess all the Maxwellian symmetries. The latter can therefore be put to heuristic use by being construed as adequacy requirements to be imposed on *all* the laws of nature; which entails a modification of Dynamics. And as a matter of fact, Einstein and Poincaré started from the well-known system **K** of Maxwell's equations; they determined the symmetry group *L* of **K** and then used *L* in order to generate new hypotheses. This is also how Planck modified the old laws of motion into Lorentz-covariant relations.

Another heuristic device consists in strengthening a covariance requirement by enlarging an existing symmetry group. For example: both for scientific and for philosophical reasons, Einstein decided to construct a generally covariant theory of gravitation. The latter had therefore to keep its form not only under the Lorentz transformations but also under all well-behaved bijections. This constraint, taken together with other requirements inherited from the Newtonian Program, determined the new field equations to within a constant (See Zahar 1989, Chapters 5, 7, 8). Yet Einstein's move appears to be forbidden by the Curie-Post principle, which is one reason why the latter had to be confined within strict limits.

(K) Some Examples from the History of Science

We shall start with the simplest examples illustrating the heuristic principles described above. In Ptolemaic Astronomy, each of the five planets performs a complex movement one of whose components duplicates the revolution of the sun about the earth. This was treated as a cosmic accident or as a series of coincidences accepted without explanation. It can mathematically be proved that, relatively to the sun, all five components would disappear at a stroke. This feature was plausibly claimed by Dreyer to have provided Copernicus with a starting point for his speculations; and it also seems to have been one reason why Aristarchus put forward his heliocentric system (See Dreyer 1953, p. 312). Whatever the case may be, Copernican astronomy does explain these coincidences by deriving them from a single source; namely from the wrong, though perfectly natural choice of the earth as our primary frame of reference.

Consider next the reduction of optics to electromagnetism. Maxwell's equations imply that all electromagnetic disturbances are propagated *in vacuo* with the velocity of light c; so Maxwell jumped to the conclusion that light must be an electromagnetic wave. Was this a sudden intuitive insight or did Maxwell simply commit the logical error of affirming the consequent? Both of these accounts strike us as implausible unless, by 'intuitive insight', a compressed and semi-conscious version of the following *argument* be meant: two distinct media, an electromagnetic ether and a luminiferous one, had been postulated; both transmit waves; it is highly unlikely that two wave processes belonging to two different domains should have identical speeds; hence optics and electromagnetism ought to be connected in some fundamental way. In section (H) above, we have already remarked that annexation is the simplest form of unification. However, one question remains: should electromagnetism be annexed to optics, or vice-versa? Maxwell had already consolidated electromagnetism into an integrated system subsuming a wide continuum of frequencies which could easily accommodate the visible spectrum. Electromagnetism was therefore bound to become the dominant theory.

Let us turn to Lorentz's hypothesis which offers another typical example of a conspiracy theory. Lorentz postulated an absolute medium which, *in the light of his own assumptions*, gradually became undetectable: compensatory factors affect our measuring instruments in such a way that every uniformly moving system behaves like the absolute frame. By establishing the first-order covariance of Maxwell's equations, Lorentz had shown that motion through the ether gives rise to no first-order effects. By first deriving the contraction of material rods, and then the retardation of clocks from his axioms, he also accounted for Michelson's null results. But Lorentz's hypothesis was fast becoming the kind of conspiracy theory which was bound to arouse Einstein's (and Poincaré's) suspicions. This is now known to have given rise to the Relativity Program. It should be added that soon after realizing that his transformations form a group—so that perfect symmetry obtains between the ether and every other inertial frame—Lorentz effectively went over to the Relativity camp: although he still hankered after the ether, he acknowledged that covariance had become the overriding heuristic principle (See Lorentz 1967, pp. 89–104, 188–204). The assumption that the presence of the ether was systematically masked by factors which happened to neutralize one another had in effect become inoperative.

At first sight, the revolutionary character of Relativity appears to preclude any attempt at explaining its origins in gradualist terms. That c should be a constant—and the same constant in all inertial frames—violates commonsense to such an extent that only inductivism, or else some form of creative intuitionism seems capable of accounting for the discovery of STR. As already mentioned: Reichenbach defended the orthodox inductivist thesis that Michelson established an experimental result which Einstein generalized and then turned into a basic postulate. But we know that there exist infinitely many ways of inducing a law from any finite set of data. It seems moreover historically certain that Michelson's experiment played no direct part in Einstein's *logic of discovery*. We seem reduced to assuming that Relativity was the product of a sudden flash of intuition. But this sort of mysticism is nothing but an admission of ignorance; and it anyway fails to make us understand why Einstein's 'intuition' was directed at one specific physical process, namely the propagation of light, whose velocity became the cornerstone of the whole of kinematics.

A gradualist account of the origins of STR can in effect be given. Let me start by making a trivial logical point: no matter how seemingly minute, an alteration of the fundamental postulates of a hypothesis may have dramatically new implications, especially at a lower logical level. Theoretical continuity is therefore consistent with revolution at the level of empirical predictions. For example: the extension of covariance from electromagnetism to the rest of physics might initially have looked like an anodyne generalization; it nevertheless entails that even the rest-mass of a particle, which was hitherto regarded as the amount of 'stuff' in a given body, could vary. This counter-intuitive consequence was later tested and corroborated; and yet it runs counter to the principle of the conservation of substance which, according to Kant, is presupposed by the very possibility of experience. As for the invariance of c, though nowadays presented as a basic premise, it was in fact the last step of a sequence of arguments involving the same principles which informed the construction of classical laws. Towards the end of the 19th century, physics was plagued by the kind of dualism to which Einstein strongly objected: mechanics, as expressed by means of ordinary second-order equations, was subject to Galilean Relativity; whereas Maxwell's theory, being formulated in terms of first-order partial differential equations, seemed to fix a unique frame and hence violate Relativity; where the privileged frame is that in which light has a constant speed c in all directions. Nature seemed split into domains obeying irreconcilable laws (or rather meta-laws). Faraday had however noted that electromagnetic induction depends, not on any absolute, but exclusively on the relative velocities of moving bodies. Thus some demon seemed bent on deceiving us about the essential asymmetry between the ether and all other inertial systems. No wonder that Einstein found this classical interpretation unconvincing. His STR was intended to restore the unity of the world-picture by ridding it of all conspiracy theories. This is why the Relativity Postulate was extended to the whole of physics and more particularly to the Maxwell-Lorentz equations; where, as already mentioned, the latter explicitly refer to the velocity of light. This immediately yields the relativity of all electromagnetic phenomena, together with the invariance—or rather the constancy—of the speed c. Hence Einstein's counter-intuitive axiom about the invariance of c was a necessary consequence of the otherwise plausible generalization of the Relativity Meta-Principle. It might of course be wondered why Einstein decided to keep Maxwell's equations unchanged, a decision which entailed a modification in depth of all mechanical laws. This was again the result not of a sudden intuition, but of long deliberation: since all attempts to reduce electromagnetism to mechanics had broken down, it seemed that the time had come for carrying out a reduction in the opposite direction. Putting it slightly differently: if one of the two systems, Newton's or Maxwell's, was to gain the upper hand, it was going to be the latter rather than the former. Using the Maxwell-Lorentz equations as a fixed point, Einstein consequently extended Lorentz-covariance, i.e. Maxwellian symmetry, to the whole of physics. Once again, annexation—by electromagnetism of the rest of physical science—turned out to be the simplest first step towards unification.

Let us turn to GTR and its relation to Classical Mechanics. According to Galileo, all bodies fall with the same constant acceleration; where this constancy is twofold: the acceleration does not vary during the time of fall and it is the same for all material objects. Only the latter form of constancy was fully accepted by Newton; but one puzzling question remained unanswered: inertia and weight were taken to represent two fundamentally different qualities of matter: the first is the resistance opposed by a body to impressed force, the second is an expression of the body's receptiveness to a gravitational field. Yet, as if by accident, these two qualities are measured by the same scalar, namely by the mass m. Thus: $m_i = m = m_g$, where m_i and m_g are the inertial and the gravitational mass respectively. The main consequence of this identity is a contingent law; namely that at any point of space, a gravitational field imparts the same acceleration to all bodies irrespective of their material composition. This law had been pondered by Newton and subsequently tested and corroborated. Refusing to believe in a mere coincidence, Einstein proposed to construct a new relativistic theory which would explain—rather than simply postulate—the identity of m_i and m_g, thereby unifying kinematics and gravitation. In view of the Correspondence Principle, he retained the empirical consequences of the equation $m_i = m_g$, more particularly the law that in a gravitational field all particles fall with the same acceleration. At the observational level, the field is therefore described by the acceleration it imparts to any test particle. Since acceleration is a kinematical, i.e. a geometrical quantity, the simplest solution consists in letting geometry annex gravity. Once again, annexation turned out to be the most straightforward form of unification. Moreover, if annexation is to have any chance of success, then kinematics ought to annex gravitation, not the other way round; for kinematics, which fixes the basic spatio-temporal framework, is the most fundamental structure within physics. As already demonstrated by Newton, the field, and hence also the new relativistic kinematics must depend on the distribution of masses in the universe; where, according to STR, every mass possesses an energy-equivalent and vice-versa. Finally, the Correspondence Principle dictates that STR should be a limiting case of the new theory. Einstein was thus guided by all these metaprinciples towards geometrizing gravity, i.e. towards constructing GTR (See below, Chapter IX; also Zahar 1989a, Chapter 8).

VII

Structural Scientific Realism (SSR)

In Chapter IX, it will be shown that orthodox metaphysical realism played a central role both in Einstein's critique of extant theories and in his logic of discovery. A more modest form of realism—referred to as Structural Scientific Realism, or SSR for short—turns out to belong to the hard core of practically all RP's (Research Programs); for SSR underpins the applicability, to the construction of new theories, of the Correspondence Principle which was seen to operate within all RP's. In using this principle, we assume not only that all strictly observational statements are true but also that the general form of the laws explaining them should be saved; i.e. that the old and highly confirmed hypotheses ought to form limiting cases of the new ones. It is therefore taken for granted that corroborated laws describe structures which are realized in the physical world—at least in some approximate form. Thus structural realism forms an integral but often implicit part of the heuristics governing all successful RP's. In this connection, the present chapter addresses the problems raised by two theses: according to the first, old-fashioned realism is dead (Laudan, Fine); and according to the second, SSR is empty (Newman, Demopoulos, Friedman and Ketland).

(A) DEFINITION OF SSR

SSR is an epistemological position whose origins go back to the philosophical insights of Pierre Duhem, Henri Poincaré and Bertrand Russell. In defining SSR, it proves useful to relate it to Quine's ontological thesis. According to a well-known Quinean slogan, to be is to be quantified over in some first-order theory. SSR reverses this doctrine by asserting that only the relations occurring in a unified and empirically successful theory mirror the ontological order of things. As for the nature of the relata, it might forever remain hidden from us. Note that Quine's position closely follows

Tarskian semantics; more precisely: the semantics of first-order languages where only individual variables occur bound (See Quine 1980b). The domain or basic ontological layer of any interpretation J of a first-order language is some set D of objects. D is the class over which the individual variables range; so that every name belonging to the primitive vocabulary denotes an element of D. As is well known, both names and function letters can be eliminated through the introduction of new predicate letters. Thus only the latter—which express relations—are indispensable. Each predicate symbol corresponds to some subset of a Cartesian product D^n of the basic domain D; where n is the number of argument-places of the predicate in question. Hence there exists, according to Quine, a fundamental asymmetry between the individual names and the predicate constants: whereas the former denote elements of the domain D, the latter do not really name anything at all; no predicate genuinely *refers* to any attribute, i.e. to the subset of D^n which ought nonetheless to correspond to it under J; we are thus in no way committed to the actual existence of any of these subsets. The reason given for this asymmetry seems to be that we have no predicate *variables* P and no second-order quantification which would enable us to assert that there is some P which has a given property, f say. I.e. $(\exists P)f(P)$ is inexpressible in a first-order theory. Quine seems in effect to take it for granted that the existence of an object of any type must be warranted by the ordinary linguistic locution: 'there exists some P such that . . .', where P is a variable of the considered type. As a consequence, the subclasses of D^n do not have the same claim to existence as do the elements of D. Should we moreover accept Quine's thesis that by virtue of its completeness, first-order logic is the only *logic* worthy of the name, then it must be concluded that only individuals exist; or at least that the latter are metaphysically more real than any relations between them.

Even if we keep to first-order logic, this dogma of ontological privilege appears difficult to defend. Yet it seems less indefensible than its opposite, namely SSR, which asserts that in a unified and highly confirmed theory, the basic relations can legitimately be held to have objective import while the relata remain inaccessible to human knowledge. This view nevertheless appears to me to be on the right track. The difficulty in defending it stems from the fact that classical semantics seems unable to interpret relations except by way of their relata. More precisely: in ascribing a truth-value to 'R(a, b)', we have *first* to determine the referents of both 'a' and 'b' in order *then* to be able to affirm or deny that <a, b> belongs to the referent of 'R'. Yet according to structural realism, we often have good reasons for supposing that 'R' reflects a real connection between entities, about whose intrinsic nature we however know next to nothing. The conditions under which we are entitled to make such a realist claim obtain whenever we have a highly unified hypothesis H which both involves R and explains a whole host of seemingly disparate facts in a non-ad hoc way. It should be kept in mind that the explanation of these facts must bring H into play (See Chapter VI, section F).

Given the absence of a structural semantics on a par with the classical one, any defense of structural realism will inevitably involve the kind of hand-waving and of reliance on specific examples which 'exact' philosophers contemptuously dismiss. I shall however not allow myself to be deterred. The relation 'R' mentioned above typically contains mathematical predicates whose form, thanks to the Correspondence Principle, remains quasi-constant across successive revolutions. By contrast, the intended referents of R's arguments often change dramatically during periods of scientific upheaval. This is illustrated by the following examples, some of which were adduced by Poincaré (Also see Worrall 1996). Though Fresnel's, Maxwell's and Lorentz's hypotheses appear to refer to very different entities, namely to a mechanical medium, to the electromagnetic ether and to a disembodied field respectively, the basic equations are approximately the same in all three cases. Another example is afforded by Newtonian mechanics which is known to have been supplanted by quantum physics: whereas Newton's laws, namely: $p_x = m.dx/dt$, $dp_x/dt = - \partial V/\partial x$, etc. connect the acceleration of a single particle with the net force acting on it, the corresponding quantum-mechanical equations: $<p_x> = m.d(<x>)/dt$, $d(<p_x>)/dt = - <\partial V/\partial x>$, etc. are relations between various expectation values, i.e., between quantities involving probabilities (See Dicke and Wittke 1960, Chapter 8). But by virtue of the Correspondence Principle, the classical and the quantum-physical equations have the same form. Thus, in all these cases, the relata appear to have changed dramatically while the relations are left almost intact by successive scientific revolutions. As for the confirmed empirical content of successive hypotheses, it has steadily increased. That it could not have decreased is anyway warranted by the Correspondence Principle.

This quasi-cumulative aspect of progress, coupled with the dramatic predictive successes achieved by the sciences, led Poincaré to formulate his no-miracles argument: short of accepting an implausible conspiracy theory, the development of science must be regarded as indicating that relations common to empirically successful laws reflect objective aspects of the ontological order of things. We have however no reason to suppose that the individual terms occurring in our theories denote separate items of reality

(See above Chapter II, A). To repeat: SSR proves more realistic with respect to universals than to individuals. And once again, the semantic difficulties mentioned above arise: how can we rationally maintain that a relation holds good when we totally ignore what its arguments denote? We might be tempted to reply that although the latter undoubtedly *possess* referents, nothing is known about these referents beyond their satisfaction of the relation in question. The difficulty with this minimalist claim is that even the logical types of the relata are often problematic. For example: in going over from classical to quantum mechanics, we find that although the form of the Hamiltonian is unchanged, its argument-places are no longer filled by quantities denoting momenta or spatio-temporal positions, but by Hermitian operators, i.e. by second-order entities. We must therefore remain cautiously agnostic about the nature of the relata while making some epistemic claims—no matter how modest—about the relations themselves. And we have already noted that no coherent semantics for this approach is as yet available (except possibly in Category Theory). Fortunately for the structuralist, mathematics provides examples where the focus shifts from the study of predicates subsuming certain entities to that of the higher-order relations between the predicates themselves. For instance: sets, i.e. properties of individuals, bear to one another certain relations which are directly investigated by Boolean Algebra. In other words: Boolean Algebra concerns itself with classes without explicitly taking account of the elements of these classes. Similarly, topologies consist of systems of open sets; where the latter have properties and bear to one another relations which can be examined abstractly, i.e. independently of the membership relation between point and set; and quantum theorists extract non-classical logics from the lattice of subspaces of a Hilbert space, all this *without* mentioning the vectors constituting these subspaces. Lattice theory can thus be viewed as a study of universals without any direct reference to individuals. Of course, such theories can in turn be expressed in first-order languages whose variables range over domains of objects; but the latter are universals rather than genuine particulars. Even from the semantic viewpoint, universals can thus be apprehended directly, i.e. without specifically mentioning the individuals falling under them. (For an excellent study of Boolean algebras and, more generally, of lattices see H. Hermes 1955).

The above considerations prove highly relevant to the genesis of the heuristics of research programs. A physical theory is a nexus of first-order relations among individuals. Through shifting the focus away from the individuals and towards the relations and their second-order properties, the scientist often manages to devise heuristic constraints which he then imposes on the form of all laws. This is hardly surprising, given that all heuristic reasoning is *metatheoretical* or second-order in character. As an example, let us cite Poincaré's logic of discovery, which largely consists of the following principles:

(a) the Correspondence Principle, together with the requirements of
(b) Lorentz-covariance, of
(c) derivability from a principle of least action and, more particularly, of
(d) the possibility of a Hamiltonian formulation of the laws to be constructed.

Let us recall that the last Chapter dealt with the Correspondence Principle as a general heuristic device. Turning to Lorentz-covariance, it can be regarded as one example of the symmetry requirements which were described above. Finally: the existence of the Hamiltonian was seen to be closely connected with the conservation of energy which flows from the Identity Principle (See Chapter II, section C).

(B) Difficulties Facing Realism

Qua epistemological position, SSR flows from two basic insights, or rather from the acceptance of two theses.

[a] Consider the characterization of realism as the belief in the existence of a mind-independent reality. This definition is unsatisfactory because it presupposes a schism between the mind on the one hand, and that which it tries to grasp on the other. By metaphysical realism I shall therefore understand the view that there exists one structured and undivided reality of which the mind is part; moreover that, far from imposing their own order on things, our mental operations are in their turn governed by the laws which describe the workings of Nature. Hence our conscious activity—or sequence of brain states—evolves according to the very laws it sets out to capture. As shown by Planck and Popper, this thesis might well entail that a total explanation of everything in the universe can never be achieved by the human mind: on pain of vicious circularity, the brain is in principle incapable of predicting its own future states. Far from being incompatible with metaphysical realism or even with determinism, this negative result could be regarded as one of the welcome consequences of realism. (M. Planck 1965b. Also K.R. Popper 1982, Chapter 3).

Methodological realism consists of the further assumption that the structure of reality is—at least in part—intelligible to the human mind. It is therefore rational for scientists to aim at grasping that reality. They may of course choose not to do so and content themselves with constructing phenomenological laws.

Henceforth referred to as SR, scientific realism adds the thesis that successful theories, i.e. those unified systems which explain the data without ad hoc assumptions, are approximately true. That is: such systems reflect the order of things as they are in themselves. Successful hypotheses thus model and in some sense 'correspond' to the real structure of the world. But as already explained, the syntactic continuity effected by the Correspondence Principle appears belied by the referential discontinuity obtaining at the ontological level. For example: irrespective of whether they really exist or not, the classical and the quantum-mechanical electrons are very different entities; the classical particle consists of a well-defined distribution of charge in space, while its quantum-mechanical counterpart is a charged mass having no sharp spatio-temporal location. Similarly, Newtonian mass represents the amount of substance in a given body while its relativistic counterpart is expressed by an inertial coefficient dependent on the speed of the mobile. In both cases, the same word, *electron* viz. *mass*, is used in order to mask an abrupt referential discontinuity. Such discontinuities have frequently occurred in the past and will probably do so in the future; yet no matter how moderate or structural, scientific realism presupposes a minimum of substantive—as opposed to merely terminological—gradualism. This is why Laudan and Fine declared realism dead (See Leplin 1984).

It has of course to be admitted that the extensions of the two notions of the classical and of the quantum-mechanical electron are disjoint; which is nonetheless perfectly compatible with the continuity of connotation, i.e. of Fregean sense (See Frege 1986). I take it that the concept of an electron can roughly be regarded as a cluster of predicates. Despite being distinct intentional objects, the classical and the quantum-mechanical electrons have several attributes in common. For example, both possess rest-mass and electric charge, both have the capacity of giving rise to an electromagnetic field, etc. Of course, if a predicate occurs in one cluster while its negation is implied by the other, the two extensions become disjoint. Yet, as we move from one hypothesis to the next, it seems reasonable to require that there be some overlap between corresponding notions which often bear the same name. But as just explained, such an overlap is not to be sought in the extensions but in the connotations of the two concepts. Even in the absence of any extensional overlap, continuity might obtain in the following way: some predicates admit of varying degrees of intensity signified by numerical indices; two such predicates, bearing different though nearly equal indices, may respectively occur in the property-clusters of the old and of the new notion. Because of this numerical difference, the extensions of the two notions will be disjoint but their meanings might nearly be qualitatively identical. For example, the classical and the relativistic masses of a body have at least one property in common: both yield a measure of the object's inertial resistance to acceleration from rest. For nonzero velocities, they represent different degrees of laziness but, provided v/c be small, this difference remains negligible (the difference $(m_0 /\sqrt{(1-v^2/c^2)}) - m_0$ between the two masses tends to zero with v/c). Thus the antirealist charge of discontinuity rests on an analysis which wrongly focuses on the denotations rather than on the meanings of certain terms.

To my mind, the insistence on *referential* continuity makes as little sense as the requirement that an old hypothesis should not only tend towards but also be logically compatible with the new one. Yet, since the demand for some overlap between the extensions of corresponding concepts seems analogous to a consistency condition, it appears to be minimal and hence highly reasonable. Alas, this is not how science progresses. Putting it bluntly: inconsistency is perfectly compatible with continuity; for it is well known that a function will generally differ from its limit, and the limiting case of a law will generally be inconsistent with the latter. We should consequently require that sequences of successful theories display a near-cumulative pattern only as regards their Fregean senses. As for the—wrong-headed—demand for referential continuity, it would inevitably lead us to adopt a principle of charity according to which Newton, Huygens, Young, Fresnel, Maxwell and Einstein were, unbeknown to themselves, talking about the self-same entity, namely the photon. This claim may be considered true in the far-fetched sense that the photon was one hidden cause of various observations made by all these scientists; but this principle of charity in no way explains the actual continuity in the development of optics from Newton to Einstein; for successive scientists have conceived of this hidden cause in logically irreconcilable ways. This is why the thesis of intensional continuity seems to me to provide the only solution to this puzzle. And this is precisely the solution offered by SSR.

Note that physical science is committed neither to the correspondence nor even to Tarski's semantic theory of truth. There is no reason why a hypothesis should mirror the world by way of the usual term-by-term mapping postulated by traditional semantics; for the structure of a scientific system can be held to reflect reality, even though the components of the system fail to refer to separate items of that reality. This is in effect the structural-realist stance denoted by 'SSR'. In its defense, it can be pointed out that traditional semantics is inspired by a commonsense ontology consisting of discrete intentional objects; where the emphasis should be placed on the word '*intentional*'. But such an ontology is not necessarily that of the *external* world. Common sense naturally tends to assimilate the transcendent to the intentional sphere, hence to posit well-circumscribed entities subsumed by various predicates. This need however not be the way in which Nature operates. As already mentioned, external objects are known to us exclusively by description, i.e. through a network of fallible conjectures; so that we are unable directly to ascertain the kind of correspondence which might obtain between our successful hypotheses and the transcendent world at which they are aimed. Only idealists like Berkeley and Husserl felt certain about the nature of such a correspondence; for idealism postulates only *immanent entities*. By contrast, the manner in which realist theories latch on to the world constitutes a *problem* for which there exist only conjectural solutions. Thus SSR should not be made to stand and fall with any specific theory of truth: all SSR asserts is that highly corroborated theories reflect the ontological order in a way which each individual scientist may—or may not—choose to specify. There is no reason why realists should not adopt a fallibilist attitude with respect both to the mode of reference and to the truth-value of their conjectures. In this connection, Duhem aptly compared scientific concepts to the flat pieces of an armor which never fits exactly the knight's body. Such concepts have a symbolic or metaphorical, rather than a strictly referential function. Poincaré's rider should nonetheless never be forgotten: the meanings and the intentional referents of the observational terms must be fixed in advance of theory. (For the important role which metaphors play in scientific explanations, see E. McMullin 1984).

Going back to the three positions outlined above, note that each is stronger than the one preceding it. This is illustrated by the following examples. It can be maintained that Kant was a metaphysical, but not a methodological realist. As for Mach and Poincaré, the former rejected realism altogether while the latter not only subscribed to, but was also one of the authors of SSR. These two philosophers are at the opposite ends of a spectrum in which Duhem occupies an intermediate position. As regards Popper: despite his outspoken methodological realism, his attitude to SR remained interestingly ambiguous. He initially based his own version of SR on a definition of verisimilitude linked to the correspondence theory of truth; but as shown in Chapter 1, David Miller undermined this approach by showing Popper's definition to be inapplicable to any false propositions. Whereas Miller accepts methodological realism whilst rejecting SR, Popper fell back on an intuitive notion of verisimilitude, thus indicating that he still adhered to SR (See Popper 1983, Introduction V).

[b] There is furthermore the realization that we are unable to ascertain the truth-value even of an atomic proposition involving 'objective' predicates, i.e. relations between terms some of which refer to transcendent entities; for of these we do not have the kind of knowledge by acquaintance which is the only one enabling us effectively to decide whether these objects bear to one another certain relations or possess some given properties. The only knowledge we can aspire to with regard to these transcendent entities is that offered by a nexus of conjectures. Should the latter prove coherent and empirically successful, then it will provide us with 'implicit definitions' of a family of domains; i.e. our conjectures will delimit a class of models one of which *might be* the real world.

In short: *SSR results from the rejection of all forms of apriorism regarding both the mode of reference and the truth of high-level scientific propositions;* it is nothing but realist—and realistic—fallibilism; which is however not to be confused with skepticism or with anti-realism.

(C) THE RAMSEY SENTENCE

A physical theory Σ is usually presented as the consequence class of finitely many proper axioms. The conjunction of the latter can therefore be written as a single formula $G(Q_1,..., Q_n, T_1,..., T_m)$, where the Q_i's denote the observational, and the T_j's the theoretical predicates of Σ (We shall write $\underline{Q}$ and $\underline{T}$ for the two sequences $Q_1,...,Q_n$ and $T_1,...,T_m$ respectively). Only in the case of the Q_i's do we have any direct access to the referents of the arguments of these predicates and are moreover able to decide whether these referents are subsumed by the Q_i's. As for the T_j's, all we can legitimately claim to know about them is that they bear to each other and to the 'observables' $\underline{Q}$ the second-order relation $G(\underline{Q}, \underline{T})$. According to SSR, the maximum amount of scientific knowledge we are entitled to lay claim to is represented by the Ramsey sentence of $G(\underline{Q}, \underline{T})$, i.e. by $(\exists \underline{t})G(\underline{Q}, \underline{t})$, where $\underline{t}$ stands for the m-tuple $(t_1,...,t_m)$, and $(\exists \underline{t})$ for $(\exists t_1,...,t_m)$.

That this conclusion is at first sight highly counter-intuitive is shown by the following example. According to classical science, physical reality consists of hard atoms construed as bits of matter possessing mass and electric charge. Scientists had in mind a concrete picture consisting of a spatio-temporal continuum containing a velocity field $\underline{V} = (v_1(\underline{x}, t), v_2(\underline{x}, t), v_3(\underline{x}, t))$ together with charge and mass densities described by two functions $\rho(\underline{x}, t)$ and $\mu(\underline{x}, t)$; where t denotes the time and $\underline{x}$ the spatial coordinates. But despite such seeming concreteness, it is obvious that a quantity like $\rho(\underline{x},t)$ is grasped exclusively by description, i.e. by means of a theoretical predicate $R(\underline{x}, t, r)$, where: r represents the function $\rho(\underline{x}, t)$ and $(\forall \underline{x})(\forall t)(\exists !r)R(\underline{x}, t, r)$ is a consequence of the underlying theory. R must therefore figure among $T_1,...,T_m$ or else be defined in terms of these predicates. Hence all our assertions about the charge, mass and velocity distributions are theoretical and must already have been packed into the matrix $G(Q, \underline{T})$; they will consequently be bound by the $(\exists \underline{t})$ in $(\exists \underline{t})G(Q, \underline{t})$.

Let us now address the problems posed by the logico-mathematical principles of a scientific system. It is well known that classical logic consists of infinitely many postulates subsumed by various schemes. But since every model of $G(Q, \underline{T})$ automatically satisfies all the logical principles, the latter need not occur explicitly in $G(Q, \underline{T})$. A serious problem however arises in connection with the mathematical axioms. As long as these were held to be analytic, they could be regarded as belonging to the logical background. But mathematics has long been acknowledged as synthetic; so its axioms must figure explicitly in $G(Q, \underline{T})$. Basic mathematical concepts like those of class and class-membership should therefore be quantified over when the transition is made from $G(Q, \underline{T})$ to the Ramsey-sentence $(\exists \underline{t})G(Q, \underline{t})$. A major difficulty stems from the fact that mathematics is normally developed within the framework of Zermelo-Fraenkel set theory (ZFC). ZFC possesses infinitely many axioms while $(\exists \underline{t})G(Q, \underline{t})$ is meant to be a finite formula of the object-language. It is therefore essential for us to show that the mathematical theories used in the empirical sciences are finitely axiomatizable.

ZFC must *prima facie* be part and parcel of every physical hypothesis H, which ought therefore to require infinitely many postulates. But in 1952, S.C. Kleene proved that through the adjunction of appropriate predicates, any axiomatizable theory H can be finitely axiomatized. Let us note right now that this result is all that needs be presupposed in vindicating the theses developed in the subsequent sections of the present Chapter. But though undoubtedly sound, Kleene's proof seems to me counter-intuitive to the point of being practically incomprehensible. This is why I decided to follow another approach—inspired by Gödelian methods—which shows how a finitely axiomatized class theory can be imbedded into *an arbitrary* empirical system. (See Appendices 1 and 2. Also K. Gödel 1940). This method possesses at least two advantages. We have just mentioned that it can be applied to any physical hypothesis. Since it moreover puts something like the Gödelian class-theoretic machinery at the physicist's disposal, it offers considerable advantages. For example: a finite number of individual names $a_1,..., a_m, u_1,..., u_s$ can be added to our primitive vocabulary where, for each $j = 1, 2,..., m$, the symbol a_j stands for the extension of the predicate T_j. In this way, class-theory can be brought to bear on all sets consisting of physical objects or of mathematical entities or of both. Thus we obtain a system of the form

$G(k, \in, a_1,..., a_m, u_1,..., u_s, Q_1,..., Q_n)$ which incorporates applied mathematics and whose Ramsey-sentence, namely $(\exists k, \in)(\exists a_1,..., a_m, u_1,...,u_s)$ $G(k, \in, a_1,..., a_m, u_1,..., u_s, Q_1,..., Q_n)$, involves the monadic predicate k and the dyadic relation $\in$. These are intuitively defined as follows: $k(x) \equiv$ [x is a class]; $(x \in y) \equiv$ [x is a member of the class y]. Now note that $(\exists k, \in)$ represents the only second-order quantification which needs to be carried out in order to obtain $(\exists k, \in)(\exists a_1,..., a_m, u_1,...,u_s) G(k, \in, a_1,..., a_m, u_1,..., u_s, Q_1,..., Q_n)$. Should the notions of *class* (k) and of *class-membership* ($\in$) be regarded as logical constants and hence as *not* to be quantified over, then the Ramsey-sentence would conveniently reduce to the *first-order* formula $(\exists a_1,..., a_m, u_1,...,u_s) G(k, \in, a_1,..., a_m, u_1,..., u_s, Q_1,..., Q_n)$. It ought nonetheless to be stressed that the conclusions drawn in the rest of this Chapter in no way depend on any *extra assumptions* about the first-order character of the Ramsey-sentence; nor, for that matter, on the results established in the Appendix. As already remarked, Kleene's finite axiomatizability theorem is all that needs be (implicitly) invoked in what follows. Moreover, in most of the examples adduced below, the considered Ramsey-sentences turn out to be *logically equivalent* to first-order formulas.

(D) Newman's Criticism of Russell's Position

Several authors have recently highlighted what they take to be a major objection to SSR, i.e. to the account of the status of theories advocated by both Poincaré and Russell. This objection is *so* major that it raises questions about the very *possibility* of structural realism.

The objection goes, essentially, as follows:

(i) For any proposition H, let H* henceforth denote the Ramsey-sentence of H. Thus: $(G(Q, \underline{T}))^* =_{Def} (\exists \underline{t}) G(Q, \underline{t})$. As already explained, SSR leads to the view that the cognitive content of any scientific theory H is fully captured by H* where, as just set out, H* is formed from H by substituting second-order variables for all the theoretical predicates involved in H and by then existentially quantifying over all these variables.

(ii) But as was allegedly first shown by the mathematician M.H.A. Newman—responding to Russell's version of structural realism—a theory's Ramsey-sentence is satisfiable in a 'trivial' way; for it imposes no more than a cardinality constraint on the scientist's domain of discourse. (Newman 1928).

(iii) However, scientific theories clearly do much more than impose constraints on the size of the universe.

(iv) So structural realism is committed to an entirely untenable account of the cognitive content of scientific theories, namely that this content is captured by the theory's Ramsey-sentence, and is itself untenable.

Newman's argument was reintroduced into the philosophy of science by Demopoulos and Friedman and, via their article, it has attracted a good deal of attention in the past few years (Demopoulos and Friedman 1985).

I shall however show that despite their apparent cogency, Newman's objections owe their *superficial* reasonableness to an oversight, or rather to an easily corrigible mistake on Russell's part. After rectifying Russell's error, it will be seen that Newman's argument in no way threatens structural realism—though consideration of this argument helps towards clarifying important aspects of SSR.

(E) RAMSIFICATION AND "TRIVIALIZATION"

Demopoulos and Friedman quote the following claim, made by Russell in *The Analysis of Matter*:

Whatever we infer from perceptions, it is only structure that we can validly infer; and structure is what can be expressed by mathematical logic (Russell 1927, p. 254).

The only legitimate attitude about the physical world seems to be one of complete agnosticism as regards all but its mathematical properties (Russell 1927, p. 270).

According to Demopoulos and Friedman, Newman, who explicitly referred to Russell, showed that any view which identifies the cognitive content of a scientific theory with that of its Ramsey sentence faces 'insurmountable difficulties'. The crucial paragraph of their paper, which in turn quotes Newman, runs as follows:

The difficulty is with the claim that *only* structure is known. On this view "the world consists of objects, forming an aggregate whose structure with respect to a certain relation R is known, say [it has] structure W; but of R nothing is known . . . but its existence; . . . all we can say is *There is* a relation R such that the structure of the external world with reference to R is W" (Newman 1928, p. 144). But "*any* collection of things can be organized so as to have the structure W, provided there are the right number of them" (p. 144, italics added). Thus, on this view, only cardinality questions are open to discovery! Every other claim about the world that can be known at all can be known a priori as a logical consequence of the existence of α-many objects. For any given set A of cardinality α can, with a minimum amount of set theory or second-order logic, establish the existence of a relation having the structure W, provided that W is compatible with the cardinality constraint that $| A | = \alpha$. (Demopoulos and M. Friedman 1985, pp. 627–28)

It was admittedly unfortunate that in his (1927) Russell spoke of a *purely* structural description being *inferred* from perceptual data. The fault lies not so much with the inductive overtones of the verb 'infer', invalid though any such inference might be; as with the implicit assumption that once the inference is carried out, an exclusively structural account is obtained, i.e. one in which no observational terms occur. In other words: after being used during the inferential process, all observational results are jettisoned, thus yielding a proposition $H(T_1,\ldots, T_m)$ where all the predicates $T_1,\ldots,T_m$ are theoretical. The proposition $H(T_1,\ldots, T_m)$ will henceforth be assumed to be a first-order sentence. Ramsifying, obtain $(\exists t_1,t_2,\ldots,t_m)$ $H(t_1,\ldots, t_m)$. Let us note that $(\exists t_1,t_2,\ldots,t_m)H(t_1,\ldots, t_m)$ expresses a mere consistency condition; it states that $H(T_1,\ldots, T_m)$ possesses at least one model. We have here a result which, should $H(T_1,\ldots, T_m)$ turn out to be consistent, is guaranteed by the Löwenheim-Skolem theorem. The latter furthermore tells us that the model in question can be assumed to be countable (See section F, [b] below).

In conformity with his overall philosophical position, Russell could nevertheless have adopted an alternative—more precisely: a hypothetico-deductivist—approach. He could have resorted to a mixed first-order proposition $G(Q_1,\ldots, Q_n, T_1,\ldots, T_m)$ where the observational terms $Q_1,\ldots,Q_n$ figure alongside the theoretical predicates $T_1,\ldots,T_m$. Being empirically falsifiable, the corresponding Ramsey-sentence, namely $(\exists t_1,t_2,\ldots,t_m)G(Q_1,\ldots, Q_n, t_1,\ldots, t_m)$, would have been far from trivially satisfiable (See section F below). Note however that this defense of Russell's structuralist thesis is predicated on a division between 'theoretical' and 'observational' terms; where the latter are taken to be understood in advance of any physical theory; that is: directly and without any involvement of description. This means that those 'antecedently understood' predicates retain their referents from interpretation to interpretation. But if our basic notions are all 'objective', i.e. transcendent and hence known exclusively by description, then we are bound to end up with an observationally untestable system of the form $H(T_1,..., T_m)$. This was in effect the conclusion reached by Neurath when he proposed a purely physicalist approach which bans the use of indexicals. In Chapter III, it was shown that like Popper after him, Neurath ascribed a—very modest—role to observation; but that being exclusively *causal*, the latter does not enable the scientist to affirm that his 'basic' statements can be *known* to be true in the sense of *corresponding* to certain experimental results. Neurath did not baulk at drawing the conclusion that every proposition, whether theoretical or 'protocol', could be struck out, kept out or else allowed into any system, provided the latter remains consistent. He thereby espoused a coherence theory of scientific truth. For his part, Popper proposed a consensual criterion for the acceptability of basic statements; a criterion which he honestly acknowledged to be conventionalist in character .

Let us show that such an *extremist* structuralist position is indeed exposed to at least one of the following two dangers: the danger of skepticism or that of utter triviality. Every scientific system $H(T_1,..., T_m)$ is supposed to contain ordinary arithmetic and to be both consistent and axiomatizable. $H(T_1,...,T_m)$ is therefore incomplete; hence, for at least one proposition A, neither A nor ¬A follows logically from $H(T_1,..., T_m)$. There is moreover no guarantee that A must necessarily be a 'theoretical' rather than a 'protocol' sentence. Be it as it may, A or alternatively ¬A can be consistently added to $H(T_1,..., T_m)$, thus yielding two new incompatible systems. Continuing in this fashion, it can be proved that there exist any number of internally consistent and mutually incompatible theories each one of which contains $H(T_1,..., T_m)$. Neurath's standpoint makes it impossible for us to give epistemological preference to any one of these systems. Thus we end up with the sort of skepticism which turns the undeniable technological progress of the sciences into an ongoing miracle.

Turning now to the danger of triviality: as already explained, if structural realism did imply that *all* that can be 'known' is structure, then it would entail that scientific hypotheses are indistinguishable from purely formal games; and so SSR would face insuperable difficulties. In fact however, the view is that while *theoretical* terms are known exclusively by description, observational entities are known both by ostension and by description—within the global context defined by the formula $G(Q_1,\ldots, Q_n, T_1,\ldots, T_m)$; for it should be noted that in $G(Q_1,\ldots, Q_n, T_1,\ldots, T_m)$, the observational Q's are indissolubly entangled with the theoretical T's. It is nowadays generally alleged that there is neither an absolute nor a sharp distinction between the theoretical and the observational predicates. Russell (along with Poincaré, as well as Grover Maxwell and Ayer) would—to the contrary—rightly identify the observational predicates with those decidable 'phenomenologically', i.e. on the basis of perception. For remember that according to Russell, we acquire knowledge by *acquaintance* as well as by description. In effect, Russell's SSR flows from the insight that while we do possess knowledge by acquaintance of percepts, our knowledge of theoretical entities is only by description (See Russell 1984, Chapter 1, also Grover Maxwell 1971).

Here however, there is no need to commit oneself to any particular account of the 'observational basis' of science. Some may wish to follow David Lewis in taking the distinction to be simply one between the 'old' predicates (taken—within the current context —*somehow or other* to be antecendently understood), and the 'new' predicates. Others might like to regard the observationally decidable predicates as those involved in Poincaré's 'crude facts'—'two points (for example the end of a meter needle and a certain point on the dial of the meter) roughly coincide'. But however exactly the distinction is understood, no serious version of structural realism can get going without some such distinction. If *all* the predicates of a scientific theory were taken to be interpreted only within the context of the claims made by the theory; if, that is, none were taken to be anchored in experience independently of our attempted descriptions of the transcendent universe, then the constraints imposed by the Ramsey-sentence (or indeed by the original theory itself) would be hopelessly weak. For the theory would then be indistinguishable from a mathematical system, the latter being subject to a mere consistency condition. The criticism of those who object to structural realism would then reduce to the ungainsayable truism that a consistent formal theory constitutes an 'implicit definition' of its primitive concepts; i.e. that it merely determines a class of models (See D. Lewis 1970).

It should be granted that Demopoulos and Friedman seem to have anticipated this counter-objection when they wrote:

More precisely, if our theory is consistent and if all its purely observational consequences are true, then the truth of the Ramsey-sentence *follows* as a theorem of set-theory or second-order logic, provided our initial domain has the right cardinality—if it doesn't, then the consistency condition of our theory again implies the existence of a domain that does. (Demopoulos and Friedman 1985, p. 635)

Thus, according to Demopoulos and Friedman: only what the Ramsey-sentence asserts *over and above its observational content* is reducible to logic or to mathematics; more precisely: to a consistency condition or to a cardinality constraint. This 'over and above' however proves to be not only badly defined but also indefinable in any non-trivial way; for on the one hand, the Ramsey-sentence generally fails to be logically implied by its empirical basis, i.e. from the set of true, empirically decidable and hence *singular* sentences (Note that every basic statement must be not only be singular but also fully empirically decidable). If, on the other hand, all the entailed but undecidable 'empirical generalizations' were included in the observational content of a theory, then the Ramsey-sentence *might well* prove to be one of them; in which case the Demopoulos–Friedman thesis would collapse into the trivial claim that the Ramsey-sentence logically entails itself.

Consider the following example—which is admittedly simplistic. Let $A \equiv [(\forall x)(F(x) \to T(x)) \wedge (\forall y)(T(y) \to K(y))]$, where T is a theoretical notion and both F and K are observational concepts. Thus $A^* \equiv (\exists t)[(\forall x)(F(x) \to t(x)) \wedge (\forall y)(t(y) \to K(y))]$. Clearly $\vdash [A^* \leftrightarrow (\forall x)(F(x) \to K(x))]$ holds; so that, in this particular case, A^* proves to be equivalent to a first-order sentence. Let $\{a_j : j \in \Delta\}$ be a set of names for all the observable entities in the universe. Δ is therefore infinite. Assume that $F(a_j) \wedge K(a_j)$ has been ascertained as true for all $j \in \Delta$. If we are to believe Demopoulos and Friedman, then what the Ramsey-sentence asserts over and above $\{F(a_j) \wedge K(a_j) : j \in \Delta\}$ is merely tautological. This claim can be easily refuted as follows. First note that the *logical* difference between two statements Y and X, i.e. the weakest formula which, in conjunction with X , entails Y, is $(\neg X \vee Y)$ or $(X \to Y)$; but we are here dealing not with the difference between A^* and a single statement, but with that between A^* and the infinite set of observation reports $\{F(a_j) \wedge K(a_j) : j \in \Delta\}$. For the sake of argument, let us suppose that the infinite conjunction $\wedge \{F(a_j) \wedge K(a_j) : j \in \Delta\}$ is syntactically well-formed; so that Demopoulos and Friedman's thesis is tantamount to the claim that $\wedge \{F(a_j) \wedge K(a_j) : j \in \Delta\} \to A^*$ is a logical truth; i.e. that $\{F(a_j) \wedge K(a_j) : j \in \Delta\} \vdash (\forall x)(F(x) \to K(x))$.

That this inference is invalid can most easily be established by invoking the compactness theorem, which yields: $\{F(a_{q(1)}) \wedge K(a_{q(2)}), \ldots, F(a_{q(n)}) \wedge K(a_{q(n)})\} \vdash (\forall x)[F(x) \rightarrow K(x)]$ for some n; whence $\vdash [(F(a_{q(1)}) \wedge K(a_{q(2)}), \ldots, F(a_{q(n)}) \wedge K(a_{q(n)})) \rightarrow (\forall x)(F(x) \rightarrow K(x))]$. It now suffices to point out that this last formula can be falsified in any domain possessing more than n elements. Thus the Ramsey sentence $(\forall x)(F(x) \rightarrow K(x))$ goes beyond the set $\{F(a_j) \wedge K(a_j) : j \in \Delta\}$ of true observation reports. Note moreover that this conclusion in no way depends on the compactness theorem; for consider any domain $\Delta'' \supset \Delta$; Δ'' clearly yields a model of $\{F(a_j) \wedge K(a_j) : j \in \Delta\}$ which falsifies $(\forall x)(F(x) \rightarrow K(x))$. (Take F to be true in Δ'', and K to be true in Δ but false in $\Delta'' \setminus \Delta$). This result flows from the impossibility of asserting, in the object-language, that x is intended to range exclusively over the denotations of the a_j's. And even if this were possible, we should have no way of knowing that the a_j's name *all* the observable entities in the universe; so that even though we might, by some superhuman effort, have actually verified A* through an infinite number $\mid \Delta \mid$ of observations, we shall still remain unaware of this fact; and our epistemological position would remain essentially unchanged.

As already mentioned, some philosophers choose to consider the 'empirical generalization' $A* \equiv (\forall x)(F(x) \rightarrow K(x))$, i.e. the Ramsey sentence itself, as belonging to the empirical basis of the hypothesis A; in which case $A*$ would trivially follow from that basis. Let us pursue this line of thought a little further. The main objection raised against SSR seems to me to flow from an unacceptable definition of what it is for a statement to be an empirical generalization. Thus: a) Following Mach, Carnap and most neopositivists regarded every first-order sentence K in which only observational predicates occur as an empirical generalization. Hence such a K would certainly have been regarded as belonging to its own empirical content (See Carnap 1966, Chapter 23). b) Let us provisionally assume that the mathematical concepts k and $\in$ are logical in character; an assumption made by practically all Neopositivists. It follows from the above that all Ramsey-sentences can be put in the first-order form $H* \equiv (\exists a_1, \ldots, a_m, u_1, \ldots, u_s) G(k, \in, a_1, \ldots, a_m, u_1, \ldots, u_s, Q_1, \ldots, Q_n)$ where only the observational predicates $Q_1, \ldots, Q_n$ occur free. *Ergo*: SSR reduces science to a sequence of H*'s and hence to a sequence of empirical generalizations; it does not therefore deserve the appellation 'Realism'.

It will however be shown that a) and b) follow from a highly misleading and hence inadmissible definition of 'empirical generalization' (See below, section H).

(F) What Cognitive Difference, If Any, Is There Between a Theory X and Its Ramsey-Sentence X*?

Summing up: we have established that as soon as a distinction is made between the theoretical notions and a fixed set of observational predicates, both the Newman and the Demopoulos-Friedman objections fail.

Let us now go back to the general case of an arbitrary hypothesis G($\underline{Q}$, $\underline{T}$) and of its Ramsey-sentence ($\exists \underline{t}$) G ($\underline{Q}$, $\underline{t}$). Again note that because they are taken to have referents fixed independently of G, the observational predicates $\underline{Q}$ are *not* quantified over. It can now easily be proved that the Ramsey-sentence ($\exists \underline{t}$)G($\underline{Q}$, $\underline{t}$) does not merely constrain the cardinality of its models—in fact, it sometimes does less than this, but generally it does much more. Comparing the logical strength of the two formulas ($\exists \underline{t}$)G($\underline{Q}$, $\underline{t}$) and G($\underline{Q},\underline{T}$), we first register, without any surprise, that:

(1) $\vdash$ [G($\underline{Q},\underline{T}$) → ($\exists \underline{t}$) G($\underline{Q},\underline{t}$)]; i.e. the original theory always entails its Ramsey-sentence.

Consider next the logical difference:

(2) [($\exists \underline{t}$)G($\underline{Q},\underline{t}$) → G($\underline{Q},\underline{T}$)] between G($\underline{Q},\underline{T}$) and ($\exists \underline{t}$)G($\underline{Q},\underline{t}$).

As is well known, Carnap looked upon (2) as an analytic meaning-postulate. He wrote:

> Thus the simplest way to formulate an A-postulate A_T for a theory *TC* is: (A_T) ^RTC → *TC* [i.e. X*→ X]. It can easily be shown that this sentence is factually empty. It tells us nothing about the world. All the factual content is in the sentence F_T, which is the Ramsey-sentence ^RTC [i.e. X*]. The sentence A_T simply asserts that *if* the Ramsey-sentence is true, we must then understand the theoretical terms in such a way that the entire theory is true. It is a purely analytic sentence, because its semantic truth is based on the meanings intended for the theoretical terms. (Carnap 1966; Chapter 28, p. 270)

From a logical viewpoint, both Carnap's notion of an analytic meaning A-postulate and his manner of arriving at the conclusion that $(X^*\rightarrow X)$ is such a postulate are highly suspect. His whole concept of analyticity—as distinct from that of logical truth—can actually be called into doubt. He surveys the sequence $Q_1,\ldots,Q_n$ of all the observational predicates occurring in a scientific hypothesis $G(Q_1,...,Q_n, T_1,...,T_m)$. Since n is usually very large, he introduces abbreviations by means of so-called D-rules which can, to my mind, be expressed only *metalinguistically*. For example: both 'animal' and 'bird' might stand for conjunctions of certain Q_i's, where the Q_i's defining 'animal' naturally figure in the definiens of 'bird'. There is of course nothing wrong with such D-rules being used in order to simplify presentation. It ought however to be kept in mind that statements containing words like 'animal' or 'bird' are not sentences of the object-language; they can be transformed into such sentences through replacing 'animal' and 'bird' by their definiens in terms of the Q_i's. Once this is done, then propositions like

(*A1*) All birds are animals

trivially turn out to be logically true. In this sense, there is no harm in calling the statement (*A1*) analytic.

Carnap however proposes to circumvent the D-rules by directly looking upon (*A1*) as analytic. But the omission of the D-rules entails that sentences like (*A1*) must now belong to the object-language; which in turn means that 'bird' and 'animal' have been surreptitiously added to our primitive vocabulary. (*A1*) ought consequently to be regarded as a synthetic judgment. In other words: once a primitive vocabulary and a list of logical constants have been selected, we can no longer *decree* what formulas should be considered analytic; for according to Carnap himself, analyticity must ultimately coincide with logical truth, i.e. with truth under all interpretations of the *primitive* descriptive terms.

By regarding (*A1*) as a *meaning*-postulate, Carnap anyway seems to me to have conflated syntax with semantics. Since notions like those of meaning, reference and truth-value are semantic in character, they cannot be adequately rendered by syntax alone; for they involve a reference both to language and—normally—to something extra-linguistic. It cannot legitimately be claimed that (*A1*) talks not only about birds and animals but also about the meanings of 'bird' and 'animal'. Here, Frege's fundamental insight ought to be strictly adhered to: no matter how much it might initially have been informed by philosophical considerations, the syntax of a language must subsequently fend for itself, that is: proceed without any backward reference to its philosophical foundations. So the best way of avoiding Carnap's ambiguities is to abolish all talk of meaning-postulates and regard (*A1*) as a synthetic proposition expressed in the primitive vocabulary of an enriched object-language. As for the Carnapian concept of a meaning-postulate, it can be retrieved through that of a *metaphysical thesis*—in Popper's sense. The meaning-postulates should be regarded as a set of axioms whose conjunction is metaphysical, i.e. observationally irrefutable. This in no way implies that such conjunctions do no empirical work, but only that they do so within the context of a more embracing system; for the omission of a metaphysical component of a theory might well diminish and even destroy the latter's observational content (See above, Chapter VI).

Let me now explain the manner in which the above considerations apply to the difference $(\exists t)G(Q, t) \to G(Q, T)$ between the theory $G(Q, T)$ and its Ramsey-sentence $(\exists t)G(Q, t)$. Here, Carnap's claim that this difference is analytic proves untenable; for otherwise, by the very definition given by Carnap, $(\exists t)G(Q, t) \to G(Q, T)$ should always be reducible—by way of the D-postulates—to a logically true formula. But this is far from being the case. To begin with, note that both the Q_i's and the T_j's can be chosen from among the primitive predicates, thus preempting any recourse to D-rules; so that we are normally in a position to determine a model of $(\exists t)G(Q, t)$ which falsifies $G(Q, T)$ and hence also $(\exists t)G(Q, t) \to G(Q, T)$. As an example, consider the theory A and its Ramsey-sentence $A*$ defined above; select any domain in which F, K and T denote the classes F_0, K_0 and T_0 respectively, where T_0 is theoretical, $F_0 \subseteq K_0$ and $\text{Not}(F_0 \subseteq T_0)$. This yields a model of $A*$ which falsifies A. Thus a theory is essentially stronger than its Ramsey-sentence; and it seems that Carnap's mistake stems from the positivist prejudice according to which all meaning ought ultimately to be anchored in perceptual experience; so that the role of (2) consists in merely conferring meanings onto the theoretical predicates T.

Let us call any sentence containing no theoretical terms an O-sentence; and let us define a basic statement as a singular O-sentences which is fully empirically decidable. It will be shown not only that (2) is empirically irrefutable and hence metaphysical, but also that it entails no synthetic O-sentence. For suppose that $\vdash [((\exists t)G(Q, t) \to G(Q, T)) \to Z]$, i.e. $\vdash [(\neg(\exists t)G(Q, t) \lor G(Q, T)) \to Z]$, where no T_j occurs in Z. Quantifying over T, obtain $\vdash [(\exists t)(\neg(\exists t)G(Q, t) \lor G(Q, t)) \to Z]$, that is: $\vdash [(\neg(\exists t)G(Q, t) \lor (\exists t)G(Q, t)) \to Z]$; whence: $\vdash Z$. Thus Z is a logical or a mathematical truth. A *fortiori*, proposition (2) metaphysical, though not analytic.

To sum up: Carnap mistakenly conflated 'analytic' with 'metaphysical'; which, given his logical empiricist stance, was almost bound to happen. For according to neopositivism, the absence of any observationally ascertainable content is tantamount to absence of content *tout court*. But this neopositivist dichotomy between the empirical and the analytic, where the latter includes all logical truths, all mathematical principles and all meaning-postulates, is wrong-headed. All we need are Popper's notions of logical truth and of metaphysical proposition. We can legitimately regard all synthetic mathematical principles as metaphysical; for when taken in isolation, they are clearly unfalsifiable. By definition, the remaining propositions, i.e. those which are neither logically true nor observationally irrefutable, will be empirically testable and hence scientific; all of which presupposes that we stick to one primitive vocabulary including a list of logical constants [In the present context, logically false statements do not form a separate category, for they are negations of logical truths]. As for Carnap's meaning-postulates concerning the observational predicates, they can be replaced by *metalinguistic* D-rules; i.e. by verbal definitions specifying how certain abbreviations are to be used. The latter do not genuinely belong to the object-language; they are in principle dispensable and therefore call for no special treatment. Finally: the difference $(X^* \rightarrow X)$ between a theory X and its Ramsey-sentence X^* does not constitute an analytic meaning-postulate, but a metaphysical proposition all of whose consequences are likewise irrefutable.

In his otherwise first-rate *Scientific Realism,* S. Psillos allowed himself to be misled by Carnap into holding that any structural realist who postulates X^* must also accept, *as merely analytic*, the proposition $(X^* \rightarrow X)$. Such a realist would therefore be forced to infer the fully-fledged theory X. When Psillos further claims that the truth of the hypothesis X is an empirical matter, he presupposes that an *interpretation,* not only of the observational, but also of the theoretical predicates occurring in X can and must be specified in terms of natural kinds (Psillos 1999, pp. 51–69). But this is precisely where the problem lies; for whereas X might be refuted by the falsification of any of its observational consequences—all of which possess fixed phenomenological meanings—*ascertaining* the truth of X as a whole involves interpreting all of its terms, observational as well as theoretical. The latter however refer to the external world; so that, barring what Putnam rightly calls a mystical insight into the nature of things, we are unable to break out of our intentional sphere and fix a semantic relation between our theoretical vocabulary and some *transcendent* reality. The structural realist in no way denies that, if true, a scientific hypothesis possesses a global referent and is therefore wholly interpret*able*; he simply points to the *epistemological* fact that we are in principle unable *effectively* to carry out an interpretation of *all* the terms occurring in the theory; and though perfectly capable of giving a syntactic–structuralist account of 'natural kinds', the realist refuses to accept *as analytic* the implication

$(X^* \rightarrow X)$; for he correctly regards $(X^* \rightarrow X)$ *as* a *synthetic*, albeit *metaphysical* proposition (See Conclusion below).

In support of the Demopoulos-Friedman thesis that X might be empirical while X^* is always trivial, Psillos adduces the following example. Let $X \equiv_{Def} [(\forall x)(F(x) \rightarrow K(x)) \wedge (\forall x)(F(x) \rightarrow P(x)) \wedge (\forall x)(K(x) \rightarrow Q(x))]$, where F and K are theoretical, while both P and Q are observational predicates. X is admittedly synthetic whereas $X^* \equiv_{Def} (\exists F, K)X$ is logically true: in order to establish $\vdash (\exists F, K)X$, it suffices to take $F \equiv_{Def} (P \wedge Q \wedge T) \equiv_{Def} K$, where T is an arbitrary (theoretical) predicate. What Psillos however fails to notice is that despite being synthetic, X is untestable and therefore non-scientific. For let $X \Rightarrow Z$ where Z is any O-sentence; i.e. Z contains neither F nor K. By Logic, infer: $(\exists F, K)X \Rightarrow Z$; like $(\exists F, K)X$, Z is therefore a logical or a mathematical truth. It follows that Z cannot be a basic statement, hence that X is metaphysical. This example illustrates a result proved above, namely that $(X^* \rightarrow X)$ is always unfalsifiable; for note that in the present case, $(X^* \rightarrow X) \Leftrightarrow (\neg X^* \vee X) \Leftrightarrow X$ since $\neg X^*$ is logically false. (The situation would have been different, had X been defined as $X \equiv_{Def} ((\forall x)(F(x) \rightarrow K(x)) \wedge (\forall x)(P(x) \rightarrow F(x)) \wedge (\forall x)(K(x) \rightarrow Q(x)))$; in which case $X^* \Leftrightarrow (\forall x)(P(x) \rightarrow Q(x))$; so that both X^* and X would have been falsifiable and hence synthetic; all this *independently of the referents of* F and K).

Let us now go back to examining, in very general terms, the various relationships between the theory $G(Q, T)$, its Ramsey-sentence $(\exists t)G(Q, t)$ and the presence or absence of observational predicates in $G(Q, T)$. It can easily be shown that $G(Q, T)$ and $(\exists t)G(Q, t)$ are not only observationally identical but that they also imply the same O-sentences.

By (1), every consequence of $(\exists t)G(Q, t)$ is trivially entailed by $G(Q, T)$. Conversely, let $H(Q, T)$ be any logical consequence of $G(Q, T)$. That is:

(3) $\vdash G(Q, T) \rightarrow H(Q, T)$. Quantifying over T, infer:

(4) $\vdash (\forall t)[G(Q, t) \rightarrow H(Q, t)]$. An immediate consequence of (4) is:

(5) $\vdash [(\exists t)G(Q, t) \rightarrow (\exists t)H(Q, t)]$.

Note first that (5) is in general much weaker than (4); secondly that in (4) we could have generalized over *all* the predicates Q_i *and* T_j. We refrained from doing so precisely because the Q_i's are observational and hence have fixed accessible meanings; so that quantifying over them—as Newman seems to have done—would involve a loss of valuable empirical information.

Two importantly different cases must now be considered.

[a] H contains no occurrences of any T_j's and is therefore an O-sentence. Thus we can write $H'(Q)$ for $H(Q, T)$. In this case, by (3): $\vdash [G(Q, T) \to H'(Q)]$, while (4) is equivalent to:

$$(6_1) \quad \vdash [(\exists t)G(Q, t) \to H'(Q)].$$

(3) and (6_1) tell us that $G(Q, T)$ and its Ramsey-sentence $(\exists t)G(Q, t)$ have the same O-consequences and are *a fortiori* observationally identical. Should $H'(Q)$ turn out to be a basic statement, then through the experimental verification of $\neg H'(Q)$, (6_1) might enable us to falsify $(\exists t)G(Q, t)$. Referring to the example given in section (E) above: both A and A^* could be refuted by any basic statement of the form $F(a) \wedge \neg K(a)$.

Thus the Ramsey-sentence of every scientific theory has empirical import and does not convey information *only* about the cardinality of its domain of discourse. To repeat: the difference $[(\exists t)G(Q, t) \to G(Q, T)]$ between a fully-fledged hypothesis $G(Q, T)$ and its Ramsey-sentence $(\exists t)G(Q, t)$ is not analytic but unfalsifiable. In fact, $[(\exists t)G(Q, t) \to G(Q, T)]$ fits exactly Popper's definition of a metaphysical thesis. At first sight, it might look as though Popper held a proposition M to be metaphysical if M is *a priori* in the sense of being totally independent of experience, i.e. of being neither provable nor falsifiable by observation. But Popper insisted *only* on the empirical irrefutability condition, thus conceding that M might be experimentally verifiable.

$[(\exists t)G(Q, t) \to G(Q, T)]$ illustrates this possibility; for we have seen that $[(\exists t)G(Q, t) \to G(Q, T)]$ entails no synthetic O-statement and is *a fortiori* untestable. $[(\exists t)G(Q, t) \to G(Q, T)]$ could however be experimentally verified through the empirical refutation of the Ramsey-sentence $(\exists t)G(Q, t)$ which was shown to be observationally equivalent to the scientific theory $G(Q, T)$. So Carnap ended up by regarding the *empirically verifiable* statement $[(\exists t)G(Q, t) \to G(Q, T)]$ as analytic and hence, according to the Neopositivists themselves, as devoid of sense. To my mind, there can be no doubt as to the superiority of Popper's trichotomy into logically true, consistent-metaphysical and consistent-scientific propositions, over Carnap's excluded middle between the analytic and the empirical.

According to SSR, there exist no experimental, theoretical or even aesthetic reason which could make us opt for $G(Q, T)$ in preference to the logically weaker Ramsey-sentence $(\exists t)G(Q, t)$; for we have seen that $G(Q, T)$ and $(\exists t)G(Q, t)$ have exactly the same O-consequences; and no unity or simplicity criteria could possibly demarcate between $G(Q, T)$ and $(\exists t)G(Q, t)$; for apart from the existential quantifier $(\exists t)$, the two formulas have essentially the same syntactical structure (In the case of the propositions A and A^* above, A^* proves to be even simpler than A).

[b] Let us now turn to the second special case of (3) where $H(\underline{Q}, \underline{T})$ is supposed to contain no occurrence of any observational predicates Q_i. We can thus write $H''(\underline{T})$ for $H(\underline{Q}, \underline{T})$, so that (5) reduces to the statement:

(6_2) $\vdash [(\exists\underline{t})G(\underline{Q}, \underline{t}) \rightarrow (\exists\underline{t})H''(\underline{t})]$.

$H''(\underline{T})$ could e.g. be the sentence $(\exists q)G(q, \underline{T})$, so that, by (6_2):

(7) $\vdash [(\exists\underline{t})G(\underline{Q},\underline{t}) \rightarrow (\exists\underline{t})(\exists q)G(q,\underline{t})]$, which is a logical truth.

This special subcase arises if all the terms contained in $G(\underline{Q}, \underline{T})$ are regarded as theory-laden and hence as essentially theoretical. As already stated above: following Brentano, Russell, Poincaré, Grover Maxwell and Ayer, I hold this 'modern' view to be deeply mistaken; for it misleads us into quantifying over *all* the predicates occurring in $G(\underline{Q}, \underline{T})$; which would yield, not $(\exists\underline{t})G(\underline{Q}, \underline{t})$, but the untestable formula $(\exists\underline{t})(\exists q)G(q, \underline{t})$ as the Ramsey-sentence of $G(\underline{Q}, \underline{T})$.

Note that $(\exists\underline{t})H''(\underline{t})$ might well express a tautology, a logical contradiction or a cardinality constraint on the underlying domain of discourse of $G(\underline{Q}, \underline{T})$. Thus, let us consider two limiting cases which might arise, should H contain no observational predicates $\underline{Q}$.

Taking m = 1 and assuming that $H''(T_1) \equiv (\forall x)[T_1(x) \leftrightarrow (x \neq x)]$, we have a situation in which $(\exists\underline{t})H''(\underline{t})$, i.e. $(\exists t_1)(\forall x)[t_1(x) \leftrightarrow (x \neq x)]$, is a logical truth (for t_1 can be chosen to be the predicate $(\lambda x)(x \neq x)$).

Another example consists in taking $H''(T_1) \equiv [(\forall x)T_1(x) \wedge (\forall x)(T_1(x) \leftrightarrow (x \neq x))]$; in which case $(\exists\underline{t})H''(\underline{t})$, i.e. $(\exists t_1)[(\forall x)t_1(x) \wedge (\forall x)(t_1(x) \leftrightarrow (x \neq x))]$, is a logical falsehood; so that our original theory, namely $G(\underline{Q}, \underline{T})$, must also be inconsistent (by (1) and (6_2)).

So far, no information about the cardinality of the domain of discourse has been conveyed. Such information will be forthcoming only in the case of finite domains; for if $H''(\underline{T})$ is first-order and has one infinite model, then $H''(\underline{T})$ and hence also $(\exists\underline{t})H''(\underline{t})$ will possess infinite models of arbitrarily large cardinalities (by the 'upward' Löwenheim-Skolem Theorem). As for the finite case, it arises if $H''(\underline{T})$ were e.g. the formula:

$[(\forall x)T_1(x) \wedge (\exists x_1, x_2, \ldots, x_r)((x_1 \neq x_2) \wedge (x_1 \neq x_3) \wedge \supset \wedge (x_{r1} \neq x_r) \wedge (\forall x)(T_1(x) \leftrightarrow ((x = x_1) \wedge (x = x_2) \wedge \supset \wedge (x = x_r)))))]$,

where r is a specific natural number. $(\exists t_1)H''(t_1)$ would then be the assertion that the domain of individuals consists of exactly r members.

The above examples expose Russell's oversight which was seized upon, first by Newman and then by Demopoulos and Friedman. As quoted above, Russell claimed that '. . . it would seem that whenever we infer from perception, it is only structure that we can validly infer; and structure is what can be expressed by mathematical logic'. This sounds as though, having used some observational results in order to arrive at a structural theory, the scientist would then leave these results behind and be left with a description of structure expressible in a purely logico-mathematical language. Such an operation can admittedly always be carried out, but it represents no serious threat to the structuralist position; for as already remarked, (5) is but a weak consequence of (4). To repeat: had Russell stuck to the original Ramsey-sentence, i.e. to the 'mixed' proposition $(\exists \underline{t})G(Q,\underline{t})$ instead of going over to $(\exists \underline{t})H''(\underline{t})$, then he would not have had to give in to Newman's 'argument'.

To sum up: the Ramsey-sentence $(\exists \underline{t})G(Q, \underline{t})$ reduces to a statement of the form $(\exists \underline{t})H''(\underline{t})$ only if n = 0; i.e. if there are no observational predicates at all, or alternatively: if no distinction be made between the observational and the theoretical terms. This is however far from being the position adopted by prominent structural realists like Poincaré, Duhem or Russell. The structural realist is committed only to regarding our knowledge of the theoretical predicates $T_1,...,T_m$ as being entirely conveyed by the nexus $G(Q_1,..., Q_n, T_1,..., T_m)$. $T_1,..., T_m$ are thus known exclusively by description, more precisely: by the manner—described by $G(Q_1,...,Q_n, T_1,..., T_m)$—in which they link up with each other and with the observational predicates $Q_1,...,Q_n$. As for the latter, they can be known *both* by description, *via* $G(Q_1,...,Q_n, T_1,..., T_m)$, and by acquaintance, i.e. phenomenologically or ostensively.

In the last analysis, the Demopoulos-Friedman objection rests on the unwarranted assumption that the structural realist denies the observational/theoretical distinction.

(G) PUTNAM'S MODEL-THEORETIC ARGUMENT(S)

At first sight, Putnam's results constitute the most powerful argument against scientific realism—whether classical or structural. Putnam showed that given *any* epistemically ideal theory T_I, we have *no* reason not to regard T_I *as true* (See H. Putnam 1983). It will furthermore be proved that given some additional cardinality constraints, T_I possesses a 'standard model' in the world, i.e. a model in which all the observational notions have their commonly accepted referents. This would entail that the Ramsey-sentence

T_I^* of T_I *can be looked upon as true simpliciter.* In order to assess the scope of Putnam's theorem, it is necessary to start by briefly examining his proof and its presuppositions. We shall then discuss the question whether structural realism is undermined by Putnam's results.

Putnam denotes by 'S' the set of all observable entities. Thus $S \subseteq W$, where 'W' denotes the whole universe. Since the results of all measurements are signified by rational numbers, S can be taken to be countable. A set of observational predicates $\{\pi_i : i \in \Omega\}$ is then posited, where for each $i \in \Omega$ and for all $\alpha, \beta, \ldots, \gamma$ in S, $\pi_i(\alpha, \beta, \ldots, \gamma)$ is empirically decidable. An epistemically ideal theory T_I is then defined as any consistent first-order system which possesses a set of terms $\{t_\alpha : \alpha \in S\}$ such that $T_I \vdash (t_\alpha \neq t_\beta)$ for any two distinct elements α and β of S. For each $i \in \Omega$, T_I is furthermore required to possess a predicate P_i which has the same number of argument-places as π_i and is such that, for all $\alpha, \beta, \ldots, \gamma$ in S, we have: $T_I \vdash P_i(t_\alpha, t_\beta, \ldots, t_\gamma)$ if $\pi_i(\alpha, \beta, \ldots, \gamma)$ is true, and $T_I \vdash \neg P_i(t_\alpha, t_\beta, \ldots, t_\gamma)$ if $\pi_i(\alpha, \beta, \ldots, \gamma)$ is false.

Let J be any model of T_I . Put:

(8) $\tau_\alpha = {}_{Def} J(t_\alpha)$ for all $\alpha \in S$.

Thus $\pi_i(\alpha, \beta, \ldots, \gamma) \equiv J(P_i)(t_\alpha, t_\beta, \ldots, t_\gamma)$ for all $\alpha, \beta, \ldots, \gamma$ in S. For suppose that $\pi_i(\alpha, \beta, \ldots, \gamma)$ is true; by hypothesis, $T_I \vdash P_i(t_\alpha, t_\beta, \ldots, t_\gamma)$; since J is a model of T_I , then $J(P_i)(J(t_\alpha), J(t_\beta), \ldots, J(t_\gamma))$, i.e. $J(P_i)(t_\alpha, t_\beta, \ldots, t_\gamma)$, is true. And if $\pi_i(\alpha, \beta, \ldots, \gamma)$ is false, then again by hypothesis, $T_I \vdash \neg P_i(t_\alpha, t_\beta, \ldots, t_\gamma)$; hence $J(\neg P_i(t_\alpha, t_\beta, \ldots, t_\gamma))$ is true; that is: $J(P_i(t_\alpha, t_\beta, \ldots, t_\gamma))$, i.e. $J(P_i)(t_\alpha, t_\beta, \ldots, t_\gamma)$, is false. Hence:

(9) $J(P_i)(t_\alpha, t_\beta, \ldots, t_\gamma) \equiv \pi_i(\alpha, \beta, \ldots, \gamma)$, for all $\alpha, \beta, \ldots, \gamma$ in S.

J is said to be standard if, for all $\alpha \in S$, we have: $J(t_\alpha) = \alpha$, i.e. if $t_\alpha = \alpha$ (Note: we do not scripturally distinguish between the formal and the intuitive equality signs). (9) entails that in a standard model:

(10) $J(P_i)(\alpha, \beta, \ldots, \gamma) \equiv \pi_i(\alpha, \beta, \ldots, \gamma)$, for all $\alpha, \beta, \ldots, \gamma$ in S. That is: for all i in Ω, $J(P_i)$ coincides with π_i on S.

Although epistemically ideal systems are practically impossible to construct, it will be assumed, if only for the sake of argument, that at least one such theory is achievable. Putnam established that every epistemically ideal T_I has a standard model; for by the Löwenheim-Skolem theorem, T_I has at least one (countable) model, J say. Letting D be the domain of J, we have, by (8): $\{\tau_\alpha: \alpha \in S\} =_{Def} \{J(t_\alpha): \alpha \in S\} \subseteq D$. Put: $\Delta = \{\tau_\alpha: \alpha \in S\}$ and $\Delta' = D\backslash\Delta = D\backslash\{\tau_\alpha: \alpha \in S\}$. Thus:

(11) $D = \Delta \cup \Delta' = \{\tau_\alpha: \alpha \in S\} \cup \Delta'$. Hence $|D| = |\Delta| + |\Delta'| = |\{\tau_\alpha: \alpha \in S\}| + |\Delta'|$.

Since $T_I \restriction t_\alpha \neq t_\beta$ for $\alpha \neq \beta$ and J is a model of T_I. then $J(t_\alpha) \neq J(t_\beta)$. That is:

(12) $\tau_\alpha \neq \tau_\beta$ for $\alpha \neq \beta$. Therefore: $|\Delta| = |\{\tau_\alpha: \alpha \in S\}| = |S|$. By the above:
(13) $|D| = |\Delta| + |\Delta'| = |S| + |\Delta'|$.

Note that if S is taken to be infinite, then D, and therefore every model J of T_I will be infinite. Now define the one-one map f as follows:

(14) $f(\tau_\alpha) = \alpha$ for all $\alpha \in S$; and for any $\mu \in \Delta'$, define $f(\mu)$ in any way consistent with the requirement that the resulting f be a bijection whose domain is the whole of D.

Now determine the interpretation J_0 as follows. The domain of J_0 will be the set:

(15) $D_0 =_{Def} S \cup f[\Delta'] = \{f(\tau_\alpha): \alpha \in S\} \cup \{f(\mu): \mu \in \Delta'\}$.

For any function letter (or name) g, let:

(16) $J_0(g)(\xi, \eta, \ldots, \zeta) =_{Def} f(J(g)(f^{-1}(\xi), f^{-1}(\eta), \ldots, f^{-1}(\zeta)))$, for any ξ, $\eta, \ldots, \zeta$ in D_0.

Finally, for any predicate R, define:

(17) $J_0(R)(\xi, \eta, \ldots, \zeta) \equiv_{Def} J(R)(f^{-1}(\xi), f^{-1}(\eta), \ldots, f^{-1}(\zeta))$, for all $\xi, \eta, \ldots,$ ζ in D_0.

As is well known, (16) entails:

(18) $J_0(u) = f(J(u))$, for all terms u.

Trivially: since J is a model of T_I, then so is J_0 (for J_0 can in effect be considered as the result of relabeling the elements of J). J_0 is furthermore a standard model, since:

(19) $J_0(t_\alpha) = f(J(t_\alpha))$ [by (18)] $=_{Def} f(\tau_\alpha) =_{Def} \alpha$ [by (14)].

This result can be strengthened by imposing further constraints on the cardinalities of various sets. Let us henceforth assume that the world W is infinite and that T_I has at least one infinite model (it suffices to suppose that S is denumerably infinite); then by the 'upward' Löwenheim-Skolem theorem, T_I has a model having cardinality | W |. In the above, it can therefore be assumed that | D | = | W |. Let us moreover suppose that | W | > | S |; which is not an unreasonable assumption, for S is countable while the set of all physical events has at least the power of the continuum. Thus:

(20) $W = S \cup S'$, where $S' =_{Def} (W \backslash S)$. Hence | W | = | S | + | S' |.

Since W is infinite and | W | > | S |, it follows that:

(21) | W | = | S' |. Thus | W | = | D | = | S | + | Δ' | [by (13)].

Since | W | is infinite and greater than | S |,

(22) | W | = | Δ' |; hence | S' | = | W | = | Δ' |; and so:
(23) $W = S \cup S'$; $D = \{\tau_\alpha : \alpha \in S\} \cup \Delta'$; where | S' | = | W | = | D | = | Δ' |.

Let Ψ be any one-one map of Δ' onto S'. Going back to (14), we see that f can be defined as follows:

(24) $f(\tau_\alpha) =_{Def} \alpha$ for all $\alpha \in S$; and for any $\mu \in \Delta'$, let $f(\mu) =_{Def} \Psi(\mu)$.

By (23) and (24), f maps $\{\tau_\alpha : \alpha \in S\} \cup \Delta' = \Delta \cup \Delta' = D$ one-one onto $S \cup S' = W$. Thus $W = [\text{Range of } f] =_{Def} D_0$. By the above, J_0 is a standard model of T_I in the world W; which clearly entails that the Ramsey-sentence T_I^* of T_I is standardly true in W.

At this point, one question arises: should the structural realist be worried about these results? We shall show that the answer is decidedly negative.

Putnam in effect provides a partial answer to the following question posed by Einstein in his *Weltbild*: is a scientific hypothesis uniquely determined by its having to account for *all* the facts? (A. Einstein 1934, pp. 175–180). Perhaps unintentionally, Putnam has shown that truth rather than uniqueness might well be attainable. More precisely: given the consistency of an epistemically ideal theory T_I, we have no empirical reason not to hold the Ramsey-sentence T_I^* of T_I to be true. Given further assumptions about the cardinalities of the world W and of the models of T_I, we are even entitled to assert the truth of T_I^*. Qua structural realists, we should thus be in a position to know that the structure described by T_I is realized in the world. A problem would arise only if there existed two ideal theories T_I and H_I with logically incompatible Ramsey-sentences T_I^* and H_I^*; but Jane English has proved that this is never the case if—as is tacitly assumed—an *epistemically ideal* theory entails no false observational statement, i.e. no false O-sentence (See Jane English 1980). It is therefore as unexceptionable for a realist to claim that the two structures displayed by T_I and by H_I are realized in W as it is for a mathematician to hold that the same set can exhibit both an algebraic and a topological structure.

The more demanding structural realist can go much further than this, but only by appealing to a metaphysical principle similar to the ones invoked by Poincaré and Einstein. The latter put it as follows: the world ought to be regarded as the realization of the mathematically simplest system. As for Poincaré, he took the degree of unity of a theory to be an index of its truth-likeness. Both scientists held unity and simplicity to be *objective* properties of scientific hypotheses; and this in the same sense in which a polynomial of the nth degree is objectively simpler than one of the $(n+1)^{st}$ degree. Note that despite being incapable of *epistemologically* distinguishing between a theory and its Ramsey-sentence, i.e. between T_I and T_I^*, we can certainly adjudicate between T_I and H_I, or rather between T_I^* and H_I^*. We might, for example, come to the conclusion that T_I^* is more unified than H_I^*; so that given the principle just stated, only T_I^* will be taken to reflect—if only approximately—the real structure of W. Thus, only in the case of T_I^* would we be prepared to accept a *realist interpretation* of the existential quantification over the theoretical predicates. According to Poincaré, we should otherwise be attributing 'too great a role to chance'; i.e. the excess 'organic compactness' of T_I^* over H_I^* would have to be regarded as an accidental feature of T_I^*; and we know that theoretical physicists of Poincaré's and Einstein's tempers of mind are most reluctant to regard such accidents as ultimately inexplicable.

(H) J. KETLAND'S LAST-DITCH DEFENSE OF THE DEMOPOULOS-FRIEDMAN THESIS

Jeffrey Ketland concludes his (2004) with the following claim:

> . . . This leaves the structural realist in a sticky position, given that the epistemological intention was to provide an interesting third way

between anti-realism and realism: the position collapses to something very close to anti-realism. As Friedman and Demopoulos put
it: Ramsification trivializes physics: it threatens to turn the *empirical* claims of science into mere *mathematical* truths. (p. 299)

The author must have known that this last thesis is false; for as acknowledged by everybody, the Ramsey-sentence H* of H has the same observational content as H. Since the latter is—by the very definition of its
scientific character—empirically falsifiable, the same applies to H*. Hence
H* cannot possibly be reduced to a mathematical truth.

Let us recall that O-propositions are defined as those sentences in which
only observational terms occur. (Such terms can be names either of observable entities or of empirically decidable predicates). As established above,
O-propositions do not all belong to the empirical basis which, taken by
itself, does not entail H* (See section E above). Thus an O-sentence like
$(\forall x)[F(x) \rightarrow G(x)]$ does not logically follow from any finite or infinite set
of basic statements $\{F(a_j) \land G(a_j): j \in \Delta\}$. In order for Ketland's position to
make sense, it must therefore be regarded as purporting to show that the
choice of H* in preference to the fully-fledged theory H involves an important loss of scientific or philosophical, as distinct from strictly empirical
content.

Let us now examine some of the details of Ketland's arguments against
SSR. He writes

To emphasize, the theory formulation language $L_2(O, M, T)$ is interpreted. By 'interpreted' we mean *semantically interpreted,* rather
than epistemologically interpreted (e.g. by Carnap-Bridgman style
correspondence rules). The worldly relations that this language is
'hooked up' to are O_i, M_i, T_i. Furthermore, we are here working
within some informal set-theoretic meta-language, and this metatheory refers to these relations too. (Ketland 2004, p. 290)

Ketland considers an extension H⁺ of H where, apart from containing H,
H⁺ is a 'Tarskian' metatheory which interprets H, thereby leading to the definition of a truth-predicate for the sentences of H. The reference to Tarski is
very apposite. As is well known, Tarski rightly held his truth-definition to
be neutral between realism and anti-realism: for he considers a purely *formal* object-language L, which he extends to an equally *formal* meta-language L_0. In L_0 every sentence A of L can be named, by $\underline{A}$ say. Tarski then
determines a predicate Tr of L_0 such that $\vdash_0 [Tr(\underline{A}) \leftrightarrow A]$. At no point in this

process is an appeal made to any 'external' state-of-affairs which might correspond to A. From a realist standpoint, the main advantage offered by Tarski's theory is that, without any presupposition as to the availability of a truth-criterion, it renders talk about truth in general, and more particularly about the truth of universal propositions meaningful; whence the importance of its role in Popper's philosophy. As for Ketland, he defines truth as follows: φ is a true sentence of $L_2(O, M, T)$ if and only if $((D_O, D_T), O, M, T) \models \varphi$.

It is tell-tale that the author uses the same symbols to signify both the predicates of his object-language and the relations these are intended to denote (See Ketland 2004, p. 289). This convention obliquely points to the following important, albeit obvious fact: despite being meant to 'hook up' H to the real world, H^+ in no way enables us to establish any correspondence between our theoretical language and its referents. This ought to be self-evident, since all theoretical terms refer to an external world which is known exclusively by description; so that we are in principle unable *effectively* to 'hook up' our theoretical language to such a transcendent reality. This is not to condemn all talk about the external world as meaningless, but only to wonder whether such talk is *scientifically* testable. That H^+ is not meant to be independently refutable anyway appears to be admitted by Ketland himself.

Ketland distinguishes between theoretical terms such as 'electron' and 'quark' on the one hand, and observational terms such as 'table', 'chair' and 'iron filings' on the other. This demarcation strikes me as highly questionable: for why should *iron filings* be any less theoretical than their constituents, i.e. than the elementary particles constituting them? When we experience colors, sounds and shapes, we normally do so as a result of a causal interaction between our nervous system and some external object, i.e. between two systems of elementary particles. Both the macroscopic objects and their constituents are transcendent entities. Only the sense-data, together with our moods and mental states, are strictly observational. At any rate, it can more guardedly be claimed that observational entities are more akin to sense-data than to tables, chairs and iron filings.

Ketland is convinced that our basic ontology is of the form $D_0 \cup D_T$, where D_0 consists of all observable, and D_T of all theoretical objects. But it can legitimately be asked: does he have any good reason for assuming that theoretical entities form a neat set D_T of individuated elements whose properties and relations are signified by subclasses of the Cartesian products D_T^n of the set D_T? The only evidence which comes to mind is a weak analogy between, on the one hand the atoms as classically pictured and, on the other, the discrete observational entities which we might carve out of our visual and tactile fields. Far from being in any way empirically confirmed, such analogies are known to be misleading; and they certainly do not in any way contribute to the empirical content of scientific hypotheses. As already explained in Chapter III, our intuitive semantics is inspired by a common-sense ontology consisting of discrete *intentional* objects. Such an ontology might however not be that of the *external* world.

Ketland resorts to a two-sorted language where some variables range over D_0 (the class of observables) and others over D_T. Even from Ketland's own viewpoint, it seems preferable to go back to a one-sorted calculus through the introduction of a predicate Ω; where $\Omega(a)$ stands for "a is an observable." For every observable relation Q, the following axiom might have to be added: $(\forall x_1, x_2, \ldots, x_n)[Q(x_1, x_2, \ldots, x_n) \rightarrow (\Omega(x_1) \wedge \Omega(x_2) \wedge \ldots \wedge \Omega(x_n))]$.

Since high-level hypotheses normally involve considerable mathematical baggage, the predicates k and $\in$ will furthermore be needed; where, as usual, k(a) and (a $\in$ b) stand for "a is a class" and "a belongs to b" respectively. A class will be mathematical if all of its ultimate elements are sets; but 'mixed' classes, as well as classes consisting exclusively of physical entities (observational or theoretical), ought also to be admitted. Thus $D_0 = \{\forall: \Omega(x)\}$ and $D_T = \{x: \neg\Omega(x) \wedge \neg k(x)\}$. Roughly speaking, a theory H will be scientific if it entails a generalization of the form $(\forall x)[F(x) \rightarrow G(x)]$, where both F and G are observational. It would follow that $(\forall x([F(x) \rightarrow (\Omega(x) \wedge G(x))])$. H could then be confirmed by a statement of the form $[F(a) \wedge \Omega(a) \wedge G(a)]$ and refuted by $[F(a) \wedge \Omega(a) \wedge \neg G(a)]$. A problem is however posed by the status of the predicates k and $\in$. They are normally looked upon as logical constants; but as explained in (C) above, they might also be regarded as theoretical predicates.

Let us now turn to Ketland's Theorem 6, the real core of his article. Using a model-theoretic argument, he establishes a proposition which can roughly be stated as follows: given a theory H and its Ramsey-sentence H*, then provided a cardinality condition be satisfied by a model of H, H* will be true if and only if H is empirically correct. There is no doubting the ingenuity and elegance of Ketland's proof; but the philosophical conclusions he tries to draw from his theorem seem to me totally unwarranted. As already quoted above:

This leaves the structural realist in a sticky position, given that the epistemological intention was to provide an interesting third way between anti-realism and realism: the position collapses to something very close to anti-realism. (p. 299)

The author does not explicitly give any good reason for his conclusion. He must presumably have taken it for granted that in the light of his theorem, all Ramsey-sentences prove to be nothing but 'empirically adequate observational' propositions; so that the structural realist is bound to reduce science to a sequence of such low-level generalizations.

Note that at least two results similar to Theorem 6 have already been mentioned. Let us first recall that Putnam defines an epistemically ideal theory T_I as one which correctly describes and logically yields *all* the observable facts. It was shown that we should then have no reason not to regard T_I^* as true. Should we moreover postulate the inequality $| W | > \aleph_0$ where $| W |$ is the cardinality of the world W, then T_I^* can be considered true *simpliciter*. There is clearly an obvious similarity between Ketland's empirically correct and Putnam's epistemically ideal theories. Secondly: in section (C) above I appear to have taken a further step towards what Ketland regards as an anti-realist position. After examining the problems posed by the mathematical principles at work within scientific systems, I showed that H could be put in the form: $H = G(k, \in, \underline{a}, \underline{u}, Q)$, where: $\underline{a}, \underline{u}, Q$ stand for the tuples $(a_1,..., a_m)$, $(u_1,...,u_s)$, $(Q_1,...,Q_n)$ respectively; and $(Q_1,...,Q_n)$ is the sequence of all the observational predicates in H. Thus H* is given by: $H^* = (\exists k, \in)(\exists \underline{x}, \underline{v})G(k, \in, \underline{x}, \underline{v}, Q)$. It was pointed out that the second-order character of the Ramsey-sentence arises exclusively from the operator $(\exists k, \in)$. Should k and $\in$ be regarded as logical constants and hence as <u>not</u> to be quantified over, then the Ramsey-sentence would reduce to the first-order formula $(\exists \underline{x}, \underline{v}) G(k, \in, \underline{x}, \underline{v}, Q)$ in which only the *observational* predicates $Q_1,...,Q_n$ occur free. Thus it looks as though the Ramsey-sentence H* *is not only verified* by empirical results but *is also in itself* an observational proposition.

As already mentioned: because of results similar to the ones just described, Ketland felt entitled to make two claims. The first is that structural realism is in effect nothing but covert anti-realism. The second is a reiteration of the Demopoulos-Friedman view that "Ramsification 'trivializes physics: it threatens to turn the *empirical* claims of science into mere *mathematical* truths'." This second thesis has already been exposed as untenable: by no stretch of the imagination can H*, which is as testable as H, be regarded as a mathematical truth. Turning to the first claim: consider the formulation $H^* = (\exists \underline{x}, \underline{v}) G(k, \in, \underline{x}, \underline{v}, Q)$ which is first-order and seems to involve no theoretical notions. It should therefore offend most strongly against the traditional realist position; for as already explained, a hardheaded realist might be tempted to regard $(\exists \underline{x}, \underline{v})G(k, \in, \underline{x}, \underline{v}, Q)$ as an observational sentence; which would vindicate Ketland's claim. The latter, as well as Demopoulos's and Friedman's claims, is in effect a reiteration of Carnap's thesis: once the theoretical predicates occurring in a hypothesis are quantified away, we are left with an empirical generalization.

It is clearly pointless to disagree over questions of pure terminology. It will nonetheless be shown that calling "$(\exists \underline{x},\underline{v})G(k, \in, \underline{x}, \underline{v}, Q)$" an observational proposition is nothing short of preposterous; for such a definition results from a wrong-headed classification of meaningful statements, a classification which flies in the face of our most elementary intuitions. To begin with: this definition does not even guarantee the scientific status of empirical conjectures; for despite containing only the observational predicates $(Q_1,...,Q_n)$, the Ramsey-sentence $H^* = (\exists \underline{x},\underline{v})G(k, \in, \underline{x}, \underline{v}, Q)$ of H, and hence H itself, might well prove untestable (See section F above). Moreover: even when refutable, a generalization like $A^* \equiv (\forall x)$ $(F(x) \rightarrow K(x))$ cannot reasonably be claimed to lie in the empirical basis of $A \equiv [(\forall x)(F(x) \rightarrow T(x)) \wedge (\forall y)(T(y) \rightarrow K(y))]$, i.e. of $[(\forall x)(F(x) \rightarrow (x \in a))$ $\wedge (\forall y)((y \in a) \rightarrow K(y))]$ where a is the extension of T. Otherwise, given that $(\forall x)(F(x) \rightarrow K(x))$ fails to be fully empirically decidable, the canons of even the most liberal version of empiricism would be transgressed. This is precisely why Schlick and other members of the Vienna Circle decided to regard synthetic universal statements as expressing inference rules rather than genuine propositions. (See Kraft 1968, pp. 121–137).

Furthermore: let $\Sigma(k, \in)$ stand for the pure class theory formulated by Gödel. By the above, we have: $(\exists \underline{x},\underline{v})G(k, \in, \underline{x}, \underline{v}, Q) \Rightarrow \Sigma(k, \in)$. It is well known that practically *every* mathematical theorem A so far established by any mathematician is provable within the framework of $\Sigma(k, \in)$. That is: $\Sigma(k, \in) \Rightarrow A$; whence $(\exists \underline{x},\underline{v})G(k, \in, \underline{x}, \underline{v}, Q) \Rightarrow A$. A might be Euclid's theorem about the existence of infinitely many primes, or Fermat's last theorem, or the fundamental theorem of algebra, or Tichonov's theorem about topological compactness, etc. Even if we decided to quantify over k and $\in$, we would still have $(\exists k,\in)(\exists \underline{x},\underline{v})G(k, \in, \underline{x}, \underline{v}, Q) \Rightarrow (\exists k, \in)(\Sigma(k, \in) \wedge A)$, where $\Sigma(k, \in)$ circumscribes the use of k and $\in$ in pure mathematics. Note that in all the cases just cited, A is not a mere tautology but a genuine synthetic mathematical truth. Should we moreover adopt Ketland's liberal definition of observability, then $(\exists \underline{x},\underline{v})G(k, \in, \underline{x}, \underline{v}, Q)$ would yield a full account of Mercury's motion, of the bending of the light rays in the neighborhood of the sun, of the Balmer series; for all these results are held by Ketland to be observable. But it seems to me that a generalization, empirically adequate though it might be, ought not to be the kind of theory which yields such high-level results including the whole of known mathematics. In epistemology as distinct from metaphysics, the main criterion for empirical correctness should be some sort of *semantic feasibility*, i.e. of effective decidability; which certainly does not apply to a hypothesis like $(\exists \underline{x},\underline{v})\mathbf{G}$ $(k, \in, \underline{x}, \underline{v}, Q)$. It is true that $(\exists \underline{x},\underline{v})\mathbf{G}(k, \in, \underline{x}, \underline{v}, Q)$ appears to involve only the observational notions denoted by Q. It should however be remembered that in opposition to classical empiricism, Popper had the great merit of tackling the status of meaningful propositions head on; that is: without any prior analysis of the concepts occurring in such propositions. Thus the empirical basis M_0 consists of all the sentences which are fully empirically decidable; these happen to be equivalent to singular statements containing only observational terms. It has already been established that despite being infinite, M_0 logically entails neither H nor H*. In this sense, neither H nor H* is observational. Next comes the set M_1 of scientific hypotheses, which are half-decidable in the sense of being empirically refutable but not verifiable. The remaining synthetic propositions form the class M' of metaphysical, i.e. of unfalsifiable statements. Strictly speaking, M' ought to be split into the sets M_2 and M_3 of verifiable and of totally undecidable sentences respectively. Now note that any concept, whether observational or abstract, can occur in any member of M_1, M_2, or M_3. For example: the statement that 'every metal has a solvent', which can be formalized as $(\forall x)(\exists y,t)(N(x) \rightarrow S(y, x, t))$, lies in M_3; and this despite N and S being normally regarded as observational; where $N(x) \equiv$ (x is a metal) and $S(y, x, t) \equiv$ (the substance y dissolves the substance x at time t). Now compare $(\forall x)(\exists y,t)[N(x) \rightarrow S(y, x, t)]$ with the Classical Absolute Time Hypothesis (ATH). As already established: when taken in isolation, (ATH) involves abstract notions and is in effect metaphysical; but it enters as an essential component into the Newtonian System where it lies at the basis of the addition law of velocities. The latter is not only refutable but has in effect been falsified. All this goes to show that the occurrence of certain quantifiers, together with their interconnections within a proposition H, plays more important a role in the determination of the status of H and hence of H*, than does the nature of the predicates contained in H.

Let us now reconsider $H = \mathbf{G}(k, \in, \underline{a}, \underline{u}, Q)$ and $H^* = (\exists \underline{x}, \underline{v})G(k, \in, \underline{x}, \underline{v}, Q)$ [or $H^* = (\exists k, \in)(\exists \underline{x}, \underline{v})\mathbf{G}(k, \in, \underline{x}, \underline{v}, Q)$]. Suppose that H is not only highly unified but also strongly and systematically confirmed by the evidence. These qualities, which will be inherited by H*, might well lead us to consider $\underline{a}$, i.e. $(a_1,..., a_m)$, as a sequence of natural kinds. Supposing that realist scientists—i.e. practically all scientists—adopted a quasi-Quinean view according to which 'to be is to be quantified over': they would then justifiably claim that $H^* = (\exists \underline{x},\underline{v})\mathbf{G}(k, \in, \underline{x}, \underline{v}, Q)$ conveys exactly what they want to assert; namely that the natural kinds $(a_1,..., a_m)$ exist *in* *reality*; which is precisely what the anti-realists are bent on denying. In other words: we can look upon the quantification $(\exists \underline{x}, \underline{v})$ in $H^* = (\exists \underline{x}, \underline{v}) G(k, \in, \underline{x}, \underline{v}, Q)$ as a means not of doing away with the theoretical entities $(a_1,...,a_m)$ but, on the contrary, of emphatically affirming their existence. And the only reason why the so-called traditional realists refuse to carry out the quantification $(\exists \underline{x}, \underline{v})$ in $H^* = (\exists \underline{x}, \underline{v}) G(k, \in, \underline{x}, \underline{v}, Q)$ is their covert belief in the existence, over and above the theory H, of some independent insight into the nature of $(a_1,...,a_m)$. This however is an illusion; for let us repeat that our knowledge of the *theoretical* entities $(a_1,...,a_m)$ is strictly *theoretical*; that is: by description and not by acquaintance; so that any further determination of $(a_1,...,a_m)$ would already have been included in H and consequently transcribed into H^*.

(I) CONCLUSION

To the above arguments both the constructive empiricist and the anti-realist might oppose the following objection: starting from the knowledge of *all* the observational facts, we can go on to construct an empirically correct hypothesis H; being aware that H is underdetermined by the evidence, we make no claim as to the truth-value of H (whatever that might mean). We know that modulo a number of constraints imposed on the cardinalities of certain classes, the Ramsey-sentence H^* is true or rather that it is adequate; provided, that is, we interpret the initial existential quantifiers of H^* in an 'as if' way. And this is all we need in order to build bridges or design accelerators, atomic reactors, etc. In all this we need appeal to no realist assumptions.

As a reply to the anti-realist, we shall first repeat that SSR is an epistemological position and that epistemology deals primarily with what we can legitimately claim to know. This is why the only allowable observability criterion is that of semantic feasibility or accessibility. So even if—counterfactually—the infinite totality of facts came to be known to us, we could never be sure that these were all the knowable facts. It is secondly clear that our evidential data-base will always remain finite and therefore incomplete. Hence none of our high-level theories H will ever yield all the potentially observable results; which is just as well since we need H to apply to future events. Some inductive principle J must therefore be presupposed. Roughly speaking, J will tell us that highly corroborated theories are more likely to be reliable than empirically undermined ones (See Chapter II above). The constructive empiricist is bound to accept J; but he is also bound to postulate J without any real argument in its favor. Note that J cannot be supported empirically without vicious circularity. Thus the only *rationale* for J is some argument connecting, in no matter how tentative a way, corroboration with verisimilitude; and no matter how intuitive, verisimilitude is founded on the notion of *truth*-likeness, hence on a realist assumption. In other words: assuming induction without verisimilitude would compel the anti-realist to accept the kind of miracle decried by Poincaré in his no-miracles-argument. As already mentioned in Chapter II, the no-miracles argument establishes a close connection between SSR and Induction:

> We have verified a simple law in a considerable number of particular cases. We refuse to admit that this coincidence, so often repeated, is a result of mere chance and we conclude that the law must be true in the general case. Kepler remarks that the positions of a planet observed by Tycho are all on the same ellipse. Not for one moment does he think that, by a singular freak of chance, Tycho had never looked at the heavens except at the very moment when the path of the planet happened to cut that ellipse. . . . We shall therefore always be able to reason in the same fashion, and if a simple law has been observed in several particular cases, we may legitimately suppose that it will still be true in analogous cases. To refuse to admit this would be to attribute an inadmissible role to chance. (Poincaré 1902, pp. 149–150)

Our considerations also show that a structural realist can account for the notion of natural kind without abandoning his syntactic-structuralist stance; for our best guide as to what kinds are natural is the degree of unity of a theory such as T_I or that of any highly successful hypothesis T in which these kinds play a central role. In other words: natural kinds are precisely those signified by the predicate and function symbols which give T its most coherent formulation. Let us repeat that both the empirical content and the so-called 'degree of internal perfection' of a theory T coincide with those of its Ramsey-sentence T^*; so there is nothing to choose between T and T^*. Note also that a most ardent defender of natural kinds, namely David Lewis, grants that those kinds are natural which are talked about by our best theories (See D. Lewis 1970, p. 428). But what are our 'best' theories if not those highly unified systems which save the facts without ad hoc assumptions? In other words: we do not possess a prior insight into natural kinds on which to base our subsequent conjectures. Instead, we start by formulating empirically adequate hypotheses *and then* select, from among these, the most unified theory, T say. T^* will then express exactly what we want to assert; namely that the theoretical predicates quantified over in T^* *denote the natural kinds which are really actualized in the world.* In this sense, only the Keplerian (near-)ellipses, as opposed to the complex curves which would have to be postulated by any Tychonic reformulation of Kepler's laws, really exist. Similarly: let E be Einstein's gravitational theory and let N denote any of its 'Euclidean reformulations'. As admitted by Einstein himself, N is empirically equivalent to E, at least within a large region of the spatio-temporal manifold. But scientists who, as a rule, are very demanding realists, do not look upon the unity displayed by the structure of E—as opposed to the ad hoc character of N—as an accidental feature of E. They hold that E describes reality more adequately than does N (See above, Chapter V, section I)

Let us—realistically—add that no ideal theory like T_I has so far been put forward; it moreover seems doubtful that such a theory could ever be achieved *in practice.* So science must content itself with provisional hypotheses, or rather with the latter's Ramsey-sentences which might at best be compatible with all *known* experimental results. It is precisely in these situations that SSR proves its mettle. Consider two such hypotheses—call them T_I and T_2—which are empirically identical. Thus both T_I and T_2 could subsequently be refuted—by the same facts. Yet T_2 —but not T_I—might possess a structure which heuristically leads to a more powerful theory, S say; where S empirically supersedes both T_I and T_2. S might, for example, explain some of the results which undermined T_I and hence also T_2; yet only the structure of T_2 survives—possibly in a modified form—in S. Once again consider the oft-cited case where: $S \equiv$ Quantum Mechanics; $T_I \equiv$ Newtonian Dynamics; and $T_2 \equiv$ (Classical) Hamiltonian Dynamics. This example is instructive, first because it does not rely on hindsight: long before the birth of Quantum Physics, Poincaré noted that despite their strict observational equivalence, T_I and T_2 have very different structures and hence make different statements about the world. Secondly: as we go over from T_2 to S, only mathematical structure, as typified by the form of the Hamiltonian function, is preserved; even the logical types of this function's arguments are modified: whereas the arguments of the classical Hamiltonian are functions of the time-variable, those of its quantum-mechanical correlate are operators, i.e. functions of functions, and hence higher-order entities. No other example illustrates more clearly the essential role played by the notion of structure in the development of fundamental science.

It might be maintained that structural *realism* does not deserve its name. This, to repeat, is a purely terminological and hence irrefutable objection. It can nonetheless be pointed out that the most prominent advocates of structural realism, namely Poincaré and Russell, were realists; they instinctively believed in the existence of a structured and mind-independent reality which the scientist tries to capture or reflect; but their ungainsayable insight was that the mode of reference of the theoretical terms is as problematic as the truth-value of the scientific hypotheses in which they occur. According to these authors as well as to a modern realist like E. McMullin, we are nonetheless entitled to regard some concepts as *metaphors* capable of more or less accurately modeling the external world; in which case there is no longer any question of a strict *term-by-term* reference to anything at all, whether it be intended or not (See E. McMullin 1984).

It is finally remarkable that both the instrumentalists and the structural realists should look upon Duhem as one of their founding fathers; which has actually led philosophers like Ketland to identify SSR with instrumentalism. It has to be admitted that reading the *Aim and Structure of Physical Theory* gives *prima facie* the impression that Duhem would have liked to vindicate instrumentalism through and through: his 'Physics of a Believer' indicates that he was a fideist intent on limiting the ambitions of theoretical science in order to make room for faith. He was, among other things, happy to point out that as long as science limited itself to classifying the phenomena without trying to explain the ultimate reality behind them, it posed no threat to the Catholic doctrine of free choice. But Duhem was too *good a scientist and too honest a thinker* not to accept the no-miracles-argument; namely that we cannot account for a hypothesis H being both highly unified and successful in predicting new types of fact *without* assuming that H approximates to a Natural Classification; where the latter reflects the ontological order as present to God's mind, without however strictly denoting that divine order. Note moreover that the notion of Natural Classification occurs in the early sections of the *Aim and Structure* and is therefore an integral part of Duhem's classic text (For an important insight into this problem, see Martin 1991, Chapter VI). For my part, I cannot understand why constructive empiricists refuse to accept this modestly realistic but central component of Duhem's system. Are they perhaps more afraid than Duhem ever was of making one concession too many to 'scientism'?

VIII

Atomism and Structural Realism

(A) METHODOLOGICAL PRELIMINARIES

In this Chapter a brief case study of classical atomic theory will illustrate
the crucial role played by metaphysics in the development of science. Once
again, we take as our starting point Popper's demarcation criterion according to which all empirically refutable hypotheses should be considered scientific. Despite its apparent banality, this definition has the merit of
readmitting metaphysical speculation into the realm of meaningful discourse (See Chapter I). We have moreover seen that, though possessing
undecidable truth-values, some ontological theses play an essential role in
the progress of science. Popper often cited atomism as the typical example
of a hypothesis which, having started life as a purely philosophical conjecture, gradually developed into a fully-fledged scientific theory. He did not
however explain how such a transmutation could take place: a statement is
after all either scientific, i.e. empirically falsifiable, or else irrefutable and
hence metaphysical; so we have here two disjoint classes which seem to
leave no room for any intermediate category.

Kuhn does no better than Popper; for he also fails to give any clear indi-
cation as to how a paradigm enables its adepts to construct new theories; he
speaks, in vague terms, of *exemplars* which scientists working within a
given paradigm attempt to emulate. Lakatos tried to remedy this defect by
distinguishing between the positive heuristic of a research program and its
hard core: the latter is kept fixed by methodological decision; the former
consists of methods designed to modify and 'sophisticate' the boundary
conditions so as to increase the testability of the underlying program.
Lakatos had in mind the Newtonian paradigm whose hard core, namely the
classical equations of motion together with the law of gravitation, remained
unaltered for more than two centuries. Unfortunately, the Lakatosian
scheme does not fit the pattern of development either of thermodynamics or
of modern atomism: from the latter's inception as a philosophical thesis, to

the classical description of elementary particles, and finally to quantum physics, we hardly find any law which remained unchanged. And yet there exists an undeniable family resemblance between all atomic hypotheses. This is one reason why I decided to regard all metaphysical hard cores, i.e. the heuristics of research programs, as consisting of meta-principles governing the form of scientific theories; so that the relation between heuristic and syntactical form is the usual one of logical subsumption. This leaves open the possibility of altering, within the same program, even the most fundamental laws entering into a scientific system; for many different statements can fall under one and the same meta-principle (See Chapter VI). A number of heuristic devices have been mentioned: the Correspondence Principle, the method of adjusting parameters to known facts, the demand that theories satisfy certain symmetry requirements and the atomistic desideratum that all hypotheses entail the discrete structure of all the basic constituents of the physical universe.

In the present chapter it will be shown that towards the end of the 19th century the methodological debate between the atomists and the classical thermodynamicists had not been definitively settled. This ambiguous situation explains why nonempirical considerations largely determined the various ways in which thermodynamical problems were tackled. Hence differing metaphysical convictions, often unrelated to experimental results, must be invoked when accounting for the decisions taken by the protagonists in this scientific debate. In other words: with regard to atomism, metaphysics acted decisively as a guide to methodology.

(B) A General Description of Atomism

The Greeks put forward atomism in response to a purely philosophical problem: that of reconciling the Parmenidean thesis of the immutability of Being with the undeniable existence of phenomenal change. Democritus was thus led to postulate a void containing a plurality of indivisible particles or *atoms,* each one of which could be assimilated to a Parmenidean sphere. Both the void and the atoms were supposed to be immutable; and the flux of appearances was to be explained in terms of different configurations of the same particles within the same empty space. Thus the only change admitted by the atomists was that of spatial position with respect to time. This hypothesis was initially untestable and hence metaphysical; for any observable state-of-affairs could be claimed to have arisen from the movement of some system of atoms, the latter being provisionally left unspecified.

After the scientific revolution and especially through the work of chemists like Boyle and Dalton, atomism was transformed into a scientific, i.e. into an empirically refutable theory. Taken in conjunction with suitable auxiliary assumptions, the atomic hypothesis could henceforth be pitted against experience; and it turned out to be a remarkably successful explanatory conjecture. But in the second half of the 19th century, atomism faced a serious challenge posed by a rival program: *phenomenological thermodynamics*. The latter was largely based on two principles: the principle of the conservation, and that of the degradation of energy. Let us denote these principles by [A] and [B] respectively. [A] hardly needs any explanation. As for [B], it can be rendered by the following proposition due to Kelvin and Planck: no process is possible whose *sole* result is a heat flow Q out of a reservoir at a single temperature and the performance of work W equal in magnitude to Q. [B] enabled Clausius to define the entropy S of a physical system Ω as a function of state which never decreases over time. In all real as opposed to *idealized* processes, S actually increases and can therefore be used to account for the unidirectionality of time. Intuitively speaking, S is a measure of the disorder within Ω; and the increase of S entails that no quantity of heat can be integrally converted into an equivalent amount of (useful) mechanical work (note that heat is, by definition, a disorderly or degraded form of energy).

Classical thermodynamics was empirically successful, but its capacity for further development remained limited: it had to rely on unexplained experimental results in obtaining the laws needed in order to arrive at verifiable predictions. For example, thermodynamicists accepted—as simply given—both the principle of the convertibility of heat into work and various equations of state like those of Boyle and van der Waals (See Clark 1976, p. 44). This did not prevent Duhem from elevating such fact-dependent methods into a heuristic principle to be used in all scientific research: through the admittedly theory-dependent and hence fallible processes of abstraction and generalization, the scientist induces laws intended to subsume a given set of scientific facts; where the latter are also theory-laden and consequently fallible. Starting from principles like [A] and [B], the scientist then constructs high-level hypotheses which, though devoid of informative content, are required to entail pre-given experimental laws. Throughout this creative process, it is not metaphysical speculation but mathematical ingenuity guided by formal analogies which plays the essential heuristic role. In his *General Theory of Knowledge,* Schlick describes this process of discovery as follows:

The different thermal sensations I have in touching a body under various conditions are correlated by the physicist with *one* identical quality; this he calls "temperature". . . .The physicist, however, utilizes a certain device to make the temperature subject to mathematical treatment. He correlates numbers with the various temperatures, and in so doing makes use of the approximate correspondence between the quality of the thermal sensation and the volume of a certain body . . . An ordering of this kind would of course not provide any knowledge of the nature of what was being correlated with numbers. At this stage, which is known as pure thermodynamics, measuring temperature would be something fundamentally different from measuring say, the length of light waves; for it would not be bound up with knowledge of the magnitude being measured. (Schlick 1974, p. 281; also Schlick 1979, p. 315)

As already mentioned, Duhem was too good a physicist not to make a concession to realism; a concession encapsulated in his notion of *natural classification*: taken as a whole, a scientific system must tend towards a classification of the phenomena which mirrors the ontological order, without however directly signifying the latter (See above, Chapter VII, Conclusion). This so-called natural classification possesses two defining characteristics. First, it displays a high degree of unity in that its components are closely interconnected; it secondly entails hitherto unknown laws which are eventually confirmed. We shall see that according to Duhem, atomism satisfies neither of these criteria (Duhem 1906 [1954, pp. 19–30]).

Atomism faced the difficult task of reducing [A] and [B] to its own principles; i.e. it had to show that [A] and [B] constitute limiting cases of some mechanical laws governing the motions of particles. [A] presents no fundamental difficulty; for according to mechanism, heat is motion. [A] should therefore follow from the law of the conservation of mechanical-cum-electromagnetic energy; where the latter is entailed by Newton's and Maxwell's hypotheses. Atomism would thus explain rather than simply postulate the convertibility of heat into work; i.e. the possibility for one form of electromechanical energy to be transformed into another.

[B] however seemed to pose insuperable problems. Let us recall that atomism was based on the thesis of the particulate nature of matter and on the laws of both mechanics and electromagnetism. It is well known that classical mechanics is not only deterministic but that it also treats prediction and retrodiction on a par. Consider any time-interval $[t_0, t_1]$. The initial conditions at t_0 not only determine, but are also uniquely determined by the final conditions at t_1. Newtonian mechanics is moreover time-reversible in the following sense. Let an isolated system of particles P_1, P_2,..., P_n describe a trajectory Γ in the time-interval $[t_0, t_1]$. Were the velocity of each P_i to be reversed at t_1, then during the interval $[t_1, 2t_1 - t_0]$ the system would retrace Γ in the reverse order; all the velocities would also be reversed at corresponding, i.e. at mirror-image points of the two trajectories. Hence, denoting by Γ^* this new (inverted) path, no mechanistic explanation of the entropy S appears to be possible; for if S were to be defined, say in terms of the positions and speeds of P_1, P_2,..., P_n, then any increase of S along Γ would be matched by an equal decrease along Γ^*. Thus, right from its inception, the kinetic program seemed doomed. Yet according to Schlick, the atomic hypothesis is the paradigm case of a successful reduction of a disparate set of phenomenological laws to one fundamental theory. Schlick writes:

> This [mechanical] theory identifies heat with the mean kinetic energy of molecules in motion—certainly an extensive magnitude. ... Temperature as a special quality is altogether eliminated from the physical world outlook. It is completely reduced to the mechanical concepts of mass, space and time; it has thus become measurable in a strict sense and its nature has become completely *known*.
> ... This process of eliminating qualities is at the heart of all advances in knowledge in the explanatory sciences. (Schlick 1974, p. 282; also Schlick 1979, p. 316)

As for the reversibility problem which plagued atomism and was underlined by Loschmidt, it will be examined in greater detail when we come to talk about Boltzmann's work.

Let me end this section by mentioning some breakthroughs and one serious empirical failure of the atomic program. Atomism not only explained the convertibility of heat into work; it also enabled its adherents to determine important equations of state like those of Boyle, Charles and van der Waals. In Maxwell's hands, it furthermore yielded the unexpected result that viscosity does not depend on density but solely on temperature. This counter-intuitive consequence was moreover confirmed (Sears and Salinger 1975, pp. 286–291). All versions of atomism however appeared to break down when it came to determining the relative specific heats of various substances. Let $\gamma = c_p/c_v$, where c_p and c_v are the specific heat capacities of a substance at constant pressure and at constant volume respectively (i.e. $c_p = (\delta q/\delta T)_p$ and $c_v = (\delta q/\delta T)_v$; where δT and δq denote the increments of the absolute temperature and of the corresponding quantity of heat per unit mass respectively; and the suffixes p and v in $(\delta q/\delta T)_p$ and in $(\delta q/\delta T)_v$ indicate that the ratio $\delta q/\delta T$ is measured at a constant pressure and at a constant volume respectively). By virtue of the law of equipartition of energy, all classical kinetic theories entail $\gamma = (f + 2)/f = (1 + 2/f)$, where f is the number of degrees of freedom of any molecule of the substance in question. For a monatomic molecule, $f = 3$ (corresponding to a purely translational kinetic energy determined by one velocity vector). Thus by the equation above, we obtain $\gamma = 1.66$ which is in good agreement with experimental results. But classical, as opposed to *quantum* mechanics generally ascribes too large a value to f. For example: in the case of diatomic molecules, $f = 7$ (3 degrees of freedom for translational kinetic energy; 2 for the rotation of the molecule, which is defined by the components of the angular velocity along 2 directions not passing through the two atoms; and 2 for the vibrational energy determined both by the distance between the two atoms and by their relative speed). This yields $\gamma = 1.29$, a value which differs sensibly from the observed one, namely 1.4. In order not to run foul of experience, the atomists had to set f equal to 5. But this was tantamount to ignoring either the rotational or the vibrational energy, whose existence was supported both by theoretical arguments and by independent evidence (Sears 1953, pp. 246–251). The kinetic program thus threatened to fall prey to its internal contradictions. 19th-Century physicists could not of course know that the villain of the piece was not the atomic hypothesis as such but the classical laws of motion. The latter, having subsequently proved inapplicable to microscopic phenomena, were replaced by wave mechanics.

The above difficulties and successes of the atomic and thermodynamic programs were not mentioned for their own sake, but with a view to bringing out an important philosophical point. We have just shown that, until the end of the 19th century, the methodological situation remained unclear. Atomism had a powerful *heuristic,* i.e. *it suggested many avenues for further research.* After some spectacular breakthroughs, it however turned out to be plagued by seemingly intractable problems. As for classical thermodynamics, though appearing to be empirically faultless, it offered only a weak heuristic. Let us recall that the hard core of every scientific program must of necessity be *metaphysical*; i.e. that, when taken in isolation, it is not *directly* testable by experience. Otherwise, no methodological fiat can immunize the core against empirical falsification (See above, Chapter VI). The core can nonetheless be *indirectly* either undermined by the experimental failures or else supported by the successes of the theories belonging to its program (For more details, see Zahar 1989a, pp. 13–38). The methodological verdict however remains inconclusive as long as a program like atomism—or thermodynamics—can both be credited with dramatic successes and impugned for a number of setbacks; for in such cases, no methodology can by itself explain an individual scientist's preference of one program over another. In order to account for such decisions, the historian has to adduce external, that is: metaphysical, moral, religious or even political *motives*. These influence the way in which, by *weighting* the available evidence, a scientist extrapolates the successes or else the failures of various programs.

I shall now examine Mach's, Duhem's, Ostwald's and Boltzmann's appraisals of atomism. My main aim is to show that because of the phenomenalist stance he derived from Kantian philosophy, Mach opposed all realist versions of atomism; that because of his fideism, Duhem, while remaining a realist, objected to all forms of reductionist materialism; that Ostwald adopted a paradoxical attitude arising from an inductivist position so naïve as to be baffling; that despite his cautious fallibilism, Boltzmann was at heart a firm believer in reductionist physicalism, as is evidenced by his unreserved adherence to Darwinism; it therefore comes as no surprise that he continued to work on the atomic program despite the latter's shortcomings.

(C) Mach's Objections to Realism

It must have struck Mach that despite theorizing about space and time, forces and atoms etc., scientists rely exclusively on their thoughts and on their sense-impressions whenever they come to test their hypotheses; i.e. they rely on mental and not on any allegedly physical processes. So why posit anything beyond our sense-data, or rather: beyond the latter's ultimate components which Mach called the *elements of sensation*? These consist of colors, smells, sounds and shapes, together with the observer's feelings, volitions and thoughts.

This Berkelian thesis can alternatively be defended by starting—as Mach himself did—from Kant's transcendental idealism according to which only appearances can be known. As for the noumena or things-in-themselves, they will always remain ineffable; or rather: all we can say about them is that they exist and that they *somehow* give rise to the appearances; but the way in which these hidden entities found the phenomena will always be a mystery to us. Since the noumena do very little work in Kant's account of theoretical reason, Mach decided to abolish them and regard ontology as consisting of a nexus of interconnected appearances. He did not realize that he was thereby adopting a strong metaphysical stance; for nothing in experience can either refute or verify the proposition that nothing exists beyond the elements of our sensations (Mach 1906, Chapter 1). Though often described as a neutral monist, Mach was in effect a thoroughgoing idealist; which is hardly surprising since he jettisoned the only realist component of Kant's philosophy. He tried to solve the mind-body problem by holding bodies to consist of relatively stable elements of sensations; where the stability is provided by a fixed system of functional relationships between these elements. For Mach as for Berkeley before him, bodies cannot be claimed to go on existing after they cease to be observed. Such a claim would actually be neither true nor false but meaningless. All we are entitled to assert is that we experience the same sense-impressions whenever we repeat, under the same conditions, some prescribed sequence of operations. Thus Mach held the task of science to consist exclusively of setting up equations of the form: $f_i(x_1,...,x_n) = 0$, $i = 1,...,m$; where $x_1,...,x_n$ range over *both* the elements of sensation constituting the so-called 'external' world—which include the observer's body—*and* the latter's thoughts, moods and volitions. We generally have fewer equations than unknowns, i.e. $m < n$. Should *any* $(n - m)$ terms among the $x_1,...,x_n$ be labeled 'causes' and provisionally fixed either theoretically or by measurement, then the equations would enable us to reconstruct or predict the remaining m elements; the latter can thus *nominalistically* be defined as the 'effects' (Mach called any such sequence of operations 'a completion of facts in thought').

Mach's objections to atomism flow from his overall philosophical position: since they have never been observed, atoms and molecules are mere mental constructs; yet some physicists illegitimately ascribe to them the spatial and tactile properties which are experienced exclusively as sensations or as relations between elements of sensation. For example: in the same way that a table is perceived as being extended and hard, we attribute both extension and impenetrability to the atoms which supposedly compose the table. Similarly: because 'macroscopic' bodies, qua complexes of sensation, bear definite spatial relations to one another, we extend these relations to all unobserved elementary particles. Notwithstanding this paradoxical extension of perceived attributes to hidden entities, the mechanists further demand that an 'explanation' be given of experienced qualities like colors and sounds in terms of the 'primary' properties of the unobservable atoms. These empirically unjustifiable requirements flow from a Cartesian prejudice; that of demanding that the whole of science be forced into the straitjacket of *mathematical* physics. Apart from its intrinsic absurdity, this project leads straight into the insoluble mind-body problem.

Mach had a third—*methodological*—objection to atomism: the decision to explain all processes in terms of mechanistic atomism drastically reduces the number of parameters available to the physicist; for he is from then on restricted to using a limited number of basic parameters; namely $<x, y, z>$ (space), t (time), $<v_x, v_y, v_z>$ (velocity), m (mass), e (charge). He is thus prevented from regarding the temperature T as an independent quantity; for mechanism compels him to look upon T as shorthand for the mean kinetic energy of a system of particles.

Another example given by Mach is as follows. Suppose we try to express all connections between the atoms exclusively in terms of the latter's spatial relations. Given any three non-collinear particles, Q_1, Q_2 and Q_3, the position of an arbitrary point P is (to within reflection in the plane $Q_1Q_2Q_3$) uniquely determined by the distances: PQ_1, PQ_2, PQ_3. All relations between P and any other point B are therefore fixed by 6 numbers, and 6 numbers only: PQ_i and BQ_i (i = 1, 2, 3); so that the decision to account for the behavior of a gas exclusively in terms of the spatial properties of its alleged constituents strongly constrains the number of allowable parameters (Mach 1909, pp. 50–57). Against Mach, it should nonetheless be noted that such constraints have the merit of limiting the ways in which a theory can be adjusted *post-hoc* to fit pre-given facts. The scientist is thus compelled to construct highly refutable hypotheses; which, from a Popperian viewpoint, is methodologically desirable. Let us moreover point out that for logical reasons, no successful scientific reduction can diminish the empirical content of any scientific laws; provided of course that the meanings of the observational terms be kept fixed. After being reduced, an old hypothesis may admittedly be refuted by new experimental results; in which case one can always go back to the original, i.e. to the unreduced theory (For more details, see Zahar 1996, section 3; also Zahar 2001, Chapter 2). Such were to be the ungainsayable reasons advanced by Boltzmann in support of atomism qua heuristic.

Before turning to Duhem's philosophy, we should mention one important concession made by Mach to atomism, or rather to atomistic *language*. He held that atomistic terminology can be legitimately used as a means of classifying certain phenomena, that is: of bringing order into the field of our sensations. Unlike the 'monstrous' concepts of absolute space and time, 'atoms' and 'electrons' might turn out to be convenient devices for organizing certain areas of knowledge; it being understood that such terms should never be given a realist interpretation (Mach 1933, Chapter 4).

(D) OSTWALD AND DUHEM

Ostwald's position is worth describing if only because it presents us with the negative image of Duhem's. Ostwald subscribed to determinism, to realism and to physicalist reductionism. But being a naive inductivist whilst holding atomism to be a gratuitous hypothesis, he regarded his own version of *energetics* as having been 'read off' directly from the facts; where energetics is the thesis that the universe is made up not of atoms, but of *interconvertible forms of energy*. Ostwald took these forms to be 'obviously' irreducible to one another because they are differently perceived by our senses (Ostwald 1937, Chapters 4, 7, 10, 11). We need not dwell on these non-sequiturs, which nonetheless have the merit of demonstrating that atomism was opposed both from a realist and from a phenomenalist angle.

Let us, once again, give a synopsis of Duhem's position. Duhem's aim was to separate sharply between science and ontology; not because he held the latter to be meaningless but because, being a devout Catholic, he was committed to one *revealed* metaphysic (See above, Chapter V). He gave the strong impression of wanting to vindicate fallibilism at all levels of scientific inquiry, thereby clipping the wings of science in order to make room for faith. He rightly denied that there could be any exact parallel between the steady progress of mathematics on the one hand, and the seemingly tortuous development of physics on the other. He nonetheless claimed that if viewed from the right perspective, the empirical sciences would display a quasi-cumulative pattern of growth. In order for such a vantage point to be gained, a price would however have to be paid, or rather an obstacle removed: given the frequent changes in our conception of ontology, any intrusion of metaphysics into science would inevitably induce instability in our perception of the development of physics; and this as long as we go on interpreting the latter realistically. Physics ought therefore to renounce all realist claims. Duhem was thus led to distinguish between the representative part of a scientific system—which he accepted—and an explanatory or interpretative part which he totally rejected. The representative component, henceforth referred to as REP, consists of purely formal relations whose only function is to entail well-tested experimental laws. As for the explanatory component, henceforth called 'EXP', it supposedly provides a realist interpretation of the whole system: it tries to anchor REP in a transcendent reality whose existence is warranted by a metaphysical hypothesis. Though describing EXP as *interpretative*, what Duhem really meant was that EXP is *reductive* in the sense of purporting to entail REP. But this was conclusively shown by him to be impossible: metaphysical conjectures are too weak to imply any testable laws, yet strong enough to conflict with genuinely scientific theories. Far from yielding any new predictions, EXP often proves hardly compatible with REP, which consequently does all the empirical work on its own (Note how close Duhem came to formulating Popper's demarcation criterion). Because of its semantic pretensions, EXP moreover misrepresents the history of science as a series of violent revolutions. Axing EXP therefore represents a double gain. First an increase in the economy of thought is achieved without any loss of empirical content. The development of science can secondly be seen as a gradual process during which, thanks to the Correspondence Principle, the mathematical form of all empirically successful laws is largely preserved. This provides a rationale for our belief that we might be moving towards a 'natural classification' (Duhem 1906 [1954, pp. 31–39]; also see Zahar 2001, Chapter 2).

Duhem went out of his way to demonstrate that most attempts at reducing physics to mechanistic atomism had been not only otiose but also counter-productive. He defined 'mechanism' as the thesis that the ultimate constituents of reality are charged particles subject the laws governing the motion of macroscopic objects. He correctly pointed out that 'mechanism' should not be confused with 'realism'. In support of his claim, he gave an example which however lacked conviction: he presented the 'English physicists' as non-realistic mechanists, for they supposedly supplemented their theories with dynamical images without regarding the latter as genuinely explanatory. Such models are offered exclusively on account of their alleged intelligibility. By contrast, Aristotle was certainly a realist but not a mechanist.

According to Duhem, the only legitimate inductive inference consists in generalizing theory-laden empirical results in a way which is also theory-dependent (See (B) above; also Chapter V, (B)). Whence a twofold fallibility of induction, which nonetheless remains the only method of acquiring new factual knowledge. Let us incidentally note that having renounced metaphysical speculation, the conventionalist is bound to resort to some form or other of inductive reasoning. Duhem again rightly distinguishes between inductivism on the one hand and mechanism on the other. Properties like shape, impenetrability and motion are admittedly revealed by the phenomena; but so are colors, smells and tastes; and experience in no way tells us that this second group of 'secondary' qualities is reducible to the 'primary' one. With some justification, Duhem maintained that his own version of energetics is closer to the domain of sense-experience than are its atomistic rivals. Though conceding that many great physicists were atomists, he denied that their metaphysical convictions helped them in any way towards achieving their breakthroughs. These scientists found it in effect difficult to reconcile their discoveries with their ontological prejudices. If we are to believe Duhem, mechanical theories possess only two advantages: they postulate very few basic predicates; the latter are moreover easy to picture, whence their appeal to the English 'ample but weak' mind.

To repeat: Duhem does not target realism as such but only reductive mechanism which, if realistically interpreted as materialist atomism, allegedly threatens Christian dogma. His criticism is nonetheless so global that it hits all reductive explanations. Because of his fideism, he gave greater weight to the difficulties facing materialist physics than to the latter's heuristic fruitfulness and its capacity for anticipating novel facts. According to realists like Boltzmann, this capacity points to the truth-likeness of atomism, whose difficulties should consequently be shelved as mere 'anomalies' to be ironed out by future research. It can thus be concluded that during periods of methodological uncertainty, metaphysics plays a dominant role in the development of the sciences. Duhem's antipathy towards all versions of dynamism accounts for his negative appraisal of practically all the theories which were to dominate twentieth century science: atomism, electromagnetic field theory, Relativity and Darwinism. The fact that despite his brilliance as a physicist and as a methodologist Duhem proved to be such a bad prophet, cannot be explained without invoking his religious convictions.

(E) BOLTZMANN, POINCARÉ AND THE DEFENSE OF ATOMISM

Boltzmann's philosophy of science can be consistently reconstructed—provided his ontology be sharply distinguished from his epistemology. Qua *metaphysician*, Boltzmann subscribed both to atomistic realism and to a Darwinian version of reductionism. He held our aesthetic and moral values, as well as our logical and supposedly apriori principles to be genetically encoded beliefs. Because of their survival value, the latter are transmitted from one generation to the next. When it came to *epistemology*, this hard-headed physicalist position was nevertheless tempered by Boltzmann's fallibilist hypothetico-deductivism. He acknowledged that in constructing his laws, the scientist must go beyond the 'facts', which always underdetermine his theories. Boltzmann rightly accused inductivists like Ostwald and idealists like Mach of ignoring these basic limitations on the certainty of all hypotheses: not only is the phenomenalist driven to solipsism but in setting up relations between his own elements of sensation, he furthermore has to rely on past, i.e. on remembered experiences. These are as imperfectly known as any 'external' objects or as the contents of other people's minds; so the scientist might just as well postulate transcendent entities rather than try—in vain—to limit himself to descriptions of his immanent states of consciousness (Boltzmann 1979, pp. 26–46).

Boltzmann tried to turn most ontological questions into *methodological* ones. He did not object to phenomenological thermodynamics as such; he simply regarded it as possessing limited heuristic power and hence as being methodologically inferior to its rivals. This is why he advised all researchers, even those who did *not believe* in atomism, to work on the atomic program; for the latter had yielded a whole host of novel laws, e.g. the equations of state of many substances and the independence of the viscosity of a gas from its density. Thus he advocated a fallibilist, anti-essentialist and pluralist methodology. In order to forestall any criticism emanating from his scientific opponents—or from the Church—he agreed to look upon all hypotheses as no more than mental images whose sole purpose is to subsume our experiences. His sincerity can however be doubted; for he concurrently maintained that if a unified theory successfully predicts unexpected empirical results, it can be taken to reflect the objective order of things. His protestations nonetheless underline an important methodological point: a scientific theory derives its high status not from any allegedly inherent 'plausibility' of its axioms, but from its internal coherence together with its entailment of verified observable consequences (Boltzmann 1979, pp. 170–189). This aspect of Boltzmann's philosophy is both ungainsayable and surprisingly modern. The problems facing him however stemmed not from his methodology, but from the logical and experimental difficulties confronting atomism. To these we must now turn.

In section (B) above, the difficulties pertaining to the specific heats of polyatomic substances were mentioned. These problems were solved through the replacement of classical by wave mechanics, whose development however postdated Boltzmann's death. But in the first decade of the twentieth century, the work of Einstein, Smoluchowski and Perrin had already provided strong support for classical atomism. By considering the fluctuations entailed by atomic theory, Einstein managed to account for the irregular movements of Brownian particles; these arise from the successive collisions of the particles with the surrounding molecules. Einstein derived a formula which was later confirmed by Perrin. This unexpected success eventually led doubters like Ostwald—but not Mach—to accept the atomic hypothesis (See Stachel 1989, pp. 206–236).

There remained one outstanding theoretical question which atomism appeared unable to answer; namely that posed by the irreversibility of most natural processes. We have already mentioned the difficulty of mechanically defining entropy in such a way that the Second Principle is verified, either exactly or approximately. Boltzmann put forward the equation: $S(q) = k.logW_q$, where k is a constant, q denotes a macrostate, and W_q a quantity proportional to the number of microstates giving rise to q. Thus, to within some constant factor, W_q represents a *thermodynamic probability*. Boltzmann initially conjectured that no physical process leads to a decrease of W_q. But could this proposition be derived from the laws of mechanics conjoined with descriptions of appropriate boundary conditions? In section (B), a bijection was established between two sets Δ and Δ^*; where Δ and Δ^* consist respectively of those initial conditions which cause an increase and those which cause a diminution of the entropy S. This result led Boltzmann to concede that while being highly improbable, a decrease of S remains possible. But instead of establishing this proposition, he *merely asserted* that his critics had failed to prove their claim; namely that a diminution of S is as likely as its increase (Brush 1966, Paper 4). Boltzmann had in effect shifted the burden of proof on to his opponents by challenging them to show that the measure of Δ^* is at least as great as that of Δ (Note that the bijection between the sets Δ and Δ^* establishes the equality of their *cardinals*, not that of their *measures*. Since the notion of measure is a generalization of that of length, of area or of volume, probabilities are proportional to measures and not to cardinalities).

Boltzmann's move seems to me highly questionable: since he set out to deduce the Second Principle from atomism, it was *up to him* to show that Δ^* is, in some sense, smaller than Δ; whereas he merely pointed to his critics' failure to establish the *incompatibility* of mechanics with thermodynamics. Be it as it may, Zermelo's objections to atomism proved even harder to rebut (Zermelo 1966, pp. 229–237). In showing the impossibility of any reduction of the Second Principle to mechanics, Zermelo invoked Poincaré's recurrence theorem (Brush 1966, Papers 5 and 7). Before examining this result, let us briefly review some tenets of Poincaré's philosophy.

(a) Unlike Duhem, Poincaré had no ulterior fideist motives. While Duhem baulked at the thesis of physical determinism which might threaten the dogma of free will, Poincaré knew that ethics had nothing to fear from science; and this—in his own words—for quasi-grammatical reasons; for, being a convinced Kantian, he subscribed to a rigorous separation between value judgments and scientific propositions (Poincaré 1913, Chapter 8).

(b) Thus Poincaré did not reject mechanistic reductionism out of hand; but only on condition that it succeed in producing unified theories predictive of crude facts. Qua structural realist, Poincaré insisted that science does not aims at 'mechanism' *per se,* but at unity coupled with empirical confirmability (See Zahar 2001, Chapter 2). As for reductive mechanism, not only had it not yet proved its mettle; it moreover seemed undermined by the theorem of eternal return.

(c) Poincaré came to believe in the existence of elementary particles; and this not only after Perrin had published results which, in Poincaré's own words, enabled the scientists to *count* the atoms; but already on account of the theory of electrons through which Lorentz had explained practically all electromagnetic phenomena, including the null outcome of Michelson's experiment. These results do not however automatically guarantee the mechanical reducibility of the second law of thermodynamics (See Zahar 1989a, Chapter 2; Poincaré 1913, Chapter 7; and Brush 1966, Papers 5 and 7).

Let us now turn to Poincaré's theorem, which can be informally stated as follows. Consider a physical system Ω together with any closed and bounded region B in the space of all possible initial conditions of Ω. Then B contains a subset $B\Omega$ of measure zero such that: if Ω is started at an arbitrary point of $B \backslash B'$, i.e. at practically any point of B, the entropy of Ω *cannot* steadily increase but might—at best—remain constant (See Appendix 6).

Boltzmann's response to this problem was unsatisfactory. He claimed that entropy could consistently be *assumed* to increase steadily, at any rate for a long time to come; after which the universe would gradually go back to a state differing from the initial one by an arbitrary positive real ε—with a corresponding diminution of entropy. Boltzmann moreover admitted that he needed to *postulate* improbable initial conditions (Brush 1966, Paper 8). These ad hoc moves might well have established the compatibility of the Second Principle of Thermodynamics with the atomic hypothesis, but certainly not the derivability of the former from the latter. Thus, in 1905, atomism had not (yet?) superseded thermodynamics. Yet because of its undeniable *empirical* successes, atomism is nowadays accepted by most physicists. So one wonders whether the unity displayed by scientific hypotheses might not, all told, play a negligible role when compared with their capacity for yielding novel experimental results.

(F) CONCLUSION

With the possible exception of Poincaré, all the scientists mentioned in this Chapter were shown to have used metaphysics as a guide to methodology. And even in the case of Poincaré—as in that of Einstein—there is an ontological presupposition, albeit an implicit one; namely that the universe possesses the simplest, i.e. the most coherent and unified structure consistent with the facts.

IX

Einstein, or the Essential Unity of Science and Philosophy

(A) INTRODUCTION

Bearing in mind the title of the Schilpp volume: *Albert Einstein: Philosopher-Scientist*, Einstein's career will be presented as a test case for the central thesis advanced in this book; namely that both science and epistemology are inseparable from general philosophy and more particularly from metaphysics.

Before Hegel, i.e. from the Presocratics to Kant, any question about the existence of some relationship between philosophy and science would immediately have been answered in the affirmative: physical science was taken to be part of philosophy; and Democritus, Aristotle, Descartes, Leibniz, Hume and Kant were philosophers as well as natural or social scientists. Kant, the last and most illustrious members of this series, did not only teach physics at the University of Königsberg; he also developed his critical philosophy largely in response to the presumed infallibility of scientific, i.e. of Newtonian knowledge. In many British universities theoretical physics has, until recently, been referred to as natural philosophy. Hegel was one of the first philosophers to throw doubt on the relevance of the mathematical disciplines to an understanding of the deep nature of things; for he held mathematics to be capable of capturing only the most abstract, and consequently the most superficial aspects of physical reality.

Throughout the 19th and 20th centuries, there have of course been many distinguished philosophers of science: Helmholtz, Mach, Whewell, Duhem, Poincaré, Meyerson, Popper, Reichenbach and most members of the Vienna Circle, to name but the most famous. They were not however regarded by their colleagues as genuine philosophers, but as philosophically inclined commentators on the foundations of physics; a view which ironically seemed confirmed by the neopositivists' own project of abolishing philosophy as a substantive discipline. In this connection, Wittgenstein claimed that even if science solved all of its outstanding problems, those of philosophy would thereby hardly have been addressed; for philosophy deals with language-games and is the kind of grammatical hygiene which can both ignore and be safely ignored by the sciences. As for the 'real' philosophers like Husserl and Heidegger, they held the sciences to be hopelessly naïve in that they abstract from the subjective activity which lies at their foundation. According to Heidegger, science is incapable of real thought since it fails to reflect on Being, Existence and Essence (See Heidegger 1953; also Husserl 1969a). Following the *Existenzphilosophen*, Sartre boldly—i.e. recklessly— tackled the problem of human freedom without taking account of any scientific laws, not even of those yielded by neurophysiology or by empirical psychology (In a later phase, he made some diffident concessions to psycho-analysis as to the only 'science' he was prepared to entertain).

(B) The Relationship Between Science and Philosophy

The above-mentioned separatist views might have been dismissed out of hand by thinkers genuinely interested in the foundations of the sciences, were it not for the fact—already alluded to—that leading members of the Vienna and Berlin Circles held strong views about a strict division of labor between science and philosophy. For example: Schlick took over Wittgenstein's thesis that philosophy puts forward, not any true-or-false propositions, but grammatical rules for the avoidance of confusions caused by a sloppy use of language (See Schlick 1986b). As for Reichenbach, his separatist position is all the more surprising since he wrote what was regarded—by Einstein himself—as one of the most impressive epistemological accounts of Relativity Theory; namely *Die Philosophie der Raum-Zeit-Lehre,* first published in 1927. Note that Einstein later disagreed with Reichenbach's empiricist stance according to which there exists a strict demarcation between the *context of discovery* and the *context of justification*. As already mentioned, Reichenbach claimed that philosophy should deal exclusively with the problem of justification and restrict itself to the logical analysis of completed theories; it ought for example to study the ways in which physical laws relate to experience. As for the genesis of scientific hypotheses, it neither calls for nor is susceptible of any rational reconstruction. What is more, any philosophical reflection on the scientist's part may have deleterious effects on his creative ability:

> The philosopher of science is not much interested in the thought processes which lead to scientific discoveries; he looks for a logical

analysis of the completed theory including the relationships establishing its validity. That is, he is not interested in the context of discovery but in the context of justification. But the critical attitude may make a man incapable of discovery; and as long as he is successful, the creative physicist may well prefer his creed to the logic of the analytic philosopher. (Schilpp 1949, p. 292)

This rigid distinction between two supposedly very different contexts was accepted by Popper—who did not use the notion of the justification but that of the empirical testing of hypotheses 'laid on the table'. For his part, Lakatos often maintained that methodologies do not offer advice but only appraisal. These separatist views were however contested by Einstein, who repeatedly claimed that Hume's and Mach's philosophical insights helped him towards discovering Relativity Theory; whence a major problem for the historians and philosophers of science.

Reichenbach might admittedly be right in holding that scientists are often unwilling or else unable to articulate the philosophical principles which guided their research; but in the same way that we often follow rules of which we can give no general account, the scientist can apply a methodology which he might be incapable of defining rigorously. As for the distinction between assessment and advice, it prompted Paul Feyerabend to the following comments. Should methodologies be treated as systems of 'norms' for the appraisal of extant theories, then they would reduce to a pointless academic exercise: that of giving various marks to known hypotheses about whose ranking physicists anyway agree. As an illustration, let us recall that although he disapproved of the methods used in QM (Quantum Mechanics), Einstein conceded that the latter had so far given the best description of atomic phenomena; it therefore looks as though Einstein did not need any 'philosophy' to tell him that QM was empirically adequate. Moreover, for every methodology M which sets out to give advice to the working physicist, there exists, according to Feyerabend, some past scientific achievement which would have been hampered by the strict application of M (See Feyerabend 1972b). Hence 'anything goes'; that is: methodology and even logic ought to be treated as handmaidens at the service of the scientist; the latter uses whatever method suits the moment: he then discards these methods in favor of other devices which might in their turn be rejected (Feyerabend 1975). As already mentioned, this view appears to have been shared by Einstein who at times defended a form of methodological opportunism. In the same vein, Max Born claimed that in his young creative period, Einstein was an out-and-out Machian positivist who later turned into a reactionary realist metaphysician. Born's comments contain more than a mere hint that these different philosophical attitudes were, if not the causes, then at any rate the symptoms of different levels of scientific creativity; it being understood that positivism and operationalism were the driving force behind Einstein's early achievements. Thus:

> I was an unconditional follower and apostle of the young Einstein and swore by his theories; I could not imagine that the old Einstein thought differently. Einstein had based Relativity Theory on the principle that concepts which refer to unobservables have no place within physics . . . Quantum Theory arose when Heisenberg applied this same theory to the electronic structure of the atom. This was a bold fundamental step, which at once struck me as self-evident and led me to put all my powers at the service of this new idea. Obviously, I found it impossible to understand that Einstein refused to accept the validity, within Quantum Theory, of the principle which he had very successfully used himself . . . In a previous letter he [Einstein] had expressed his views by saying that he was averse to the philosophy of the "esse est percipi." (Einstein and Born 1969, pp. 299–300. My translation)

To sum up: according to well-known philosophers, science and philosophy deal with disjoint domains, not to say with different levels of intellectual activity. According to other thinkers, scientists no doubt make use of philosophies, but only in the guise of disposable methodological instruments; these change with the circumstances and possess no special status.

(C) THE PROBLEM OF FALSE CONSCIOUSNESS

In the rest of this chapter I propose to refute the above separatist views by defending the following thesis: throughout his life, Einstein adhered essentially to the same *intuitive* philosophy; the latter not only provided him with heuristic guidelines towards the discovery of STR and GTR; it also determined the standpoint he adopted both in criticizing QM and in formulating the Einstein-Podolsky-Rosen (EPR) paradox.

It is well known that Einstein found QM wanting; so he put forward his own program of deriving the existence of particles from a *realistically* interpreted field theory. The fact that despite being based on an approach which had proved its mettle in the construction of electrodynamic and gravitational theories, this program ultimately failed, is irrelevant to the problem posed by the relationship between science and philosophy; for it should be remembered that, starting from a philosophy giving rise to a heuristic, the scientist might be in a position to propose, but it is only Nature which disposes.

In what follows my main references will be articles written by Einstein in the 1930s. I chose this period for a specific reason. In the 30s, after a long creative period, Einstein seems to have taken a step back in order to reflect on his own achievements as well as on those of his contemporaries; also to identify the principles which had underlain his discoveries and the moral values to which he still adhered. Finally, in the EPR paper, he used both methodology and a realist brand of metaphysics in order to show the incompleteness of QM and then to go, beyond the latter, towards a determinist theory of atomic processes. Of great significance are Einstein's efforts throughout this difficult period to express his philosophical convictions while analyzing the way in which they enabled him to create Relativity Theory.

Superficially, it can easily be shown that philosophical speculation played an important part in Einstein's scientific thinking. At first sight, all that needs to be done is to quote the numerous passages in which Einstein refers to Schopenhauer's determinism, to Spinoza's pantheism, to Hume's critique of the principle of induction, to Kant's transcendental system, to Mach's operationalism and finally to Poincaré's views about both the foundations of geometry and the role of conventions in physics. For example:

I do not at all believe in human freedom in the philosophical sense. Everybody acts not only under external compulsion, but also with inner necessity. Schopenhauer's saying 'A man can do what he wants but not want what he wants' has been a very real inspiration to me since my youth; it has been a continual consolation in the face of life's hardships, my own and others', and an unfailing well-spring of tolerance. (Einstein 1994a, p. 9)

And:

One sees that in this paradox the germ of the Special Theory of Relativity is already contained. Today everybody knows, of course, that all attempts to clarify this paradox satisfactorily were condemned to failure as long as the axiom of the absolute character of time, viz. of simultaneity, unrecognizedly was anchored in con-

sciousness. Clearly to recognize this axiom and its arbitrary character already entails the solution to the problem. The type of critical
reasoning which was required for the discovery of this central point
was decisively furthered, in my case, especially by reading David
Hume's and Ernst Mach's philosophical writings. (Schilpp 1949, p.
53)

Concerning Poincaré's influence on Einstein, the latter is known to have
read *Science and Hypothesis* where both Classical Relativity and Lorentz's
theory are discussed at great length. Moreover, Einstein's *Geometry and
Experience* bristles with references to Poincaré's theses about the conventionality of geometry and the possibility of providing the non-Euclidean
axioms with a physical interpretation (See Einstein 1994a, p. 254).

The above quotations however do not satisfactorily answer any serious
question about the *logical* interdependence between philosophy and science; for as already explained, every thinker confronts a problem of false
consciousness whenever he tries to give an account of the heuristics he
actually used in making his discoveries; and we have noted that according
to Einstein himself, we ought always to examine what the physicist actually
did and not what he claims to have done. After putting forward his hypotheses, the scientist is therefore as able—or as unable—to describe his intuitive
methodology as is the historian who attempts to reconstruct his heuristics.
In this connection, one point deserves special attention: Einstein was later
to claim that realism played a central role in his logic of discovery; but if
we are to believe Duhem, though regarded as true by many physicists,
metaphysical realism hardly helped any working scientist towards discovering any new laws. Arthur Fine made a similar, albeit more extreme point
about Einstein's realism, which he alleged to have had a *motivational* but
no *cognitive* content:

The particular psychoanalytic concept that seems to me most apt for
Einstein's realism is the concept of an imago—the complex ideal of
the parent, rooted in the unconscious elaborated by childhood fan-
tasies, and bound with the strong affect of that childhood period. The
parental image lies behind and drives certain of our behavior just as
Einstein tells us that realism 'lurks' behind and drives our work as
scientists . . . . (Fine 1986, pp. 109–111)

I admit to feeling scandalized whenever I read passages like this last
one. This is not because I hold psychoanalytic speculation to be *per se*

absurd or unilluminating; but the latter should not be invoked exclusively in order to bolster up some pre-given methodology which, in Fine's case, is the so-called Natural Ontological Attitude (NOA). As already explained, externalist explanations ought to be supported by independent evidence; and Fine offers next to none for his psychoanalytic account, which is anyway easily refuted by the following considerations.

(D) HUME'S, KANT'S AND MACH'S REAL INFLUENCE ON EINSTEIN

We have already said that a scientist's explicit philosophy, as formulated after his creative work has come to an end, is often a caricature of his intuitive methodology; that we can nonetheless learn many important things from such caricatures; for these present us with images, albeit distorted ones, of the scientist's real 'logic' of discovery (See above Chapter VI, section B).

Of course, these considerations apply to Einstein. In his so-called Machian period, he went as far as claiming that *all* scientific concepts could and should express direct relations between sense-impressions; which is nothing but an exaggerated version—or caricature—of the method he actually used; for in STR, the invariance of c can be confirmed by measuring round-trip velocities and is put forward *before* any convention for synchronizing clocks, i.e. for defining coordinate time is proposed. Moreover, only in the light of the postulated invariance of c does the convention of clock-synchronism make real sense, i.e. prove convenient (For more details, see Zahar 1989, Chapter 4). The following excerpt demonstrates that theoretical considerations—totally unrelated to sense-experience—both preceded and founded Einstein's 'operational' definition of distant simultaneity:

The successes of the Maxwell-Lorentz theory have given great confidence in the validity of the electromagnetic equations for empty space and hence, in particular, to the statement that light travels 'in space' with a constant speed c. Is this law of the invariability of light velocity in relation to any desired inertial system valid? If it were not, then one specific inertial system or, more accurately, one specific state of motion (of a body of reference), would be distinguished from all others. In opposition to this idea, however, stand all the mechanical and electromagnetic-optical facts of our experience. (Einstein 1967, p. 77)

Note that the facts adduced by Einstein—which might incidentally include the results of the Michelson-Morley experiment—do not involve the notion of distant simultaneity but that of round-trip speeds; so no convention concerning clock-synchronization needed to be invoked in order to kick-start the Relativity Program. As for reducing GTR to a system of relations between sense-data, it was neither undertaken nor even seriously envisaged by Einstein; for, by his own admission, the new theory had made the connection between measurement and the generalized coordinates more problematic. This is clearly expressed in the following passage:

> The foregoing improvement in the interpretation of the mechanical basis must, however, be paid for in that—as becomes evident on closer scrutiny—the new coordinates could no longer be interpreted as results of measurements by rigid bodies and clocks, as they could in the original system (an inertial system with vanishing gravitational field). (Einstein 1967, p. 79)

In other words: General Relativity had greatly increased the logical distance between theory and observation. Was Einstein therefore deluding himself when he maintained that:

> . . . in contrast to psychology, physics treats directly only of sense-experiences and of the 'understanding' of their connection. But even the concept of the 'real external world' of everyday thinking rests exclusively on sense impressions. (Einstein 1967, p. 79)

Is this mere lip-service paid to crude Machism? I think not, or rather: not entirely. In order to understand why not, we must start by considering Hume's influence on Einstein. It was really Hume who convinced Einstein that no causal laws could be directly induced from any facts, whether the latter be considered objective or merely perceptual: causal connections do not inhere in the phenomena as they present themselves to us; they are added by the mind's operations to the results yielded by observation (See e.g. Einstein 1994a, p. 23). Thus in Einstein's philosophy of science, we find on the one hand an insistence on the *epistemological primacy* of concepts directly connected with sense-experience; and on the other, the recognition that science operates with notions which, though ultimately linked to sense-data, remain logically independent of the latter. Such abstract concepts are free creations of the human mind; they are simply posited, but their justification ultimately flows from their capacity for ordering and pre-dicting our mental experience:

> ... this proves at the same time that every attempt at a logical deduc-tion of the basic concepts and postulates of mechanics from ele-mentary experiences is doomed to failure. (Einstein 1994a, p. 300)

Unlike Hume, Einstein was however not driven to skepticism by the bankruptcy of the inductive method. For a time, he was drawn to Kant's the-sis that the possibility of science is guaranteed by the existence of synthetic a priori principles: these are alleged to be imposed, with absolute necessity, by the mind on the material provided by the senses. Thus the Kantian a pri-ori offered a means of bridging the gap opened by Hume between theory and perceptual experience:

> The following however appears to me to be correct in Kant's state-ment of the problem: in thinking we use, with a certain 'right', con-cepts to which there is no access from the materials of sensory experience, if the situation is viewed from the logical point of view.
>
> As a matter of fact, I am convinced that even much more is to be asserted: the concepts which arise in our thought and in our linguis-tic expressions are all—when viewed logically—the free creations of thought which cannot inductively be gained from sense experi-ences. (Einstein 1994a, pp. 23–24)

At this point, Mach, who had been an orthodox Kantian, had the merit of demonstrating that the possibility of experience presupposes the full strength neither of the Absolute Space and Time hypotheses nor of the categories of substance and causality. He went of course much further by trying to show that the very *notions* of Absolute Space and Time were monstrous impossi-bilities; also that experience was theory-independent and that science ought to limit itself to establishing connections between various elements of sen-sation (See above, Chapter VIII, section C). In these extreme claims, he undoubtedly failed; and Einstein anyway never seriously undertook to inter-pret his field equations in terms of relations between sense-data. Mach had however unwittingly shown that if any laws were at all presupposed by experience, then they were so low-level as to be neutral between Newtonian Mechanics and any new physics which might explain inertia in terms of rota-tions relatively to the stars. He had also demonstrated that experience involves the intuition, not of absolute, but of clock-time; moreover, that the notion of absolute space is in no way implicated in the perception of moving bodies. What Mach achieved vis-à-vis Einstein was nevertheless contrary to Mach's own intention of banning metaphysics from science. By analyzing what we do when we observe, Mach in effect liberated physics from its Kantian straightjacket; he thereby set Einstein free to speculate at the highest level of scientific theorizing and hence alter dogmas about space and time which had hitherto been considered sacrosanct.

When Einstein faced the incompatibility of the following three principles:

The Relativity Postulate,
Maxwell's equations (viz. the constancy of c)
The Galilean Transformation,

he knew from Mach's teaching that he could alter the Galilean Transformation, and more particularly the absoluteness of time, without necessarily falling foul of experience. The way in which this modification ought to be carried out was however determined, not by any phenomenalist analysis of experience, but by examining the symmetry properties of Maxwell's equations, and hence the possibility of turning c into an invariant. Thus Mach negatively helped Einstein by showing him that absolute time could be dispensed with; but Machism, i.e. Mach's explicitly formulated antirealist philosophy, offered no positive assistance when Einstein embarked on constructing a law which would supplant the Galilean equations. The Lorentz-transformation was determined by the requirement that apart from being linear, it ought to turn Maxwell's theory into a set of covariant relations. *Mathematics* therefore provided the heuristics leading to the discovery of STR.

To repeat: by showing how little is dictated by perceptual experience, Mach did not ban 'metaphysics' from the domain of science. On the contrary, he opened the flood-gates to imaginative speculation at the most fundamental level of scientific theorizing. The only constraint on such seemingly unbridled conjecturing is the well-known Popperian one: no matter how free the speculation, it must still be capable of contact—more precisely: of possible conflict—with experience. That the parallel with Popper is indeed close is evidenced by the following excerpt from Einstein's 'Deduktion und Induktion', which appeared in the *Berliner Tageblatt* of 1919 (I take this opportunity for thanking Prof. J. Stachel, who sent me the German text). In this article, Einstein clearly expressed his adherence to a hypothetico-deductivist, fallibilist and openly anti-inductivist logic of discovery:

The truly great steps forward in the understanding of nature occurred in a way almost diametrically opposite to that of induction. An intuitive grasp of what is essential in a complex of facts leads the researcher to set up a fundamental hypothetical law, or many such laws. From the fundamental law (Axiom system), he draws consequences in a purely hypothetico-deductive fashion, and in as complete a way as possible. These consequences, which are derived from the fundamental law exclusively by means of lengthy developments and calculations, allow of being compared with experience and thus yield a criterion for the justification of the assumed fundamental law. The fundamental law (the axioms), together with its consequences, constitutes what we call a "theory." Every expert knows that all the greatest advances in our knowledge of nature, e.g. Newton's gravitational theory, thermodynamics, the kinetic theory of gases, modern electrodynamics etc. arose in this way; and that the foundations of these theories have an essentially hypothetical character. The researcher admittedly starts from the facts the discovery of whose connections is the aim of his endeavors. He does not however arrive at his conceptual system in a methodical, inductive way; he keeps close to the facts while choosing between various conceivable axiomatic systems. A theory can therefore be recognized as incorrect if deductions from it contain a logical error, or as inapplicable [*unzutreffend*] if a fact is incompatible with one of its consequences. But the truth of a theory can never be demonstrated. For one can never know that, in the future, no experimental result will come to be known which contradicts the consequences of the theory; . . . . (My translation. See Appendix 3)

Note first that Einstein's remarks are similar to those made by Poincaré in his (1902) and by Duhem in his (1914). Secondly: the passage above demonstrates that right from the beginning of his career and though held to be a Machian positivist, Einstein never proceeded inductively from sense-impressions to experimental laws.

There remains the question whether Mach's influence on Einstein was purely negative—in the sense explained above. The answer will be in the negative, but only provided a distinction be made between two different areas in which Mach positively influenced Einstein's scientific thought. The first area is that in which Mach's *intuitive* philosophy—as implicitly used in his physics—got the better of his *professed phenomenalism*. In his (1909) as well as in his (1933) Mach not only failed to adhere to any phenomenalist philosophy; he moreover adopted an instinctively realist attitude with respect both to macroscopic objects and to scientific laws. He wrote:

> Obviously it does not matter whether we think of the earth as turning round its axis, or at rest while the celestial bodies revolve round it. Geometrically, these are exactly the same case of a relative rotation of the earth and of the celestial bodies with respect to one another. Only, the first representation is astronomically more convenient and simpler. But if we think of the earth as at rest and the other celestial bodies as revolving round it, there is no flattening of the earth, no Foucault's pendulum and so on, at least according to our usual conception of the law of inertia. Now one can solve the difficulty in two ways: either all motion is absolute, or our law of inertia is wrongly expressed. Neumann preferred the first proposition, I, the second. *The law of inertia must be so conceived that exactly the same thing results from the second supposition as from the first.* By this it will be evident that, in its expression, regard must be paid to the masses of the universe. (Mach 1909, pp. 76–77, my italics.)

Mach can thus legitimately be held to have put forward general covariance as a condition to be imposed on all physical theories; as a result, the oblateness of the earth ought to be explicable, whether the earth or the stars be adopted as providing the 'primary' frame of reference. He does not explicitly assert that the explanations must assume the same form in the two cases. Some such assertion is nonetheless implicit in the above passage; for Mach knew full well that provided an inertial field be invoked, all classical laws can be referred to an arbitrary coordinate system; where, in the case of astronomy, the field is determined by the relative motion of the earth and the stars. It was also well known that the basic equations of physics take on a form more complex in the case of an accelerating, than in that of a uniformly moving frame. This was after all the essential content of Newton's conclusions regarding the bucket experiment. In order to make sense of the above passage, i.e. in order to make it non-vacuous, we must therefore suppose that in Mach's view, physical hypotheses should be made to assume the same form in all frames. In other words: all laws should be generally covariant; a condition which Newton's equations fail to satisfy. Thus Einstein was right in claiming that

> Mach clearly recognized the weak spots in Classical Mechanics and was not far from requiring a General Theory of Relativity, all this

about half a century ago. (Einstein, as quoted in G. Heller 1960, pp.
153–56. My translation)

Einstein's arguments in support of general covariance are well known
and can be summarized as follows. Theories have an ontological status
alongside the observables among which they establish connections.
Simplicity and unity are moreover objective properties of scientific laws.
Should scientific theories assume a particularly simple form in some
frames, then the latter would derive a privileged status from this simplicity.
But according to the Relativity Postulate, no such frames exist; hence all
hypotheses must have the same form in all coordinate systems. Note that
this argument involves the central assumption that theories, together with
their form, possess an objective status. Yet according to Machism—as distinct from Mach's intuitive methodology—a law is nothing more than a
computational device, so that the device and its degree of convenience have
only subjective import. Hence the simplicity of scientific hypotheses can in
no way be taken to indicate that the chosen frame is *ontologically* privileged. In fact, being unobservable, the frame does not belong to Machian
ontology, which consists exclusively of elements of sensation. From such a
positivist viewpoint, there is no good reason why the choice of one coordinate system should not prove more *convenient* or more *economical* than that
of another. On the contrary, an instrumentalist has every reason for con-
gratulating scientists like Copernicus and Newton for having determined a
convenient frame for the most economical formulation of astronomical
laws. In putting forward general covariance, Mach was therefore violating
a central tenet of his own brand of phenomenalism. He was in effect following the scientist's intuitively realist philosophy with all its Platonistic
undertones: apart from subsuming various elements of sensation, scientific
hypotheses are intended to describe the structure of a mind-independent
world. Hence not only do our theories have ontological import, but their
form also reveals an objective property of the frame to which all physical
entities are referred. Similarly to Duhem and Poincaré, Mach had instinctively adopted a structural realist stance, thus revealing the gap between the
scientist's natural thought-processes and his overtly professed philosophy.
    Another area in which Mach influenced Einstein pertains to the empiri-
cal basis of the sciences. Time and again, Einstein repeated that the basic
statements of physics are reports about sense-impressions; that they do not
express transcendent propositions the knowledge of whose truth-values
would have to remain conjectural. In Einstein's writings there is, on the one
hand a Machian insistence on the epistemic primacy of concepts directly

connected with sense-experience; and on the other, a clear recognition that science involves notions which, despite being ultimately linked to perception, remain logically independent of the latter. To repeat: these high-level concepts are taken to be free creations of the human mind:

> The layers (of concepts) are furthermore not clearly separated. It is not even absolutely clear which concepts belong to the primary layer. As a matter of fact, we are dealing with freely formed concepts which, with a certainty sufficient for practical use, are intuitively connected with complexes of sense experiences in such a manner that, in any given case of experience, there is no uncertainty as to the applicability or non-applicability of the statement. (Einstein 1967, p. 63)

In this passage, two Einsteinian theses stand out clearly. First: most of the concepts entering into high-level theories are independent of sense-experience. As for the theories themselves, they are simply laid down as postulates. Secondly, the hypotheses must entail empirically decidable basic statements. These are not conventionally accepted propositions but level-0 reports whose truth-value can be incorrigibly established by observation. It should be pointed out that by observation, Einstein means a strictly *perceptual* or *experiential process*. According to this view, the empirical basis coincides neither with Neurath's set of protocol sentences nor with Popper's family of potential falsifiers: Einstein's basic statements are not *any* singular consequences—or negations of such consequences—drawn from a theory and *provisionally* accepted by the scientific community; nor are they Neurath's protocol sentences, which can be accepted or rejected with the only proviso that the ensuing system remain *coherent*. On the contrary: Einstein's observation statements bear a close resemblance to Schlick's *Konstatierungen*, to Poincaré's crude factual reports and even to Husserl's phenomenologically reduced propositions; where all these statements have indubitably ascertainable truth-values. This conception of the empirical basis is further clarified by the following passage:

> Concepts can only acquire content when they are connected, however indirectly, with sensible experience. But no logical investigation can reveal this connection; it can only be experienced. And yet it is this connection that determines the cognitive value of systems of concepts. (Einstein 1994a, p. 303)

Einstein could not have expressed more clearly his Machian belief that no matter how high-level, scientific hypotheses must in the end be connected to subjective experience. A theory should not only bring order into the field of our sense-data; it ought also to be appraised by means of its *experiential,* as distinct from its merely *experimental* basis. To repeat: Einstein did not, and in effect could not present his laws as systems of Machian relations between elements of sensation. But at a time when Neurath, Popper, Wittgenstein and even Carnap were turning away from autopsychological reports and towards intersubjectively testable physicalist statements, Einstein underlined the subjective-perceptual character which the empirical basis must retain. It should however be noted that the word 'subjective' applies not to the truth-values but only to the referents of the basic statements. Although the latter are about the observer's subjective experiences, they are regarded as possessing absolute truth-values. In fact, Einstein's position parallels Poincaré's in many respects. According to Poincaré, high-level hypotheses should be appraised exclusively by means of two criteria: first, their capacity for entailing 'crude' factual propositions without recourse to ad hoc assumptions; secondly, their degree of convenience (*commodité*), i.e. their unity and organic compactness. Thus the components of a theoretical system must be so tightly knit that a change in any one of them automatically induces modifications in all the others (See above, Chapter II, section A). This is also why Einstein adopted an uncompromisingly falsificationist attitude *vis-à-vis* scientific hypotheses:

> The great attraction [of GTR] is its logical consistency. If any deduction from it should prove untenable, it must be given up. A modification of it seems impossible without destruction of the whole. (Einstein 1967, p. 58)

This out-and-out falsificationism *à la* Popper naturally includes a ban on conventionalist stratagems; and the passage just quoted brings to mind similar methodological *desiderata* put forward by Poincaré in his 1904 Saint Louis address: should the laws of Classical Mechanics prove empirically inadequate, then we must refrain from merely tinkering with them; for we should otherwise run the risk of destroying the unity of the classical system. We ought rather to recast our whole kinematical framework, which is in effect what Poincaré achieved in 1905, and Einstein in 1915 (See Poincaré 1906, pp. 109–110).

The above considerations concerning the influence exerted on Einstein's scientific thinking by the philosophies of Hume, Kant, Mach and Poincaré therefore justify Einstein's claim:

The reader has already guessed that I am here alluding to certain
concepts of the theories of space, time and mechanics which have
undergone modifications through the theory of relativity. Nobody
can take away from the epistemologists the merit of having helped
towards the new developments in these areas; from my own experience I know that I have been, directly or indirectly, aided by epistemologists, especially by Hume and Mach . . . . (Heller 1960, p. 153.
My translation)

(E) EINSTEIN'S PANMATHEMATICISM

As shown above, Einstein was a fallibilist, hypothetico-deductivist philosopher who held scientific hypotheses to be unverifiable but empirically
refutable propositions. By itself, hypothetico-deductivism is however con-
fronted us with difficulties which, at first sight, seem insuperable (See
above, Chapter VI, section F). Given the underdetermination of theories by
facts and therefore the need of what Einstein called a degree of empathy with
nature, are we not forced into acknowledging Reichenbach's strict distinction between the context of discovery and the context of justification? In
other words: because of the gap between hypothesis and observation, would
it not be hopeless to embark on giving a rational account of the process of
theory-construction? Should we not limit methodologies to being pure 'logics of appraisal' which have nothing to do with the genesis of scientific
hypotheses? My answer will again be in the negative; for it can be shown
that the hiatus between fact and general law is considerably narrowed by the
imposition of mathematical constraints (See also Chapter VII above).

As already mentioned, one of the cardinal errors made by the Vienna
Circle was to look upon all mathematical theorems as analytic propositions.
More generally: as long as any axiom system remained observationally
uninterpreted, the neopositivists regarded it as logically true; which seems
to me to be a grave non-sequitur. Trivially, all theorems of a theory are—by
definition—implicitly contained in the latter's system of axioms. But also
by definition, an analytic formula is a statement which must prove true
under all interpretations of its descriptive terms; and there is no guarantee
that all the axioms of an arbitrary formal system, and hence all of its theorems must turn out to be logically true. For example, not only the postulates
of geometry but also those of set theory fail to be analytic. Of course, even
a system expressed in mathematical language has to be regarded as interpreted before it can say something about the world; but such an interpreta-

tion needs be neither effectively nor even exclusively given in terms of observables. For example: a mathematical function enabling us to make empirical predictions may well possess a referent, though not necessarily a physical one (See Chapter VI above). Even the gravitational field, when taken by itself, is not an observable entity which can ostensively be pointed to. Yet the conjecture that the field is co-extensive with the metric of space-time puts mathematical constraints on gravitational theories; for all metric geometries are taken to have a Riemannian structure, an assumption which is far from being trivial or 'analytic'. It entails that gravity must largely determine our kinematics; so that all other phenomena, e.g. all electromagnetic and atomic processes, are altered by the presence of the gravitational field. This *physical* result is implied by a seemingly innocuous mathematical assumption, namely that gravity possesses a kinematical character. Thus mathematics provides us not only with a language, but also with a surplus structure which restricts the number of hypotheses compatible with the evidence. This is clearly expressed in the following passage, which contains the whole essence of Einstein's methodology:

> If, then, it is true that the axiomatic basis of theoretical physics cannot be extracted from experience but must be freely invented, can we ever hope to find the right way? Nay, more, has this right way any existence outside our illusions? Can we hope to be guided safely by experience at all when there exist theories (such as classical mechanics) which to a large extent do justice to experience , without getting to the root of the matter? I answer without hesitation that there is, in my opinion, a right way and that we are capable of finding it. Our experience hitherto justifies us in believing that nature is the realization of the simplest conceivable mathematical ideas. I am convinced that we can discover by means of purely mathematical constructions the concepts and the laws connecting them with each other, which furnish the key to the understanding of natural phenomena. Experience may suggest the appropriate mathematical concepts, but these certainly cannot be deduced from it. Experience remains, of course, the sole criterion of the physical utility of a mathematical construction. But the creative principle resides in mathematics. In a certain sense therefore, I hold it true that pure thought can grasp reality, as the Ancients dreamed. (Einstein 1994a, p. 300)

Thus mathematics takes over the function assigned to those a priori principles which were held to bridge the gap between subjective perception on the one hand, and science or objective experience on the other. But there remains one essential difference between the axioms of physics and Kant's synthetic a priori propositions: since empirical hypotheses are almost never uniquely determined by mathematical constraints, a posteriori considerations must play a central role in theory-choice. The relationship between mathematics and physics is best described in dialectical terms: it consists in a to-and-fro movement between two poles; one moves from low-level generalizations to idealizing mathematical assumptions which generally possess extra content; then back to some more down-to-earth physics; then forward to fresh mathematical innovations with ever increasing surplus structure. The so-called harmony between mathematics and physics is not pre-established; it is the result of an arduous process of mutual adaptation.

The last passage quoted above constitutes one of Einstein's most overtly Platonist and realist-deterministic declarations of faith. But in line with his and with Duhem's injunctions, we ought once again to check whether Einstein's explicit philosophical position played any part in the genesis or in the appraisal of the hypotheses which he envisaged. It should not be forgotten that 'On the Method of Theoretical Physics' was published in 1930, i.e. long after Einstein's most creative scientific period. We have already mentioned that he appeared then to have rethought his whole philosophical position and, more particularly, to have distanced himself from the 'positivist' stance he took in his youth. Thus we have to examine whether the following account is not, on his part, a 'rational reconstruction' in the pejorative sense of reading newly adopted views into past achievements:

> In order to justify this confidence, I am compelled to make use of a mathematical concept. The physical world is represented as a four-dimensional continuum. If I assume a Riemannian metric in it and ask what are the simplest laws which such a metric can satisfy, I arrive at the relativistic theory of gravitation in empty space. If in that space I assume a vector field or an anti-symmetrical tensor field which can be derived from it, and ask what are the simplest laws which such a field can satisfy, I arrive at Maxwell's equations for empty space. (Einstein 1994a, p. 300)

Comparing this quotation with the article written by Einstein and Grossmann in 1913, and then with the sequence of papers published in the *Sitzungsberichte der preußischen Akademie der Wissenschaften* between 1913 and 1915, we find that Einstein's account faithfully retraces his and Grossmann's path to the discovery of GTR (See Einstein and Grossmann

1913). The two physicists actually proceeded in a manner reminiscent of Galileo's method; that is: they considered, in turn, the simplest hypotheses which seemed consistent with the known facts. It is well known that Galileo started by envisaging the equation v [= $_{Def.}$ velocity] = constant, as the law of free fall. This first hypothesis predicts an impact independent both of the time t and of the distance traversed x; a consequence known to be experimentally refuted. So Galileo moved to the next simplest law, according to which v is a linear function of some independent variable. To begin with, he took the latter to be the distance traversed. He then corrected this second conjecture by assuming v to be a linear function of the time t. Having corroborated this last law, he considered the more complex case where both gravity and air resistance act on the mobile; and so on. Similarly, Einstein and Grossmann first envisaged the field equations B^a_{pqb} = 0 for free space, where B^a_{pqb} is the curvature tensor. This is however too stringent a law since it yields a flat metric and hence a reducible field, i.e. one which can globally be transformed away by one change of coordinates. This Einstein knew to be impossible, since eliminating the earth's field at one point entails piling it up at the antipodes. So he tried the next best, or rather the next simplest putative solution. Given the constraint of covariance, he obtained R_{pq} = 0, where R_{pq} is the Ricci tensor obtained by contraction from B^a_{bpq}; i.e. R_{pq} = $_{Def.}$ B^a_{pqa}. This equation, first proposed by Grossmann in 1913, was shown to yield a satisfactory explanation of the precession of Mercury's perihelion. When it came to the more general field equations, it is well known that they cost Einstein years of intense effort. Through considering the contribution of gravity to the total energy of a physical system, he finally arrived at what is nowadays held to be the correct solution, namely $R_{pq} - (1/2)g_{pq}.R = - kT_{pq}$. It should be added that unbeknown to Einstein, the mathematics, taken together with minimal physical constraints, determines an essentially unique solution: in accordance with the conservation laws, the divergence of the tensor T_{pq} must vanish; and it can be mathematically proved that the most general divergeless tensor which can be built from the g_{pq}'s and from their partial derivatives, which is moreover second-order and linear in the second derivatives, must be of the form $[R_{pq} - (1/2)g_{pq}.R + \lambda.g_{pq}]$. Note that $\lambda.g_{pq}$ is the cosmological term which was later added by Einstein to his equations. As for writing Maxwell's equations in generally covariant form and thus displaying their dependence on the metric, it presented no serious technical difficulties. These developments show that Einstein's confidence in the heuristic power of mathematics was not the product of hindsight; for it helped him to construct one of the most beautiful physical theories ever proposed, namely GTR (For more details, see Zahar 1989a, Chapter 8).

(F) Determinism and Realism

Einstein undoubtedly believed in reductionism and in strict determinism governing not only all physical and biological, but also all mental phenomena. We have already mentioned his adherence to Schopenhauer's philosophy which is further confirmed by the following quotation:

> Buddhism, as we have learnt especially from the wonderful writings of Schopenhauer, contains a much stronger element of this [cosmic religion]. . . .The man who is thoroughly convinced of the universal operation of the law of causation cannot for a moment entertain the idea of a being who interferes in the course of events . . . . He has no use for the religion of fear and equally little for social or moral religion. A God who rewards and punishes is inconceivable to him for the simple reason that a man's actions are determined by necessity, external and internal, so that in God's eyes he cannot be responsible, any more than an inanimate object is responsible for the motions it undergoes. (Einstein 1994a, pp. 41–42)

The reference to Schopenhauer is no doubt appropriate, but only in so far as the latter subscribed to an iron-hard version of determinism. According to Schopenhauer, determinism however applies exclusively to the world qua representation, i.e. to a domain of appearances indistinguishable from a coherent dream-sequence. There is a unique thing-in-itself which Schopenhauer identifies with one universal Will; i.e. with an irrational entity which, though lying outside space, time and the scope of causality, creates a deterministic dream-world as a means of its own objectification. It goes without saying that Einstein did not share Schopenhauer's idealism, for he regarded physical reality as constituting the fundamental ontological layer. In the Einsteinian universe only energy exists—in various forms some of which give rise to mental processes; and it manifests itself in conformity with immanent deterministic laws governing the behavior of all existents. Such laws do not apply to mere 'appearances' but to a universe embodying the mathematically most coherent structure. This position is therefore closer to Spinoza's than to Schopenhauer's world-view; except that Einstein's philosophy is even more monistic than Spinoza's: God—or Nature—can be conceived, not under *several aspects,* but under *one* and only *one all-embracing scheme*; where the latter subsumes physical as well as mental phenomena. Still, for both philosophers, science consists in an intellectual love of God.

Let me now show that Einstein did not pay mere lip-service to Schopenhauer's comprehensive principle of causality but that the latter exerted a significant influence on his scientific thinking. Throughout his life, Einstein remained faithful to a realist-deterministic ideal which led him to reject QM; but this only in so far as the latter was construed as *a fundamental* theory. He firmly believed that the probabilities involved in QM would one day be derived from deeper deterministic laws taken in conjunction with suitable boundary conditions; so that QM could eventually be interpreted as a statistical mechanics of microprocesses. It should nonetheless be repeated that Einstein was aware of the methodological superiority of QM over its extant rivals. With regard to the relationship between theory and experience, he therefore took methodology to be neutral vis-à-vis metaphysics. In 1926, he wrote to Max Born:

Quantum Mechanics is certainly imposing. But an inner voice tells me that it is not yet the real thing. The theory says a lot, but does not bring us any closer to the secret of the 'old one'. I, at any rate, am convinced that *He* is not playing at dice. (Born-Einstein Letters, p. 91)

In other words: while conceding that QM is impressive, Einstein had metaphysical objections to it; objections based on his belief in a deterministic God who, qua guarantor of order and harmony in the universe, refuses to play dice with its constituents. Furthermore, this brand of realist determinism was not a matter of subjective preference, for it had proved immensely successful as a positive heuristic in the Relativity Program and in all Unified Field Theories. Note moreover that Einstein's attempts to derive particles from fields had not yet come to be regarded as doomed to failure; all of which goes to show that metaphysical doctrines need not be treated as a priori dogmas; for when operating as heuristic tools in scientific research, they can be indirectly supported (or undermined) by the empirical successes (viz. failures) of their associated programs.

(G) The EPR Paradox

No account of Einstein's philosophical position would be complete without a discussion of the EPR paradox. In a paper published in 1935, Einstein, Podolsky and Rosen set out to show that when construed as a theory about single entities rather than about statistical ensembles, QM is incomplete. In what follows, I shall try to reconstruct their arguments without assuming the latter to be valid. My concern will be to show that realism informed Einstein's reasoning and guided him towards conclusions which were later addressed by leading physicists.

In a series of letters, Wolfgang Pauli pointed out to Max Born that realism rather than fully-fledged determinism was the cornerstone of Einstein's position and more particularly of his objections to QM:

> Now from my conversations with Einstein I have seen that he takes exception to the assumption, essential to quantum mechanics, that the *state of a system is defined only by specification of an experimental arrangement.* [By the way, Einstein says instead of 'specification of the experimental arrangement': 'that the state of a system depends on the way one looks at it'. But it boils down to the same thing. Max Born.] *Einstein wants to know nothing of this.* If one were able to measure with sufficient accuracy, this would of course be as true for small macroscopic spheres as for electrons. (Born-Einstein Letters, p. 218)

And:

> . . . In particular, Einstein does not consider the concept of 'determinism' to be as fundamental as it is frequently held to be (as he told me emphatically many times), and he denied energetically that he had ever put up a postulate such as (your letter, para. 3): 'the sequence of such conditions must also be objective and real, that is, automatic, machine-like, deterministic'. In the same way, he *disputes* that he uses as criterion for the admissibility of a theory the question: 'Is it rigorously deterministic?'
>
> Einstein's point of departure is 'realistic' rather than 'deterministic', which means that his philosophical prejudice is a different one. (Born-Einstein Letters, p. 221)

Thus Einstein regarded realism rather than determinism as a prerequisite of scientific theorizing. We shall therefore have to examine the methodological 'cash-value' of realism with regard to the EPR paradox. Instead of setting out, right from the beginning, all the hidden lemmas presupposed in Einstein's incompleteness proof, I shall proceed analytically and in stages. Each stage will consist of a tighter specification of an appropriate experimental set up, together with the assumptions implicitly or overtly made by Einstein in his derivation of the EPR paradox.

(a) Consider two systems W_1 and W_2 which "interact from the time t = 0 to t = T, after which time we suppose that there is no longer any interaction between the two parts" (EPR 1935, p. 777). Einstein's anti-idealist position has the following implication: no measurement of any observable P_1, which I might either *envisage* or actually *carry out* on W_1 at time t_1, can give rise to, affect or even define any property of W_2 at t_2, *unless* the measurement of P_1 at t_1 could have physically interfered with W_2 at, or before t_2. Note that while arguing against Bohr's position, Einstein conceded that an experimental outcome might conceivably depend on a practically uncontrollable interaction between an object and some measuring apparatus:

> Did the respective individual system have this q-value before the measurement? To this question there is no definite answer within the framework of the (existing) theory, since measurement is a process which implies a finite disturbance of the system from the outside; it would therefore be thinkable that the system obtains a definite numerical value for q (or p), the measured numerical value, only through the measurement itself. (Schilpp 1949, p. 83)

To repeat: what Einstein categorically rejects is the thesis that any decision on our part to perform certain operations can in any way alter the properties of an object which has not been *physically* disturbed by these operations. More particularly: when taken by themselves, our mental acts do not define or throw into existence attributes or relations which have—so to speak—to wait for our decisions in order to make their appearance in the physical world.

(b) More specifically: let us examine, not the example described in the EPR paper, but the one given by David Bohm in 1951 and then analyzed by M. Redhead in his (1987).

Let W_1 and W_2 be two spatially separated spin-$(1/2)$ particles in the singlet state Ψ of their total spin. Thus: $\Psi = (1/\sqrt{2}).[\mu(1)\beta(2) - \beta(1)\mu(2)]$, where $\mu(j)$ and $\beta(j)$ denote the spin eigenfunctions for the z-component S_{zj} of the spin of W_j with eigenvalues ($h/4\pi$ and $(-h/4\pi)$ respectively ($j = 1,2$). Since Ψ is spherically symmetric, it can also be expressed as:

$\Psi = (1/\sqrt{2}).[\alpha(1)\gamma(2) - \gamma(1)\alpha(2)]$, where α and γ denote the spin eigenfunctions for the x-component S_x of the spin of an individual particle with eigenvalues $(+ h/4\pi)$ and $(- h/4\pi)$ respectively.

Suppose that at time t_1 we measure the z-component S_{z1} of the spin of W_1 and thereby obtain the result (+h/4π). By (1), it follows that if S_{z2} is measured at $t > t_1$, then the result will, with probability 1, be (– h/4π). Similarly: had we obtained (– h/4π) as the outcome of measuring S_{z1} at t_1, then we would univocally have predicted (+ h/4π) as the outcome of measuring S_{z2} at $t > t_1$. At this point, we shall invoke two theses put forward by Einstein. The first was expressed in EPR as follows:

> *If, without in any way disturbing a system, we can predict with certainty (i.e. with probability equal to unity) the value of a physical quantity, then there exists an element of physical reality corresponding to this physical quantity.* (EPR 1935, p. 777)

The second principle is the locality condition which flows from Einstein's interpretation of STR; namely that no causal action can be propagated at a velocity greater than c = speed of light. In EPR, he wrote:

> We see therefore that, as a consequence of two different measurements performed on the first system, the second system may be left in states with two different state functions. On the other hand, since at the time of measurement the two systems no longer interact, no real change can take place in the second system in consequence of anything that may be done to the first system. (EPR 1935, p. 779)

Thus Einstein's realist stance led him to advance the following claim: should I decide to carry out a measurement on W_1 and even should the result depend both on the state of W_1 and on the measuring device; then provided I be in a position to predict with probability 1 the magnitude of a quantity attached to W_2, I would be entitled to assert that W_2 objectively possesses a property signified by the quantity in question; for the observation made on W_1 could not have interfered with a system like W_2 which is separated from W_1 in the sense explained above. As for my decision to carry out on W_1 one type of operation rather than another, it does not, *by itself,* endow W_2 with a property which would otherwise have remained unpossessed or undefined.

Several points can be made in connection with the two theses stated above. There is first Einstein's insistence on the condition of certainty, i.e. on the prediction being made with a probability equal to 1. He regarded probabilities as objective attributes of statistical ensembles. But he seems to have held an ignorance, i.e. a Laplacean view of probabilities whenever the latter are applied to single cases: such probabilities arise out of our incomplete knowledge of the total state of an individual system. Single case probabilities therefore possess an exclusively *epistemological* and even *subjective* aspect, which vanishes only at the limit where certainty is attained. Secondly, Einstein insists on the system W_2 not being disturbed by the prediction; otherwise, as seen above, the predicted quantity would have to be ascribed, not to the system as originally considered, but to one already altered by the process of prediction. That no disturbance could have occurred in the case of the system W_2 is insured by our attributing to W_2 a quantity *purely inferred* from a measurement carried out on the spatially separate system W_1. W_2 could therefore not have been interfered with, for by hypothesis, it would not have been subjected to any measurement. This is why, in the quotation above, Einstein speaks of the 'value of a physical quantity', not of the *measured magnitude* of such a quantity; for an *observable* on W_2 might still express a relation between a possible observer and some observed entity, even though the truth-value of such a relation might be predictable with certainty. Thus Einstein may already have violated one of Bohr's central tenets according to which QM does not ascribe to any objects a property independent on some mode of measurement. This is why, in his final analyzes, Bohr always refers to the 'total experimental arrangement'. A defender of the Copenhagen Interpretation will maintain that a property of W_2, even though it be inferred from a measurement made on W_1, still pertains to a possible subsequent observation to be made on W_2. Thus, we are still dealing with an interaction between W_2 (or between a set up including W_2) and some measuring device; except that in the present case, the outcome of the experiment on W_2 can be anticipated with probability one.

We shall now examine, in greater detail, the sense in which Einstein's two principles entail that S_{z2} possesses a definite value at some instant t, where $t < t_1$. Let us suppose that the behavior of each of the two particles, W_1 and W_2, is causally affected *only* by that of the other.

First Proof: let k(t) be the distance between W_1 and W_2 at (coordinate) time t. k(t) is assumed to be a continuous function. Since W_1 and W_2 are spatially separated, we have $k(t_1) > 0$. By continuity, there exists a positive real a such that $k(t) > 0$ for all $t \in [t_1 - a, t_1 + a]$. Let λ be the minimum value of k(t) in $[t_1 - a, t_1 + a]$. By continuity, we know that λ is a value assumed by the function k(t) at some point of $[t_1 - a, t_1 + a]$; whence $\lambda > 0$. Choose b to be any positive real such that $b \le a$ and $t_1 - b + (\lambda/c) > t_1 + b$; i.e. $b < \lambda/(2c)$. Put: $t_2 = t_1 + b$ and $t_3 = t_1 - b$.

Now let t be such that $t_1 - b = t_3 \le t \le t_1 + b = t_2$; and consider any causal action K which originates from W_1 at time t. The time it takes K to reach

W_2 is at the very least equal to $t + \lambda/c$; where we note that: $t + \lambda/c \geq t_1 - b + \lambda/c > t_1 + b = t_2$. By Einstein's locality principle, nothing which happens to W_1 in $[t_3, t_2]$ can therefore affect W_2 in the same interval of time $[t_3, t_2]$. Suppose all we do in $[t_3, t_2]$ is measure S_{z1} at t_1; and let, once again, $h/(4\pi)$ be the result thus obtained. As already mentioned, we can predict—with certainty—that a measurement of S_{z2} at t_2 will yield $-h/(4\pi)$. By locality, W_2 would have to have had the value $-h/(4\pi)$ throughout $[t_3, t_2]$ since nothing would have interfered with W_2 during $[t_3, t_2]$; so there would have existed, at t_3, an element of reality corresponding to $S_{z1} = -h/(4\pi)$. Similarly: had the measurement of S_{z1} at t_1 yielded $-h/(4\pi)$, then there would have had to be an element of reality corresponding to the value $h/(4\pi)$ of S_{z2} at t_3. But since $t_3 < t_1 =$ (time of measuring S_{z1} and hence of collapsing Ψ), it follows by (1) that Ψ does not predict any determinate value of S_{z2} at t_3.

QM is therefore incomplete.

ALITER: Any causal action emanating from W_1 at time t_1 will reach W_2 at $t'_1 > t_1$, where $t'_1 \geq t_1 + L/c$, L being the distance traversed. Consider the interval (t_1, t_2), where t_2 is such that $t_2 > t'_1$; whence $t'_1 \in (t_1, t_2)$. By continuity, there exist a t_0 and a t_3 such that: $t_0 < t_1 < t_3$ and, for any $t \in (t_0, t_3)$, a causal action leaving W_1 at t will reach W_2 at time $t' \in (t_1, t_2)$. Since $t' > t_1$ and $(t_0, t_1) \subseteq (t_0, t_3)$, then nothing having causally happened to W_1 during (t_0, t_1) can interfere with W_2 in the same time-interval (t_0, t_1). It follows that since the spin of W_2 has a sharp value at t_1, it will have the same sharp value throughout (t_0, t_1), and *a fortiori* for any $t \in (t_0, t_1)$, i.e. for any t such that $t_0 < t < t_1$; but the collapse of the wave function Ψ occurs only at $t_1 > t$; so that, by (1) above, Ψ cannot ascribe a sharp value to the spin of W_2 at t; whence the incompleteness of QM.

(c) As a matter of fact, in EPR, Einstein envisaged two noncommuting operators on each of W_1 and W_2. In the example just adduced, this might, for instance, correspond to measuring *either* the z- *or* the x-component of the spin of a particle at t_1. Thus, if the above argument is repeated for the x–component of the spin and use is made of expansion (2), it can be concluded that during some (t_0, t_1), i.e. before carrying out any measurement either on W_1 or on W_2, the x–component of W_2 had a definite value; which the function Ψ does not however enable us to determine uniquely. Once again, we can conclude that QM is incomplete; but as pointed out by Redhead and as shown above: from an Einsteinian realist viewpoint, the consideration of just one measurement suffices to establish the incompleteness of QM. By resorting to two noncommuting operators, we can however establish the paradoxical—though not strictly contradictory—character of QM.

Thus take P_j and Q_j to be any two noncommuting Hermitian operators which represent two observables on W_j ($j = 1$, 2). Einstein actually took these observables to be the momentum and the position of W_j. Beyond P_jQ_j $\neq Q_jP_j$, P_j and Q_j can however be left unspecified. So since $P_2Q_2 \neq Q_2P_2$, P_2 and Q_2 cannot have all eigenstates in common. Without loss of generality, suppose that φ_2 is an eigenfunction of P_2 but not of Q_2; and let a_2 be the eigenvalue of φ_2. Suppose further that a_2 is non-degenerate and hence that a_2 uniquely determines φ_2—of course, to within a constant factor. It is not only conceivable but also physically possible for a measurement of P_1 to have yielded a value a_1 of P_1 enabling us to predict, with certainty, that P_2 must have the value a_2. We should thus have inferred that W_2 is in the eigenstate φ_2 of P_2. But had we decided to measure Q_1 instead of P_1, then we would have concluded that W_2 is in some eigenstate of Q_2 having eigenvalue b_2; which is logically impossible, or at any rate paradoxical, since φ_2 differs from every eigenstate of Q_2. There is however a paradox *only* if we take 'being in a given eigenstate of some operator' to be a property attributable to a single system.

As is well known, Bohr's answer was that a_2 must be attributed not to W_2 alone, but to a whole experimental arrangement consisting of: W_1 + (Device for measuring P_1) + W_2, or rather of: W_1 + (Measurement of P_1) + W_2 + (Device for measuring P_2 immediately after having measured P_1).

Similarly, b_2 expresses a property of: W_1 + (Measurement of Q_1) + W_2 + (Device for measuring Q_2 immediately after having measured Q_1). Hence no paradox arises since no incompatible properties are attributed to the *same* object.

Note that Bohr's viewpoint goes beyond the kind of holism according to which the system $W_1\&W_2$ forms one indivisible object of inquiry; i.e. that W_1 and W_2 are not separable; for Bohr insists on regarding the whole *experimental* set up as being the proper subject of discourse of QM. As for Einstein, he anyway realized that non-separability—or else instantaneous action-at-a-distance—might constitute a *logically* consistent solution of the EPR paradox; a solution which he nonetheless totally rejected, no doubt in the name of his non-mystical version of realism:

One can escape from this conclusion only by either assuming that the measurement of S_1 (telepathically) changes the real situation of S_2 or by denying independent real situations to things which are spatially separated from each other. Both alternatives appear to me entirely unacceptable. (Schilpp 1949, p. 84. Note: by S_j Einstein means what, in the text, we have denoted by W_j; $j = 1,2$.)

To sum up: in order to show the incompleteness, as distinct from the paradoxical character of QM, we need consider only one operator; or rather the two correlated operators P_1 and P_2 defined on W_1 and W_2 respectively: measuring P_1 at t_1 enables us to conclude that W_2 possesses a sharp value of P_2 at *and shortly before* t_1; for since there exists no instantaneous causal action-at-a-distance, nothing could, in the meantime, have interfered with W_2. Thus W_2 possessed a sharp value of P_2 before t_1; and yet, before t_1, i.e. before any measurement is carried out on W_1, the system $W_1 \& W_2$ was in a singlet state which generally ascribes no unique value to P_2. The information provided by a quantum-mechanical description of W_2 is therefore incomplete. Moreover, by considering two non-commuting operators P_j and Q_j ($j = 1, 2$), we have also shown that QM is not merely incomplete but also paradoxical. (Note however that since our argument for the paradoxical character of QM involves counter-factuals, it falls short of showing QM to be inconsistent).

(H) CONCLUSION

It has been shown that in the case both of the Relativity and of the Quantum Mechanical Programs, Metaphysical Realism provided Einstein with essential guidelines not only in his construction of a new system and in his overall criticism of Quantum Theory, but also in the discovery of a 'paradox' which modern physicists are still trying to unravel. Hence, no matter whether one accepts or rejects Einstein's scientific conclusions, there is no denying that metaphysics played a central role in his logic of research as well as in his theory of knowledge.

APPENDIX 1

General Considerations Concerning the Need for Finitely Axiomatizing Mathematics

(I) Despite all the efforts made to reduce it to Logic, Mathematics stubbornly continues to be a synthetic discipline. Moreover, its basic notions, namely those of class [k] and of class-membership [∈], can hardly be claimed to be known by acquaintance. Thus, in as far as they fail to be logical constants, k and ∈ must be regarded as theoretical predicates. The conjunction **M** of all mathematical postulates ought therefore to form an explicit part of every physical system **G**; so that k and ∈ should either be quantified over or else be treated as logical relations within the Ramsey-sentence **G*** of **G**.

(II) As usually formulated, **M** consists of an infinite number of axioms, namely those of ZFC, whereas **G** is taken to be a finite (first-order) formula.

(III) Some method of finitely axiomatizing **M** must therefore be found. In the case of pure mathematics, this has already been achieved by Gödel in his (1940). Gödel's basic idea was as follows. Let us, for example, consider the Replacement Scheme which, in **ZFC**, subsumes a denumerable infinity of axioms, each of the form: $(\forall u)[(\forall x)(\exists^*y)B(y, x) \rightarrow (\exists v)(\forall y)((y \in v) \leftrightarrow (\exists x \in u)B(y, x))]$; where $B(y, x)$ is an arbitrary wff. of **ZFC**. Gödel's method was to introduce the notion k of 'class' where every set was to constitute a special kind of class, whilst $\{<x, y>: B(x, y)\}$ would always be a class, though not necessarily a set. Thus the above scheme could be replaced by the single sentence: $(\forall u, B)[(\forall x, y, z) (((<y, x> \in B) \wedge (<z, x> \in B)) \rightarrow (y = z)) \rightarrow (\exists v)(\forall y)((y \in v) \leftrightarrow (\exists x \in u)(<y, x> \in B))]$, where lower-case variables range over sets, and capital letters over classes.

(IV) Note first that in $B(y, x)$ which is taken to be a wff. of ZFC, only sets are quantified over; secondly, that in order to guarantee that the extension, in x and y, of every $B(y, x)$ is a class, Gödel had to start by postulating that the extension of every atomic wff. is a class. He had then to see to it that the basic logical operations (negation, conjunction and existential quantification *over sets*) lead from classes to other classes. Practically all of the formation rules of the language of ZFC therefore had to be mirrored in the axiom system of Gödel's (1940).

(**V**) Gödel was also aware of the need to ensure that the elements of n-tuples subsumed by any class could be permuted at will. He—surprisingly—managed to show that only 3 axioms were needed, where the latter involve ordered 2- and 3-tuples (*Note: for my part, I failed to get by without the introduction of a fourth axiom involving 4-tuples*).

(**VI**) My problem has been to try and extend Gödel's finite axiomatization methods to the case of applied mathematics; i.e. of the mathematics used in the physical sciences, where we face a richer ontology containing entities which might be non-classes and hence non-sets. Such entities are often referred to as *Urelemente*. Furthermore: over and above the basic predicates k and $\in$, other primitive notions like those represented by $T_1,...,T_m$ and $Q_1,...,Q_n$ had to be dealt with. Thanks to class theory, $T_1,...,T_m$ can then be construed as classes of tuples. Thus, for each T_j, an individual name a_j can be introduced, where: a_j denotes the class of all p_j-tuples satisfying T_j, p_j being the number of argument-places of T_j. As for the observational predicates $Q_1,...,Q_n$, since they are not to be quantified over, they must all be regarded as primitive (For otherwise, a basic statement like Q(d) would have to be interpreted as (d $\in$ Q); Q however expresses an observational concept, while $\in$ might be regarded as a theoretical notion to be quantified over when we come to construct the Ramsey-sentence **G*** of **G**. So there would be no basic statements free from theoretical predicates; which, from an empiricist viewpoint, is unacceptable).

(**VII**) Let us put: $e(t) =_{Def} (\exists y)(t \in y)$. Thus e(t) means that t is an element of some class—provided we postulate: $(\forall x, y)[(x \in y)\rightarrow k(y)]$, i.e. only classes possess elements. The concept of set is then defined by: $s(t) =_{Def} [e(t) \wedge k(t)] =_{Def} [(\exists y)(t \in y) \wedge k(t)]$; i.e. a set is a class which is an element of at least one other class. As for any *Urelement* w, it is an element which is not a class; i.e. we have, in this case: $[e(w) \wedge \neg k(w)] =_{Def} [(\exists y)(w \in y) \wedge \neg k(w)]$.

For reasons of convenience, we use $\emptyset$ as a name for the empty set. We then put: $\{t_1, t_2\} =_{Def}$ [set consisting of the 2 elements t_1 & t_2 (if t_1 & t_2 are elements)]; $<t> =_{Def} t$; $<t_1, t_2> =_{Def} \{\{t_1, t_1\}, \{t_1, t_2\}\}$; then, by meta-induction, define: $<t_1, t_2,..., t_q> =_{Def} <t_1, <t_2,..., t_q>>$ (*or alternatively* $<t_1, t_2,..., t_q> =_{Def} <t_1, t_2,..., t_{q-1}>, t_q>$). We know that, within set theory, $\emptyset$ and $\{...\}$ are eliminable (incomplete) symbols.

(**VIII**) Having formulated the usual axioms of set theory (using class language), let α, β and γ be any (primitive) individual names. The next step is to make sure that all the atomic wffs. are extensional; i.e. that when considered as propositional functions in some or in all of their *element* variables, the following formulas have classes as extensions: $(x = y)$; $(x = x)$; $(x = \alpha)$; $k(x)$; $(x \in y)$; $(x \in x)$; $(x \in \alpha)$; $(\alpha \in x)$; and finally, $Q_m(t_1, \ldots, t_p)$ for each $m = 1, \ldots, n$; where every t_i is either a name or an element variable.

(IX) As already indicated, we then have to require that: corresponding to negation, every class possesses a complement; corresponding to conjunction, any 2 classes possess an intersection and, corresponding to the existential quantifier, we have: $(\forall x)[k(x) \rightarrow (\exists b)(k(b) \wedge (\forall z)((z \in b) \leftrightarrow (e(z) \wedge (\exists y)(e(y) \wedge (<y, z> \in x)))))]$ *(See* [13]–[15] *below).*

After formulating other obvious postulates, we finally arrive at the permutation axioms [24]–[27] (See below). Let us now give a more formal treatment of these guidelines.

APPENDIX 2

The System Σ

A finite list of axioms will be given for a Gödel-Bernays type of class-theory intended to be part of any scientific system $G(k, \in, \underline{h}, \emptyset, a_1,..., a_m, Q_1,..., Q_n)$, whose observational and theoretical predicates are $Q_1,...,Q_n$ and $T_1,...,T_m$ respectively. $a_1,...,a_m$ are individual class names for the extensions of the predicates $T_1,...,T_m$ respectively. The (intuitive) meanings and the role of the symbols k, $\in$, $\underline{h}$ and $\emptyset$ will be explained below.

(i) Adopt the Gödel-Bernays finitely axiomatized class theory S with its two basic notions of class $[k(x) \equiv (x \text{ is a class})]$ and class-membership $[(x \in y) \equiv (x \text{ is a member of the class } y)]$.

(ii) Extend S first by adding to its vocabulary the name $\emptyset$ and the binary function letter $\underline{h}$. ($\emptyset$ and $\underline{h}(t_1, t_2)$ denote—respectively—the empty set and the set whose only elements are t_1 and t_2; $\{t_1, t_2\}$ often stands for $\underline{h}(t_1, t_2)$).

(iii) For each theoretical term T_j having, say, p_j argument-places, enter a class name a_j, where a_j is the class of p_j-tuples subsumed by T_j .

Also add a finite number of element names $u_1, u_2,..., u_s$ to the primitive vocabulary. The latter will therefore contain a *finite* number of individual names; namely: $\emptyset, a_1,..., a_m, u_1,..., u_s$.

The predicates $Q_1,...,Q_n$ will finally be adjoined to our primitive vocabulary.

(IV) ABBREVIATIONS

The basic propositional connectives will be taken to be $\neg$ (negation) and $\wedge$ (conjunction), all the other connectives being considered as mere abbreviations, e.g.: $(\Psi \to \Xi) =_{\text{Def.}} \neg(\Psi \wedge \neg \Xi)$; $(\Psi \vee \Xi) =_{\text{Def.}} \neg(\neg \Psi \wedge \neg \Xi)$; $(\Psi \leftrightarrow \Xi) =_{\text{Def.}} [\neg(\Psi \wedge \neg \Xi) \wedge \neg(\neg \Psi \wedge \Xi)]$. We take the existential quantifier $\exists$ to be basic and define $(\forall x)\Psi =_{\text{Def.}} \neg(\exists x)\neg \Psi$.

We shall also make use of the following abbreviations: $e(t) =_{\text{Def}} (\exists y)[t \in y]$; $s(t) =_{\text{Def}} [e(t) \wedge k(t)] =_{\text{Def}} [(\exists y)(t \in y) \wedge k(t)]$; $\{t_1, t_2\} =_{\text{Def}} \underline{h}(t_1, t_2)$;

$\{t\} =_{\text{Def.}} \{t, t\} =_{\text{Def.}} \underline{h}(t, t)$; $<t> =_{\text{Def.}} t$; $<t_1, t_2> =_{\text{Def}} \{\{t_1, t_1\}, \{t_1, t_2\}\} =_{\text{Def}}$ $\underline{h}(\underline{h}(t_1, t_1), \underline{h}(t_1, t_2))$; then, by meta-induction, define: $<t_1, t_2, ..., t_q> =_{\text{Def.}} <t_1, <t_2, ..., t_q>>$.

Thus, by Logic alone: $\vdash [(t_1 \in t_2) \rightarrow e(t_1)]$; $\vdash [s(t) \rightarrow e(t)]$; $\vdash [s(t) \rightarrow k(t)]$. where t, t_1, t_2 are three arbitrary terms.

Also: $[t_1 \subseteq t_2] =_{\text{Def}} (\forall v)[e(v) \rightarrow ((v \in t_1) \rightarrow (v \in t_2))]$ and $[t_1 \subset t_2] =_{\text{Def}}$ $[(t_1 \subseteq t_2) \wedge (t_1 \neq t_2)]$; whence, by Logic: $\vdash [(t_1 \subseteq t_2) \leftrightarrow (\forall v)((v \in t_1) \rightarrow (v \in t_2))]$; i.e. $\vdash [(t_1 \subseteq t_2) \leftrightarrow (\forall v \in t_1)(v \in t_2)]$.

And: $Un(t) =_{\text{Def}} [k(t) \wedge (\forall z)((e(z) \wedge (z \in t)) \rightarrow (\exists x,y)(e(x) \wedge e(y) \wedge (z = <x,y>))) \wedge (\forall x,y,z)((e(x) \wedge e(y) \wedge e(z) \wedge (<x,z> \in t) \wedge (<y, z> \in t)) \rightarrow (x = y))]$; hence: $\vdash Un(t) \leftrightarrow [k(t) \wedge (\forall z \in t)(\exists x,y)(e(x) \wedge e(y) \wedge (z = <x,y>)) \wedge (\forall x,y,z)((e(x) \wedge e(y) \wedge e(z) \wedge (<x,z> \in t) \wedge (<y,z> \in t)) \rightarrow (x = y))]$.

Note that by Logic: $\vdash [Un(t) \rightarrow k(t)]$.

We shall sometimes write $A \Rightarrow B$ and $A \Leftrightarrow B$ for $\vdash (A \rightarrow B)$ and $\vdash (A \leftrightarrow B)$ respectively .

(v) AXIOMS

The (finitely many) mathematical axioms of our system—henceforth denoted by Σ—are as follows (Let us immediately point out that the axioms below are not all logically independent of each other; moreover that an attempt has been made to quantify, wherever possible, exclusively over element variables):

[1] $k(a_i)$; and $e(u_j)$ for all $i = 1, ..., m$ & all $j = 1, ..., s$. Thus, by definition $\vdash (\exists y)(u_j \in y)$ for all j.

[2] $(\forall x, y)[(x \in y) \rightarrow k(y)]$. (*This proposition follows from the meaning of 'class': only classes can have elements*).

Hence, by (iv): $\vdash (\forall x, y)[(x \in y) \rightarrow (e(x) \wedge k(y))]$.

[3] $(\forall x,y)[(k(x) \wedge k(y) \wedge (\forall z)(e(z) \rightarrow ((z \in x) \leftrightarrow (z \in y)))) \rightarrow (x = y)]$. (*This the postulate of the extensionality of all classes*).

By (iv): $\vdash (\forall x,y)[(k(x) \wedge k(y) \wedge (\forall z)((z \in x) \leftrightarrow (z \in y))) \rightarrow (x = y)]$. By Logic: $\vdash (\forall x,y)[(k(x) \wedge k(y)) \rightarrow ((\forall z)((z \in x) \leftrightarrow (z \in y)) \leftrightarrow (x = y))]$.

[4] $[e(\emptyset) \wedge k(\emptyset) \wedge (\forall z)(e(z) \rightarrow (z \notin \emptyset))]$. (*Existence of the empty set*).

In view of (iv): $\vdash [e(\emptyset) \wedge k(\emptyset) \wedge (\forall z)(z \notin \emptyset)]$; i.e. $\vdash [s(\emptyset) \wedge (\forall z)(z \notin \emptyset)]$.

[5] $(\forall x,y)[e(\{x,y\}) \wedge k(\{x,y\}) \wedge (\forall z)(e(z) \rightarrow ((z \in \{x, y\}) \leftrightarrow ((z = x) \vee (z = y))))]$. (*Pairing Axiom*).

Once again, by virtue of (iv): $\vdash(\forall x, y)[s(\{x, y\}) \wedge (\forall z)((z \in \{x, y\}) \leftrightarrow (e(z) \wedge ((z = x) \vee (z = y)))))]$.

By Logic: $\vdash (\forall x, y)[s(\{x, y\}) \wedge (\forall z)((z \in \{x, y\}) \leftrightarrow ((e(x) \wedge (z = x)) \vee (e(y) \wedge (z = y))))]$.

We can in fact dispense with $\emptyset$ and with $\underline{h}$ as primitive symbols through replacing **[3]** and **[4]** by the following axioms **[3′]** and **[4′]**:

[4′] $(\exists x)[e(x) \wedge k(x) \wedge (\forall z)(e(z) \rightarrow (z \notin x))]$. I.e. $(\exists x)[s(x) \wedge (\forall z)(e(z) \wedge (z \notin x))]$; whence, by (iv): $\vdash (\exists x)[s(x) \wedge (\forall z)(z \notin x)]$.

[5′] $(\forall x,y)(\forall v)[e(v) \wedge k(v) \wedge (\forall z)(e(z) \rightarrow ((z \in v) \leftrightarrow ((z = x) \wedge (z = y))))]$. By (iv):

$\vdash (\forall x,y)(\exists v)[e(v) \wedge k(v) \wedge (\forall z)((z \in v) \leftrightarrow (e(z) \wedge ((z = x) \vee (z = y))))]$. By Logic: $\vdash(\forall x,y)(\exists v)[e(v) \wedge k(v) \wedge (\forall z)((z \in v) \leftrightarrow ((e(x) \wedge (z = x)) \vee (e(y) \wedge (z = y))))]$. That is: $\vdash(\forall x,y)(\exists v)[s(v) \wedge (\forall z)((z \in v) \leftrightarrow ((e(x) \wedge (z = x)) \vee (e(y) \wedge (z = y))))]$.

Thus $\emptyset$ and $\underline{h}(t_1, t_2)$, i.e. $\{t_1, t_2\}$ and hence also $<t_1, t_2>$, can be taken to be incomplete and therefore eliminable symbols.

[6] $(\forall x,b)[(e(x) \wedge k(x) \wedge Un(b) \wedge k(b)) \rightarrow (\exists y)(e(y) \wedge k(y) \wedge (\forall z)(e(z) \rightarrow ((z \in y) \leftrightarrow (\exists v)(e(v) \wedge (v \in x) \wedge (<z,v> \in b)))))]$. (*Axiom of Replacement*).

That is:$(\forall x,b)[(s(x) \wedge Un(b)) \rightarrow (\exists y)(s(y) \wedge (\forall z)(e(z) \rightarrow ((z \in y) \leftrightarrow (\exists v)(e(v) \wedge (v \in x) \wedge (<z,v> \in b)))))]$.

In view of (iv): $\vdash (\forall x,b)[(s(x) \wedge Un(b)) \rightarrow (\exists y)(s(y) \wedge (\forall z)((z \in y) \leftrightarrow (e(z) \wedge (\exists v) ((v \in x) \wedge (<z,v> \in b)))))]$.

[7] $(\forall x,b)[(s(x) \wedge k(b)) \rightarrow (\exists y)(s(y) \wedge (\forall z)(e(z) \rightarrow ((z \in y) \leftrightarrow ((z \in x) \wedge (z \in b)))))]$. (*Axiom of Separation*).

By (iv): $\vdash (\forall x,b)[(s(x) \wedge k(b)) \rightarrow (\exists y)(s(y) \wedge (\forall z)((z \in y) \leftrightarrow ((z \in x) \wedge (z \in b))))]$.

[8] $(\forall x)[(s(x) \wedge (\forall y \in x)(e(y) \rightarrow k(y))) \rightarrow (\exists z)(s(z) \wedge (\forall v)(e(v) \rightarrow ((v \in z) \leftrightarrow (\exists y)(e(y) \wedge (v \in y \in x)))))]$. (*Axiom of the Union*).

By (iv): $\vdash (\forall x)[(s(x) \wedge (\forall y \in x)k(y)) \rightarrow (\exists z)(s(z) \wedge (\forall v)((v \in z) \leftrightarrow (\exists y)(v \in y \in x)))]$.

[9] $(\forall x)[s(x) \rightarrow (\exists y)(s(y) \wedge (\forall z)(e(z) \rightarrow ((z \in y) \leftrightarrow (k(z) \wedge (z \subseteq x)))))]$ (*Power Set Axiom*).

By (iv) and by definition of s(t) and of $\subseteq$:
$\vdash (\forall x)[s(x) \rightarrow (\exists y)(s(y) \wedge (\forall z)((z \in y) \leftrightarrow (s(z) \wedge (\forall v \in z)(v \in x))))]$.

[10] $(\exists d)[Un(d) \wedge (\forall x)((e(x) \wedge (\exists y)(e(y) \wedge (y \in x))) \rightarrow (\exists z)(e(z) \wedge (z \in x) \wedge (<z,x> \in d))))]$. (*Strong version of the Axiom of Choice*).

By (iv): $\vdash (\exists d)[Un(d) \wedge (\forall x)((e(x) \wedge (\exists y)(y \in x)) \rightarrow (\exists z)((z \in x) \wedge (<z,x> \in d))))]$.

[11] $(\forall b)[(\exists x)(x \in b) \rightarrow (\exists y)((y \in b) \wedge \neg (\exists z \in b)(z \in y))]$. (*Axiom of Foundation*).

[12] $(\exists x)[s(x) \wedge (\forall y \in x)(s(y) \wedge (y \subseteq x)) \wedge (\exists y \in x)(\forall z)(z \notin y) \wedge (\forall y \in x) (\exists z \in x)(\forall v)((v \in z) \leftrightarrow (e(v) \wedge ((v \in y) \vee (v = y))))]$. (*Axiom of Infinity*).

By (iv): $\vdash (\exists x)[s(x) \wedge (\forall y \in x)(s(y) \wedge (y \subseteq x)) \wedge (\exists y \in x)(\forall z)(z \notin y) \wedge (\forall y \in x)(\exists z \in x)(\forall v)((v \in z) \leftrightarrow ((v \in y) \vee (v = y)))]$.

Now we come to the axioms which ensure the extensional character of the basic—logical as well as non-logical—notions.

[13] $(\forall x)[k(x) \rightarrow (\exists b)(k(b) \wedge (\forall y)((y \in b) \leftrightarrow (e(y) \wedge (y \notin x))))]$.
(*Extensionality of negation, i.e. of* $\neg$).

[14] $(\forall x,y)[(k(x) \wedge k(y)) \rightarrow (\exists b)(k(b) \wedge (\forall z)((z \in b) \leftrightarrow ((z \in x) \wedge (z \in y))))]$. (*Extensionality of the conjunction* $\wedge$).

[15] $(\forall x)[k(x) \rightarrow (\exists b)(k(b) \wedge (\forall z)((z \in b) \leftrightarrow (e(z) \wedge (\exists y)(e(y) \wedge (<y, z> \in x)))))]$. (*Extensionality of the existential quantifier* $\exists$).

[16] $(\forall x,y)[(k(x) \wedge e(y)) \rightarrow (\exists b)(k(b) \wedge (\forall z)(e(z) \rightarrow ((z \in b) \leftrightarrow (<z, y> \in x))))]$.

By virtue of (iv): $\vdash (\forall x,y)[(k(x) \wedge e(y)) \rightarrow (\exists b)(k(b) \wedge (\forall z)((z \in b) \leftrightarrow (e(z) \wedge (<z, y> \in x))))]$.

[17] $(\forall x)[k(x) \rightarrow (\exists b)(k(b) \wedge (\forall y,z)((e(y) \wedge e(z)) \rightarrow ((<y, z> \in b) \leftrightarrow (z \in x))))]$. (*Existence of the Cartesian product* $V \times x$, *V being the universal class, i.e. the class of all elements*).

By (iv): $\vdash (\forall x)[k(x) \rightarrow (\exists b)(k(b) \wedge (\forall y, z)((e(y) \wedge e(z)) \wedge (<y, z> \in b)) \leftrightarrow (e(y) \wedge (z \in x))))]$.

[18] $(\exists b)[k(b)\wedge(\forall x)(e(x) \rightarrow (x \in b))]$.
(*This axiom entails the extensionality of* $e(x)$ *and of* $(x = x)$).
[19] $(\exists b)[k(b)\wedge(\forall x, y)((e(x)\wedge e(y))\rightarrow((<x, y> \in b) \leftrightarrow (x = y)))]$.
(*Extensionality of the identity* $(x = y)$).
[20] $(\exists b)[k(b)\wedge(\forall x)(e(x) \rightarrow ((x \in b)\leftrightarrow(x \in x)))]$. (*Extensionality of* $x \in x$).
By (iv): $\vdash (\exists b)[k(b)\wedge(\forall x)((x \in b) \leftrightarrow (x \in x))]$.
[21] $(\exists b)[k(b)\wedge(\forall x, y)((e(x)\wedge e(y)) \rightarrow ((<x, y> \in b) \leftrightarrow (x \in y)))]$.
(*Extensionality of* $x \in y$).
[22] $(\exists b)[k(b)\wedge(\forall x)(e(x) \rightarrow ((x \in b) \leftrightarrow k(x)))]$. (*Extensionality of* k).

By (iv): $\vdash (\exists b)[k(b)\wedge(\forall x)((x \in b) \leftrightarrow (e(x)\wedge k(x)))]$. Hence, by definition of s: $\vdash (\exists b)[k(b)\wedge(\forall x)((x \in b) \leftrightarrow s(x))]$. (*Extensionality of* s).

[23] Consider any primitive descriptive predicate R having, say , r argument-places (R could be one of the observational predicates $Q_1,...,Q_n$ of our underlying physical theory).

Choose, and then fix, any (r+1) distinct variables: b, x_1, x_2,..., x_r . Let t_1, t_2,..., t_r be any sequence of (not necessarily distinct) symbols chosen from among x_1, x_2,...,x_r, $\emptyset$, a_1,...,a_m, u_1,...,u_s. (Thus there exist $(r + m + s + 1)^r$ distinct sequences having this property). For a given sequence t_1, t_2,..., t_r, let q be the number of its (distinct) members which are variables, i.e. which figure among x_1, x_2,...,x_r . Hence $q \leq r$. Let y_1, y_2,...,y_q be any sequence of these variables (a given sequence t_1, t_2,..., t_r determines q and consequently q! sequences of the form y_1, y_2,...,y_q). For every p such that $0 \leq p \leq q - 1$, we postulate:

$(\forall y_1, y_2,...,y_p)(\exists b)[k(b)\wedge(\forall y_{p+1}, y_{p+2},...,y_q)((e(y_{p+1})\wedge e(y_{p+2})\wedge...\wedge e(y_q))$
$\rightarrow ((<y_{p+1}, y_{p+2},..., y_q> \in b) \leftrightarrow R(t_1, t_2,..., t_r)))]$. (*Here we have a finite number N_R of formulas, where $N_R \leq (r+m+s+1)^r.r!.r$*).

Let us finally go over to the permutation axioms, i.e. to those enabling us to permute the free variables of any propositional function.

[24] $(\forall d)[k(d) \rightarrow (\exists b)(k(b)\wedge(\forall x,y)((e(x)\wedge e(y)) \rightarrow ((<x,y> \in d) \leftrightarrow (<y,x> \in b)))]$. (*Axiom of Commutativity*) .

[25] $(\forall d)[k(d) \rightarrow (\exists b)(k(b)\wedge(\forall x, y, z)((e(x)\wedge e(y)\wedge e(z)) \rightarrow ((<x, y, z> \in d) \leftrightarrow (<z, x, y> \in b)))]$.

[26] $(\forall d)[k(d) \rightarrow (\exists b)(k(b) \wedge (\forall x, y, z)((e(x) \wedge e(y) \wedge e(z)) \rightarrow ((<x, y, z> \in d) \leftrightarrow (<x, z, y> \in b)))]$.

[27] $(\forall d)[k(d) \rightarrow (\exists b)(k(b) \wedge (\forall x, y, z, u)((e(x) \wedge e(y) \wedge e(z) \wedge e(u)) \rightarrow ((<x, y, z, u> \in d) \leftrightarrow (<x, z, y, u> \in b)))]$.

We have thus determined a finite number of axioms whose conjunction will be denoted by M. M can be added to the empirical postulates of any scientific theory, thus yielding the system Σ mentioned above. Σ can thus be put in the form $\mathbf{G}(k, \in, \underline{h}, \emptyset, a_1,..., a_m, u_1,..., u_s, Q_1,..., Q_n)$, whose Ramsey-sentence is $(\exists k, \in, \underline{h})(\exists \emptyset, a_1,...,a_m, u_1,...,u_s)\mathbf{G}(k, \in, \underline{h}, \emptyset, a_1,..., a_m, u_1,..., u_s, Q_1,..., Q_n)$.

Note that the second-order character of this last formula derives exclusively from the presence of the operator $(\exists k, \in, \underline{h})$ among its quantifiers. We have anyway seen that both the name $\emptyset$ and the function letter $\underline{h}$ are in principle eliminable; which would leave us with the theory $\mathbf{G}(k, \in, a_1,..., a_m, u_1,..., u_s, Q_1,..., Q_n)$, or rather with its Ramsey-sentence $(\exists k, \in)(\exists a_1,..., a_m, u_1,..., u_s)\mathbf{G}(k, \in, a_1,..., a_m, u_1,..., u_s, Q_1,..., Q_n)$. Should we be prepared to accept k and $\in$ as logical constants, then we would have to deal exclusively with a first-order proposition, namely with $(\exists a_1,..., a_m, u_1,..., u_s)\mathbf{G}(k, \in, a_1,..., a_m, u_1,..., u_s, Q_1,..., Q_n)$.

APPENDIX 3

Einstein's Anti-Inductivism

Prof. John Stachel kindly drew my attention to an text written by Einstein which appeared in the *Berliner Tageblatt* on the 25–12–1919. I have been unable to trace the German original. The quotation which is cited in Chapter IX is my English translation of a passage taken from the following German text, a passage which I have underlined. For the sake of thoroughness, I have decided to quote the latter in full:

> Die einfachste Vorstellung, die man sich von der Entstehung einer Erfahrungswissenschaft bilden kann, ist die der induktiven Methode. Einzeltatsachen werden so gewählt und gruppiert, daß der gesetzmäßige Zusammenhang zwischen denselben klar hervortritt. Durch Gruppierung dieser Gesetzmäßigkeiten lassen sich wieder allgemeinere Gesetzmäßigkeiten erzielen, bis ein mehr oder weniger enheitliches System zu der vorhandenen Menge der Einzeltatsachen geschaffen wäre von der Art, daß der rückschauende Geist aus den so gewonnenen Verallgemeinerungen auf umgekehrtem rein gedanklichem Wege wieder zu den einzelnen Tatsachen gelangen könnte.
>
> Schon ein flüchtiges Blick auf die tatsächliche Entwicklung lehrt, daß die großen Fortschritte wissenschaftlicher Erkenntnis nur zum kleinen Teil auf diese Weise entstanden sind. Wenn nämlich der Forscher ohne irgendwelche vorgefaßte Meinung an die Dinge heranginge, wie sollte er aus der ungeheuren Fülle kompliziertester Erfahrung überhaupt Tatsachen herausgreifen können, die einfach genug sind, um gestzmäßige Zusammenhänge offenbar werden zu laßen? Galilei hätte niemals das Gesetz des freien Falles finden können ohne die vorgefaßte Meinung, daß die Verhältniße, welche wir tatsächlich vorfinden, durch die Wirkungen des Luftwiderstandes kompliziert seien, daß man also Fälle ins Auge faßen müße, bei denen dieser eine möglichst geringe Rolle spielt.

Die wahrhaft großen Fortschritte der Naturerkenntnis sind auf einem der Induktion fast diametral entgegengesetzten Wege entstanden. Intuitive Erfassung des Wesentlichen eines großen Tatsachenkomplexes führt den Forscher zur Aufstellung eines hypothetischen Grundgesetzes oder meherer. Aus dem Grundgesetz (System der Axiome) zieht er auf rein logisch-deduktivem Wege möglichst vollständig die Folgerungen. Diese oft erst durch langwierige Entwicklungen und Rechnungen aus dem Grundgesetz abzuleitenden Folgerungen lassen sich dann mit den Erfahrungen vergleichen und liefern so ein Kriterium für die Berechtigung des angenommenen Grundgesetzes. Grundgesetz (Axiome) und Folgerungen bilden das, was man eine "Theorie" nennt. Jeder Kundige weiß, daß die größten Fortschritte der Naturerkenntnis, zum Beispiel Newtons Gravitationstheo-rie, die Thermodynamik, die kinetische Gastheorie, die moderne Elektrodynamik usw., alle auf solchem Wege entstanden sind, und daß ihrer Grundlage jener prinzipiell hypothetische Charakter zukommt. Der Forscher geht also zwar stets von den Tatsachen aus, deren Verknüpfung das Ziel seiner Bemühungen bildet. Aber er gelangt nicht auf methodischem, induktivem Wege zu seinem Gedankensysteme, sondern er schmiegt sich den Tatsachen an durch intuitive Auswahl unter den denkbaren, auf Axiomen beruhenden Theorien. Eine Theorie kann also als unrichtig erkannt werden, wenn in ihren Deduktionen ein logischer Fehler ist, oder als unzutreffend, wenn eine Tatsache mit einer ihrer Folgerungen nicht im Einklang ist. Niemals aber kann die Wahrheit einer Theorie erwiesen werden. Denn niemals weiß man, daß auch in Zukunft keine Erfahrung bekannt werden wird, die ihren Folgerungen widerspricht; und stets sind noch andere Gedankensysteme denkbar, welche imstande sind, dieselben gegebenen Tatsachen zu verknüpfen. Stehen zwei Theorien zur Verfügung, welche beide mit dem gegebenen Tatsachenmaterial vereinbar sind, so gibt es kein anderes Kriterium für die Bevorzugung der einen oder der anderen als den intuitiven Blick des Forschers. So ist es zu verstehen, daß scharfsinnige Forscher die Theorien und Tatsachen beherrschen, doch leidenschaftliche Anhänger gegensätzlicher Theorien sein können.

Ich bringe dem Leser in dieser aufgeregten Zeit diese kleine objektive leidenschaftslose Betrachtung, weil ich der Meinung bin, daß man mit stiller Hingabe an die ewigen Ziele, die allen Kulturmenschen gemeinsam sind, der politischen Gesundung heute wirksamer dienen kann als durch politishe [*hier fehlt ein Wort*] und Bekenntniße.

It also seemed appropriate that I should translate the German article in its entirety:

The simplest image one can form of the origins of an empirical science is by way of the inductive method. Individual facts are chosen and grouped in such a way that the law-like connections between them clearly stand out. Through grouping such laws, other more general laws can be obtained, until a more or less unified system subsuming the set of individual facts is created; so that by looking back at this process and proceeding, in thought, in the opposite direction, our mind can get back at the singular facts.

However, a cursory glance at the development of science suffices to inform us that only a small proportion of the advances achieved in scientific knowledge have taken place in this way. Had the researcher tackled things without preconceived opinions, then how could he, out of the overwhelming variety of a most complex experience, have singled out those facts which are simple enough to reveal the existence of law-like connections? Galileo could never have discovered the law of free fall, were it not for his preconceived opinion that the states-of-affairs we actually find before us are complicated by effects due to air resistance, that we should therefore direct our attention to cases in which these effects play as negligible a role as possible.

The truly great steps forward in the understanding of nature occurred in a way almost diametrically opposite to that of induction. An intuitive grasp of what is essential in a complex of facts leads the researcher to set up a fundamental hypothetical law, or many such laws. From the fundamental law (Axiom system), he draws consequences in a purely hypothetico-deductive fashion, and in as complete a way as possible. These consequences, which are derived from the fundamental law exclusively by means of lengthy developments and calculations, allow of being compared with experience and thus yield a criterion for the justification of the assumed fundamental law. The fundamental law (the axioms), together with its consequences, constitutes what we call a "theory." Every expert knows that all the greatest advances in our knowledge of nature, e.g. Newton's gravitational theory, thermodynamics, the kinetic theory of gases, modern electrodynamics etc. arose in this way; and that the foundations of these theories have an essentially hypothetical character. The researcher admittedly starts from the facts the discovery of whose connections is the aim of his endeavors. He does not however arrive at his conceptual system in a methodical, inductive way; he keeps close to the facts while choosing between various conceivable axiomatic systems. A theory can therefore be recognized as incorrect if deductions from it contain a logical error, or as inapplicable [unzutreffend] if a fact is incompatible with one of its consequences. But the truth of a theory can never be demonstrated. For one can never know that, in the future, no experimental result will come to be known which contradicts the consequences of the theory; and there always are other conceivable systems of thought capable of establishing connections between the same given facts. Should we have at our disposal two theories both of which are compatible with the given collection of facts, then there is no other criterion for preferring the one to the other than the researcher's intuitive insight. It is thus understandable that different deep-thinking researchers are able to master theories and facts and yet can passionately subscribe to incompatible theories.

In our troubled times, I present the reader with these modest objective considerations because I hold that a quiet dedication to the timeless aims common to all cultured people can have a more healing political effect than political [speeches] and confessions.

APPENDIX 4

Induction and the Uniformity of Nature

In the main text, a metatheoretic approach to the problem of induction was adopted: the principle $(\forall H, K, \Delta) J(H, K, \Delta)$ talks *about* hypotheses, their applicability to certain areas and *about* the degrees of their corroboration. This problem has however traditionally been approached through asking whether the discrepancy between facts and generalizations might not be bridged by an appeal to a so-called Principle of the Uniformity of Nature; where the latter was to be expressed *in the object-language*. There arises the question of how this principle—henceforth denoted by U—is to be worded.

Let us start by reformulating the problem of induction in simple, not to say simplistic terms. This problem results from the logical hiatus between the conjunction E of all the known singular factual statements and any universal generalization H purporting to 'explain' E. Since the content of H goes well beyond that of E, the truth of E does not guarantee that of H. It follows that (E→H) is not analytic; whence the question as to the possible existence of some principle Z such that: Z, E ⊢ H. Thus: $Z \Rightarrow (E \rightarrow H)$; i.e. Z must be at least as logically strong as (E → H). Trivially: Z could be taken to be identical with (E → H); for (E → H) $\Rightarrow$ (E → H).

Our intention is to choose Z to be as weak or as near-tautological as possible; so it appears as though $Z \equiv_{Def.} (E \rightarrow H)$ constitutes the most rational solution to this problem. But can (E → H) be inductively confirmed? Note that (E → H) $\Leftrightarrow$ (¬E∨H), where (¬E∨H) is a scientific proposition; for since H is universal and E singular, the whole of (¬E∨H) can be given a universal form; remembering that E is held to be empirically decidable, (¬E∨H) could moreover be refuted by the verification of both E and some basic statement incompatible with H.

Let us recall that E represents the sum total of our ascertained factual knowledge; so that (E → H), i.e. (¬E∨H), might *prima facie* be expected to be strongly supported by the total evidence E. This was however refuted by a result established by David Miller; namely that: $p(\neg E \vee H, E) \le p(\neg E \vee H)$. Here is a proof of this highly counter-intuitive result: since $((\neg E \vee H) \wedge E) \Leftrightarrow$

(H∧E), we have: p(¬E∨H, E) = $_{Def.}$ p((¬E∨H)∧E)/p(E) = p(H∧E)/p(E) = $_{Def.}$ p(H, E). But since (¬E∨H) ⇔ (¬E∨(H∧E)), we also have: p(¬E∨H) = p(¬E) + p(H∧E) = 1 − p(E) + p(H∧E). Subtracting, obtain: p(¬E∨H) − p(¬E∨H, E) = [1 − p(E)].[1 − p(H∧E)/p(E)]. Now note that since p is a probability measure, p(E) ≤ 1; moreover: [p(H∧E)/p(E)] ≤ 1 because (H∧E) ⇒ E; so: p(¬E∧H) − p(¬E∧H, E) ≥ 0; i.e. p(¬E∧H, E) ≤ p(¬E∧H). The probability of (¬E∧H), given E, is therefore smaller than, or at most equal to the prior probability of (¬E∧H). Thus (¬E∧H) is never supported, and might even be undermined by E.

Of course, nothing compels us to identify Z with (¬E∨H); but as shown above, whatever solution we adopt, we must have: Z ⇒ (E→H), i.e. Z ⇒ (¬E∨H). Since (¬E∨H) is refutable and hence scientific, then so is Z; and again the question arises as to how well Z is supported by the facts, i.e. by E. Note that since Z ⇒ (¬E∨H), then: (Z∧E) ⇒ [(¬E∨H)∧E] ⇔ (H∧E); whence: p(Z∧E) ≤ p(H∧E), so that: p(Z, E) = $_{Def.}$ p(Z∧E)/p(E) ≤ p(H∧E)/p(E) = $_{Def.}$ p(H, E); hence Z cannot receive more inductive support from the evidence E than does H.

In so far as it calls upon us to find good *logical* reasons for accepting Z, the problem of induction is therefore insoluble; which entails that the acceptance of a proposition like Z, while not necessarily irrational, is nonetheless non-rational.

Two reactions to this so-called Scandal of Reason will now be examined: David Miller's counter-solution and the solution described by Alain Boyer (See D. Miller, 1995 and Boyer, 1997). In the main text, I have tried to rebut Miller's claim that technology needs no principle of induction. (See Chapter II above). In another of his papers, Miller sets out to show that if a principle Z of the 'Uniformity of Nature' were to be accepted, then Z would have to be so absurdly strong as to become unbelievable; which is why the article ends with the remark that 'induction is a bit of a joke'.

According to the classical solution defended by A. Boyer—which appears to me to be on the right track—every time we decide to apply a highly corroborated law, we resort to a *scheme* founded on a general principle; namely the principle that a certain set provides a representative sample for a hypothesis laid on the table. This is a clearly inductive solution, or rather an obviously inductive postulate. Note however that there is no question of the sample—by itself—leading the scientist to any explanatory hypothesis. In other words, there is no psychological process of inductive reasoning à la Hume: repetitions do not give rise to laws; they are, on the contrary, characterized as repetitions against a given background of theoretical knowledge. But somewhat in the manner described by the meta-principle *J*, the scheme put forward by Boyer enables us to effect a transition from the past corroboration of a theory to the expectation of its future confirmation. This solution will be rigorously formulated below in the course of discussing Miller's viewpoint. Suffice it to say that according to the classical approach defended by Boyer, the human mind follows—if only implicitly—a uniform procedure when it comes to selecting the theory deemed to be the most reliable; or, in negative Popperian terms: the theory judged to be the least likely to break down. As for justifying such a choice, no miracle should be expected ; for we have seen that no matter what solution is adopted, it must take the form of a principle Z such that $Z \Rightarrow (\neg E \vee H)$; where $(\neg E \vee H)$ is a scientific conjecture. It follows that Z is not only synthetic but also empirically falsifiable. Trying to justify Z would therefore land us either in a vicious circle or in an infinite regress. It seems to me that Z should be subject to at least two conditions:

[a] Z ought to be susceptible of a uniform characterization; and:

[b] Z should have been actually—though not always consciously—applied in the selection of the supposedly most reliable laws.

There is a third requirement on which David Miller insists, namely:

[c] When expressed in prenex normal form– in some appropriate first-order language—Z should be a strictly universal sentence; i.e. it should start with a quantifier of the form $(\forall v_1, v_2, \ldots, v_n)$.

We shall see that the classical solution satisfies conditions [a] and [b] but not [c]. Let me however give an exposé, and then a critique of Miller's position. As already mentioned, Miller proposes to show that a Principle of the Uniformity of Nature—or PUN for short—must be absurdly strong and hence counter-intuitive. $x_1, x_2, \ldots, x_m$ being any finite sequence of distinct individual variables, let us define:

(1) $D(x_1, x_2, \ldots, x_m) =_{\text{Def.}} [(x_1 \neq x_2) \wedge (x_1 \neq x_2) \wedge \ldots \wedge (x_{m-1} \neq x_m)] = \Pi_{p<q} (x_p \neq x_q)$; that is: $D(x_1, x_2, \ldots, x_m)$ tells us that $x_1, x_2, \ldots, x_m$ stand for m distinct entities.

By Logic:

(2) For any $m \leq n$: $\vdash (\forall x_1, x_2, \ldots, x_m)[D(x_1, x_2, \ldots, x_n) \rightarrow D(x_1, x_2, \ldots, x_m)]$; since any conjunct $(x_p \neq x_q)$ occurring in $D(x_1, x_2, , x_m)$ is also a conjunct of $D(x_1, x_2, \ldots, x_n)$.

(3) For any formula $H(y)$, define: $(\exists^m x)H(x) =_{\text{Def.}} (\exists x_1, x_2, \ldots, x_m)[D(x_1, x_2, \ldots, x_m) \wedge H(x_1) \wedge H(x_2) \wedge H(x_m)]$. Thus: $(\exists^1 x)H(x) =_{\text{Def.}} (\exists x)H(x)$.

By Logic:

(4) For any m: $(\forall x)[H(x) \to M(x)] \Rightarrow [(\exists^m x)H(x) \to (\exists^m x)M(x)]$; and:

(5) For $m \leq n$: $(\exists^n x)H(x) \Rightarrow (\exists^m x)H(x)$. Combining (4) and (5):

(6) For $m \leq n$: $(\forall x)[H(x) \to M(x)] \Rightarrow [(\exists^n x)H(x) \to (\exists^m x)M(x)]$.

For the sake of simplicity, take the domain of discourse of our first-order language to be that of all ravens. Put $\Omega(x) \equiv$ (x has been observed), and $B(x) \equiv$ (x is black). Miller takes the factual premise of the inductive inference to be:

(7) $E_m =_{\text{Def.}} [(\exists^m x)\Omega(x) \wedge (\forall y)(\Omega(y) \to B(y))]$.

Thus $(\forall y)B(y)$ is the conclusion which is to be drawn from E_m. Miller—brilliantly—established that, in a first-order language containing neither names nor function letters, the *weakest universal proposition* which, taken in conjunction with E_m, logically implies $(\forall y)B(y)$ is:

(8) $G_m =_{\text{Def.}} [(\exists^m x)(\Omega(x) \wedge B(x)) \to (\forall y,z)((\Omega(y) \wedge \neg\Omega(z)) \to (B(y) \to B(z)))]$.

Miller interprets $(\forall y,z)[(\Omega(y) \wedge \neg\Omega(z)) \to (B(y) \to B(z))]$ as asserting that "unobserved ravens are not less black than observed ones are", which sounds plausible until one realizes that:

(9) $(\forall y,z)[(\Omega(y) \wedge \neg\Omega(z)) \to (B(y) \to B(z))] \Leftrightarrow [(\exists y)(\Omega(y) \wedge B(y)) \to (\forall z)(\neg\Omega(z) \to B(z))] \Leftrightarrow_{\text{Def.}} [(\exists^1 y)(\Omega(y) \wedge B(y)) \to (\forall z)(\neg\Omega(z) \to B(z))]$. This means that the blackness of *one* observed raven entails that of *all* the unobserved ones; a wildly inductive conjecture.

Substituting in (8) and making use of (5), obtain:

(10) $G_m \Leftrightarrow [(\exists^m x)(\Omega(x) \wedge B(x)) \to (\forall z)(\neg\Omega(z) \to B(z))]$.

G_m tells us that if m black ravens have been observed, then (irrespective of other considerations) all unobserved ravens will be black. As already mentioned, Miller showed that G_m is the only admissible *universal* PUN (Principle of the Uniformity of Nature). Note that G_m is clearly universal in the predicate-logical sense, since:

(11) $G_m \Leftrightarrow [\neg(\exists^m x)(\Omega(x) \wedge B(x)) \vee (\forall z)(\neg\Omega(z) \rightarrow B(z))]$. Moreover, by (5):

(12) For $m \leq n$, we have: $G_m \Rightarrow G_n$.

At first sight, G_m appears to be a reasonable PUN which enables us to infer, from the observation of m black ravens, the proposition that all the unobserved ravens are also black. (12) moreover tells us that the logical strength of the inductive assumption G_m, which is needed in order to justify the generalization $(\forall x)B(x)$, decreases with the accumulation of the evidence in favor of $(\forall x)B(x)$; which again seems consonant with scientific common sense. But because it fails to mention the totality of the available evidence, G_m has highly paradoxical consequences. For example, G_m logically implies:

$$F_{mr} =_{Def} [((\exists^m x)(\Omega(x) \wedge B(x)) \wedge (\exists^r x)(\Omega(x) \wedge W(x))) \rightarrow (\forall z)(\neg\Omega(z) \rightarrow B(z))];$$

where we can take: $W(x) =_{Def.}$ (x is white), and r to be an arbitrary positive integer. Thus: if m+r ravens are observed of which m are black and r white, then all the unobserved ravens must be black; which, from an inductive viewpoint, is clearly unacceptable.

From the above results one might be tempted to conclude that inductivism is even more untenable than even Miller expected; but one could alternatively—and more reasonably—assume that there is something seriously wrong with the assumption either that PUN must be universal in *the predicate-logical sense*; or that the underlying language should contain *neither names nor definite descriptions*; or finally that *the property expressed by $\Omega(x)$ should be atemporal.*

(A) The Universality Condition

Note first that there is nothing natural, let alone self-evident, about the universality condition as conceived by Miller; for as already mentioned, such universality has a formal meaning rather than that of a general applicability to all empirical situations, i.e. of a scheme subsuming *all* predicates R and B. As already mentioned, the *weakest* assumption which, taken in conjunction with E_m, yields $(\forall x)B(x)$ is:

(13) $G'_m =_{Def.} [E_m \rightarrow (\forall z)B(z)] =_{Def.} [((\exists^m x)\Omega(x) \wedge (\forall y)(\Omega(y) \rightarrow B(y))) \rightarrow (\forall z)B(z)] \Leftrightarrow [(\exists^m x)\Omega(x) \rightarrow ((\forall y)(\Omega(y) \rightarrow B(y)) \rightarrow (\forall z)B(z))] \Leftrightarrow [(\exists^m x)\Omega(x) \rightarrow ((\forall y)(\Omega(y) \rightarrow B(y)) \rightarrow (\forall z)(\neg\Omega(z) \rightarrow B(z)))]$.

Of course, because of the occurrence of $(\forall y)(\Omega(y) \to B(y))$ in its antecedent, G'_m is not universal in the predicate-logical sense; for it is easily seen that:

(14) $G'_m \Leftrightarrow (\forall x_1, x_2, \ldots, x_m)(\exists y)(\forall z)[(D(x_1, x_2, \ldots, x_m) \wedge \Omega(x_1) \wedge \ldots \wedge \Omega(x_m) \wedge (\Omega(y) \to B(y))) \to B(z)]$

Note however that G'_m is a general scheme which can be used in all relevant experimental situations. In order to simplify our presentation, we have so far taken our domain of discourse to be that of all ravens; which seems to restrict the general applicability of a principle like G'_m. But we could alternatively have left the underlying domain unspecified and introduced a monadic predicate R for ravenness. The principle of induction would then have assumed the form:

(15) $G^*_m = {}_{\text{Def.}} [((\exists^m x)(\Omega(x) \wedge R(x)) \wedge (\forall y)((\Omega(y) \wedge R(y)) \to B(y))) \to (\forall z)(R(z) \to B(z))] \Leftrightarrow [(\exists^m x)(\exists(x)\Omega R(x)) \to ((\forall y)((\Omega(y) \wedge R(y)) \to B(y))) \to (\forall z)((\neg\Omega(z) \wedge R(z)) \to B(z)))].$

Keeping in mind that the notion of observability expressed by Ω has a fixed meaning, G^*_m can be said to be a scheme applicable to all attributes R and B and not only to ravenness and blackness.

(B) Should Ω Be a Timed Predicate?

Let us recall that $\Omega(x) = {}_{\text{Def.}}$ (x is observed); which suggests that Miller takes Ω to be an atemporal, or else an omnitemporal predicate. Thus $\Omega(x)$ might stand for: x either was, or is, or will be observed; in which case $(\forall y)[(\Omega(y) \wedge R(y)) \to B(y)]$ could at no point of time be *known* to be true. $(\forall y)[(\Omega(y) \wedge R(y)) \to B(y)]$ should therefore not form part of the base E_m from which any inductive inference could legitimately start. This is why it seems appropriate to introduce, for each real number t, a predicate Ω_t, where $\Omega_t(x) = {}_{\text{Def.}}$ (x has, by time t, already been observed). As part of background knowledge, we therefore have: for any $t \le u$, $(\forall x)[\Omega_t(x) \to \Omega_u(x)]$ holds good; moreover, for every t and every predicate F, the set $\{x: \Omega_t(x) \wedge F(x)\}$ is finite. Thus, at any time t, the sum total of our empirical knowledge about ravens and their color is expressible by a sentence of the form S_t, where, noting that t uniquely determines m:

(16) S_t = $_{Def.}$ $(\exists x_1, x_2,...,x_m)[D(x_1, x_2,..., x_m) \wedge (\Lambda_{1 \leq j \leq m} B(x_j)) \wedge (\forall y)$
$((\Omega_t(y) \wedge R(y)) \leftrightarrow ((y = x_1) \vee (y = x_2) \vee ... \vee (y = x_m)))]$.

As for our PUN, it would then take the form of the following principle:

(17) G''_t = $_{Def.}$ $[S_t \rightarrow (\forall z)(R(z) \rightarrow B(z))]$.

Once again, note that G''_t is the weakest assumption which, taken in conjunction with S_t, logically implies the generalization $(\forall z)[R(z) \rightarrow B(z)]$. Given the occurrence in S_t of the universal quantifier $(\forall y)$, G''_t is universal, not in the formal sense of first-order logic, but in that of the general applicability of the scheme G''_t to all monadic predicates R and B.

(C) THE USE OF DEFINITE DESCRIPTIONS.

As already mentioned, the first-order vocabulary so far considered does not contain names, function letters or the definite description sign ι. Let us now reformulate the inductive principles G^*_m and G''_t in the language of set theory. The latter normally makes use of definite descriptions which enable us to write the class of all objects satisfying some propositional function H(y) as $\{y: H(y)\}$ = $_{Def.}$ $(\iota z)[k(z) \wedge (\forall y)((y \in z) \leftrightarrow H(y))]$; where k(z) stands for: z is a class. We also write $\{x_1, x_2,...,x_m\}$ = $_{Def.}$ $\{y: (y = x_1) \vee (y = x_2) \vee ... \vee (y = x_m)\}$. Thus G^*_m, S_t and G''_t can respectively be reexpressed as:

(18) $\underline{G}^*_m$ = $_{Def.}$ $[((\exists^m x)(\Omega(x) \wedge R(x)) \wedge (\{y: \Omega(y) \wedge R(y)\}$ = $\{y: \Omega(y)$
$\wedge R(y) \wedge B(y)\})) \rightarrow (\forall z)(R(z) \rightarrow B(z))] \Leftrightarrow (\forall x_1, x_2,...,x_m, z)[(D(x_1, x_2,...,$
$x_m) \wedge \Lambda_{1 \leq j \leq m}(\Omega(x_j) \wedge R(x_j)) \wedge (\{y: \Omega(y \wedge R(y)\}$ = $\{y: \Omega(y) \wedge R(y) \wedge B(y)\})$
$\wedge R(z)) \rightarrow B(z)]$.

(19) $\underline{S}_t$ = $_{Def.}$ $(\exists x_1, x_2,...,x_m)[D(x_1, x_2,..., x_m) \wedge (\Lambda_{1 \leq j \leq m} B(x_j)) \wedge (\{y: \Omega_t(y)$
$\wedge R(y)\}$ = $\{x_1, x_2,...,x_m\})]$.

(20) $\underline{G}''_t$ = $_{Def.}$ $(\forall x_1, x_2,...,x_m, z)[(D(x_1, x_2,..., x_m) \wedge \Lambda_{1 \leq j \leq m} B(x_j) \wedge (\{y:$
$\Omega_t(y) \wedge R(y)\}$ = $\{x_1, x_2,..., x_m\}) \wedge R(z)) \rightarrow B(z)]$.

Now note that unlike G^*_m and G''_t, the two PUN's $\underline{G}'_m$ and $\underline{G}_t''$ are in universal prenex form, albeit in a language involving definite descriptions; which seems to indicate that formal universality is not of the essence. Moreover, the above interpretations of inductive inferences are clearly non-paradoxical, which shows that induction is far from being a ridiculous principle.

APPENDIX 5

Comments on $(\forall H, K, \Delta) J(H, K, \Delta)$

Let me try to explain—somewhat more rigorously—what is meant by H being less likely (in the long run) to break down in Δ. Suppose that H and K yield the generalizations $(\forall \underline{x},t)[A(\underline{x}, t) \to C(\underline{x}, t)]$ and $(\forall \underline{x},t)[B(\underline{x}, t) \to C(\underline{x}, t)]$ respectively; where the $(\underline{x}, t)$'s are spatio-temporal variables belonging to the domain Δ. We assume that A, B and C are observational predicates; moreover that, unlike $C(\underline{x}, t)$, both $A(\underline{x}, t)$ and $B(\underline{x},t)$ can be actualized at will. Suppose further that in Δ, K has been refuted through the verification, say, of $[B(\underline{x}_0, t_0) \wedge \neg C(\underline{x}_0, t_0) \to B(\underline{x}_1, t_1) \wedge \neg C(\underline{x}_1, t_1) \wedge ... \wedge B(\underline{x}_n, t_n) \wedge \neg C(\underline{x}_n, t_n)]$; while H has been corroborated by $[A(\underline{y}_0, t_0) \wedge C(\underline{y}_0, t_0) \wedge A(\underline{y}_1, t_1) \wedge C(\underline{y}_1, t_1) \wedge ... \wedge A(\underline{y}_n, t_n) \wedge C(\underline{y}_n, t_n)]$. Consider any infinite series of (future) points $(\underline{z}_0, t'_0), (\underline{z}_1, t'_1),..., (\underline{z}_m, t'_m),...$ all lying in Δ. That is, assume that $Max(t_0, t_1,..., t_n) < t'_0 < t'_1 < ... < t'_m < t'_{m+1} < ...$. For each m, define the two natural numbers p_m and q_m as follows: p_m is the number of the $(\underline{z}_j, t'_j)$ among $(\underline{z}_0, t'_0), (\underline{z}_1, t'_1),..., (\underline{z}_m, t'_m)$ such that: should we realize $B(\underline{z}_j, t'_j)$ (viz. $A(\underline{z}_j, t'_j)$), then we would obtain (viz. fail to obtain) $C(\underline{z}_j, t'_j)$; i.e. p_m is the number of future points at which K, as opposed to H, would be confirmed: while q_m is the number of the $(\underline{z}_j, t'_j)$ among $(\underline{z}_0, t'_0), (\underline{z}_1, t'_1),..., (\underline{z}_m, t'_m)$ such that: should we realize $A(\underline{z}_j, t'_j)$ (viz. $B(\underline{z}_j, t'_j)$), then we would obtain (viz. fail to obtain) $C(\underline{z}_j, t'_j)$; i.e. q_m is the number of points at which H, as opposed to K, would be confirmed. In this situation, $J(H, K, \Delta)$ tells us that, as m increases indefinitely, p_m/q_m will remain smaller than a number (much) smaller than 1.

APPENDIX 6

Poincaré's Theorem

Consider a system Ω of particles $P_1,\ldots,P_n$, whose velocities and positions are bounded and which are subject to forces dependent exclusively on position. Let Φ be any Euclidean 6n-dimensional space. Every P_i gives rise to six coordinates $<x_i\, y_i\, z_i\, v_{xi}\, v_{yi}\, v_{zi}>$, where $<x_i\, y_i\, z_i>$ denotes the position, and $<v_{xi}\, v_{yi}\, v_{zi}>$ the velocity of P_i. Thus every point $q \in \Phi$ represents a possible (micro)state of Ω. Fix any initial instant t_0. For any t and any $q \in \Phi$, denote by $q(t)$ the state in which Ω would find itself if q represented the initial conditions of Ω at t_0. Put $\Gamma_q = \{<t, q(t)>: (t \geq t_0)\}$; thus: $q(t_0) = q$, and Γ_q is the trajectory of Ω starting from the initial conditions q. Let G be any bounded region of Φ. Poincaré showed that for arbitrarily large t and almost all $q \in G$, Γ_q returns to G for some $t_1 > t$; i.e. $(\exists t_1 > t)[q(t_1) \in G]$.

More precisely: for any (Lebesgue) measurable $X \subseteq \Phi$, let us denote the measure of X by $\mu(X)$. Poincaré can be taken to have established that:

[1] $(\forall t \geq t_0)(\exists X \subseteq G)[(\mu(X) = 0)\&(\forall q \in G\backslash X)(\exists t' \geq t)(q(t') \in G)]$.

From this theorem, let us infer the stronger result:

[2] $(\exists X \subseteq G)[(\mu(X) = 0)\&(\forall q \in G\backslash X)(\forall t \geq t_0)(\exists t' \geq t)(q(t') \in G)]$.

Consider any increasing sequence: $t_0 < t_1 < \ldots < t_i < t_{i+1} < \ldots$ such that $t_i \to \infty$ as $i \to \infty$. For each t_i, choose X_i to be such that: $[(X_i \subseteq G)\&(\mu(X_i) = 0)\&(\forall q \in G\backslash X_i)(\exists t' \geq t_i)(q(t') \in G)]$.

Put $E = \cup \{X_i: i \in \omega\}$. That is: $E = X_0 \cup X_1 \cup X_2 \cup \ldots$ It follows from measure theory that since $\mu(X_i) = 0$ for all i, then $\mu(E) = 0$. Moreover: $E \subseteq G$ since $X_i \subseteq G$ for each i. So it suffices to show that $(\forall q \in G\backslash E)(\forall t \geq t_0)(\exists t \geq t)[q(t') \in G]$.

Let $q \in G\backslash E$, $t \geq t_0$. Thus $q \in G$ and $q \notin E = \cup \{X_i: i \in \omega\}$; hence $q \notin X_i$ for all i. It follows that $q \in G\backslash X_i$ for all i. Moreover, since $t_i \to \infty$ with i, then we must have, for some j, $t \leq t_j$. Thus $q \in G\backslash X_j$. So, by the definition of X_j, $q(t') \in$ G for some $t' \geq t_j$. Thus $t' \geq t_j \geq t$; hence $t' \geq t$; from which our result follows.

Now let B be a bounded closed subdomain of Φ and S(q) any function continuous on B. [S(q) could e.g. be the entropy of Φ in state q]. We propose to show that:

[3] $(\forall \xi > 0)(\exists X \subseteq B)[(\mu(X) = 0)$ & $(\forall q \in B\backslash X)((S$ decreases nowhere along $\Gamma_q) \Rightarrow (\forall t \geq t_0)(0 \leq S(q(t)) - S(q) \leq \xi)]$.

ξ being any positive real, then by uniform continuity: there exists a function $\eta(\xi)$ of ξ alone such that: $\eta(\xi) > 0$ and $(\forall p \in B)(\forall b \in B)[(d(p,b) \leq \eta(\xi)) \Rightarrow (| S(p) - S(b) | < \xi)]$, where d(p, b) denotes the distance between p and b. Let $K(p, \alpha)$ and $\underline{K}(p, \alpha)$ be the open and the closed spheres centre $p \in \Phi$ and radius $\alpha \geq 0$ respectively. By compactness, there exist finitely many points $p_1,\ldots, p_m$ in B such that:

[4] $B \subseteq [K(p_1, \eta(\xi)/2) \cup \ldots \cup K(p_m, \eta(\xi)/2)] \subseteq [\underline{K}(p_1, \eta(\xi)/2) \cup \ldots \cup \underline{K}(p_m, \eta(\xi)/2)]$.

For every i, put $B_i = B \cap \underline{K}(p_i, \eta(\xi)/2)$. Thus B_i is both bounded and closed; and by [4]:

[5] $B = B_1 \cup B_2 \ldots \cup B_m$. By the above:
[6] $(\forall a \in B_i)(\forall k \in B_i)[|S(a) - S(k)| < \xi]$, since $d(a,k) \leq d(a, p_i) + d(p_i, k) \leq 2\eta(\xi)/2 = \eta(\xi)$.

By [2]: for each i, there exists an H_i such that:

[7] $[(H_i \subseteq B_i)$&$(\mu(H_i) = 0)$&$(\forall q \in B_i\backslash H_i)(\forall t \geq t_0)(\exists t' \geq t)(q(t') \in B_i)]$.

If $q \in B_i\backslash H_i \subseteq B_i$ and $q(t') \in B_i$, then by [6]: $| S(q(t')) - S(q) | < \xi$. But by definition, $q = q(t_0)$; hence, by [7]:

[8] $[(H_i \subseteq B_i)$&$(\mu(H_i) = 0)$&$(\forall q \in B_i\backslash H_i)(\forall t \geq t_0)(\exists t' \geq t)(| S(q(t')) - S(q(t_0)) | < \xi)]$.

Put $H = H_1 \cup H_2 \ldots \cup H_m$. Thus $\mu(H) = 0$ because $\mu(H_i) = 0$ for all i. Moreover: since $H_i \subseteq B_i$ for all i, $H \subseteq B_1 \cup \ldots \cup B_m = B$ (See [8] and [5]).

We propose to show that: $(\forall q \in B\backslash H)(\forall t \geq t_0)(\exists t' \geq t)[| S(q(t')) - S(q(t_0)) | < \xi]$. Let $q \in B\backslash H$, $t \geq t_0$; thus: $q \in B = B_1 \cup \ldots \cup B_m$ and $q \notin H$

$= H_1 \cup \ldots \cup H_m$; i.e. $q \in B_j$ for some j and $q \notin H_i$ for all i. Hence $q \notin H_j$, so that $q \in (B_j \backslash H_j)$; therefore, by [8], $| S(q(t')) - S((q(t_0)) | < \xi$ for some $t' \geq t$. We have therefore established:

[9] $[(H \subseteq B) \& (\mu(H) = 0) \& (\forall q \in B \backslash H)(\forall t \geq t_0)(\exists t' \geq t)(| S(q(t')) - S(q(t_0)) | < \xi)]$.

For every $\xi > 0$, choose $H(\xi)$ to be any H satisfying [9]. Thus:

[10] $(\forall \xi > 0)[(H(\xi) \subseteq B) \& (\mu(H(\xi)) = 0) \& (\forall q \in B \backslash H(\xi))(\forall t \geq t_0)(\exists t' \geq t)(| S(q(t')) - S(q(t_0)) | < \xi)]$.

Consider any sequence $0 > \xi_0 > \xi_1 > \ldots > \xi_i > \xi_{i+1} > \ldots$ such that $\xi_i \to 0$ as $i \to \infty$. For each $i \in \omega$, put $Q_i = H(\xi_i)$. By [10]:

[11] $[(Q_i \subseteq B) \& (\mu(Q_i) = 0) \& (\forall q \in B \backslash Q_i)(\forall t \geq t_0)(\exists t' \geq t)(| S(q(t')) - S(q(t_0)) | < \xi_i)]$.

Define $Q = \cup \{Q_i : i \in \omega,\}$. Thus: $Q \subseteq B$ and $\mu(Q) = 0$. Let us show that:

[12] $(\forall q \in B \backslash Q)[(S$ decreases nowhere along $\Gamma_q) \Rightarrow (\forall t \geq t_0)(S(q(t)) = S(q(t_0)))]$.

Suppose that $q \in B \backslash Q$ and that S decreases nowhere along Γ_q; and let $t \geq t_0$. Thus $q \in B \backslash Q = B \backslash \cup \{Q_i : i \in \omega\}$. Hence $q \in B \backslash Q_i$ for all $i \in \omega$. Keep i fixed for the time being. By [11]: for some $t' \geq t$, $| S(q(t')) - S(q(t_0)) | < \xi_i$. Since $t' \geq t \geq t_0$ and since S decreases nowhere along $\Gamma_q = \{<t, q(t)>: t \geq t_0\}$, we have: $S(q(t')) \geq S(q(t)) \geq S(q(t_0))$. Therefore: $0 \leq S(q(t)) - S(q(t_0)) \leq S(q(t')) - S(q(t_0)) = |S(q(t')) - S(q(t_0))|$. So, by the above: $0 \leq S(q(t)) - S(q(t_0)) < \xi_i$. Now vary i and let $i \to \infty$; since $\xi_i \to 0$, it can be concluded that $S(q(t)) - S(q(t_0)) = 0$; which establishes [12]. But [12] tells us that for any $q \in B \backslash Q$, (the entropy) S cannot strictly increase along Γ_q, where Q is of *zero measure*; i.e. either S decreases somewhere along Γ_q or else S is (at best) constant along Γ_q. From the viewpoint of any mechanistic reduction of the Second Principle, this is a highly paradoxical result.

Bibliography

Adler, R., Bazin, M. and Schiffer, M. 1965. *Introduction to General Relativity*. New York: McGraw-Hill.

Albert, H. 1975. *Traktat über kritische Vernunft*. Tübingen: Mohr (Siebeck).

Ayer, A.J. 1956. *The Problem of Knowledge*. London: Penguin.

————., ed. 1959. *Logical Positivism*. USA: The Free Press.

Bachelard, G. 1949. The Philosophic Dialectic of the Concepts of Relativity. In Schilpp 1949.

Böhm, J., Holweg, H. and Hoock, C. (eds.) 2002. *Karl Poppers kritischer Rationalismus heute*. Tübingen; Mohr(Siebeck).

Boltzmann, L. 1891. *Vorlesungen über Maxwells Theorie der Elektricität und des Lichts* Leipzig: J.Barth.

————. 1896. *Vorlesungen über Gastheorie*, Leipzig: J.Barth.

————. 1979. *Populäre Schriften*, Braunschweig/Wiesbaden: Vieweg.

Born, M. 1964. *Natural Philosophy of Cause and Chance*. New York: Dover.

The Born-Einstein Letters 1971. Macmillan: London.

Bovens, L. and Hartmann, S. 2003. *Bayesian Epistemology*. Oxford: Clarendon Press.

Boyer, A. 1992. Physique de croyant? Duhem et l'autonomie de la science. *Revue internationale de philosophie* 92, Vol. 46, No. 182 .

————. 1997. Induction as Fairness. In Zahar 1997, Appendix 1, p. 135.

Brecht, B. 1963. *Leben des Galilei*. Frankfurt a. Main: Suhrkamp.

Brentano, F. 1924. *Psychologie vom empirischen Standpunkt (Band 1)*. Hamburg: Felix Meiner.

————. 1930. *Wahrheit und Evidenz*. Hamburg: Felix Meiner.

————. 1968. *Psychologie vom empirischen Standpunkt (Band 3)*. Hamburg: Felix Meiner.

————. 1982. *Deskriptive Psychologie*. Hamburg: Felix Meiner.

Bridgman, P.W. 1936. *The Nature of Physical Theory*. New York: Wiley.

Brush, S.J. 1966. *Kinetic Theory 2*, Oxford and London: Pergamon.

Calaprice, A. (ed.) 1996. *The Quotable Einstein*. Princeton: Princeton University Press.

Carnap, R. 1932. Über Protokollsätze. *Erkenntnis III*, 1932–33.

——. 1966. *Philosophical Foundations of Physics.* New York: Basic Books.

Catton, P. and Macdonald, G. 2004. *Karl Popper: Critical Appraisals.* London and New York: Routledge.

Clark, P. 1976. 'Atomism versus Thermodynamics', in C. Howson (ed.) *Method and Appraisal in the Physical Sciences,* Cambridge: Cambridge University Press.

D'Agostino, F. and Jarvie, I.C. eds. 1989. *Freedom and Rationality: Essays in Honor of John Watkins.* London: Kluwer.

Demopoulos, D., and Friedman, M. 1985. Critical Notice: Bertrand Russell's "The Analysis of Matter": Its Historical Context and Contemporary Interest. *Philosophy of Science,* 52; pp. 621–63.

Descartes, R. 1986. *Meditations on First Philosophy.* Trans. J. Cottingham. Cambridge: Cambridge University Press.

Dicke, R.H., and Wittke, J.P. 1960. *Introduction to Quantum Mechanics.* Reading, Madison/Palo Alto/London: Addison-Wesley.

Dorling, J. 1979. Bayesian Personalism, the Methodology of Research Programmes and Duhem's Problem. *Studies in History and Philosophy of Science,* vol. 10, pp. 177–87.

Dreyer, J.L.E. 1953. *A History of Astronomy from Thales to Kepler.* New York: Dover.

Duhem, P. 1911. *Traité d'énergétique ou de thermodynamique générale.* Paris: Gauthier-Villars.

——. 1913. *Le Système du Monde.* Paris: Hermann.

——. 1914. *La théorie physique: son objet, sa structure.* Paris: Marcel Rivière.

——. 1954. *The Aim and Structure of Physical Theory.* New Jersey: Princeton University Press.

Eddington, A.S. 1920. *Space, Time and Gravitation.* Cambridge: Cambridge University Press.

——. 1923. *The Mathematical Theory of Relativity.* Cambridge: Cambridge University Press.

——. 1958. *The Philosophy of Physical Science.* Ann Arbor: The University of Michigan Press.

Einstein, A. 1923. The Foundations of the General Theory of Relativity. In A. Einstein et al. 1923.

——. 1934a. *Mein Weltbild.* Frankfurt am Main: Ullstein.

——. 1934b. Geometrie und Erfahrung. In Einstein 1934a.

——. 1934c. Prinzipien der Forschung. In Einstein 1934a.

——. 1949. Autobiographical Notes. In Schilpp 1949.

——. 1967. *Out of my Later Years.* New Jersey: Littlefields, Adams and Co.

——. 1994a. *Ideas and Opinions.* New York: The Modern Library.

——. 1994b. On the Method of Theoretical Physics. In Einstein 1994a.

Einstein, A. and Grossmann, M. 1913. Entwurf einer verallgemeinerten Relativitäts-theorie und einer Theorie der Gravitation. *Zeitschrift für Mathematik und Physik,* 62.

Einstein, A., et al. 1923. *The Principle of Relativity.* New York: Dover.

Einstein, A., Podolsky, B. and Rosen, N. 1935. Can Quantum-Mechanical Description of Physical Reality be Considered Complete? *Physical Review* 47, pp. 777–80.

Einstein, A., Born, M. and Born, H. 1969. *Briefwechsel 1916–1955.* München: Nymphenburger Verlagshandlung.

English, J. 1980. Underdetermination: Craig and Ramsey. *The Journal of Philosophy,* pp. 453–462.

Feyerabend, P.K. 1972a. *Der wissenschaftstheoretische Realismus und die Autorität der Wissenschaften.* Braunschweig: Vieweg.

Feyerabend, P.K. 1972b. Von der beschränkten Gültigkeit methodologischer Regeln. In Feyerabend 1972a.

———. 1975. *Against Method.* London: Humanities Press.

———. 1980. Zahar on Mach, Einstein and Modern Science. *British Journal for the Philosophy of Science, 31.*

Field, H. 1980. *Science Without Numbers.* Oxford: Blackwell.

Fine, A. 1986. *The Shaky Game.* Chicago: Chicago University Press.

Frege, G. 1986. *Funktion, Begriff, Bedeutung.* Göttingen: Vandenhoeck und Ruprecht.

Gödel, K. 1940. *The Consistency of the Continuum Hypothesis.* Princeton, New Jersey: Princeton University Press.

Greffe, J.L., Heinzmann, G. and Lorentz, K. eds. 1996. *Henri Poincaré: Science and Philosophy.* Berlin: Akademie Verlag.

Grossmann, R. 1984. *Phenomenology and Existentialism.* London: Routledge and Kegan Paul.

Grünbaum, A. 1973. *Philosophical Problems of Space and Time.* Dordrecht: Reidel.

Heidegger, M. 1953. *Einführung in die Metaphysik.* Tübingen: Niemeyer.

Heller, G. 1960. *Ernst Mach.* Berlin: Springer.

Hermes, H. 1955. *Einführung in die Verbandstheorie.* Berlin: Springer.

———. 1965. *Enumerability, Decidability, Computability.* Berlin, Heidelberg, New York: Springer.

Holton, G. 1969. Einstein, Michelson and the 'Crucial' Experiment. *Isis, 60.*

Husserl, E. 1928. *Ideen (I).* Tübingen: Niemeyer.

Howson, C. and Urbach, P. 1993. *Scientific Reasoning: the Bayesian Approach.* La Salle, Illinois: Open Court.

Husserl, E. 1929. *Formale und transzendentale Logik.* Tübingen: Niemeyer.

———. 1939. *Erfahrung und Urteil.* Hamburg: Felix Meiner.

———. 1969a. *Die Krisis der europäischen Wissenschaften und die transzendentale Phänomenologie.* Hamburg: Felix Meiner.

———. 1969b. *Cartesianische Meditationen.* Hamburg: Felix Meiner.

Jarvie, I.C. and Laor, N. eds. 1995. *Critical Rationalism, Metaphysics and science.* Dordrecht: Kluwer.

Kant, I. 1787. *Kritik der reinen Vernunft.* Hamburg: Felix Meiner.

————. 1953. *Prolegomena to any Future Metaphysics*. Manchester: Manchester University Press.

————. 1957. *Metaphysische Anfangsgründe der Naturwissenschaft*. Wiesbaden: Insel Verlag.

Kilmister, C.W. 1984. *Russell*. Brighton: The Harvester Press.

Ketland, J. 2004. Empirical Adequacy and Ramsification. *The British Journal for the Philosophy of Science*, 55.

Kraft, V. 1968. *Der Wiener Kreis*. Wien and New York: Springer Verlag.

Kretschmann, K. 1917. Über den physikalischen Sinn der Relativitätspostulate, A. Einsteins neue und seine ursprüngliche Relativitätstheorie. *Annalen der Physik* 53.

Kripke, S. 1972. *Naming and Necessity*. Oxford: Basil Blackwell.

Kuhn, T.S. 1970. *The Structure of Scientific Revolutions*. Chicago: University of Chicago Press.

Lakatos, I. 1970. Falsification and the Methodology of Scientific Research Programmes. In Lakatos and Musgrave 1970.

————. 1976. *Proofs and Refutations*. Cambridge: Cambridge University Press.

————. 1978a. *Philosophical Papers 1*. Cambridge: Cambridge University Press.

————. 1978b. Popper on Demarcation and Induction. In Lakatos 1978a.

Lakatos, I. and Musgrave, A. eds. 1970. *Criticism and the Growth of Knowledge*. Cambridge: Cambridge University Press.

Lakatos, I. and Zahar, E. 1978. Why did Copernicus's Programme supersede Ptolemy's? In Lakatos 1978a.

Leplin, J., ed. 1984. *Scientific Realism*. Berkeley: University of California Press.

Lewis, D. 1970. How to Define Theoretical Terms. *The Journal of Philosophy*, Vol. 57, no. 13; pp. 427–446.

Lipton, P. 2004. *Inference to the Best Explanation*. London and New York: Routledge.

Lorentz, H.A. 1895. *Versuch einer Theorie der electrishen und optischen Erscheinungen in bewegten Körpern*. Reprinted in Lorentz 1934.

Lorentz, H.A. 1934. *Collected Papers*. The Hague: Nijhoff.

————. 1967. *Problems of Modern Physics*. New York: Dover.

Mach, E. 1906. *The Analysis of Sensations*. New York: Dover.

————. 1909. *The History and the Root of the Principle of the Conservation of Energy*. La Salle, Illinois: Open Court.

————. 1922. *Die Anlyse der Empfindungen*. Darmstadt: Wissenschaftliche Buchgesellschaft.

————. 1926. *Erkenntnis und Irrtum*. Leipzig: J.A. Barth.

————. 1933. *Die Mechanik*. Darmstadt: Wissenschaftliche Buchgesellschaft.

McMullin, E. 1984. A Case for Scientific Realism. In Leplin 1984, pp. 30–36.

McGuinness, B.F. 1967. *Friedrich Waismann: Wittgenstein und der Wiener Kreis*. Oxford: Blackwell.

Malament, D. 1982. Review of Field's Science Without Numbers. *Journal of Philosophy*, no. 79, pp. 523–534.

Maxwell, G.1971. Structural Realism and the Meaning of Theoretical Terms. In Radner, M., and Minokur, S., eds. 1971. *Minnesota Studies in the Philosophy of Science*, Vol. 8, pp. 181–192.

Martin, R.N.D. 1991. *Pierre Duhem. Philosophy and History in the Work of a Believing Physicist.* La Salle, Illinois: Open Court.

Meyerson, E. 1907. *Identité et réalité.* Paris: Payot.

———. 1921. *De l'explication dans les sciences.* Paris: Payot.

Miller, D. 2002. Induction: a Problem Solved. In Böhm et al. 2002.

———. 1995. How Little Uniformity Need an Inductive Inference Presuppose? In Jarvie and Laor 1995.

Musgrave, A. 2004. How Popper (might have) solved the problem of induction. In Catton and Macdonald, pp. 16–27.

Newman, M.H.A. 1928. Mr. Russell's "Causal Theory of Perception." *Mind,* Vol. 37, No. 146, pp. 137–148.

Newton, I. 1686. *Principia Mathematica.* Berkeley: University of California Press.

Ostwald, W. (1937). *L'Énergie.* Paris: Flammarion.

Papineau, D., ed. 1996. *The Philosophy of Science.* Oxford: Oxford University Press.

Paty, M. 1988. *La matière dérobée.* Paris: Archives contemporaines.

Piaget, J. 1970. *L'épistémologie génétique.* Paris: Presses Universitaires de France.

Planck, M. 1965a. *Vorträge und Erinnerungen.* Darmstadt: Wissenschaftliche Buchgesellschaft.

———. 1965b. Die Einheit des physikalischen Weltbildes. In Planck 1965a.

———. 1965c. Sinn und Grenzen der exakten Wissenschaft. In Planck 1965a.

———. 1965d. Kausalgesetz und Willensfreiheit. In Planck 1965a.

Poincaré, H. 1902. *La science et l'hypothèse.* Paris: Flammarion. All page references are to the English translation (1952. *Science and Hypothesis.* New York: Dover).

———. 1906a: *La valeur de la science.* Paris: Flammarion. All page references are to the English translation (1958. *The Value of Science.* New York: Dover).

———. 1906b: Sur la dynamique de l'électron. *Rendiconti del Circolo Matematico di Palermo.*

———. 1908. *Science et méthode.* Paris: Flammarion. All page references are to the English translation (1958. *Science and Method.* New York: Dover).

———. 1913: *Dernières Pensées.* Paris: Flammarion. All page references are to the English translation (1963. *Last Essays.* New York: Dover).

Popper, K.R. 1959. *The Logic of Scientific Discovery.* London: Hutchinson.

———. 1963. *Conjectures and Refutations.* London: Routledge.

———. 1972. *Objective Knowledge.* Oxford: Oxford University Press.

———. 1974. Replies to my Critics. In Schilpp 1974, pp. 659–1197.

———. 1979. *Die beiden Grundprobleme der Erkenntnistheorie.* Tübingen: Mohr (Siebeck).

———. 1982. *The Open Universe.* London: Hutchinson.

———. 1983. *Realism and the Aim of Science.* London: Hutchinson.

Psillos, S. 1999. *Scientific Realism.* London and New York: Routledge.

Putnam, H. 1983a. *Realism and Reason.* Cambridge: Cambridge University Press.

———. 1983b. Models and Reality. In Putnam 1983a.

Quine, W.v.O. 1980a. *From a Logical Point of View.* Cambridge (USA): Harvard University Press.

———. 1980b. On What There Is. In: Quine 1980a.

———. 1980c. Two Dogmas of Empiricism. In Quine 1980a.

Redhead, M. 1975. Symmetry in Intertheory Relations. *Synthese 32.* Dordrecht: Reidel.

———. 1987. *Incompleteness, Nonlocality and Realism.* Oxford: Oxford University Press.

———. 1995. *From Physics to Metaphysics.* Cambridge: Cambridge University Press.

Reichenbach, H. 1928. *Philosophie der Raum-Zeit-Lehre.* Berlin: Walter de Gruyter.

———. 1958. *The Philosophy of Space and Time.* New York: Dover.

Russell, B. 1927. *The Analysis of Matter.* London: Allen and Unwin.

———. 1962. *The Problems of Philosophy.* Oxford: Oxford University Press.

———. 1973. *Essays in Analysis.* London: Allen and Unwin.

———. 1984. *The Theory of Knowledge. The 1913 Manuscript.* London: Allen and Unwin.

Sartre, J.-P. 1981. *La transcendance de l'égo.* Paris: Vrin.

Schilpp, P.A., ed. 1949. *Einstein: Philosopher-Scientist.* New York: Tudor.

———., ed. 1974. *The Philosophy of Karl Popper*, 2 vols. La Salle, Illinois: Open Court.

———., ed. 1949. *Albert Einstein: Philosopher-Scientist.* New York: Tudor.

Schlick, M. 1920. *Space & Time.* New York: Dover.

———. 1938. *Gesammelte Aufsätze.* Wien: Springer.

———. 1974. *General Theory of Knowledge.* Wien and New York: Springer-Verlag.

———. 1979. *Allgemeine Erkenntnislehre.* Frankfurt am Main: Suhrkamp.

———. 1986a. *Die Probleme der Philosophie in ihrem Zusammenhang.* Frankfurt am Main: Suhrkamp.

———. 1986b. Die philosophische Fragestellung. In Schlick 1986a.

———. 1986c. Das Wesen des Logischen. In Schlick 1986a.

Schrödinger, E. 1950. *Space-time Structure.* Cambridge: Cambridge University Press.

Sears, W. 1953. *Thermodynamics, the Kinetic Theory of Gases and Statistical Mechanics.* Reading (Mass.): Addison-Wesley.

Sears, W. and Salinger, G.L. 1975. *Thermodynamics.* Reading (Mass.): Addison-Wesley.

Stachel, J., ed. 1989. *The Collected Works of Albert Einstein*, Vol. 2. Princeton, NJ: Princeton University Press.

Watkins, J.W.N. 1984. *Science and Skepticism.* Princeton, NJ: Princeton University Press.

Worrall, J. 1996. Structural Realism. In Papineau 1996.

Zahar, E. 1977. Mach, Einstein and the Rise of Modern Science. *The British Journal for the Philosophy of Science,* 28.

———. 1989a. *Einstein's Revolution: A Study in Heuristic.* La Salle, Illinois: Open Court.

———. 1989b. John Watkins on the Empirical Basis and the Corroboration of Scientific Theories. In D'Agostino and Jarvie 1989.

———. 1991. Natural Axiomatization: a Revision of Wajsberg's Requirement. *The British Journal for the Philosophy of Science,* 42.

———. 1996. Poincaré's Structural Realism and his Logic of Discovery. In Greffe, Heinzmann and Lorentz 1996.

———. 1997. *Leçons d'épistémologie.* Palaiseau: Imprimerie de l'École Polytechnique.

———. 2000. *Essai d'épistémologie réaliste.* Paris:Vrin.

———. 2001. *Poincaré's Philosophy: from Conventionalism to Phenomenology.* La Salle, Illinois: Open Court.

Zermelo, E. 1966. On the Mechanical Explanation of Irreversible Processes. In Brush 1966.

Index

a = b, as identity statement, 97–99
Albert, Hans, 79
Albert Einstein: Philosopher-Scientist,
    223
Ampère, André Marie, 128
analytic propositions
    meaning in
        ostensive, 102, 104–105
        verbal, 102
    nature of, 101–102
    paradox of, 102
a priori
    different senses of, 2–3
    and mathematics, 3
Aristarchus, 161
Aristotle, 223
atomism
    acceptance of, 221
    appraisals of, 213
    breakthroughs of, 211
    description of, 208–209
    difficulties for, 210–211, 219–20
    empirical failure of, 211–12
    metaphysics as guide in, 208
    support for, 219
autopsychological reports. *See also*
level-0 propositions
    features of, 69–70
    psychologistic view of, as false, 70
    referents of, 62
    special status of, 61
Ayer, A. J., 60, 61, 69, 181, 190
    on autopsychological propositions,
        62–63
    on basic statements, 59

Bachelard, G., 131
basic statements, as theory-laden, 50, 54

Bayesianism, 110
    critique of, 113–14
    and objectivism, 111
    subjective interpretation of
        probability in, 111
Bayes's theorem, 110
Berkeley, George, 174, 214
Bohm, David, 245
Bohr, Niels, 81, 245, 247, 249
Boltzmann, L., 211, 213, 220
    atomistic realism of, 218–20
    on entropy, 221
Bolzano, Bernard, 33
Born, Max, 84, 86, 87, 133, 134, 225,
    243, 244
Bovens, L., 111
Boyer, Alain, 8, 132, 265–66
Boyle, Robert, 20, 2009, 211
Brahe, Tycho, 143
Brecht, Bertolt, 51
Brentano, Franz, 70, 190
    on consciousness, 63, 66–67
    Evidenzlehre of, 62
    on intentional entities, 63
    on sense-data, 63, 64
    theory of self-evidence, 61–62
Bridgman, P. W., 139
Brownian motion, 107

Carnap, R., 34, 83, 94, 114, 183, 200,
    237
    on analytic meaning A-postulate,
        184–86
    analytic/metaphysical conflation in,
        186–87, 189
    critique of
        on analyticity, 184–85
        on physical language, 42–43